CASES AND MATERIALS ON FEDERAL CONSTITUTIONAL LAW

Volume IV

Federalism Limitations on State and Federal Power

CASES AND MATERIALS ON FEDERAL CONSTITUTIONAL LAW

Volume IV
Federalism Limitations on
State and Federal Power

SECOND EDITION

Scott W. Gaylord
Christopher R. Green
Lee J. Strang

Carolina Academic Press
Durham, North Carolina

ISBN: 978-1-5310-0646-4
eISBN: 978-1-53100-647-1
LCCN: 2017955579

Carolina Academic Press, LLC
700 Kent Street
Durham, North Carolina 27701
Telephone (919) 489-7486
Fax (919) 493-5668
www.cap-press.com

INTRODUCTION TO THE MODULAR CASEBOOK SERIES

By now you have realized that the course materials assigned by your instructor have a very different form than traditional casebooks. The *Modular Casebook Series* is intentionally designed to break the mold. Course materials consist of one or more separate volumes selected from among a larger and growing set of volumes. Each volume is relatively short so that an instructor may "mix and match" a suitable number of volumes for a course of varying length and focus.

Each volume is designed to serve an instructional purpose rather than as a treatise; as a result, the *Modular Casebook Series* is published in soft cover. Publication of the separate volumes in soft cover also permits course materials to be revised more easily so that they will incorporate recent developments. Moreover, by purchasing only the assigned volumes for a given course, students are likely to recognize significant savings over the cost of a traditional casebook.

Traditional casebooks are often massive tomes, frequently exceeding 1000 or even 1500 pages. Traditional casebooks are lengthy because they attempt to cover the entire breadth of material that *might* be useful to an instructor for a two-semester course of five or six credits. Even with six credits, different instructors will cover different portions of a traditional casebook within the time available. As a consequence, traditional casebooks include a range of materials that may leave hundreds of unexplored pages in any particular six-credit class. Especially for a student in a three or four credit course, such a book is hardly an efficient means of delivering the needed materials. Students purchase much more book than they need, at great expense. And students carry large, heavy books for months at a time.

Traditional casebooks are usually hard cover publications. It seems as though they are constructed to last as a reference work throughout decades of practice. In fact, as the presence of annual supplements to casebooks makes clear, portions of casebooks become obsolete very shortly after publication. Treatises and hornbooks are designed to serve as reference works; casebooks serve a different purpose. Once again, the traditional format of casebooks seems to impose significant added costs on students for little reason.

The form of traditional casebooks increases the probability that the content will become obsolete shortly after publication. The publication of lengthy texts in hardcover produces substantial delay between the time the author completes the final draft and the time the book reaches the hands of students. In addition, the broader scope of material addressed in a 1,000 or 1,500 page text means that portions of the text are more likely to be superseded by later developments than any particular narrowly-tailored volume in the *Modular Casebook Series*. Because individual volumes in the *Modular Casebook Series* may be revised without requiring revision of other volumes, the materials for any particular course will be less likely to require supplementation.

Most importantly, the cases and accompanying exercises provide students with the opportunity to learn and deploy the standard arguments in the various subject matters of constitutional law. Each case is edited to emphasize the key arguments made by the Court and justices. For instance, in many older cases, headings were added to note a new or related argument. Furthermore, the exercises following each case focus on identifying and critiquing the Court's and justices' arguments. The exercises also form the basis for rich class discussion. All of this introduces students to the most important facet of constitutional law: the deployment of standard arguments in each doctrinal context and across constitutional law doctrines.

We hope you enjoy this innovative approach to course materials.

Dedication

To Pamela and our family and to all the families who serve and
sacrifice to protect the Constitution.
S.W.G.

To Bonnie and Justice John Marshall Harlan I.
C.R.G.

To Elizabeth and Saint Thomas Aquinas.
L.J.S.

Acknowledgments

We would like to thank Tom Odom for proposing and initiating the Modular Casebook Series, and for inviting us to participate in the Series, and, for research leave and support, to the Elon University School of Law, the Jamie Lloyd Whitten Chair of Law and Government Endowment at the University of Mississippi School of Law, and the University of Toledo College of Law. The hard work and excellent research of Paul Cordell is reflected in this Volume. Without our wives' loving support, this project would not have been completed.

Preface to the Second Edition

Technological improvements permit the compilation of resources in a manner unthinkable when we were law students. Materials that permit further examination of assigned reading can be delivered in a cost-effective manner and in a format more likely to be useful in practice than reams of photocopies.

With regard to assigned reading, there is no good reason to burden students with stacks of hand-outs or expensive annual supplements. Publication through the *Modular Casebook Series* ensures that even very recent developments may be incorporated prior to publication. Moreover, if important cases are decided after publication of the latest edition of the volume, they will be included on the series website. Cases and materials that shed additional light on matter in the hard copy casebook are also included.

We welcome comments from readers so that we may make further improvements in the next edition of this publication.

Scott W. Gaylord

Christopher R. Green

Lee J. Strang

TECHNICAL NOTE FROM THE EDITORS

The cases and other materials excerpted in this Volume have been edited in an effort to enhance readability. Citations of multiple cases for a single proposition have been shortened in many places to reference only one or two prominent authorities. In some places, archaic language or spelling has been revised. Headings were added to some of the longer decisions to permit ease of reference to various parts of the opinion. Such headings may also assist the reader in identifying a transition from one point to another.

Cases have been edited to a suitable length. In order to achieve that result, many interesting but tangential points have been omitted. The length of some opinions also hindered the inclusion of excerpts from concurring or dissenting opinions. We have noted in the text where such opinions have been omitted.

In editing these cases, we have not indicated the portions of cases that have been deleted unless such deletion with the absence of ellipses would have been misleading. However, any time material has been inserted into a case, we indicated the insertion with the use of brackets.

Scott W. Gaylord

Christopher R. Green

Lee J. Strang

Table of Contents

Introduction to Volume 4

The term *"Federalism"* refers to the collection of doctrines that govern the relationship between the central government and the several states. This Volume addresses constitutional limitations that Federalism imposes upon states and the central government. In particular, it explains four of the limits on state and federal power derived from the original Constitution, that is, the Constitution prior to the Reconstruction Amendments (which are addressed in Volume 5).

A. Express Constitutional Limitations Upon States

1. Limitations to Ensure Exclusive Federal Authority

The Constitution of 1789 contained several express limitations upon states. In several instances, an affirmative grant of authority to the central government is joined with a prohibition on the individual states exercising any parallel authority. As a result, the Constitution directly vests exclusive authority over these matters in the central government.

For example, the treaty power is affirmatively vested in the central government. Under Article II, § 2, cl. 2, the President has the "Power, by and with the Advice and Consent of the Senate, to make Treaties, provided two thirds of the Senators present concur; and he shall nominate, and by and with the Advice and Consent of the Senate, shall appoint Ambassadors, other public Ministers and Consuls. . . ." Under Article I, § 10, "No State shall enter into any Treaty, Alliance, or Confederation." Even in the absence of action by the central government, states are constitutionally prohibited from pursuing opportunities to establish treaties with foreign nations.

Similarly, Congress not only is granted authority to declare war, but also is expressly granted the authority to issue Letters of Marque and Reprisal in Article I, § 8, cl. 11. Because authorizing such action likely would constitute an act of war, Article I, § 10 precludes states from issuing such letters: "No State shall . . . grant Letters of Marque and Reprisal."

So too, Article I, § 10, provides that states may not "coin Money" while Congress is granted the power "To coin Money, regulate the Value thereof, and foreign Coin, and fix the Standard of Weights and Measures" in Article I, § 8, cl. 5.

These limitations upon state authority provoke little controversy.

2. Limitations on States Parallel to Limitations on the Central Government

The Constitution of 1789 contains several other express limitations on states that parallel prohibitions on the central government. For example, both the states and the central government are prohibited from (1) enacting any Bill of Attainder, (2) promulgating any *ex post facto* law, and (3) "grant[ing] any Title of Nobility." *Compare* Art. I, § 9, cls. 3 & 8, *with* Art. I, § 10, cl. 1. Because these provisions are more appropriately viewed as preserving individual rights (protecting individuals from state and federal action), they are beyond the scope of this Volume.

3. Unique Limitations on States

The Constitution of 1789 includes only a few express limitations on state autonomy that have no parallel provision that either grants exclusive authority to the central government or that equally prohibits action by the central government. One such provision is the requirement that states may not "pass any . . . Law impairing the Obligation of Contracts." Art. I, § 10, cl 1. The Contracts Clause is the subject of **Chapter 1.**

B. Implied Constitutional Limitations Upon States

Even when the Constitution of 1789 does not expressly limit the several states, there are limited situations where the grant of power to the central government necessarily implies a denial to the several states of any parallel authority.

1. Express Grants of Exclusive Authority to the Central Government

The grant of "exclusive" authority over the District of Columbia and federal enclaves, *see* Art. I, § 8, cl. 17, necessarily implies that the several states cannot exercise any competing authority. For these provisions to apply, however, the appropriate state must cede jurisdiction over the property; the central government's acquisition of the property, either by purchase or eminent domain, does not itself confer exclusive jurisdiction. *See, e.g., Kohl v. United States*, 91 U.S. 367, 371 (1875). Without a cessation of jurisdiction, the United States holds property within a state as "an ordinary proprietor." *James v. Dravo Contracting Co.*, 302 U.S. 134, 141–42 (1937).

Even grants of authority to Congress to establish "uniform" laws or to grant "exclusive" rights may not imply a prohibition on the several states. For example, Congress is granted authority to "establish . . . uniform Laws on the subject of Bankruptcies throughout the United States," *see* Art. I, § 8, cl. 4, and one might reason that a uniform law necessarily displaces the separate non-uniform laws of the several states. In the absence of congressional *exercise* of this power, though, does the mere *existence* of the power serve to divest states of the authority to establish laws on the subject that vary from state to state? In a relatively early decision, the Supreme Court answered that question in the negative:

> Congress is not authorized merely to pass laws, the operation of which shall be uniform, but to establish uniform laws on the subject throughout the United States. This establishment of uniformity is, perhaps, incompatible with state legislation, on that part of the subject to which the acts of Congress may extend.
>
> It does not appear to be a violent construction of the Constitution, and is certainly a convenient one, to consider the power of the States as existing

over such cases as the laws of the Union may not reach. But be this as it may, the power granted to Congress may be exercised or declined, as the wisdom of that body shall decide. If, in the opinion of Congress, uniform laws concerning bankruptcies ought not to be established, it does not follow, that partial laws may not exist, or that State legislation on the subject must cease. It is not the mere existence of the power, but its exercise, which is incompatible with the exercise of the same power by the States. It is not the right to establish these uniform laws, but their actual establishment, which is inconsistent with the partial acts of the States.

Sturges v. Crowninshield, 17 U.S. (4 Wheat.) 120, 193-94 (1819) (Marshall, C.J.).

A similar situation presented itself in the immigration context. Because Congress did not enact the first statute broadly regulating immigration until 1875, Act of Mar. 3, 1875, ch. 141, 18 Stat. 477; *see INS v. St. Cyr*, 533 U.S. 289, 305 (2001), prior to that federal statute there was no basis for preemption, leaving state laws to be challenged solely on whether the subject was vested exclusively in the central government.

From the earliest days under the Constitution, various states enacted limitations on immigration of criminals, *see* Gerald L. Neuman, *The Lost Century of American Immigration Law (1776–1875)*, 93 COLUM. L. REV. 1833, 1843 (1993), the destitute, *see id.* at 1848–59, and individuals infected with contagious diseases — a basis for "State authority . . . [which] had long enjoyed the unequivocal endorsement of the federal government." *Id.* at 1864. As Professor Neuman observed, initially, a majority of the Supreme Court endorsed the concurrent authority of states. *See, e.g., Gibbons v. Ogden*, 22 U.S. (9 Wheat.) 1, 203–06 (1824) (Marshall, C.J.) (expressly endorsing state quarantine and health laws in the absence of actual conflict with federal law); *Mayor of New York v. Miln*, 36 U.S. (11 Pet.) 102, 142–43 (1837) (approving state laws addressed to "paupers, vagabonds, and possibly convicts" in addition to individuals "laboring under an infectious disease"); *Prigg v. Pennsylvania*, 41 U.S. 16 Pet.) 539, 625 (1842) (recognizing state authority to exclude "runaway slaves" as well as "idlers, vagabonds, and paupers"); *Moore v. Illinois*, 55 U.S. (14 How.) 13, 18 (1853) (endorsing state authority to criminalize the introduction of "paupers, criminals, or fugitive slaves"). In addition to support for that view from the federal judiciary, Congress enacted laws and the Executive engaged in diplomatic efforts designed to reinforce state regulation. *See* Neuman, *supra*, at 1883. Only after the Civil War did the U.S. Supreme Court assert that "[t]he authority to control immigration — to admit or exclude aliens — is vested solely in the Federal Government," *Truax v. Raich*, 239 U.S. 33, 42 (1915), beginning its retreat with cases like *Henderson v. Mayor of New York*, 92 U.S. 259 (1876) and *Chy Lung v. Freeman*, 92 U.S. 275 (1876).

In light of the breadth of federal legislation in the fields of bankruptcy and immigration, as well as the resulting preemption, the question whether the Constitution prohibits states from exercising concurrent authority in those areas is of diminished importance.

2. The Supremacy of Federal Law

When the central government acts pursuant to its own constitutional authority, the Supremacy Clause dictates that the central government may displace state law. Such "preemption" of state law is addressed in **Chapter 2.**

C. Implied Grant of Exclusive Authority to the Central Government

The text of the Commerce Clause does not purport to grant exclusive authority to the central government. Not only is there no explicit prohibition on concurrent state regulation of commerce, certain specific prohibitions upon states would become superfluous if the Clause were so construed. U.S. Const., Art. I, § 10, cl. 2. Despite early precedent to the contrary, the U.S. Supreme Court eventually articulated the doctrine of the "dormant" Commerce Clause. Under that view, certain aspects of the regulation of commerce are vested exclusively in the central government so that even when Congress does not affirmatively legislate, states nonetheless lack the concurrent authority to regulate. The dormant Commerce Clause is the subject of **Chapter 3.**

D. Federalism Limits on the Central Government

The federal structure established by the Constitution also limits the central government. The most important aspect of federalism limits on the federal government is the doctrine of limited and enumerated powers. The Tenth Amendment is the focus of debates over the scope of that doctrine and is the subject of **Chapter 4.** The Court has been sharply divided over the nature and purpose of the Tenth Amendment. In recent cases, such as *Bond v. United States*, 134 S.Ct. 2077 (2014) and *Shelby County v. Holder*, 133 S.Ct. 2612 (2013), a majority of the Court has invoked Federalism as a robust rule of construction to limit the scope of federal statutes without ostensibly restricting Congress's enumerated powers.

Federalism limits on the central government have manifested in other areas of case law as well. Most prominently, the Supreme Court reinvigorated limits on Congress' Commerce Clause authority in *United States v. Lopez*, 514 U.S. 549 (1995), *United States v. Morrison*, 529 U.S. 598 (2000), and *NFIB v. Sebelius*, 567 U.S. 519 (2012). The Court also restricted the scope of Congress' Section 5 powers in *Boerne v. Flores*, 521 U.S. 57 (1997), and, in a related line of cases beginning with *Seminal Tribe v. Florida*, 517 U.S. 44 (1996), expanded the scope of state sovereign immunity from suit. These limits are discussed in Volume 3.

The Constitution of the United States

We the People of the United States, in order to form a more perfect nion, establish Justice, insure domestic Tranquility, provide for the common defence, promote the general Welfare, and secure the Blessings of Liberty to ourselves and our Posterity, do ordain and establish this Constitution for the United States of America.

Article I

Section 1. All legislative Powers herein granted shall be vested in a Congress of the United States, which shall consist of a Senate and House of Representatives.

Section 2. The House of Representatives shall be composed of Members chosen every second Year by the People of the several States, and the Electors in each State shall have the Qualifications requisite for Electors of the most numerous Branch of the State Legislature.

No person shall be a Representative who shall not have attained to the Age of twenty five Years, and been seven Years a Citizen of the United States, and who shall not, when elected, be an Inhabitant of that State in which he shall be chosen.

Representatives and direct Taxes shall be apportioned among the several States which may be included within this Union, according to their respective Numbers, which shall be determined by adding to the whole Number of free Persons, including those bound to Service for a Term of Years, and excluding Indians not taxed, three fifths of all other Persons. The actual Enumeration shall be made within three Years after the first Meeting of the Congress of the United States, and within every subsequent Term of ten Years, in such Manner as they shall by Law direct. The Number of Representatives shall not exceed one for every thirty Thousand, but each State shall have at Least one Representative; and until such enumeration shall be made, the State of New Hampshire shall be entitled to chuse three, Massachusetts eight, Rhode-Island and Providence Plantations one, Connecticut five, New-York six, New Jersey four, Pennsylvania eight, Delaware one, Maryland six, Virginia ten, North Carolina five, South Carolina five, and Georgia three.

When vacancies happen in the Representation from any State, the Executive Authority thereof shall issue Writs of Election to fill such Vacancies.

The House of Representatives shall chuse their Speaker and other Officers; and shall have the sole Power of Impeachment.

Section 3. The Senate of the United States shall be composed of two Senators from each State, chosen by the Legislature thereof, for six Years; and each Senator shall have one Vote.

Immediately after they shall be assembled in Consequence of the first Election, they shall be divided as equally as may be into three Classes. The Seats of the

Senators of the first Class shall be vacated at the Expiration of the second Year, of the second Class at the Expiration of the fourth Year, and of the third Class at the Expiration of the sixth Year, so that one third may be chosen every second Year; and if Vacancies happen by Resignation, or otherwise, during the Recess of the Legislature of any State, the Executive thereof may make temporary Appointments until the next Meeting of the Legislature, which shall then fill such Vacancies.

No Person shall be a Senator who shall not have attained to the Age of thirty Years, and been nine Years a Citizen of the United States, and who shall not, when elected, be an Inhabitant of that State for which he shall be chosen.

The Vice President of the United States shall be President of the Senate, but shall have no Vote, unless they be equally divided.

The Senate shall choose their other Officers, and also a President pro tempore, in the Absence of the Vice President, or when he shall exercise the Office of President of the United States.

The Senate shall have the sole Power to try all Impeachments. When sitting for that Purpose, they shall be on Oath or Affirmation. When the President of the United States is tried, the Chief Justice shall preside: and no Person shall be convicted without the Concurrence of two thirds of the Members present.

Judgment in Cases of Impeachment shall not extend further than to removal from Office, and disqualification to hold and enjoy any Office of honor, Trust or Profit under the United States: but the Party convicted shall nevertheless be liable and subject to Indictment, Trial, Judgment and Punishment, according to Law.

Section 4. The Times, Places and Manner of holding Elections for Senators and Representatives, shall be prescribed in each State by the Legislature thereof; but the Congress may at any time by Law make or alter such Regulations, except as to the Places of chusing Senators.

The Congress shall assemble at least once in every Year, and such Meeting shall be on the first Monday in December, unless they shall by Law appoint a different Day.

Section 5. Each House shall be the Judge of the Elections, Returns and Qualifications of its own Members, and a Majority of each shall constitute a Quorum to do Business; but a smaller Number may adjourn from day to day, and may be authorized to compel the Attendance of absent Members, in such Manner, and under such Penalties as each House may provide.

Each House may determine the Rules of its Proceedings, punish its Members for disorderly Behaviour, and, with the Concurrence of two thirds, expel a Member.

Each House shall keep a Journal of its Proceedings, and from time to time publish the same, excepting such Parts as may in their Judgment require Secrecy; and the Yeas and Nays of the Members of either House on any question shall, at the Desire of one fifth of those Present, be entered on the Journal.

Section 6. The Senators and Representatives shall receive a Compensation for their Services, to be ascertained by Law, and paid out of the Treasury of the United

States. They shall in all Cases, except Treason, Felony and Breach of the Peace, be privileged from Arrest during their Attendance at the Session of their respective Houses, and in going to and returning from the same; and for any Speech or Debate in either House, they shall not be questioned in any other Place.

No Senator or Representative shall, during the Time for which he was elected, be appointed to any civil Office under the Authority of the United States, which shall have been created, or the Emoluments whereof shall have been encreased during such time; and no Person holding any Office under the United States, shall be a Member of either House during his Continuance in Office.

Section 7. All Bills for raising Revenue shall originate in the House of Representatives; but the Senate may propose or concur with Amendments as on other Bills.

Every Bill which shall have passed the House of Representatives and the Senate, shall, before it become a Law, be presented to the President of the United States; If he approve he shall sign it, but if not he shall return it, with his Objections to that House in which it shall have originated, who shall enter the Objections at large on their Journal, and proceed to reconsider it. If after such Reconsideration two thirds of that House shall agree to pass the Bill, it shall be sent, together with the Objections, to the other House, by which it shall likewise be reconsidered, and if approved by two thirds of that House, it shall become a Law. But in all such Cases the Votes of both Houses shall be determined by yeas and Nays, and the Names of the Persons voting for and against the Bill shall be entered on the Journal of each House respectively. If any Bill shall not be returned by the President within ten days (Sundays excepted) after it shall have been presented to him, the Same shall be a Law, in like Manner as if he had signed it, unless the Congress by their Adjournment prevent its Return in which Case it shall not be a Law.

Every Order, Resolution, or Vote to which the Concurrence of the Senate and House of Representatives may be necessary (except on a question of Adjournment) shall be presented to the President of the United States; and before the Same shall take Effect, shall be approved by him, or being disapproved by him, shall be repassed by two thirds of the Senate and House of Representatives, according to the Rules and Limitations prescribed in the Case of a Bill.

Section 8. The Congress shall have Power To lay and collect Taxes, Duties, Imposts and Excises, to pay the Debts and provide for the common Defence and general Welfare of the United States; but all Duties, Imposts and Excises shall be uniform throughout the United States;

To borrow Money on the credit of the United States;

To regulate Commerce with foreign Nations, and among the several States, and with the Indian Tribes;

To establish an uniform Rule of Naturalization, and uniform Laws on the subject of Bankruptcies throughout the United States;

To coin Money, regulate the Value thereof, and foreign Coin, and fix the Standard of Weights and Measures;

To provide for the Punishment of counterfeiting the Securities and current Coin of the United States;

To establish Post Offices and post Roads;

To promote the Progress of Science and useful Arts, by securing for limited Times to Authors and Inventors the exclusive Right to their respective Writings and Discoveries;

To constitute Tribunals inferior to the supreme Court;

To define and punish Piracies and Felonies committed on the high Seas, and Offences against the Law of Nations;

To declare War, grant Letters of Marque and Reprisal, and make Rules concerning Captures on Land and Water;

To raise and support Armies, but no Appropriation of Money to that Use shall be for a longer Term than two Years;

To provide and maintain a Navy;

To make Rules for the Government and Regulation of the land and naval Forces;

To provide for calling forth the Militia to execute the Laws of the Union, suppress Insurrections and repel Invasions;

To provide for organizing, arming, and disciplining, the Militia, and for governing such Part of them as may be employed in the Service of the United States, reserving to the States respectively, the Appointment of the Officers, and the Authority of training the Militia according to the discipline prescribed by Congress;

To exercise exclusive Legislation in all Cases whatsoever, over such District (not exceeding ten Miles square) as may, by Cession of particular States, and the Acceptance of Congress, become the Seat of the Government of the United States, and to exercise like Authority over all Places purchased by the Consent of the Legislature of the State in which the Same shall be, for the Erection of Forts, Magazines, Arsenals, dock-Yards, and other needful Buildings;—And

To make all Laws which shall be necessary and proper for carrying into Execution the foregoing Powers, and all other Powers vested by this Constitution in the Government of the United States, or in any Department or Officer thereof.

Section 9. The Migration or Importation of such Persons as any of the States now existing shall think proper to admit, shall not be prohibited by the Congress prior to the Year one thousand eight hundred and eight, but a Tax or duty may be imposed on such Importation, not exceeding ten dollars for each Person.

The Privilege of the Writ of Habeas Corpus shall not be suspended, unless when in Cases of Rebellion or Invasion the public Safety may require it.

No Bill of Attainder or ex post facto Law shall be passed.

No Capitation, or other direct, Tax shall be laid, unless in Proportion to the Census or Enumeration herein before directed to be taken.

No Tax or Duty shall be laid on.Articles exported from any State.

No Preference shall be given by any Regulation of Commerce or Revenue to the Ports of one State over those of another; nor shall Vessels bound to, or from, one State, be obliged to enter, clear, or pay Duties in another.

No Money shall be drawn from the Treasury, but in Consequence of Appropriations made by Law; and a regular Statement and Account of the Receipts and Expenditures of all public Money shall be published from time to time.

No Title of Nobility shall be granted by the United States: And no Person holding any Office of Profit or Trust under them, shall, without the Consent of the Congress, accept of any present, Emolument, Office, or Title, of any kind whatever, from any King, Prince, or foreign State.

Section 10. No State shall enter into any Treaty, Alliance, or Confederation; grant Letters of Marque and Reprisal; coin Money; emit Bills of Credit; make any Thing but gold and silver Coin a Tender in Payment of Debts; pass any Bill of Attainder, ex post facto Law, or Law impairing the Obligation of Contracts, or grant any Title of Nobility.

No State shall, without the Consent of the Congress, lay any Imposts or Duties on Imports or Exports, except what may be absolutely necessary for executing it's inspection Laws: and the net Produce of all Duties and Imposts, laid by any State on Imports or Exports, shall be for the Use of the Treasury of the United. States; and all such Laws shall be subject to the Revision and Controul of the Congress.

No State shall, without the Consent of Congress, lay any Duty of Tonnage, keep Troops, or Ships of War in time of Peace, enter into any Agreement or Compact with another State, or with a foreign Power, or engage in War, unless actually invaded, or in such imminent Danger as will not admit of delay.

Article II

Section 1. The executive Power shall be vested in a President of the United States of America. He shall hold his Office during the Term of four Years, and, together with the Vice President, chosen for the same Term, be elected as follows

Each State shall appoint, in such Manner as the Legislature thereof may direct, a Number of Electors, equal to the whole Number of Senators and Representatives to which the State may be entitled in the Congress: but no Senator or Representative, or Person holding an Office of Trust or Profit under the United States, shall be appointed an Elector.

The Electors shall meet in their respective States, and vote by Ballot for two Persons, of whom one at least shall not be an Inhabitant of the same State with themselves. And they shall make a List of all the Persons voted for, and of the Number of Votes for each; which List they shall sign and certify, and transmit sealed to the Seat

INTRODUCTION TO VOLUME 4

of the Government of the United States, directed to the President of the Senate. The President of the Senate shall, in the Presence of the Senate and House of Representatives, open all the Certificates, and the Votes shall then be counted. The Person having the greatest Number of Votes shall be the President, if such Number be a Majority of the whole Number of Electors appointed; and if there be more than one who have such Majority, and have an equal Number of Votes, then the House of Representatives shall immediately chuse by Ballot one of them for President; and if no Person have a Majority, then from the five highest on the List the said House shall in like Manner chuse the President. But in chusing the President, the Votes shall be taken by States, the Representation from each State having one Vote; A quorum for this Purpose shall consist of a Member or Members from two thirds of the States, and a Majority of all the States shall be necessary to a Choice. In every Case, after the Choice of the President, the Person having the greatest Number of Votes of the Electors shall be the Vice President. But if there should remain two or more who have equal Votes, the Senate shall chuse from them by Ballot the Vice President.

The Congress may determine the Time of chusing the Electors, and the Day on which they shall give their Votes; which Day shall be the same throughout the United States.

No Person except a natural born Citizen, or a Citizen of the United States, at the time of the Adoption of this Constitution, shall be eligible to the Office of President; neither shall any Person be eligible to that Office who shall not have attained to the Age of thirty five Years, and been fourteen Years a Resident within the United States.

In the Case of the Removal of the President from Office, or of his Death, Resignation, or Inability to discharge the Powers and Duties of the said Office, the Same shall devolve on the Vice President, and the Congress may by Law provide for the Case of Removal, Death, Resignation or Inability, both of the President and Vice President, declaring what Officer shall then act as President, and such Officer shall act accordingly, until the Disability be removed, or a President shall be elected.

The President shall, at stated Times, receive for his Services, a Compensation, which shall neither be encreased nor diminished during the Period for which he shall have been elected, and he shall not receive within that Period any other Emolument from the United States, or any of them.

Before he enter on the Execution of his Office, he shall take the following Oath or Affirmation:—"I do solemnly swear (or affirm) that I will faithfully execute the Office of the President of the United States, and will to the best of my Ability, preserve, protect and defend the Constitution of the United States."

Section 2. The President shall be the Commander in Chief of the Army and Navy of the United States, and of the Militia of the several States, when called into the actual service of the United States; he may require the Opinion, in writing, of the principal Officer in each of the executive Departments, upon any Subject relating to the Duties of their respective Offices, and he shall have Power to grant Reprieves and Pardons for Offenses against the United States, except in Cases of Impeachment.

He shall have Power, by and with the Advice and Consent of the Senate, to make Treaties, provided two thirds of the Senators present concur; and he shall nominate, and by and with the Advice and Consent of the Senate, shall appoint Ambassadors, other public Ministers and Consuls, Judges of the supreme Court, and all other Officers of the United States, whose Appointments are not herein otherwise provided for, and which shall be established by Law but the Congress may by Law vest the Appointment of such inferior Officers, as they think proper, in the President alone, in the Courts of Law, or in the Heads of Departments.

The President shall have Power to fill up all Vacancies that may happen during the Recess of the Senate, by granting Commissions which shall expire at the End of their next Session.

Section 3. He shall from time to time give to the Congress Information of the State of the Union, and recommend to their Consideration such Measures as he shall judge necessary and expedient; he may, on extraordinary Occasions, convene both Houses, or either of them, and in Case of Disagreement between them, with Respect to the Time of Adjournment, he may adjourn them to such Time as he shall think proper; he shall receive Ambassadors and other public Ministers; he shall take Care that the Laws be faithfully executed, and shall Commission all the Officers of the United States.

Section 4. The President, Vice President and all civil Officers of the United States, shall be removed from Office on Impeachment for, and Conviction of, Treason, Bribery, or other high Crimes and Misdemeanors.

Article III

Section 1. The judicial Power of the United States, shall be vested in one supreme Court, and in such inferior Courts as the Congress may from time to time ordain and establish. The Judges, both of the supreme and inferior Courts, shall hold their Offices during good Behaviour, and shall, at stated Times, receive for their Services, a Compensation, which shall not be diminished during their Continuance in Office.

Section 2. The judicial Power shall extend to all Cases, in Law and Equity, arising under this Constitution, the Laws of the United States, and Treaties made, or which shall be made, under their Authority;—to all Cases affecting Ambassadors, other public Ministers and Consuls;—to all Cases of admiralty and maritime Jurisdiction;—to Controversies to which the United States shall be a Party;—to Controversies between two or more States;—between a State and Citizens of another State;—between Citizens of different States;—between Citizens of the same State claiming Lands under Grants of different States, and between a State, or the Citizens thereof, and foreign States, Citizens or Subjects.

In all cases affecting Ambassadors, other public Ministers and Consuls, and those in which a State shall be a Party, the supreme Court shall have original Jurisdiction. In all the other Cases before mentioned, the supreme Court shall have appellate Jurisdiction, both as to Law and Fact, with such Exceptions, and under such Regulations as the Congress shall make.

The Trial of all Crimes, except in Cases of Impeachment, shall be by Jury; and such Trial shall be held in the State where the said Crimes shall have been committed; but when not committed within any State, the Trial shall be at such Place or Places as the Congress may by Law have directed.

Section 3. Treason against the United States, shall consist only in levying War against them, or in adhering to their Enemies, giving them Aid or Comfort. No Person shall be convicted of Treason unless on the Testimony of two Witnesses to the same overt Act, or on Confession in open Court.

The Congress shall have Power to declare the Punishment of Treason, but no Attainder of Treason shall work Corruption of Blood, or Forfeiture except during the Life of the Person attainted.

Article IV

Section 1. Full Faith and Credit shall be given in each State to the public Acts, Records, and judicial Proceedings of every other State. And the Congress may by general Laws prescribe the Manner in which such Acts, Records and Proceedings shall be proved, and the Effect thereof.

Section 2. The Citizens of each State shall be entitled to all Privileges and Immunities of Citizens in the several States.

A Person charged in any State with Treason, Felony, or other Crime, who shall flee from Justice, and be found in another State, shall on Demand of the executive Authority of the State from which he fled, be delivered up, to be removed to the State having Jurisdiction of the Crime.

No Person held to Service or Labour in one State, under the Laws thereof, escaping into another, shall, in Consequence of any Law or Regulation therein, be discharged from such Service or Labour, but shall be delivered up on Claim of the Party to whom such Service or Labour may be due.

Section 3. New States may be admitted by the Congress into this Union; but no new State shall be formed or erected within the Jurisdiction of any other State; nor any State be formed by the Junction of two or more States, or Parts of States, without the Consent of the Legislatures of the States concerned as well as of the Congress.

The Congress shall have Power to dispose of and make all needful Rules and Regulations respecting the Territory or other Property belonging to the United States; and nothing in this Constitution shall be so construed to Prejudice any Claims of the United States, or of any particular State.

Section 4. The United States shall guarantee to every State in this Union a Republican Form of Government, and shall protect each of them against Invasion; and on

Application of the Legislature, or of the Executive (when the Legislature cannot be convened) against domestic Violence.

Article V

The Congress, whenever two thirds of both Houses shall deem it necessary, shall propose Amendments to this Constitution, or, on the Application of the Legislatures of two thirds of the several States, shall call a Convention for proposing Amendments, which, in either Case, shall be valid to all Intents and Purposes, as Part of this Constitution, when ratified by the Legislatures of three fourths of the several States, or by Conventions in three fourths thereof, as the one or the other Mode of Ratification may be proposed by the Congress; provided that no Amendment which may be made prior to the Year One thousand eight hundred and eight shall in any Manner affect the first and fourth Clauses in the Ninth Section of the first Article; and that no State, without its Consent, shall be deprived of its equal Suffrage in the Senate.

Article VI

All Debts contracted and Engagements entered into, before the adoption of this Constitution, shall be as valid against the United States under this Constitution, as under the Confederation.

This Constitution, and the Laws of the United States which shall be made in Pursuance thereof; and all Treaties made, or which shall be made, under the Authority of the United States, shall be the supreme Law of the Land; and the Judges in every State shall be bound thereby, any Thing in the Constitution or Laws of any State to the Contrary notwithstanding.

The Senators and Representatives before mentioned, and the members of the several State Legislatures, and all executive and judicial Officers, both of the United States and of the several States, shall be bound by Oath or Affirmation, to support this Constitution; but no religious Test shall ever be required as a Qualification to any Office or public Trust under the United States.

Article VII

The Ratification of the Conventions of nine States, shall be sufficient for the Establishment of this Constitution between the States so ratifying the Same.

Go. Washington—Presidt.

And deputy from Virginia

New Hampshire
John Langdon
Nicholas Gilman

New Jersey
Wil: Livingston
David Brearley
Wm. Paterson
Jona: Dayton

Massachusetts
Nathaniel Gorham
Rufus King

Connecticut
Wm. Saml. Johnson
Roger Sherman

New York
Alexander Hamilton

Pennsylvania
B Franklin
Thomas Mifflin
Robt. Morris
Geo. Clymer
Thos. Fitzsimons
Jared Ingersoll
James Wilson
Gouv Morris

Delaware
Geo: Read
Cunning Bedford jun
John Dickinson
Richard Bassett
Jaco: Broom

North Carolina
Wm: Blount.
Richd. Dobbs Spaight
Hu Williamson

Maryland
James McHenry
Dan of St. Thos. Jenifer
Danl. Carroll

South Carolina
J. Rutledge
Charles Cotesworth Pinckney
Pierce Butler

Virginia
John Blair
James Madison Jr.

Georgia
William Few
Abr Baldwin

The Bill of Rights

(1791)

Amendment I

Congress shall make no law respecting an establishment of religion, or prohibiting the free exercise thereof; or abridging the freedom of speech, or of the press; or the right of the people peaceably to assemble, and to petition the government for a redress of grievances.

Amendment II

A well regulated militia, being necessary to the security of a free state, the right of the people to keep and bear arms, shall not be infringed.

Amendment III

No soldier shall, in time of peace be quartered in any house, without the consent of the owner, nor in time of war, but in a manner to be prescribed by law.

Amendment IV

The right of the people to be secure in their persons, houses, papers, and effects, against unreasonable searches and seizures, shall not be violated, and no warrants shall issue, but upon probable cause, supported by oath or affirmation, and particularly describing the place to be searched, and the persons or things to be seized.

Amendment V

No person shall be held to answer for a capital, or otherwise infamous crime, unless on a presentment or indictment of a grand jury, except in cases arising in the land or naval forces, or in the militia, when in actual service in time of war or public danger; nor shall any person be subject for the same offense to be twice put in jeopardy of life or limb; nor shall be compelled in any criminal case to be a witness against himself, nor be deprived of life, liberty, or property, without due process of law; nor shall private property be taken for public use, without just compensation.

Amendment VI

In all criminal prosecutions, the accused shall enjoy the right to a speedy and public trial, by an impartial jury of the state and district wherein the crime shall have been committed, which district shall have been previously ascertained by law, and to be informed of the nature and cause of the accusation; to be confronted with the witnesses against him; to have compulsory process for obtaining witnesses in his favor, and to have the assistance of counsel for his defense.

Amendment VII

In suits at common law, where the value in controversy shall exceed twenty dollars, the right of trial by jury shall be preserved, and no fact tried by a jury, shall be otherwise reexamined in any court of the United States, then according to the rules of the common law.

Amendment VIII

Excessive bail shall not be required, nor excessive fines imposed, nor cruel and unusual punishments inflicted.

Amendment IX

The enumeration in the Constitution, of certain rights, shall not be construed to deny or disparage others retained by the people.

Amendment X

The powers not delegated to the United States by the Constitution, nor prohibited by it to the states, are reserved to the states respectively, or to the people.

Later Amendments

Amendment XI

(1798)

The judicial power of the United States shall not be construed to extend to any suit in law or equity, commenced or prosecuted against one of the United States by Citizens of another State, or by Citizens or Subjects of any Foreign State.

Amendment XII

(1804)

The Electors shall meet in their respective states and vote by ballot for President and Vice-President, one of whom, at least, shall not be an inhabitant of the same state with themselves; they shall name in their ballots the person voted for as President, and in distinct ballots the person voted for as Vice-President, and they shall make distinct lists of all persons voted for as President, and of all persons voted for as Vice-President, and of the number of votes for each, which lists they shall sign and certify, and transmit sealed to the seat of the government of the United States, directed to the President of the Senate;—The President of the Senate shall, in the presence of the Senate and House of Representatives, open all the certificates and the votes shall then be counted;—the person having the greatest number of votes for President, shall be the President, if such number be a majority of the whole number of Electors appointed; and if no person have such majority, then from the persons having the highest numbers not exceeding three on the list of those voted for as President, the House of Representatives shall choose immediately, by ballot, the President. But in choosing the President, the votes shall be taken by states, the representation from each state having one vote; a quorum for this purpose shall consist of a member or members from two-thirds of the states, and a majority of all the states shall be necessary to a choice. And if the House of Representatives shall not choose a President whenever the right of choice shall devolve upon them, before the fourth day of March next following, then the Vice-President shall act as President, as in the case of the death or other constitutional disability of the President. The person having the greatest number of votes as Vice-President, shall be the Vice-President, if such number be a majority of the whole number of Electors appointed, and if no person have a majority, then from the two highest numbers on the list, the Senate shall choose the Vice-President; a quorum for the purpose shall consist of two-thirds of the whole number of Senators, and a majority of the whole number shall be necessary to a choice. But no person constitutionally ineligible to the office of President shall be eligible to that of Vice-President of the United States.

Amendment XIII

(1865)

Section 1. Neither slavery nor involuntary servitude, except as a punishment for crime whereof the party shall have been duly convicted, shall exist within the United States, or any place subject to their jurisdiction.

Section 2. Congress shall have power to enforce this article by appropriate legislation.

Amendment XIV

(1868)

Section 1. All persons born or naturalized in the United States, and subject to the jurisdiction thereof, are citizens of the United States and of the State wherein they reside. No State shall make or enforce any law which shall abridge the privileges or immunities of citizens of the United States; nor shall any State deprive any person of life, liberty, or property, without due process of law; nor deny to any person within its jurisdiction the equal protection of the laws.

Section 2. Representatives shall be apportioned among the several States according to their respective numbers, counting the whole number of persons in each State, excluding Indians not taxed. But when the right to vote at any election for the choice of electors for President and Vice President of the United States, Representatives in Congress, the Executive and Judicial.officers of a State, or the members of the Legislature thereof, is denied to any of the male inhabitants of such State, being twenty-one years of age, and citizens of the United States, or in any way abridged, except for participation in rebellion, or other crime, the basis of representation therein shall be reduced in the proportion which the number of such male citizens shall bear to the whole number of male citizens twenty-one years of age in such State.

Section 3. No person shall be a Senator or Representative in Congress, or elector of President and Vice President, or hold any office, civil or military, under the United States, or under any State, who, having previously taken an oath, as a member of Congress, or as an officer of the United States, or as a member of any State legislature, or as an executive or judicial officer of any State, to support the Constitution of the United States, shall have engaged in insurrection or rebellion against the same, or given aid or comfort to the enemies thereof. But Congress may by a vote of two-thirds of each House, remove such disability.

Section 4. The validity of the public debt of the United States, authorized by law, including debts incurred for payment of pensions and bounties for services in suppressing insurrection or rebellion, shall not be questioned. But neither the United States nor any State shall assume or pay any debt or obligation incurred in aid of insurrection or rebellion against the United States, or any claim for the loss or emancipation of any slave; but all such debts, obligations and claims shall be held illegal and void.

Section 5. The Congress shall have power to enforce, by appropriate legislation, the provisions of this article.

Amendment XV

(1870)

Section 1. The right of citizens of the United States to vote shall not be denied or abridged by the United States or by any State on account of race, color, or previous condition of servitude.

Section 2. The Congress shall have power to enforce this article by appropriate legislation.

Amendment XVI

(1913)

The Congress shall have power to lay and collect taxes on incomes, from whatever source derived, without apportionment among the several States, and without regard to any census or enumeration.

Amendment XVII

(1913)

The Senate of the United States shall be composed of two Senators from each State, elected by the people thereof, for six years; and each Senator shall have one vote. The electors in each State shall have the qualifications requisite for electors of the most numerous branch of the State legislature.

When vacancies happen in the representation of any State in the Senate, the executive authority of such State shall issue writs of election to fill such vacancies: *Provided*, That the legislature of any State may empower the executive thereof to make temporary appointments until the people fill the vacancies by election as the legislature may direct.

This amendment shall not be so construed as to affect the election or term of any Senator chosen before it becomes valid as part of the Constitution.

Amendment XVIII

(1919)

Section 1. After one year from the ratification of this article the manufacture, sale, or transportation of intoxicating liquors within, the importation thereof into, or the exportation thereof from the United States and all territory subject to the jurisdiction thereof for beverage purposes is hereby prohibited.

Section 2. The Congress and the several States shall have concurrent power to enforce this article by appropriate legislation.

Section 3. This article shall be inoperative unless it shall have been ratified as an amendment to the Constitution by the legislatures of the several States, as provided in the Constitution, within seven years from the date of the submission hereof to the States by the Congress.

Amendment XIX

(1920)

The right of citizens of the United States to vote shall not be denied or abridged by the United States or by any State on account of sex.

Congress shall have power to enforce this article by appropriate legislation.

Amendment XX

(1933)

Section 1. The terms of the President and Vice President shall end at noon on the 20th day of January, and the terms of Senators and Representatives at noon on the 3d day of January, of the years in which such terms would have ended if this article had not been ratified; and the terms of their successors shall then begin.

Section 2. The Congress shall assemble at least once in every year, and such meeting shall begin at noon on the 3d day of January, unless they shall by law appoint a different day.

Section 3. If, at the time fixed for the beginning of the term of the President, the President elect shall have died, the Vice President elect shall become President. If a President shall not have been chosen before the time fixed for the beginning of his term, or if the President elect shall have failed to qualify, then the Vice President elect shall act as President until a President shall have qualified; and the Congress may by law provide for the case wherein neither a President elect nor a Vice President elect shall have qualified, declaring who shall then act as President, or the manner in which one who is to act shall be selected, and such person shall act accordingly until a President or Vice President shall have qualified.

Section 4. The Congress may by law provide for the case of the death of any of the persons from whom the House of Representatives may choose a President whenever the right of choice shall have devolved upon them, and for the case of the death of any of the persons from whom the Senate may choose a Vice President whenever the right of choice shall have devolved upon them.

Section 5. Sections 1 and 2 shall take effect on the 15th day of October following the ratification of this article.

Section 6. This article shall be inoperative unless it shall have been ratified as an amendment to the Constitution by the legislatures of three-fourths of the several States within seven years from the date of its submission.

Amendment XXI
(1933)

Section 1. The eighteenth article of amendment to the Constitution of the United States is hereby repealed.

Section 2. The transportation or importation into any State, territory, or possession of the United States for delivery or use therein of intoxicating liquors, in violation of the laws thereof, is hereby prohibited.

Section 3. This article shall be inoperative unless it shall have been ratified as an amendment to the Constitution by conventions in the several States, as provided in the Constitution, within seven years from the date of the submission hereof to the States by the Congress.

Amendment XXII
(1951)

Section 1. No person shall be elected to the office of the President more than twice, and no person who has held the office of President, or acted as President, for more than two years of a term to which some other person was elected President shall be elected to the office of the President more than once. But this article shall not apply to any person holding the office of President when this article was proposed by the Congress, and shall not prevent any person who may be holding the office of President, or acting as President, during the term within which this article becomes operative from holding the office of President or acting as President during the remainder of such term.

Section 2. This article shall be inoperative unless it shall have been ratified as an amendment to the Constitution by the legislatures of three-fourths of the several States within seven years from the date of its submission to the States by the Congress.

Amendment XXIII

(1961)

Section 1. The District constituting the seat of government of the United States shall appoint in such manner as the Congress may direct:

A number of electors of President and Vice President equal to the whole number of Senators and Representatives in Congress to which the District would be entitled if it were a State, but in no event more than the least populous State; they shall be in addition to those appointed by the States, but they shall be considered, for the purposes of the election of the President and Vice President, to be electors appointed by a State; and they shall meet in the District and perform such duties as provided by the twelfth article of amendment.

Section 2. The Congress shall have power to enforce this article by appropriate legislation.

Amendment XXIV

(1964)

Section 1. The right of citizens of the United States to vote in any primary or other election for President or Vice President, for electors for President or Vice President, or for Senator or Representative in Congress, shall not be denied or abridged by the United States or any State by reason of failure to pay any poll tax or other tax.

Section 2. The Congress shall have the power to enforce this article by appropriate legislation.

Amendment XXV

(1967)

Section 1. In case of the removal of the President from office or his death or resignation, the Vice President shall become President.

Section 2. Whenever there is a vacancy in the office of the Vice President, the President shall nominate a Vice President who shall take office upon confirmation by a majority vote of both Houses of Congress.

Section 3. Whenever the President transmits to the President pro tempore of the Senate and the Speaker of the House of Representatives his written declaration that he is unable to discharge the powers and duties of his office, and until he transmits to them a written declaration to the contrary, such powers and duties shall be discharged by the Vice President as Acting President.

Section 4. Whenever the Vice President and a majority of either the principal officers of the executive departments or such other body as Congress may by law provide, transmit to the President pro tempore of the Senate and the Speaker of the House of Representatives their written declaration that the President is unable to discharge the powers and duties of his office, the Vice President shall immediately assume the powers and duties of the office as Acting President.

Thereafter, when the President transmits to the President pro tempore of the Senate and the Speaker of the House of Representatives his written declaration that no inability exists, he shall resume the powers and duties of his office unless the Vice President and a majority of either the principal officers of the executive department or of such other body as Congress may by law provide, transmit within four days to the President pro tempore of the Senate and the Speaker of the House of Representatives their written declaration that the President is unable to discharge the powers and duties of his office. Thereupon Congress shall decide the issue, assembling within forty-eight hours for that purpose if not in session. If the Congress, within twenty-one days after receipt of the latter written declaration, or, if Congress is not in session, within twenty-one days after Congress is required to assemble, determine by two-thirds vote of both Houses that the President is unable to discharge the powers and duties of his office, the Vice President shall continue to discharge the same as Acting President; otherwise, the President shall resume the powers and duties of his office.

Amendment XXVI

(1971)

Section 1. The right of citizens of the United States, who are 18 years of age or older, to vote, shall not be denied or abridged by the United States or any State on account of age.

Section 2. The Congress shall have the power to enforce this article by appropriate legislation.

Amendment XXVII

(1992)

No law varying the compensation for the services of the Senators and Representatives shall take effect until an election of Representatives shall have intervened.

Chapter 1

THE CONTRACTS CLAUSE

A. INTRODUCTION

The Contracts Clause prohibits states from passing any "Law impairing the Obligation of Contract." U.S. Const. Art. I, § 10, cl. 1. The Supreme Court's interpretation of the Clause has varied from an initially robust interpretation to today's relatively narrow interpretation.

EXERCISE 1:

Volume I in this series introduced five commonly-accepted forms of argument in constitutional interpretation. They include: (1) the Constitution's text; (2) the structure of the government created and contemplated by the Constitution; (3) the historical setting from which the Constitution emerged and the text's meaning as articulated in that setting; (4) the traditional understanding of the Constitution on a particular matter; and (5) judicial precedent.

Apply the first four forms of argument to the Contracts Clause:

1. Looking at the Contracts Clause itself, the text of the rest of Article I, § 10, cl. 1, and the text of Article I, § 10, what do you learn about the Contract Clause's meaning?

2. Looking at the Constitution's structure, and particularly at the federal system it creates, what do you learn about the Contract Clause's meaning?

3. Reviewing materials from the ratification debates (on the course website), what do they tell you about that meaning?

4. What insight do the materials following adoption of the Constitution (including early treatises on the course website) offer into the Contract Clause's meaning?

As you read the materials throughout the rest of this Chapter, some of the issues to consider include:

Does the Contracts Clause apply to the Federal government?

Does the Contracts Clause apply only to contracts between private parties, or does it also apply to contracts to which a state is a party?

Are there — or should there be — any differences in treatment between private and government contracts?

Is the distinction between laws that impair *obligations* of contract and laws that impair *remedies* relevant under today's law?

Is the distinction between laws impairing obligations and laws impairing remedies one of kind or degree?

What is the Supreme Court's current interpretation of the Contracts Clause?

How does the Supreme Court's current interpretation of the Contracts Clause differ from its previous interpretation(s)?

What is the basis for the Supreme Court's modern interpretation of the Contracts Clause?

Which of the Supreme Court's interpretations of the Contracts Clause has the most support from the five forms of argument?

B. ORIGINS

The Contracts Clause was drafted and inserted into the Constitution to prohibit states from passing debtor relief legislation which had become, in the view of the Framers, an all-too-common practice. During the period prior to the adoption of the Constitution, state legislatures, subject to pressure, especially from farmer-debtors, had passed a variety of laws making it difficult for creditors to collect the full value of what was owed them. The Contracts Clause was designed to prevent states from retroactively eliminating or reducing the contractual rights of creditors.[1]

In the first sixty years of the Constitution, the Contracts Clause was frequently litigated. But by the 1950s, largely due to case law articulated during the New Deal, the Supreme Court construed the Clause so narrowly that it became more of an historic relic, though there was a brief revival in the late 1970s. In this Section, we are concerned only with the history and development of the Contracts Clause through the Framing and Ratification.

The Contracts Clause is important for at least two reasons. First, it is one of the few clauses in the Constitution of 1789 that protected individual rights. Second, it was one of the few provisions that was a direct limitation on the states prior to the adoption of the Fourteenth Amendment.[2] There are many factors that contributed to the framing and subsequent incorporation of the Contracts Clause into the U.S. Constitution.

The Framers held the widely believed view that the security of private property was essential to individual liberty. John Locke's *Second Treatise* had influenced the Framers to beware of the evils of "[arbitrariness] over the lives and fortunes of the people."[3]

---

1. Douglas W. Kmiec & John O. McGinnis, *The Contracts Clause: A Return to the Original Understanding*, 14 Hast. Const. L.Q. 525, 533–34 (1987).

2. Article I, Section 10 of the Constitution includes other provisions restricting state power.

3. John Locke, Two Treatises of Government § 135 (1680–90).

The emergent economic theory of the time, now called classical economics, as embodied in Adam Smith's *Wealth of Nations*, had convinced many of the Framers of the boons of state non-interference in commerce.[4] By the time of the Philadelphia Convention, the Framers had practical experience to support these theoretical points.

Under the Articles of Confederation, states had adopted pro-debtor laws making it easy for debtors to pay off creditors either through inflated—i.e., devalued—currency or by seeking debt relief from state legislatures.[5] Partly as a result, the country's economy was in disarray.[6] James Madison, in his famous *Federalist No. 10*, described

---

4. For a detailed discussion, see CHARLES A. BEARD, AN ECONOMIC INTERPRETATION OF THE CONSTITUTION OF THE UNITED STATES 31–32 (1913) ("[P]aper money, stay laws, pine barren acts, and other devices for depreciating the currency or delaying the collection of debts [led to] a widespread derangement of the monetary system."); *see also* Kmiec & McGinnis, *supra*, at 526 (describing the Clause as prohibiting "retrospective, redistributive legislation").

5. JAMES MADISON, NOTES OF DEBATES IN THE FEDERAL CONVENTION OF 1787, at 15 (1966) ("In the internal administration of the States a violation of Contracts had become familiar in the form of depreciated paper made a legal tender, of property substituted for money, of Instalment laws, and of the occlusions of the Courts of Justice; although evident that all such interferences affected the rights of other States, relatively creditor, as well as Citizens Creditors within the State."); *see also* 3 THE RECORDS OF THE FEDERAL CONVENTION OF 1787, at 548 (Max Ferrand ed., 1966); 5 THE DEBATES IN THE SEVERAL STATE CONVENTIONS ON THE ADOPTION OF THE FEDERAL CONSTITUTION AS RECOMMENDED BY THE GENERAL CONVENTION AT PHILADELPHIA IN 1787, at 120 (Jonathan Elliot, ed., 1974) (hereinafter "ELLIOT'S DEBATES"); JOHN R. VILE, THE CONSTITUTIONAL CONVENTION OF 1787: A COMPREHENSIVE ENCYCLOPEDIA OF AMERICA'S FOUNDING 190 (2005). *See generally* CHARLES WARREN, THE MAKING OF THE CONSTITUTION 5–6 (1928) ("[T]he State laws particularly complained of [were] those staying process of the Courts, making property a tender in payment of debts, issuing paper money, interfering with foreclosure of mortgages."); JOHN FISKE, THE CRITICAL PERIOD OF AMERICAN HISTORY 168 (1888) ("By 1786, under the universal depression and want of confidence, all trade had ... stopped, and political quackery, with its cheap and dirty remedies, had full control of the field .... [P]aper money [and] a Barmecide feast of economic vagaries [were prevalent].").

6. CHRISTOPHER COLLIER & JAMES L. COLLIER, DECISION IN PHILADELPHIA, THE CONSTITUTIONAL CONVENTION OF 1787, at 10–11 (1986). Collier vividly illustrates this point:

> [T]he disappearance of hard currency from the American states was bound to cause problems. The British manufacturers leaned on the American importers for payment, and they in turn leaned on the local shopkeepers, who leaned on the local farmers. But too frequently the farmers had no money. The storekeepers then went to court and sent sheriffs out to attach a farmer's plow or horse or even his farm; and if that was not enough, the courts might actually put the farmer in jail. From 1784 to 1786 in Hampshire County, Massachusetts, nearly a third of the males over sixteen were involved in debt cases. The figure was typical of the whole country. Sheriff's auctions were commonplace. Here you would see for sale your neighbor's ox, your cousin's plow, your brother's barrels of cider. Farms were foreclosed and hundreds of men were thrown into debtor's prisons—seventy-three men in Hampshire County between July 1784 and December 1786.
>
> Those in trouble were frantic, and like trapped animals, they sprang at anything that looked like a way out. They began demanding that their state legislatures save them. They asked for stay laws, which would postpone all debt collection for some period of time, typically a year. They wanted more paper money, backed only by faith, but this currency tended to depreciate even as it came from the press. They wanted tender laws, which would require creditors to accept payment in this depreciated money.

the harm caused by property redistributing legislation of which debtor relief laws were the paradigm example.[7] He maintained that legislation seeking to redistribute resources between factions—in this case from creditors to debtors—by voiding contractual obligations, oppressed minority factions.[8]

Thus, there was a consensus on limiting state power to retroactively impair contracts.[9] However, it was widely believed that the *Ex Post Facto* Clause applied only to criminal cases.[10] Hence, there arose the need for the Contracts Clause, which would limit retroactive laws in civil matters, and delegates to the Philadelphia Convention introduced a provision to prohibit retrospective laws in civil matters.[11]

The Contracts Clause was therefore part of a wider scheme of prohibitions on the states. Coupled with the prohibitions in the *Ex Post Facto* Clause and against bills of attainder,[12] along with Congress' power to enact bankruptcy laws[13] and Article VI's preservation of pre-existing debts,[14] the Contracts Clause incorporated the notion into the Constitution of ensuring that people had a fair opportunity to organize their affairs without fear of retroactive state intervention.

The Contracts Clause was not introduced until late in the Federal Convention.[15] Rufus King, a delegate from Massachusetts, was the first to propose a provision

---

Creditors fought bitterly against these laws, which seemed to them little more than legal robbery. In states where they were able to dominate the legislatures they prevented passage of the laws. The farmers, left without legal redress, turned to illegal ones. From 1784 on, in New Jersey, South Carolina, Pennsylvania, Virginia, and Maryland, bands of insurgent farmers gathered at courts and sheriff's auctions and closed them down. In some places they set fire to courthouses, destroying records of debt cases.

Id. at 11.

7. The Federalist No. 10 (James Madison) ("Is a law proposed concerning private debts? It is a question to which the creditors are parties on one side and the debtors on the other.").

8. Kmiec & McGinnis, *supra*, at 528–29.

9. *Id.* at 527–28.

10. *See* Volume 1 (*Calder v. Bull* and accompanying discussion); *see also* Forrest McDonald, Novus Ordo Seclorum, the Intellectual Origins of the Constitution 208 (1985); Vile, *supra*, at 190.

11. Vile, *supra*, at 190.

12. U.S. Const. art I, § 10, cl. 1.

13. U.S. Const. art. I, § 8, cl. 4.

14. U.S. Const. art. VI, cl. 1.

15. The Contracts Clause was absent from the August 6, 1787, draft of the Constitution, and the only precursor to the current Article I, Section 10 was "Article XII: No State shall coin money; nor grant letters of marque and reprisal; nor enter into any Treaty, alliance, or confederation; nor grant any title of Nobility." Madison, *supra*, at 385–96. Mr. King moved to introduce a rudimentary contracts clause on August 28, 1787. *Id.* at 542 ("Mr. King moved to add, in the words used in the Ordinance of Cong[ress] establishing new States, a prohibition on the States to interfere in private contracts."). However, this proposal was quashed with an 8–3 vote. *Id.* at 543. The Contracts Clause finally made its way into the September 12, 1787, version of the Constitution, but was amended on September 14, 1787. *Id.* at 621, 641–42. With other minor modifications, the Constitution was signed in Convention on September 17, 1787. *Id.* at 652.

prohibiting states from interfering in private contracts.[16] King modeled the clause on a similar provision in the Northwest Ordinance of 1787.[17] The Continental Congress enacted the Northwest Ordinance on July 13, 1787, about six weeks before King proposed a contracts clause. Those at the Convention who opposed what became the Contracts Clause objected that it was "[c]arrying restraint too far because of unforeseen emergencies,"[18] and that it infringed on the right of the majority to govern.[19]

However, James Madison's argument that any inconvenience caused by the Contracts Clause would be outweighed by its utility ultimately gained support.[20] (Madison extended this argument in *Federalist No. 10*.[21]) Pennsylvania delegate James Wilson's argument also was persuasive. He contended that since the Contracts Clause did not prohibit prospective relief, it would prevent oppression of minority factions as well as the uncertainty and arbitrariness of retrospective legislation, while at the same time leaving the door open for prospective legislation which is better controlled by the natural political process.[22]

The Contracts Clause was subsequently adopted.[23] Interestingly, the Constitutional Convention did not expressly restrict Congress from retrospectively impairing the obligation of contracts, but this omission occurred without discussion.[24]

---

16. *See* 3 The Documentary History of the Ratification of the Constitution 352 (Merrill Jensen ed., 1978) ("The restraint on the legislatures of the several states respecting . . . impairing the obligation of contracts by *ex post facto* laws was thought necessary as a security to commerce, in which the interest of foreigners as well as citizens of different states may be affected."); 2 The Records of the Federal Convention of 1787, at 439–40, 448–49; *see also* Vile, *supra*, at 190.

17. An Ordinance for the Government of the Territory of the United States North-West of the River Ohio, 1 Stat. 51 (1789) ("And in the just preservation of rights and property, it is understood and declared, that no law ought ever to be made, or have force in the said territory, that shall in any manner whatever interfere with, or affect private contracts, or engagements, bona fide, and without fraud previously formed."). For a detailed history of the Northwest Ordinance, see Peter S. Onuf, Statehood and Union: A History of the Northwest Ordinance xiii (1987); *see also* The Northwest Ordinance 1787: A Bicentennial Handbook (Robert M. Taylor, ed., 1987); Northwest Ordinance: Essays on Its Formulation, Provisions and Legacy (Frederick D. Williams, ed., 1988).

18. Madison, *supra*, at 439.

19. *Id.*

20. Vile, *supra*, at 190.

21. "Complaints are everywhere heard . . . that the public good is disregarded in the conflicts of rival parties, and that measures are too often decided, not according to the rules of justice and the rights of the minor party, but by the superior force of an interested and overbearing majority. . . . These must be chiefly, if not wholly, effects of the unsteadiness and injustice with which a factious spirit has tainted our public administrations." The Federalist No. 10 (J. Madison).

22. Vile, *supra*, at 190.

23. For a full discussion of events leading up to the inclusion of the Contracts Clause, see McDonald, *supra*, at 270–75.

24. 3 Documentary History of the Constitution of the United States of America 749 ("Mr. Gerry entered into observations inculcating the importance of public faith, and the propriety of the restraint put on the States from impairing the obligation of contracts—Alledging that Congress ought to be laid under the like prohibitions. [H]e made a motion to that effect. He was not [seconded].").

The debates in the various state conventions also evidenced the common under-standing of the Contracts Clause. The most widely accepted meaning of the Contracts Clause in the state conventions was that it was "necessary as a security to commerce."[25] In North Carolina, for instance, the fear of South Carolina impairing its contracts was palpable. North Carolina, thus, was supportive of the Contracts Clause.[26]

Debates in North Carolina further suggest that the Ratifiers in that state believed that law generally may have no retrospective application, whether civil or criminal.[27] Therefore, an express provision prohibiting states from retrospectively impairing obligations of contract was viewed as no more than codification of an established principle of jurisprudence.[28]

South Carolina was supportive of the Contracts Clause, mainly because of Charles Pinckney, who was supportive of the Clause in the Federal Convention. His influen-tial speech in the ratification convention prevented any protracted debate on the Clause in South Carolina.[29]

---

25. "The restraint on the legislatures of the several states respecting emitting bills of credit, making any thing but money a tender in payment of debts, or impairing the obligation of contracts by ex post facto laws, was thought necessary as a security to commerce, in which the interest of foreigners, as well as of the citizens of different states, may be affected." *Letter from Hon. Roger Sherman, and the Hon. Oliver Ellsworth, Esquires, to Gov. of Connecticut*, 1 ELLIOT'S DEBATES 492.

26. Mr. Davie, speaking about the federal judiciary, spoke in favor of Section 10's restrictions on states thus:

> These restrictions ought to supersede the laws of particular states .... Paper money and private contracts were in the same condition. Without a general controlling judici-ary, laws might be made in particular states to enable its citizens to defraud the citizens of other states. Is it probable, if a citizen of South Carolina owed a sum of money to a citizen of this state, that the latter would be certain of recovering the full value in their courts? That state might in future, as they have already done, make pine-barren acts to discharge their debts. They might say that our citizen should be paid in sterile, inarable lands, at an extravagant price. They might pass the most iniquitous instalment laws, procrastinating the payment of debts due from their citizens, for years—nay, for ages. Is it probable that we should get justice from their own judiciary, who might consider themselves obliged to obey the laws of their own state? Where, then, are we to look for justice? To the judiciary of the United States.

4 ELLIOT'S DEBATES 156–57.

27. Mr. Maclaine, in answering Mr. Bloodworth's arguments against Article 1, Section 10, said: "It is contrary to the universal principles of jurisprudence, that a law or constitution should have a retrospective operation, unless it be expressly provided that it shall." 4 ELLIOT'S DEBATES 181; *see also* THE FEDERALIST No. 44 (J. Madison) ("[L]aws impairing the obligation of contracts[] are con-trary to the first principles of the social compact and to every principle of sound legislation.").

28. 4 ELLIOT'S DEBATES 181.

29. "I consider [Article I, Section 10] as the soul of the Constitution .... If we consider the situ-ation of the United States as they are at present, either individually or as members of a general confederacy, we shall find it extremely improper [the States] should ever be intrusted with the power of emitting money, or interfering in private contracts; or, by means of tender-laws, impair-ing the obligation of contracts." 4 ELLIOT'S DEBATES 333–34.

In Massachusetts, the debate regarding Article I, § 10, revolved around the operation of checks and balances.[30] Mr. Thatcher was of the opinion that the checks and balances introduced in the Constitution would protect the states, even if Section 10 took away some of the states' powers.[31] He referenced what the states had done when Section 10 was not in place.[32] Pennsylvania also supported the Contracts Clause.[33]

This is not to say that the Contracts Clause enjoyed universal acceptance. Some viewed it as injurious to the states' ability to shoulder debts.[34] Virginia, for instance, was skeptical about Article I, § 10, because it was a large creditor state. The noted Anti-Federalist, Patrick Henry, chided Virginia for subscribing to the Constitution in general and to Article I, § 10 in particular.[35] Mr. Henry repeatedly voiced his fears regarding Section 10, especially concerning Virginia's ability to pay its share of Continental debt.[36]

---

30. 2 ELLIOT'S DEBATES 141–48.

31. *Id.* at 144–45.

32. "Massachusetts was on the point of civil war. In Vermont and New Hampshire, a great disaffection to their several governments prevailed among the people. New York absolutely refused complying with the requisitions of Congress. In Virginia, armed men endeavored to stop the courts of justice. In South Carolina, creditors, by law, were obliged to receive barren and useless land for contracts made in silver and gold. I pass over the instance of Rhode Island: their conduct was notorious." 2 ELLIOT'S DEBATES 144.

33. "I think it would be worth our adoption. . . . Fatal experience has taught us, dearly taught us, the value of [Section 10] restraints. What is the consequence even at this moment? It is true, we have no tender law in Pennsylvania; but the moment you are conveyed across the Delaware, you find it haunt your journey, and follow close upon your heels." 2 ELLIOT'S DEBATES 486.

34. Mr. J. Galloway, voicing concerns on the question of North Carolina's ability to shoulder redemption of paper money, if the Contracts Clause became effective, said:

> I wish the committee to attend to that part of [Article 1, Section 10] which provides that no state shall pass any law which will impair the obligation of contracts. Our public securities are at a low ebb, and have been so for many years. We well know that this country has taken those securities as specie. This hangs over our heads as a contract. There is a million and a half in circulation at least. That clause of the Constitution may compel us to make good the nominal value of these securities . . . . I therefore wish the committee to consider whether North Carolina can redeem those securities in the manner most agreeable to her citizens, and justifiable to the world, if this Constitution is adopted.

4 ELLIOT'S DEBATES 190–91.

35. 3 ELLIOT'S DEBATES 471.

36. "[T]his state would be obliged to pay for her share of the Continental money, shilling for shilling." 3 ELLIOT'S DEBATES 471; *see also id.* at 474 ("The expression includes public, as well as private contracts between individuals. Notwithstanding the sagacity of [Mr. Madison], he cannot prove its exclusive relation to private contracts. Here is an enormous demand, which your children, to the tenth generation, will not be able to pay. Should we ask if there be any obligation in justice to pay more than the depreciated value, we shall be told that contracts must not be impaired.").

Debates in Connecticut,[37] New Hampshire[38] and Maryland[39] were relatively cursory, except for the powerful Anti-Federalist argument, propounded by Luther Martin in the Maryland convention. Martin argued that:

> [T]here might be times of such *great public calamities* and *distress*, and such *extreme scarcity* of *specie* as should render it the *duty* of a government, for the *preservation* of even the *most valuable part* of its citizens in some measure to interfere in their favor, by passing laws *totally* or *partially stopping* the courts of justice, or authorizing the debtor to pay by *installments*, or by delivering up his property to the creditors at a *reasonable* and *honest* valuation. The times have been such as to render regulation of this kind necessary in most, or all of the States, to prevent the *wealthy creditor* and the *monied man* from *totally* destroying the *poor* though even *industrious* debtor— *Such times* may *again* arrive. I therefore voted against depriving the States of this power, a power which I am decided they ought to possess, but which I admit ought only to be exercised on very important and urgent occasions. I apprehend, Sir, the principal cause of complaint among the people at large is, the public and private debt with which they are oppressed, and which, in the present scarcity of cash, threatens them with destruction, unless they can obtain so much indulgence in point of time that by industry and frugality they may extricate themselves.[40]

In New York, there was no debate on the Contracts Clause in the ratification convention, though there was debate in the broader society.[41] In particular, James Madison prominently argued in *Federalist No. 44* that the Contracts Clause prohibited retroactive infringement of contract rights.[42] Madison recounted the harm caused by state debtor relief laws and how the Clause would help remedy those problems:

> The sober people of America are weary of the fluctuating policy which has directed the public councils. They have seen with regret and indignation that sudden changes and legislative interferences, in cases affecting personal rights, become jobs in the hands of enterprising and influential speculators, and snares to the more-industrious and less-informed part of the community. They have seen, too, that one legislative interference is but the first link

---

37. 2 ELLIOT'S DEBATES 185–202.

38. *Id.* at 203–04.

39. *Id.* at 547–66.

40. Luther Martin, *Information to the General Assembly of the State of Maryland* (1788), *reprinted in* 2 THE COMPLETE ANTI-FEDERALIST 4.77–.78 (H. Storing ed. 1981) (italics in original); *see also* 3 THE RECORDS OF THE FEDERAL CONVENTION OF 1787, at 214–15.

41. "The committee then proceeded through sections 8, 9 and 10, of this article, and the whole of the next, with little or no debate." 2 ELLIOT'S DEBATES 406. Thus, five of the nine states whose ratification was required to make the Constitution operative, debated on the meaning of the Contracts Clause. Four (Connecticut, New Hampshire, Maryland and New York) of the nine states had little or no discussion on the Contracts Clause. Excluding Virginia, four states (North Carolina, South Carolina, Massachusetts and Pennsylvania) were in favor of the clause.

42. THE FEDERALIST No. 44 (J. Madison).

of a long chain of repetitions, every subsequent interference being naturally produced by the effects of the preceding. They very rightly infer, therefore, that some thorough reform is wanting, which will banish speculations on public measures, inspire general prudence and industry, and give a regular course to the business of society.[43]

Formative Period

During his tenure on the Supreme Court, Chief Justice John Marshall utilized the Contracts Clause as the chief limitation on state power.[44] As you will see in the subsequent cases below, the Marshall Court initially interpreted the Contracts Clause robustly as a limitation on states. The Taney Court, though composed of justices from different political parties and with different political views than the Marshall Court justices, largely continued the same course. As you read the Taney Court decisions reproduced below, note in what ways the Supreme Court moved to a slightly less robust interpretation of the Contracts Clause.

Chief Justice Marshall's first opportunity to employ the Contracts Clause arose in *Fletcher v. Peck*, 10 U.S. (6 Cranch) 87 (1810). *Fletcher* involved a 1795 land grant by Georgia to private parties. The Court, speaking through Marshall, was ambiguous regarding whether the Contracts Clause voided a later Georgia statute purporting to rescind the initial statutory land grant.

FLETCHER v. PECK
10 U.S. (6 Cranch) 87 (1810)

[In 1795, the Georgia legislature authorized the transfer of valuable farmland—known as the Yazoo Lands—to a group of private individuals who had bribed several legislators, and the Governor signed the documents of transfer. The private individuals then sold the land to speculators. The bribery was uncovered and, in the wake of the ensuing scandal, the Georgia electorate selected a large number of new legislators rather than return the incumbents to office. When the new legislature convened, it repealed the authorization for sale of the lands. In 1803, one of the speculators, Peck, transferred title to a portion of the lands to Fletcher. The deed included an express warranty that the legislative repeal did not interfere with Peck's title to the land. Fletcher sued Peck for breach of that express warranty.]

CHIEF JUSTICE MARSHALL delivered the opinion of the Court.

---

43. *Id.*

44. An early precursor to Chief Justice Marshall's robust interpretation of the Contracts Clause is found in *VanHorne's Lessee v. Dorrance*, 28 F. Cas. 1012 (C.C.D. Pa. 1795) (No. 16,857) (ruling that the Contracts Clause voided a Pennsylvania statute that quieted title to land).

[I]

The 4th covenant in the deed is, that the title to the premises has been, in no way, constitutionally or legally impaired by virtue of any subsequent act of any subsequent legislature of the state of Georgia.

The principle is this; that a legislature may, by its own act, devest the vested estate of any man whatever, for reasons which shall, by itself, be deemed sufficient. Is the power of the legislature competent to the annihilation of such title, and to a resumption of the property thus held?

The principle asserted is, that one legislature is competent to repeal any act which a former legislature was competent to pass; and that one legislature cannot abridge the powers of a succeeding legislature. The correctness of this principle, so far as respects general legislation, can never be controverted. But, if an act be done under a law, a succeeding legislature cannot undo it. The past cannot be recalled by the most absolute power. Conveyances have been made, those conveyances have vested legal estate, and, if those estates may be seized by the sovereign authority, still, that they originally vested is a fact, and cannot cease to be a fact.

When, then, a law is in its nature a contract, when absolute rights have vested under that contract, a repeal of the law cannot devest those rights; and the act of annulling them, if legitimate, is rendered so by a power applicable to the case of every individual in the community.

It may well be doubted whether the nature of society and of government does not prescribe some limits to the legislative power; and, if any be prescribed, where are they to be found, if the property of an individual, fairly and honestly acquired, may be seized without compensation. To the legislature all legislative power is granted; but the question, whether the act of transferring the property of an individual to the public, be in the nature of the legislative power, is well worthy of serious reflection.

[II]

The validity of this rescinding act, then, might well be doubted, were Georgia a single sovereign power. But Georgia cannot be viewed as a single, unconnected, sovereign power, on whose legislature no other restrictions are imposed than may be found in its own constitution. She is a part of a large empire; she is a member of the American union; and that union has a constitution the supremacy of which all acknowledge, and which imposes limits to the legislatures of the several states, which none claim a right to pass. The constitution of the United States declares that no state shall pass any bill of attainder, *ex post facto* law, or law impairing the obligation of contracts.

Does the case now under consideration come within this prohibitory section of the constitution?

[A]

In considering this very interesting question, we immediately ask ourselves what is a contract? Is a grant a contract?

A contract is a compact between two or more parties, and is either executory or executed. An executory contract is one in which a party binds himself to do, or not to do, a particular thing; such was the law under which the conveyance was made by the governor. A contract executed is one in which the object of contract is performed; and this, says Blackstone, differs in nothing from a grant. The contract between Georgia and the purchasers was executed by the grant. A contract executed, as well as one which is executory, contains obligations binding on the parties. A grant, in its own nature, amounts to an extinguishment of the right of the grantor, and implies a contract not to reassert that right. A party is, therefore, always estopped by his own grant.

Since, then, in fact, a grant is a contract executed, the obligation of which still continues, and since the constitution uses the general term contract, without distinguishing between those which are executory and those which are executed, it must be construed to comprehend the latter as well as the former. It would be strange if a contract to convey was secured by the constitution, while an absolute conveyance remained unprotected.

[B]

If, under a fair construction the constitution, grants are comprehended under the terms contracts, is a grant from the state excluded from the operation of the provision? Is the clause to be considered as inhibiting the state from impairing the obligation of contracts between two individuals, but as excluding from that inhibition contracts made with itself?

The words themselves contain no such distinction. They are general, and are applicable to contracts of every description. If contracts made with the state are to be exempted from their operation, the exception must arise from the character of the contracting party, not from the words which are employed.

Whatever respect might have been felt for the state sovereignties, it is not to be disguised that the framers of the constitution viewed, with some apprehension, the violent acts which might grow out of the feelings of the moment; and that the people of the United States, in adopting that instrument, have manifested a determination to shield themselves and their property from the effects of those sudden and strong passions to which men are exposed. The restrictions on the legislative power of the states are obviously founded in this sentiment; and the constitution of the United States contains what may be deemed a bill of rights for the people of each state.

No state shall pass any bill of attainder, *ex post facto* law, or law impairing the obligation of contracts.

A bill of attainder may affect the life of an individual, or may confiscate his property, or may do both. In this form the power of the legislature over the lives and fortunes of individuals is expressly restrained. What motive, then, for implying, in words which import a general prohibition to impair the obligation of contracts, an exception in favour of the right to impair the obligation of those contracts into which the state may enter?

The state legislatures can pass no *ex post facto* law. An *ex post facto* law is one which renders an act punishable in a manner in which it was not punishable when it was committed. Such a law may inflict penalties on the person, or may inflict pecuniary penalties which swell the public treasury. The legislature is then prohibited from passing a law by which a man's estate, or any part of it, shall be seized for a crime which was not declared, by some previous law, to render him liable to that punishment. Why, then, should violence be done to the natural meaning of words for the purpose of leaving to the legislature the power of seizing, for public use, the estate of an individual in the form of a law annulling the title by which he holds that estate? The court can perceive no sufficient grounds for making this distinction. This rescinding act would have the effect of an *ex post facto* law. It forfeits the estate of Fletcher for a crime not committed by himself, but by those from whom he purchased. This cannot be effected in the form of an *ex post facto* law, or bill of attainder; why, then, is it allowable in the form of a law annulling the original grant?

The argument in favour of presuming an intention to except a case, not excepted by the words of the constitution, is susceptible of some illustration from a principle originally ingrafted in that instrument, though no longer a part of it. The constitution, as passed, gave the courts of the United States jurisdiction in suits brought against individual states. A state, then, which violated its own contract was suable in the courts of the United States for that violation. Would it have been a defence in such a suit to say that the state had passed a law absolving itself from the contract? It is scarcely to be conceived that such a defence could be set up. And yet, if a state is neither restrained by the general principles of our political institutions, nor by the words of the constitution, from impairing the obligation of its own contracts, such a defence would be a valid one. This feature is no longer found in the constitution; but it aids in the construction of those clauses with which it was originally associated.

It is, then, the unanimous opinion of the court, that, in this case, the estate having passed into the hands of a purchaser for a valuable consideration, without notice, the state of Georgia was restrained, either by general principles which are common to our free institutions, or by the particular provisions of the constitution of the United States, from passing a law whereby the estate of the plaintiff in the premises so purchased could be constitutionally and legally impaired and rendered null and void.

Judgment affirmed with costs.

JUSTICE JOHNSON, concurring. [omitted]

EXERCISE 2:

1. What was the basis of the Court's invalidation of Georgia's statute purporting to repeal the 1795 statutory grant? Describe how the Court utilized some of the five forms of argument.

2. Are you persuaded that state land grants are included within the scope of the Contracts Clause?

3. Why did the Court not use the fifth mode of argument: judicial precedent?

4. Was Chief Justice Marshall's Contracts Clause argument consistent with the Clause's original meaning?

5. What policy reason might argue for including contracts to which a state is a party within the purview of the Contracts Clause? Does this reasoning find expression in the Court's decision?

6. What did Chief Justice Marshall mean when he concluded his opinion with: "the state of Georgia was restrained . . . by general principles which are common to our free institutions . . . from passing a law whereby the estate of the plaintiff in the premises so purchased could be constitutionally and legally impaired and rendered null and void"? What are these general principles? Where do they come from? What is their content? How does one know them? Why are they judicially enforceable?

7. There is evidence that *Fletcher v. Peck* was a case of collusion. Many have argued that Marshall, a land speculator himself, ruled the way he did because he identified with the landholders who would lose their investments if Georgia was permitted to revoke its grant. This view may be supported by a case from the trilogy of Marshall Court Indian law cases, *Johnson v. M'Intosh*, 21 U.S. (8 Wheat.) 543 (1823). There, the Court, speaking through Marshall, ruled in favor of the party holding title from the United States against the party holding title from the Indian tribe. This case was perceived as favorable to land speculators. Many have argued that *Johnson* is another example of collusion in order to have the Supreme Court render a definitive statement on an issue.

The Supreme Court definitively determined that the Contracts Clause applied to private charters in *Trustees of Dartmouth College v. Woodward*, 17 U.S. (4 Wheat.) 518 (1819). After the Board of Trustees removed the president of Dartmouth College, the New Hampshire legislature attempted to alter Dartmouth's original corporate charter, which King George III had granted to the college in 1769. In particular, the legislature sought to convert Dartmouth into a public institution, giving the governor of New Hampshire the authority to appoint trustees, reinstating the removed president, and establishing a state board of visitors with veto power over the trustees' decisions. Chief Justice Marshall, writing for the Court, held that Dartmouth's corporate charter was a contract between private parties, the King and the college's trustees, and that, consequently, the Contract Clause precluded New Hampshire's interference with the charter. In so holding, Chief Justice Marshall also set the foundation for the modern business corporation, establishing that corporations are "persons" in the eyes of the law: "[a] corporation is an artificial being, invisible, intangible, and existing only in contemplation of law . . . . Among the most important [qualities of corporations] are immortality, and, if the expression may be allowed, individuality; properties by which a perpetual succession of many persons are considered as the same, and may act as a single individual." *Id.* at 635. As a result, *Dartmouth College* marks a landmark decision with respect to the Contracts Clause and corporate law.

The Supreme Court subsequently concluded that the Contracts Clause prohibited states from impairing contracts between private parties generally and not just private charters. Even though, as we saw above, the motivating goal of the Framers and Ratifiers was elimination of state legislation that helped debtors at the expense of creditors, it was not until *Sturges v. Crowninshield*, 17 U.S. (4 Wheat.) 122, 196 (1819), that the Court directly faced such a case, striking down a New York law that sought to "liberate[] the person of the debtor, and discharge[] him from all liability for any debt previously contracted."

* * *

The Supreme Court under Chief Justice Taney, despite its members' Jacksonian political sympathies, basically continued the path that the Marshall Court laid out, with some modifications. Three changes in particular constrained the possible breadth of the principles laid down under Chief Justice Marshall's tenure. First, the Taney Court determined that in contracts to which states were a party, the contracts would be construed in favor of states retaining authority to modify them. Second, the Court held that certain state powers — police powers — were inalienable, and hence states could abrogate (provisions of) contracts that purported to limit state exercise of these powers. Third, the Court distinguished between contractual *obligations*, which states could not impair, and *remedies* for breach of contract, which states could modify. The first is found in *Charles River Bridge v. Warren Bridge*, 36 U.S. (11 Pet.) 420 (1837), the second in *West River Bridge Co. v. Dix*, 47 U.S. (6 How.) 507 (1848), and the third in *Bronson v. Kinzie*, 42 U.S. (1 How.) 311 (1843). *West River Bridge* is reprinted, and *Charles River Bridge* is discussed, below.

In the *Charles River Bridge* case, Massachusetts had granted a corporate charter to operate a bridge across the Charles River between Cambridge and Boston. The grant effectively gave the Charles River Bridge Company a monopoly on bridge traffic across the river for which the Company charged a toll and made a sizeable profit. Later, the state granted a similar charter to a rival company to operate a bridge, the Warren Bridge, across the Charles River a short distance from the Charles River Bridge. To add insult to injury, Massachusetts provided that the Warren Bridge would cease charging a toll after a specified period of time. Later, the Warren Bridge ceased charging a toll and became a free public bridge. Of course, this destroyed the Charles River Bridge Company's business. So, the Company sued, claiming that the state had unconstitutionally impaired its contract by granting a charter to construct the Warren Bridge. The Company argued that its corporate charter was a contract between it and the state and that the state promised the company a monopoly, a promise the state breached when it granted the charter to the Warren Bridge Company.

The Supreme Court, with Chief Justice Taney writing, ruled that Massachusetts had not violated the Contracts Clause. The Court invoked a rule of construction — contracts between states and private parties must be construed favorably to the state — and found that since the Charles River Bridge Company's charter did not *explicitly* make its grant exclusive, the grant was not exclusive. Massachusetts, therefore, could issue a rival charter.

In a key passage, Chief Justice Taney articulated the rationale behind this rule of construction:

> [T]he object and end of all government is to promote the happiness and prosperity of the community by which it is established; and it can never be assumed, that the government intended to diminish its power of accomplishing the end for which it was created. And in a country like ours, free, active and enterprising, continually advancing in numbers and wealth, new channels of communication are daily found necessary, both for travel and trade, and are essential to the comfort, convenience and prosperity of the people. A state ought never to be presumed to surrender this power, because the whole community have an interest in preserving it undiminished. And when a corporation alleges, that a state has surrendered, for seventy years, its power of improvement and public accommodation, in a great and important line of travel, along which a vast number of its citizens must daily pass, the community have a right to insist, that its abandonment ought not to be presumed, in a case, in which the deliberate purpose of the state to abandon it does not appear. The continued existence of a government would be of no great value, if, by implications and presumptions, it was disarmed of the powers necessary to accomplish the ends of its creation, and the functions it was designed to perform, transferred to the hands of privileged corporations.

> The rule of construction was distinctly placed on the ground, that the interests of the community were concerned in preserving, undiminished, the power then in question; and whenever any power of the state is said to be surrendered or diminished, whether it be the taxing power, or any other affecting the public interest, the same principle applies, and the rule of construction must be the same. No one will question, that the interests of the great body of the people of the state, would, in this instance, be affected by the surrender of this great line of travel to a single corporation, with the right to exact toll, and exclude competition, for seventy years. While the rights of private property are sacredly guarded, we must not forget, that the community also have rights, and that the happiness and well-being of every citizen depends on their faithful preservation.

Charles River Bridge v. Warren Bridge, 36 U.S. (11 Pet.) 420, 547–48 (1837). This ratio-nale found its strongest expression in *West River Bridge Co. v. Dix*, reprinted below.

EXERCISE 3:

1. Is the *Charles River Bridge* case faithful to the Contracts Clause's original meaning?

2. Is it faithful to the Marshall Court's precedent?

3. Is it an attractive rule of construction for contracts to which a State is a party?

WEST RIVER BRIDGE CO. v. DIX
47 U.S. (6 How.) 507 (1848)

Justice Daniel delivered the opinion of the Court.

The[se cases] are brought before us in order to test the conformity with the Con-stitution of the United States of certain statutes of Vermont; laws that have been sus-tained by the Supreme Court of Vermont, but which it is alleged are repugnant to [Article I, Section 10] of the Constitution, prohibiting the passage of State laws impairing the obligation of contracts.

It appears from the records of these causes, that, in the year 1795, the [incorpora-tors of the West River Bridge Company] were, by act of the legislature of Vermont, created a corporation, and invested with the exclusive privilege of erecting a bridge over West River, and with the right of taking tolls for passing the same. The fran-chise granted this corporation was to continue for one hundred years, and the period originally prescribed for its duration has not yet expired. The corporation erected their bridge, have maintained and used it, and enjoyed the franchise granted to them by law, until the institution of the proceeding now under review.

By the general law of Vermont relating to roads, passed November [19], 1839, the County Courts are authorized, upon petition, to appoint commissioners to lay out highways within their respective counties, and to assess the damages which may accrue to landholders by the opening of roads, and these courts, upon the reports of the commissioners so appointed, are empowered to establish roads within the bounds of their local jurisdiction.

Under the authority of these statutes, and in the modes therein prescribed, a pro-ceeding was instituted in the County Court of Windham, upon the petition of Joseph Dix and others, in which, by the judgment of that court, a public road was extended and established between certain termini, passing over and upon the bridge of the plaintiffs, and converting it into a free public highway. By the proceedings and judg-ment just mentioned, compensation was assessed and awarded to the plaintiffs for this appropriation of their property, and for the consequent extinguishment of their franchise. The judgment of the County Court, having been carried by certiorari before the Supreme Court of the State, was by the latter tribunal affirmed.

In considering the question propounded in these causes, there can be no doubt, nor has it been doubted in argument, on either side of this controversy, that the charter of incorporation granted to the plaintiffs in 1793, with the rights and privileges it declared or implied, formed a contract between the plaintiffs and the State of Vermont, which the latter, under the inhibition in [Article I, Section 10] of the Constitution, could have no power to impair. Yet this proposition, though taken as a postulate on both sides, determines nothing as to the real merits of these causes. No State, it is declared, shall pass a law impairing the obligation of contracts; yet, with this concession constantly yielded, it cannot be justly disputed, that in every political sovereign community there inheres necessarily the right and the duty of guarding its own existence, and of protecting and promoting the interests and welfare of the community at large. This power and this duty are to be exerted not only in the highest acts of sovereignty, and in the external relations of governments; they reach and comprehend likewise the interior polity and relations of social life, which should be regulated with reference to the advantage of the whole society. This power, denominated the *eminent domain* of the State, is, as its name imports, paramount to all private rights vested under the government, and these last are, by necessary implication, held in subordination to this power, and must yield in every instance to its proper exercise.

The Constitution of the United States, although adopted by the sovereign States of this Union, and proclaimed in its own language to be the supreme law for their government, can, by no rational interpretation, be brought to conflict with this attribute in the States; there is no express delegation of it by the Constitution; and it would imply an incredible fatuity in the States, to ascribe to them the intention to relinquish the power of self-government and self-preservation. A correct view of this matter must demonstrate, moreover, that the right of eminent domain in government in no wise interferes with the inviolability of contracts; that the most sanctimonious regard for the one is perfectly consistent with the possession and exercise of the other.

Under every established government, the tenure of property is derived mediately or immediately from the sovereign power of the political body, organized in such mode or exerted in such way as the community or State may have thought proper to ordain. It can rest on no other foundation, can have no other guarantee. It is owing to these characteristics only, in the original nature of tenure, that appeals can be made to the laws either for the protection or assertion of the rights of property. Upon any other hypothesis, the law of property would be simply the law of force. Now it is undeniable, that the investment of property in the citizen by the government, whether made for a pecuniary consideration or founded on conditions of civil or political duty, is a contract between the State, or the government acting as its agent, and the grantee; and both the parties thereto are bound in good faith to fulfil it. But into all contracts, whether made between States and individuals or between individuals only, there enter conditions which arise not out of the literal terms of the contract itself; they are superinduced by the preexisting and higher authority of the laws of nature, of nations, or of the community to which the parties belong; they are always presumed, and must be presumed, to be known and recognized by all, are binding upon all, and need never, therefore, be carried into express stipulation, for this could add nothing to their force. Every contract is made in subordination to them, and must yield to their control, as conditions inherent and paramount, wherever a necessity for their execution shall occur. Such a condition is the right of eminent domain. This right does not operate to impair the contract effected by it, but recognizes its obligation in the fullest extent, claiming only the fulfilment of an essential and inseparable condition. The impairing of contracts inhibited by the Constitution can scarcely, by the greatest violence of construction, be made applicable to the enforcing of the terms or necessary import of a contract; the language and meaning of the inhibition were designed to embrace proceedings attempting the interpolation of some new term of condition foreign to the original agreement, and therefore inconsistent with and violative thereof.

It, then, being clear that the power in question not being within the purview of the restriction imposed by [Article I, Section 10] of the Constitution, it remains with the States to the full extent in which it inheres in every sovereign government, to be exercised by them in that degree that shall by them be deemed commensurate with public necessity. So long as they shall steer clear of the single predicament denounced by the Constitution, shall avoid interference with the obligation of contracts, the wisdom, the modes, the policy, the hardship of any exertion of this power are subjects not within the proper cognizance of this court. This is, in truth, purely a question of power; and, conceding the power to reside in the State government, this concession would seem to close the door upon all further controversy in connection with it.

A franchise to erect a bridge, to construct a road, to keep a ferry, and to collect tolls upon them, granted by the authority of the State, we regard as occupying the same position, with respect to the paramount power and duty of the State to promote and protect the public good, as does the right of the citizen to the possession and enjoyment of his land under his patent or contract with the State, and it can no more interpose any obstruction in the way of their just exertion. Such exertion we hold to be not within the inhibition of the Constitution, and no violation of a contract. The power of a State, in the exercise of eminent domain, to extinguish immediately a franchise it had granted, appears never to have been directly brought here for adjudication, and consequently has not been heretofore formally propounded from this court; but in England, this power, to the fullest extent, was recognized in the case of the Governor and Company of the Cast Plate Manufacturers *v.* Meredith, and Lord Kenyon, especially in that case, founded solely upon this power the entire policy and authority of all the road and canal laws of the kingdom.

Upon the whole, we consider the authority claimed for the State of Vermont, and the exertion of that authority which has occurred under the provisions of the statutes above mentioned, by the extinguishment of the franchise previously granted the plaintiffs, as set forth upon the records before us, as presenting no instance of the impairing of a contract, within the meaning of [Article I, Section 10] of the

Constitution, and consequently no case which is proper for the interposition of this court. The decisions of the Supreme Court of Vermont are therefore affirmed.

JUSTICE MCLEAN, concurring. [omitted]

JUSTICE WOODBURY, concurring. [omitted]

JUSTICE WAYNE, dissenting. [omitted]

EXERCISE 4:

1. This case presents another example of a suit against a state for impairing one of its own contracts, specifically a corporate charter or franchise. Under the Supreme Court's reasoning, could New Hampshire have used its eminent domain power to take the Dartmouth College property without violating the Contracts Clause? If so, is there any reason to uphold the latter approach and not the former?

2. The Supreme Court rested its decision on the claim that states cannot bargain away portions of their sovereignty, their authority to make laws for the common good of their people. Where is *this* rule found? In the Constitution? Somewhere else? If so, how can it trump the Constitution's textual mandate that states not impair contractual obligations?

3. Articulate the manner in which the Court applied its rule of construction.

4. As the nineteenth century wore on, the Supreme Court came to label the residual state authority to enact legislation for the good of its citizens a state's "police power." *Stone v. Mississippi*, 101 U.S. (11 Otto) 814, 817 (1880). The police power was regularly characterized as including the protection of its citizens' "lives, health, morals, comfort, and the general welfare of the people." *Manigault v. Springs*, 199 U.S. 473, 480 (1905). For an excellent discussion of the history and meaning of the police power, see D. Benjamin Barros, *The Police Power and the Taking Clause*, 58 U. MIAMI L. REV. 471 (2004).

5. What is the limit to the Court's reasoning? Below, we will see that the Court's reasoning in *West River Bridge* is utilized to substantially lessen the Contracts Clause's restrictiveness on states during the New Deal.

6. Why did the Court not rely on the *Charles River Bridge* case as a precedent?

In *Bronson v. Kinzie*, 42 U.S. (1 How.) 311 (1843), the Court distinguished between remedies under a contract and the underlying obligations of that contract. While states generally could exercise their police power to change the *remedies* under past or future contracts, they could not materially alter the *obligations* of pre-existing contracts: "Whatever belongs merely to the remedy may be altered according to the will of the state, . . . [but i]f these acts so change the nature and extent of existing remedies as materially to impair the rights and interests of the owner, they are just as much a violation of the compact as if they directly overturned his rights and interests." *Id.* at 316.

In *Bronson*, two Illinois statutes imposed restrictions on mortgage foreclosure sales and gave mortgagors greater rights to redeem foreclosed property. The Illinois statutes also were retroactive, ostensibly applying to the mortgage that John H.

Kinzie (the mortgagor) had given to Arthur Bronson (the mortgagee) prior to enactment of the Illinois legislation. Mr. Bronson sought to foreclose on the mortgage free of the Illinois limitations. Chief Justice Taney, writing for the Court, acknowledged that it might be "difficult . . . to draw a line that would be applicable in all cases between legitimate alterations of the remedy and provisions which . . . impair the right," but he concluded that the Illinois statutes violated the Contracts Clause because they did "not . . . act merely on the remedy, but directly upon the contract itself, . . . engraft[ing] upon [the mortgage] new conditions injurious and unjust to the mortgagee." *Id.* at 317, 319. As discussed below, however, although the *Bronson* Court used the distinction between remedies and obligations to limit Illinois's ability to retroactively impose new conditions on the contracting parties, the elusiveness of this distinction set the groundwork for the Court's expansion of the states' police powers in relation to contracts in *Blaisdell*.

C. LATE-NINETEENTH CENTURY

The Contracts Clause was the primary tool that the Supreme Court utilized in the Antebellum period to limit state legislative activity and protect propertied interests. As we saw, the Court, under Chief Justice Taney, articulated the distinction between remedy and obligation, along with the notion of reserved state police powers that a state could not bargain away.

This distinction gave states relatively robust freedom under the Contracts Clause that they exercised in the latter portion of the nineteenth century. For instance, in *Stone v. Mississippi*, 101 U.S. (11 Otto) 814 (1880), the Court rejected a Contracts Clause challenge to a state statute outlawing state lotteries after the state had chartered a lottery company for that purpose. The Court reasoned that one legislature cannot eliminate the power of later legislatures to legislate for the purpose of protecting its people's health, safety, and morals. *Id.* at 817–18.

Another development that caused the Contracts Clause to recede to the background was the rise of the Supreme Court's use of the Fourteenth Amendment's Due Process Clause. Following the Court's limited interpretation of the Privileges or Immunities Clause of the Fourteenth Amendment in the *Slaughter-House Cases*, 83 U.S. (16 Wall.) 36 (1872), the Supreme Court began employing the Due Process Clause to protect private property and to limit state legislative authority.

The Supreme Court seemed to prefer this approach over the Contracts Clause for a number of reasons. First, it protected all contracts, not only those made prior to enactment of the challenged statute. Second, it offered a relatively wide-open field that was predicated on a relatively indeterminate text and history and that was unpopulated by precedent. Third, the Due Process Clause, as interpreted by the Supreme Court, did not contain a police powers "exception" like the Contracts Clause; in fact, the Due Process Clause was used to limit the states' exercise of their police powers.

The Supreme Court continued to invoke the Contracts Clause infrequently during the late-nineteenth and early-twentieth centuries. The decisive change occurred, as it did in many areas of law, during the New Deal. In the Contracts Clause context, *Home Bldg. & Loan Ass'n v. Blaisdell*, 290 U.S. 398 (1934), is the key case.

D. NEW DEAL—DECLINE OF THE CONTRACTS CLAUSE AS A LIMIT ON STATES

HOME BUILDING & LOAN ASS'N v. BLAISDELL
290 U.S. 398 (1934)

CHIEF JUSTICE HUGHES delivered the opinion of the Court.

Appellant contests the validity of the Minnesota Mortgage Moratorium Law [approved April 18, 1933,] as being repugnant to the contract clause and the due process and equal protection clauses of the Fourteenth Amendment of the Federal Constitution.

The act provides that, during the emergency declared to exist, relief may be had through authorized judicial proceedings with respect to foreclosures of mortgages, and execution sales, of real estate; that sales may be postponed and periods of redemption may be extended. The act is to remain in effect "only during the continuance of the emergency and in no event beyond May 1, 1935." No extension of the period for redemption and no postponement of sale is to be allowed which would have the effect of extending the period of redemption beyond that date.

We are here concerned with the provisions of [the Act] authorizing the district court of the county to extend the period of redemption from foreclosure sales "for such additional time as the court may deem just and equitable," subject to the above-described limitation. The extension is to be made upon application to the court, on notice, for an order determining the reasonable value of the income on the property involved in the sale, or, if it has no income, then the reasonable rental value of the property, and directing the mortgagor "to pay all or a reasonable part of such income or rental value, in or toward the payment of taxes, insurance, interest, mortgage . . . indebtedness at such times and in such manner" as shall be determined by the court. The section also provides that the time for redemption from foreclosure sales theretofore made, which otherwise would expire less than thirty days after the approval of the act, shall be extended to a date thirty days after its approval, and application may be made to the court within that time for a further extension as provided in the section. By another provision of the act, no action, prior to May 1, 1935, may be maintained for a deficiency judgment until the period of redemption as allowed by existing law or as extended under the provisions of the act has expired. Prior to the expiration of the extended period of redemption, the court may revise or alter the terms of the extension as changed circumstances may require.

Invoking the relevant provision of the statute, appellees applied to the district court of Hennepin county for an order extending the period of redemption from a foreclosure sale. Their petition stated that they owned a lot in Minneapolis which they had mortgaged to appellant; that the mortgage contained a valid power of sale by advertisement, and that by reason of their default the mortgage had been foreclosed and sold to appellant on May 2, 1932, for $3,700.98; that appellant was the holder of the sheriff's certificate of sale; that, because of the economic depression, appellees had been unable to obtain a new loan or to redeem, and that, unless the period of redemption were extended, the property would be irretrievably lost; and that the reasonable value of the property greatly exceeded the amount due on the mortgage, including all liens, costs, and expenses.

The court entered its judgment extending the period of redemption to May 1, 1935, subject to the condition that the appellees should pay to the appellant $40 a month through the extended period from May 2, 1933. [T]his judgment [was] sustained by the Supreme Court of the state.

We approach the questions thus presented upon the assumption made below, as required by the law of the state, that the mortgage contained a valid power of sale to be exercised in case of default; that this power was validly exercised; that under the law then applicable the period of redemption from the sale was one year, and that it has been extended by the judgment of the court over the opposition of the mortgagee-purchaser; and that, during the period thus extended, and unless the order for extension is modified, the mortgagee-purchaser will be unable to obtain possession, or to obtain or convey title in fee, as he would have been able to do had the statute not been enacted. The statute does not impair the integrity of the mortgage indebtedness. The obligation for interest remains. The statute does not affect the validity of the sale or the right of a mortgagee-purchaser to title in fee, or his right to obtain a deficiency judgment, if the mortgagor fails to redeem within the prescribed period. Aside from the extension of time, the other conditions of redemption are unaltered. While the mortgagor remains in possession, he must pay the rental value as that value has been determined, upon notice and hearing, by the court. The rental value so paid is devoted to the carrying of the property by the application of the required payments to taxes, insurance, and interest on the mortgage indebtedness. While the mortgagee-purchaser is debarred from actual possession, he has, so far as rental value is concerned, the equivalent of possession during the extended period.

[II]

In determining whether the provision for this temporary and conditional relief exceeds the power of the state by reason of the clause in the Federal Constitution prohibiting impairment of the obligations of contracts, we must consider the relation of emergency to constitutional power, the historical setting of the contract clause, the development of the jurisprudence of this Court in the construction of that clause, and the principles of construction which we may consider to be established.

[A]

Emergency does not create power. Emergency does not increase granted power or remove or diminish the restrictions imposed upon power granted or reserved. The Constitution was adopted in a period of grave emergency. Its grants of power to the federal government and its limitations of the power of the States were determined in the light of emergency, and they are not altered by emergency. What power was thus granted and what limitations were thus imposed are questions which have always been, and always will be, the subject of close examination under our constitutional system.

While emergency does not create power, emergency may furnish the occasion for the exercise of power. The constitutional question presented in the light of an emergency is whether the power possessed embraces the particular exercise of it in response to particular conditions. Thus, the war power of the federal government is not created by the emergency of war, but it is a power given to meet that emergency. It is a power to wage war sucessfully, and thus it permits the harnessing of the entire energies of the people in a supreme co-operative effort to preserve the nation. But even the war power does not remove constitutional limitations safeguarding essential liberties. When the provisions of the Constitution, in grant or restriction, are specific, so particularized as not to admit of construction, no question is presented. Thus, emergency would not permit a state to have more than two Senators in the Congress, or permit the election of President by a general popular vote without regard to the number of electors to which the States are respectively entitled, or permit the States to "coin money" or to "make anything but gold and silver coin a tender in payment of debts." But, where constitutional grants and limitations of power are set forth in general clauses, which afford a broad outline, the process of construction is essential to fill in the details. That is true of the contract clause. The necessity of construction is not obviated by the fact that the contract clause is associated in the same section with other and more specific prohibitions. Even the grouping of subjects in the same clause may not require the same application to each of the subjects, regardless of differences in their nature.

[B]

In the construction of the contract clause, the debates in the Constitutional Convention are of little aid. But the reasons which led to the adoption of that clause, and of the other prohibitions of [Article I, Section 10], are not left in doubt. The widespread distress following the revolutionary period and the plight of debtors had called forth in the States an ignoble array of legislative schemes for the defeat of creditors and the invasion of contractual obligations. Legislative interferences had been so numerous and extreme that the confidence essential to prosperous trade had been undermined and the utter destruction of credit was threatened. "The sober people of America" were convinced that some "thorough reform" was needed which would "inspire a general prudence and industry, and give a regular course to the business of society." THE FEDERALIST, No. 44. It was necessary to interpose the restraining power of a central authority in order to secure the foundations even of "private faith." The occasion and general purpose of the contract clause are summed up [by] Chief Justice Marshall in *Ogden v. Saunders*, [25 U.S. (12 Wheat.) 213 (1827)].

But full recognition of the occasion and general purpose of the clause does not suffice to fix its precise scope. Nor does an examination of the details of prior legislation in the States yield criteria which can be considered controlling. To ascertain the scope of the constitutional prohibition, we examine the course of judicial decisions in its application. These put it beyond question that the prohibition is not an absolute and is not to be read with literal exactness like a mathematical formula. The inescapable problems of construction have been: What is a contract? What are the obligations of contracts? What constitutes impairment of these obligations? What residuum of power is there still in the States, in relation to the operation of contracts, to protect the vital interests of the community?

The obligation of a contract is the law which binds the parties to perform their agreement. But this broad language cannot be taken without qualification. Chief Justice Marshall pointed out the distinction between obligation and remedy. *Sturges v. Crowninshield*, 17 U.S. (4 Wheat.) 122 (1819). And in *Von Hoffman v. City of Quincy*, 71 U.S. 535 (1866), the general statement above quoted was limited by the further observation that

> it is competent for the States to change the form of the remedy, or to modify it otherwise, as they may see fit, provided no substantial right secured by the contract is thereby impaired. No attempt has been made to fix definitely the line between alterations of the remedy, which are to be deemed legitimate, and those which, under the form of modifying the remedy, impair substantial rights. Every case must be determined upon its own circumstances.

And CHIEF JUSTICE WAITE, quoting this language in *Antoni v. Greenhow*, 107 U.S. 769 (1882), added: "In all such cases the question becomes, therefore, one of reasonableness, and of that the legislature is primarily the judge."

The obligations of a contract are impaired by a law which renders them invalid, or releases or extinguishes them and impairment, has been predicated of laws which without destroying contracts derogate from substantial contractual rights. *Sturges v. Crowninshield*.

None of these cases, and we have cited those upon which appellant chiefly relies, is directly applicable to the question now before us in view of the conditions with which the Minnesota statute seeks to safeguard the interests of the mortgagee-purchaser during the extended period. And broad expressions contained in some of these opinions went beyond the requirements of the decision, and are not controlling.

[D]

Not only is the constitutional provision qualified by the measure of control which the state retains over remedial processes, but the state also continues to possess authority to safeguard the vital interests of its people. It does not matter that legislation appropriate to that end "has the result of modifying or abrogating contracts already in effect." Not only are existing laws read into contracts in order to fix obligations as between the parties, but the reservation of essential attributes of sovereign power is also read into contracts as a postulate of the legal order. The policy of protecting contracts against impairment presupposes the maintenance of a government by virtue of which contractual relations are worth while—a government which retains adequate authority to secure the peace and good order of society. This principle of harmonizing the constitutional prohibition with the necessary residuum of state power has had progressive recognition in the decisions of this Court.

While the charters of private corporations constitute contracts, a grant of exclusive privilege is not to be implied as against the state. *Charles River Bridge v. Warren Bridge*, 36 U.S. (11 Pet.) 420 (1837). And all contracts are subject to the right of eminent domain. *West River Bridge v. Dix*, 47 U.S. (6 How.) 507 (1848). The reservation of this necessary authority of the state is deemed to be a part of the contract. The Legislature cannot "bargain away the public health or the public morals." Thus the constitutional provision against the impairment of contracts was held not to be violated by an amendment of the state Constitution which put an end to a lottery theretofore authorized by the Legislature. *Stone v. Mississippi*, 101 U.S. (11 Otto) 814, 817 (1880).

The economic interests of the state may justify the exercise of its continuing and dominant protective power notwithstanding interference with contracts.

The argument is pressed that in the cases we have cited the obligation of contracts was affected only incidentally. This argument proceeds upon a misconception. The question is not whether the legislative action affects contracts incidentally, or directly or indirectly, but whether the legislation is addressed to a legitimate end and the measures taken are reasonable and appropriate to that end.

Undoubtedly, whatever is reserved of state power must be consistent with the fair intent of the constitutional limitation of that power. The reserved power cannot be construed so as to destroy the limitation, nor is the limitation to be construed to destroy the reserved power in its essential aspects. They must be construed in harmony with each other. This principle precludes a construction which would permit the state to adopt as its policy the repudiation of debts or the destruction of contracts or the denial of means to enforce them. But it does not follow that conditions may not arise in which a temporary restraint of enforcement may be consistent with the spirit and purpose of the constitutional provision and thus be found to be within the range of the reserved power of the state to protect the vital interests of the community. It cannot be maintained that the constitutional prohibition should be so construed as to prevent limited and temporary interpositions with respect to the enforcement of contracts if made necessary by a great public calamity such as fire, flood, or earthquake. The reservation of state power appropriate to such extraordinary conditions may be deemed to be as much a part of all contracts as is the reservation of state power to protect the public interest in the other situations to which we have referred. And, if state power exists to give temporary relief from the enforcement of contracts in the presence of disasters due to physical causes such as fire, flood, or earthquake, that power cannot be said to be nonexistent when the urgent public need demanding such relief is produced by other and economic causes.

[E]

It is manifest from this review of our decisions that there has been a growing appreciation of public needs and of the necessity of finding ground for a rational compromise between individual rights and public welfare. The settlement and consequent contraction of the public domain, the pressure of a constantly increasing density of population, the interrelation of the activities of our people and the complexity of our economic interests, have inevitably led to an increased use of the organization of society in order to protect the very bases of individual opportunity. Where, in earlier days, it was thought that only the concerns of individuals or of classes were involved, and that those of the state itself were touched only remotely, it has later been found that the fundamental interests of the state are directly affected; and that the question is no longer merely that of one party to a contract as against another, but of the use of reasonable means to safeguard the economic structure upon which the good of all depends.

It is no answer to say that this public need was not apprehended a century ago, or to insist that what the provision of the Constitution meant to the vision of that day it must mean to the vision of our time. If by the statement that what the Constitution meant at the time of its adoption it means to-day, it is intended to say that the great clauses of the Constitution must be confined to the interpretation which the framers, with the conditions and outlook of their time, would have placed upon them, the statement carries its own refutation. It was to guard against such a narrow conception that Chief Justice Marshall uttered the memorable warning: "We must never forget, that it is a constitution we are expounding" *McCulloch v. Maryland*, 17 U.S. (4 Wheat.) 316 (1819); "a constitution intended to endure for ages to come, and, consequently, to be adapted to the various crises of human affairs." When we are dealing with the words of the Constitution, said this Court in *Missouri v. Holland*, 252 U.S. 416 (1920), "we must realize that they have called into life a being the development of which could not have been foreseen completely by the most gifted of its begetters. . . . The case before us must be considered in the light of our whole experience and not merely in that of what was said a hundred years ago."

Nor is it helpful to attempt to draw a fine distinction between the intended meaning of the words of the Constitution and their intended application. The vast body of law which has been developed was unknown to the fathers, but it is believed to have preserved the essential content and the spirit of the Constitution. With a growing recognition of public needs and the relation of individual right to public security, the court has sought to prevent the perversion of the clause through its use as an instrument to throttle the capacity of the states to protect their fundamental interests. This development is a growth from the seeds which the fathers planted. And the germs of the later decisions are found in the early cases of the *Charles River Bridge* and the *West River Bridge*, which upheld the public right against strong insistence upon the contract clause. The principle of this development is, as we have seen, that the reservation of the reasonable exercise of the protective power of the state is read into all contracts, and there is no reason for refusing to apply this principle to Minnesota mortgages.

[III]

Applying the criteria established by our decisions, we conclude:

1. An emergency existed in Minnesota which furnished a proper occasion for the exercise of the reserved power of the state to protect the vital interests of the community. The declarations of the existence of this emergency by the Legislature and by the Supreme Court of Minnesota cannot be regarded as a subterfuge or as lacking in adequate basis. The finding of the Legislature and state court has support in the facts of which we take judicial notice. That there were in Minnesota conditions urgently demanding relief, if power existed to give it, is beyond cavil.

2. The legislation was addressed to a legitimate end; that is, the legislation was not for the mere advantage of particular individuals but for the protection of a basic interest of society.

3. In view of the nature of the contracts in question — mortgages of unquestionable validity — the relief afforded and justified by the emergency, in order not to contravene the constitutional provision, could only be of a character appropriate to that emergency, and could be granted only upon reasonable conditions.

4. The conditions upon which the period of redemption is extended do not appear to be unreasonable. The initial extension of the time of redemption for thirty days from the approval of the act was obviously to give a reasonable opportunity for the authorized application to the court. As already noted, the integrity of the mortgage indebtedness is not impaired; interest continues to run; the validity of the sale and the right of a mortgagee-purchaser to title or to obtain a deficiency judgment, if the mortgagor fails to redeem within the extended period, are maintained; and the conditions of redemption, if redemption there be, stand as they were under the prior law. The mortgagor during the extended period is not ousted from possession, but he must pay the rental value of the premises as ascertained in judicial proceedings and this amount is applied to the carrying of the property and to interest upon the indebtedness. The mortgagee-purchaser during the time that he cannot obtain possession thus is not left without compensation for the withholding of possession. Also important is the fact that mortgagees, as is shown by official reports of which we may take notice, are predominantly corporations, such as insurance companies, banks, and investment and mortgage companies. These, and such individual mortgagees as are small investors, are not seeking homes or the opportunity to engage in farming. Their chief concern is the reasonable protection of their investment security. It does not matter that there are, or may be, individual cases of another aspect. The Legislature was entitled

to deal with the general or typical situation. The relief afforded by the statute has regard to the interest of mortgagees as well as to the interest of mortgagors. The legislation seeks to prevent the impending ruin of both by a considerate measure of relief.

5. The legislation is temporary in operation. It is limited to the exigency which called it forth. While the postponement of the period of redemption from the foreclosure sale is to May 1, 1935, that period may be reduced by the order of the court under the statute, in case of a change in circumstances, and the operation of the statute itself could not validly outlast the emergency or be so extended as virtually to destroy the contracts.

We are of the opinion that the Minnesota statute as here applied does not violate the contract clause of the Federal Constitution. Whether the legislation is wise or unwise as a matter of policy is a question with which we are not concerned.

Judgment affirmed.

Justice Sutherland, dissenting.

Few questions of greater moment than that just decided have been submitted for judicial inquiry during this generation. He simply closes his eyes to the necessary implications of the decision who fails to see in it the potentiality of future gradual but ever-advancing encroachments upon the sanctity of private and public contracts. The effect of the Minnesota legislation, though serious enough in itself, is of trivial significance compared with the far more serious and dangerous inroads upon the limitations of the Constitution which are almost certain to ensue as a consequence naturally following any step beyond the boundaries fixed by that instrument. And those of us who are thus apprehensive of the effect of this decision would, in a matter so important, be neglectful of our duty should we fail to spread upon the permanent records of the court the reasons which move us to the opposite view.

[I]

A provision of the Constitution, it is hardly necessary to say, does not admit of two distinctly opposite interpretations. It does not mean one thing at one time and an entirely different thing at another time. If the contract impairment clause, when framed and adopted, meant that the terms of a contract for the payment of money could not be altered in invitum by a state statute enacted for the relief of hardly pressed debtors to the end and with the effect of postponing payment or enforcement during and because of an economic or financial emergency, it is but to state the obvious to say that it means the same now. This view, at once so rational in its application to the written word, and so necessary to the stability of constitutional principles, though from time to time challenged, has never, unless recently, been put within the realm of doubt by the decisions of this court.

[T]he provisions of the Constitution [have] been expressed by our ancestors in such plain English words that it would seem the ingenuity of man could not evade them. "Those great and good men," the Court said [in *Ex parte Milligan*], "foresaw that troublous times would arise, when rules and people would become restive under restraint, and seek by sharp and decisive measures to accomplish ends deemed just and proper; and that the principles of constitutional liberty would be in peril, unless established by irrepealable law. The history of the world had taught them that what was done in the past might be attempted in the future." 71 U.S. (4 Wall.) 2, 120 (1866). "The Constitution of the United States is a law for rulers and people, equally in war and in peace, and covers with the shield of its protection all classes of men, at all times, and under all circumstances. No doctrine, involving more pernicious consequences, was ever invented by the wit of man than that any of its provisions can be suspended during any of the great exigencies of government. Such a doctrine leads directly to anarchy or despotism." *Id.* at 121.

Chief Justice Taney, in *Dred Scott v. Sandford*, 60 U.S. (17 How.) 393 (1856), said that, while the Constitution remains unaltered, it must be construed now as it was understood at the time of its adoption; that it is not only the same in words but the same in meaning, "and as long as it continues to exist in its present form, it speaks not only in the same words, but with the same meaning and intent with which it spoke when it came from the hands of its framers, and was voted on and adopted by the people of the United States. Any other rule of construction would abrogate the judicial character of this court, and make it the mere reflex of the popular opinion or passion of the day."

The provisions of the Federal Constitution, undoubtedly, are pliable in the sense that in appropriate cases they have the capacity of bringing within their grasp every new condition which falls within their meaning.[1] But, their meaning is changeless; it is only their application which is extensible. Constitutional grants of power and restrictions upon the exercise of power are not flexible as the doctrines of the common law are flexible. These doctrines, upon the principles of the common law itself, modify or abrogate themselves whenever they are or whenever they become plainly unsuited to different or changed conditions.

The whole aim of construction, as applied to a provision of the Constitution, is to discover the meaning, to ascertain and give effect to the intent of its framers and the people who adopted it. The necessities which gave rise to the provision, the controversies which preceded, as well as the conflicts of opinion which were settled by its adoption, are matters to be considered to enable us to arrive at a correct result. The history of the times, the state of things existing when the provision was framed and adopted should be looked to in order to ascertain the mischief and the remedy. As nearly as possible we should place ourselves in the condition of those who framed and adopted it. And, if the meaning be at all doubtful, the doubt should be resolved,

---

1. In such cases it is no more necessary to modify constitutional rules to govern new conditions than it is to create new words to describe them. The commerce clause is a good example. When that was adopted, its application was necessarily confined to the regulation of the primitive methods of transportation then employed; but railroads, automobiles, and aircraft automatically were brought within the scope and subject to the terms of the commerce clause the moment these new means of transportation came into existence, just as they were at once brought within the meaning of the word "carrier," as defined by the dictionaries.

wherever reasonably possible to do so, in a way to forward the evident purpose with which the provision was adopted.

[II]

[A]

An application of these principles to the question under review removes any doubt, if otherwise there would be any, that the contract impairment clause denies to the several states the power to mitigate hard consequences resulting to debtors from financial or economic exigencies by an impairment of the obligation of contracts of indebtedness. A candid consideration of the history and circumstances which led up to and accompanied the framing and adoption of this clause will demonstrate conclusively that it was framed and adopted with the specific and studied purpose of preventing legislation designed to relieve debtors especially in time of financial distress.

* * *

If it be possible by resort to the testimony of history to put any question of constitutional intent beyond the domain of uncertainty, the [Clause's history] leaves no reasonable ground upon which to base a denial that the clause was meant to foreclose state action impairing the obligation of contracts primarily and especially in respect of such action aimed at giving relief to debtors in time of emergency. And, if further proof be required to strengthen what already is inexpugnable, such proof will be found in the previous decisions of this court [such as] *Bronson v. Kinzie*, 42 U.S. (1 How.) 311 (1843).

[B]

The present exigency is nothing new. From the beginning of our existence as a nation, periods of depression, of industrial failure, of financial distress, of unpaid and unpayable indebtedness, have alternated with years of plenty. The vital lesson that expenditure beyond income begets poverty, that public or private extravagance, financed by promises to pay, either must end in complete or partial repudiation or the promises be fulfilled by self-denial and painful effort, though constantly taught by bitter experience, seems never to be learned; and the attempt by legislative devices to shift the misfortune of the debtor to the shoulders of the creditor without coming into conflict with the contract impairment clause has been persistent and oft-repeated.

The defense of the Minnesota law is made upon grounds which were discountenanced by the makers of the Constitution and have many times been rejected by this Court. That defense should not now succeed because it constitutes an effort to overthrow the constitutional provision by an appeal to facts and circumstances identical with those which brought it into existence. With due regard for the processes of logical thinking, it legitimately cannot be urged that conditions which produced the rule may now be invoked to destroy it.

It is quite true that an emergency may supply the occasion for the exercise of power, dependent upon the nature of the power and the intent of the Constitution with respect thereto. The emergency of war furnishes an occasion for the exercise of certain of the war powers. This the Constitution contemplates, since they cannot be exercised upon any other occasion. But we are here dealing, not with a power granted by the Federal Constitution, but with the state police power, which exists in its own right. Hence the question is, not whether an emergency furnishes the occasion for the exercise of that state power, but whether an emergency furnishes an occasion for the relaxation of the restrictions upon the power imposed by the contract impairment clause; and the difficulty is that the contract impairment clause forbids state action under any circumstances, if it have the effect of impairing the obligation of contracts. That clause restricts every state power in the particular specified, no matter what may be the occasion. It does not contemplate that an emergency shall furnish an occasion for softening the restriction or making it any the less a restriction upon state action in that contingency than it is under strictly normal conditions.

The Minnesota statute either impairs the obligation of contracts or it does not. If it does not, the occasion to which it relates becomes immaterial, since then the passage of the statute is the exercise of a normal, unrestricted, state power and requires no special occasion to render it effective. If it does, the emergency no more furnishes a proper occasion for its exercise than if the emergency were nonexistent. And so, while, in form, the suggested distinction seems to put us forward in a straight line, in reality it simply carries us back in a circle, like bewildered travelers lost in a wood, to the point where we parted company with the view of the state court.

[C]

If what has now been said is sound, as I think it is, we come to what really is the vital question in the case: Does the Minnesota statute constitute an impairment of the obligation of the contract now under review?

In answering that question, we must first of all distinguish the present legislation from those statutes which, although interfering in some degree with the terms of contracts, or having the effect of entirely destroying them, have nevertheless been sustained as not impairing the obligation of contracts in the constitutional sense. Among these statutes are such as affect the remedy merely [including] *Bronson v. Kinzie.*

It is quite true also that "the reservation of essential attributes of sovereign power is also read into contracts"; and that the Legislature cannot "bargain away the public health or the public morals." General statutes to put an end to lotteries, the sale or manufacture of intoxicating liquors, the maintenance of nuisances, to protect the public safety, etc., although they have the indirect effect of absolutely destroying private contracts previously made in contemplation of a continuance of the state of affairs then in existence but subsequently prohibited, have been uniformly upheld as not violating the contract impairment clause. The distinction between legislation of that character and the Minnesota statute, however, is readily observable. It may be demonstrated by an example. A, engaged in the business of manufacturing

intoxicating liquor within a state, makes a contract, we will suppose, with B to manufacture and deliver at a stipulated price and at some date in the future a quantity
of whisky. Before the day arrives for the performance of the contract, the state passes
a law prohibiting the manufacture and sale of intoxicating liquor. The contract immediately falls because its performance has ceased to be lawful. This is so because the
contract is made upon the implied condition that a particular state of things shall
continue to exist, "and when that state of things ceases to exist the bargain itself ceases
to exist."

The same distinction properly may be made as to the contract impairment clause,
in respect of subsequent state legislation rendering unlawful a state of things which
was lawful when an obligation relating thereto was contracted. By such legislation
the obligation is not impaired in the constitutional sense. The contract is frustrated—
it disappears in virtue of an implied condition to that effect read into the contract
itself.

Bearing in mind these aids toward determining whether such an implied condition may be read into a particular contract, let us revert to the example already given
with respect to an agreement for the manufacture and sale of intoxicating liquor. And
let us suppose that the state, instead of passing legislation prohibiting the manufacture and sale of the commodity, in which event the doctrine of implied conditions
would be pertinent, continues to recognize the general lawfulness of the business,
but, because of what it conceives to be a justifying emergency, provides that the time
for the performance of existing contracts for future manufacture and sale shall
be extended for a specified period of time. It is perfectly admissible, in view of the
state power to prohibit the business, to read into the contract an implied proviso to
the effect that the business of manufacturing and selling intoxicating liquors shall
not, prior to the date when performance is due, become unlawful; but in the case last
put, to read into the contract a pertinent provisional exception in the event of inter-
meddling state action would be more than unreasonable, it would be absurd, since
we must assume that the contract was made on the footing that, so long as the obligation remained lawful, the impairment clause would effectively preclude a law
altering or nullifying it however exigent the occasion might be.

That, in principle, is precisely the case here. The contract is to repay a loan within
a fixed time, with the express condition that upon failure the property given as security shall be sold, and that, in the absence of a timely redemption, title shall be
vested absolutely in the purchaser. This contract was lawful when made; and it has
never been anything else. What the Legislature has done is to pass a statute which
does not have the effect of frustrating the contract by rendering its performance
unlawful, but one which, at the election of one of the parties, postpones for a time the
effective enforcement of the contractual obligation, notwithstanding the obligation,
under the exact terms of the contract, remains lawful and possible of performance
after the passage of the statute as it was before.

We come back, then, directly, to the question of impairment. As to that, the conclusion reached by the court here seems to be that the relief afforded by the statute does not contravene the constitutional provision because it is of a character appropriate to the emergency and allowed upon what are said to be reasonable conditions.

It will be observed that, whether the statute operated directly upon the contract or indirectly by modifying the remedy, its effect was to extend the period of redemption absolutely for a period of sixteen days, and conditionally for a period of two years. That this brought about a substantial change in the terms of the contract reasonably cannot be denied. If the statute was meant to operate only upon the remedy, it nevertheless, as applied, had the effect of destroying for two years the right of the creditor to enjoy the ownership of the property, and consequently the correlative power, for that period, to occupy, sell, or otherwise dispose of it as might seem fit. This postponement, if it had been unconditional, undoubtedly would have constituted an unconstitutional impairment of the obligation. This Court so decided in *Bronson v. Kinzie*, where the period of redemption was extended for a period of only twelve months after a sale under a decree; in *Howard v. Bugbee*, 65 U.S. 461 (1861), where the extension was for two years; and in *Barnitz v. Beverly*, 163 U.S. 118 (1896), where the period was extended for eighteen months. Those cases, we may assume, still embody the law, since they are not overruled.

A statute which materially delays enforcement of the mortgagee's contractual right of ownership and possession does not modify the remedy merely; it destroys, for the period of delay, all remedy so far as the enforcement of that right is concerned. The phrase "obligation of a contract" in the constitutional sense imports a legal duty to perform the specified obligation of that contract, not to substitute and perform, against the will of one of the parties, a different, albeit equally valuable, obligation. And a state, under the contract impairment clause, has no more power to accomplish such a substitution than has one of the parties to the contract against the will of the other. It cannot do so either by acting directly upon the contract or by bringing about the result under the guise of a statute in form acting only upon the remedy. If it could, the efficacy of the constitutional restriction would, in large measure, be made to disappear.

I quite agree with the opinion of the Court that whether the legislation under review is wise or unwise is a matter with which we have nothing to do. Whether it is likely to work well or work ill presents a question entirely irrelevant to the issue. The only legitimate inquiry we can make is whether it is constitutional. If it is not, its virtues, if it have any, cannot save it; if it is, its faults cannot be invoked to accomplish its destruction. If the provisions of the Constitution be not upheld when they pinch as well as when they comfort, they may as well be abandoned. Being unable to reach any other conclusion than that the Minnesota statute infringes the constitutional restriction under review, I have no choice but to say so.

EXERCISE 5:

1. What factual circumstances did the Supreme Court consider in determining that the Minnesota act was constitutional? Why are these factors important to determining whether the Contracts Clause forbids the moratorium? Should these factors play a role in the Supreme Court's decision?

2. How important are these facts to the analyses of the Court and the dissent, respectively? The Court states that "[i]t does not matter that there are, or may be, individual cases of another respect." Yet, the Court then concludes the statute "as applied" is constitutional. Is this a facial or an "as applied" analysis? Can the Court properly address cases that may present different factual bases or should any such statement be considered dicta?

3. What if the moratorium did not have a definite end date? Instead, what if the moratorium ended when the emergency ended?

4. What modes of interpretation did the majority and dissent utilize to support their respective conclusions?

5. Justice Sutherland quoted a statement by Chief Justice Taney in *Dred Scott*. *Dred Scott*, covered in Volume 5, was a thoroughly discredited opinion that held that free black Americans could not become U.S. citizens. Does the fact that Justice Sutherland employed a mode of interpretation used by the Supreme Court in *Dred Scott* undermine the validity of that method of interpretation?

6. Justice Sutherland argued that the Court could not interpret the Constitution differently than it had in the past, in part because of the harmful consequences that would occur if the Constitution was interpreted in a flexible manner. What are those harmful consequences predicted by Justice Sutherland? Have they come to pass as Justice Sutherland predicted? What are the benefits of a flexible interpretation that Justice Sutherland did not mention? Which of these considerations is more weighty? May one's choice of interpretative method properly consider the consequences of the method?

7. What did the Court mean when it stated that, while an emergency cannot create a power, an emergency can occasion the exercise of power?

8. Is *Blaisdell* an innovative decision, or is it consistent with the Contracts Clause's text and history, as well as the structure of government?

9. Is *Blaisdell* an innovative decision, or is it consistent with the Supreme Court's precedent?

10. Using the rationale articulated in *West River Bridge Co.*, can you support the *Blaisdell* decision?

11. Using the rationale articulated in *Bronson*, can you support the *Blaisdell* decision?

12. Justice Sutherland distinguished certain precedents as involving state laws that prohibited a general class of activity and thereby indirectly frustrated performing the

particular contract in question. Is that a persuasive basis for distinguishing those cases? Why or why not?

13. Are you persuaded by Justice Sutherland's conclusion that the Contracts Clause was intended to eliminate the exact type of law enacted by Minnesota? If one is persuaded by Justice Sutherland, must one reach his conclusion in this case?

14. Do you agree with Chief Justice Hughes' statement that:

> It is no answer . . . to insist that what the provision of the Constitution meant to the vision of that day it must mean to the vision of our time. If by the statement that what the Constitution meant at the time of its adoption it means to-day, it is intended to say that the great clauses of the Constitution must be confined to the interpretation which the framers, with the conditions and outlook of their time, would have placed upon them, the statement carries its own refutation. The case before us must be considered in the light of our whole experience and not merely in that of what was said a hundred years ago.

Blaisdell, 290 U.S. at 442–43.

15. Is the Contracts Clause's original meaning, as followed by Justice Sutherland, too restrictive for today's society? If so, what follows constitutionally?

16. What limits does the Contracts Clause impose on states following *Blaisdell*? Under what circumstances would a state statute run afoul of this prohibition?

17. In the majority's view, what is the relationship between a state's police power and individual rights? Is this the right way to look at that relationship?

18. One of the common critiques utilized by the group of legal scholars known as "legal realists" was that the legal categories the Supreme Court utilized prior to the New Deal covered or hid the real decision-making processes of the Court. In many areas of constitutional law, the realists argued, the Supreme Court had articulated a categorical approach where a state law was valid or invalid depending on whether it fell into or out of a category.

For example, in the Commerce Clause context, covered in Volume 3, the Supreme Court prior to the New Deal had held that Congress could not regulate manufacturing. *See United States v. E.C. Knight Co.*, 156 U.S. 1 (1895). As a result, any laws that fell into that category—regulating "manufacturing"—were beyond Congress' Commerce Clause power. The realists contended that, in fact, the Court was balancing different values. The Supreme Court balanced the need for federal regulation, on the one hand, against the value of retained state autonomy on the other. Then, following this balancing, the Court labeled the activity "manufacturing" or "commerce."

The *Blaisdell* Court explicitly stated that the remedies and obligations of contract are not distinct categories. Instead, the line is one of judgment, one of balancing. What conclusion did this lead the Court to draw regarding which institution was best suited to draw such lines, and why? Are those persuasive reasons?

E. TODAY

Since *Blaisdell,* the Supreme Court has rarely used the Contracts Clause to strike down state legislation. Instead, *Blaisdell* has come to stand for the proposition that states may regulate activities otherwise governed by contract under retained police power, which *Blaisdell* broadly defined. *See City of El Paso v. Simmons,* 379 U.S. 497 (1965) (ruling that a Texas statute, which limited the right of reinstatement to five years for land forfeited back to the state for failure to pay interest, did not violate the Contracts Clause).

The Supreme Court has articulated a distinction between legislation that impairs contracts involving only private parties and those involving a state and private parties. The Court has ruled that it will scrutinize the latter more rigorously than the former. The following two cases exemplify this distinction.

UNITED STATES TRUST COMPANY OF NEW YORK v. NEW JERSEY

431 U.S. 1 (1977)

Mr. Justice Blackmun delivered the opinion of the Court.

Plaintiff-appellant sued as trustee for two series of Port Authority Consolidated Bonds, as a holder of Port Authority Consolidated Bonds and on behalf of all holders of such bonds.

After a trial, the Superior Court ruled that the statutory repeal was a reasonable exercise of New Jersey's police power and declared that it was not prohibited by the Contract Clause. The Supreme Court of New Jersey affirmed.

I

BACKGROUND

The Port Authority was established in 1921 by a bistate compact [between New York and New Jersey]. The compact granted the Port Authority [broad authority, including the authority to operate public transportation facilities].

The Port Authority was conceived as a financially independent entity, with funds primarily derived from private investors. [T]he Port Authority was given power to mortgage its facilities and to pledge its revenues to secure the payment of bonds issued to private investors.

Four bridges for motor vehicles were constructed by the Port Authority. A separate series of revenue bonds was issued for each bridge.

The States in 1931 enacted statutes creating the general reserve fund of the Port Authority. Surplus revenues from all Port Authority facilities were to be pooled in the fund to create an irrevocably pledged reserve equal to one-tenth of the par value of the Port Authority's outstanding bonds. In 1952, the Port Authority's Consolidated

Bond Resolution established the present method of financing its activities; under this method its bonds are secured by a pledge of the general reserve fund.

In 1960 the takeover of the Hudson & Manhattan Railroad by the Port Authority was proposed. This was a privately owned interstate electric commuter system. A special committee of the New Jersey Senate was formed to determine whether the Port Authority was "fulfilling its statutory duties and obligations." The committee concluded that the solution to bondholder concern [over purchasing Port Authority bonds] was "[l]imiting by a constitutionally protected statutory covenant with Port Authority bondholders the extent to which the Port Authority revenues and reserves pledged to such bondholders can in the future be applied to the deficits of possible future Port Authority passenger railroad facilities beyond the original Hudson & Manhattan Railroad system." And the trial court found that the 1962 New Jersey Legislature "concluded it was necessary to place a limitation on mass transit deficit operations to be undertaken by the Authority in the future so as to promote continued investor confidence in the Authority."

The statutory covenant of 1962 was the result. The covenant itself was part of the bistate legislation authorizing the Port Authority to acquire, construct, and operate the Hudson & Manhattan Railroad and the World Trade Center. The statute in relevant part read:

> "The 2 States covenant and agree with each other and with the holders of any affected bonds, as hereinafter defined, that so long as any of such bonds remain outstanding and unpaid and the holders thereof shall not have given their consent as provided in their contract with the port authority, . . . (b) neither the States nor the port authority nor any subsidiary corporation incorporated for any of the purposes of this act will apply any of the rentals, tolls, fares, fees, charges, revenues or reserves, which have been or shall be pledged in whole or in part as security for such bonds, for any railroad purposes whatsoever . . . ."

The terms of the covenant were self-evident. Within its conditions the covenant permitted, and perhaps even contemplated, additional Port Authority involvement in deficit rail mass transit as its financial position strengthened, since the limitation of the covenant was linked to, and would expand with, the general reserve fund.

With the legislation embracing the covenant thus effective, the Port Authority on September 1, 1962, assumed the ownership and operating responsibilities of the Hudson & Manhattan through a wholly owned subsidiary, Port Authority Trans-Hudson Corporation (PATH). Funds necessary for this were realized by the successful sale of bonds to private investors accompanied by the certification required by the Consolidated Bond Resolution that the operation would not materially impair the credit standing of the Port Authority, the investment status of the Consolidated Bonds, or the ability of the Port Authority to fulfill its commitments to bondholders.

The PATH fare in 1962 was 30 cents and has remained at that figure despite recommendations for increase. As a result of the continuation of the low fare, PATH deficits have far exceeded the initial projection. In accordance with a stipulation of the parties, the trial court found that the PATH deficit so exceeded the covenant's level of permitted deficits that the Port Authority was unable to issue bonds for any new passenger railroad facility that was not self-supporting.

Governor Cahill of New Jersey and Governor Rockefeller of New York in April 1970 jointly sought increased Port Authority participation in mass transit. In November 1972 they agreed upon a plan for expansion of the PATH system. This included the initiation of direct rail service to Kennedy Airport and the construction of a line to Plainfield, N.J., by way of Newark Airport. The plan anticipated a Port Authority investment of something less than $300 million. It also proposed to make the covenant inapplicable with respect to bonds issued after the legislation went into effect. This program was enacted, effective May 10, 1973, and the 1962 covenant was thereby rendered inapplicable, or in effect repealed, with respect to bonds issued subsequent to the effective date of the new legislation.

New Jersey had previously prevented outright repeal of the 1962 covenant, but its attitude changed with the election of a new Governor in 1973. In early 1974, when bills were pending in the two States' legislatures to repeal the covenant retroactively, a national energy crisis was developing. This time, proposals for retroactive repeal of the 1962 covenant were passed by the legislature and signed by the Governor of each State.[12]

II

Home Building & Loan Assn. v. Blaisdell, 290 U.S. 398 (1934), is regarded as the leading case in the modern era of Contract Clause interpretation. This Court's most recent Contract Clause decision is *El Paso v. Simmons*, 379 U.S. 497 (1965). Both of these cases eschewed a rigid application of the Contract Clause to invalidate state legislation. Yet neither indicated that the Contract Clause was without meaning in modern constitutional jurisprudence, or that its limitation on state power was illusory. Whether or not the protection of contract rights comports with current views of wise public policy, the Contract Clause remains a part of our written Constitution. We therefore must attempt to apply that constitutional provision to the instant case with due respect for its purpose and the prior decisions of this Court.

---

12. Governor Wilson of New York, upon signing that State's repealer, observed:
   "It is with great reluctance that I approve a bill that overturns a solemn pledge of the State. I take this extraordinary step only because it will lead to an end of the existing controversy over the validity of the statutory covenant, a controversy that can only have an adverse affect (sic) upon the administration and financing of the Port Authority, and because it will lead to a speedy resolution by the courts of the questions and issues concerning the validity of the statutory covenant. Because it is the province of the courts to decide questions of constitutionality, I will not prevent the covenant issue from being brought before them."

III

We first examine appellant's general claim that repeal of the 1962 covenant impaired the obligation of the States' contract with the bondholders. It long has been established that the Contract Clause limits the power of the States to modify their own contracts as well as to regulate those between private parties. *Fletcher v. Peck*, 6 U.S. (6 Cranch) 87, 137–39 (1810); *Dartmouth College v. Woodward*, 17 U.S. (4 Wheat.) 518 (1819). Yet the Contract Clause does not prohibit the States from repealing or amending statutes generally, or from enacting legislation with retroactive effects. Thus, as a preliminary matter, appellant's claim requires a determination that the repeal has the effect of impairing a contractual obligation.

In this case the obligation was itself created by a statute, the 1962 legislative covenant. The intent to make a contract is clear from the statutory language: "The 2 States covenant and agree with each other and with the holders of any affected bonds." Moreover, as the chronology set forth above reveals, the purpose of the covenant was to invoke the constitutional protection of the Contract Clause as security against repeal. In return for their promise, the States received the benefit they bargained for: public marketability of Port Authority bonds. We therefore have no doubt that the 1962 covenant has been properly characterized as a contractual obligation of the two States.

As a security provision, the covenant was not superfluous; it limited the Port Authority's deficits and thus protected the general reserve fund from depletion. Nor was the covenant merely modified or replaced by an arguably comparable security provision. Its outright repeal totally eliminated an important security provision and thus impaired the obligation of the States' contract.[17] The trial court recognized that there was an impairment in this case.

Having thus established that the repeal impaired a contractual obligation of the States, we turn to the question whether that impairment violated the Contract Clause.

IV

Although the Contract Clause appears literally to proscribe "any" impairment, this Court observed in *Blaisdell* that "the prohibition is not an absolute one and is not to be read with literal exactness like a mathematical formula." Thus, a finding that there has been a technical impairment is merely a preliminary step in resolving the

---

17. More recent decisions have not relied on the remedy/obligation distinction, primarily because it is now recognized that obligations as well as remedies may be modified without necessarily violating the Contract Clause. *El Paso v. Simmons; Home Building & Loan Assn. v. Blaisdell.*

Although now largely an outdated formalism, the remedy/obligation distinction may be viewed as approximating the result of a more particularized inquiry into the legitimate expectations of the contracting parties. The parties may rely on the continued existence of adequate statutory remedies for enforcing their agreement, but they are unlikely to expect that state law will remain entirely static. Thus, a reasonable modification of statutes governing contract remedies is much less likely to upset expectations than a law adjusting the express terms of an agreement. In this respect, the repeal of the 1962 covenant is to be seen as a serious disruption of the bondholders' expectations.

more difficult question whether that impairment is permitted under the Constitution. In the instant case, as in *Blaisdell*, we must attempt to reconcile the strictures of the Contract Clause with the "essential attributes of sovereign power" necessarily reserved by the States to safeguard the welfare of their citizens.

The trial court concluded that repeal of the 1962 covenant was a valid exercise of New Jersey's police power because repeal served important public interests in mass transportation, energy conservation, and environmental protection. Yet the Contract Clause limits otherwise legitimate exercises of state legislative authority, and the existence of an important public interest is not always sufficient to overcome that limitation. Moreover, the scope of the State's reserved power depends on the nature of the contractual relationship with which the challenged law conflicts.

The States must possess broad power to adopt general regulatory measures without being concerned that private contracts will be impaired, or even destroyed, as a result. Otherwise, one would be able to obtain immunity from the state regulation by making private contractual arrangements.

Yet private contracts are not subject to unlimited modification under the police power. The Court in *Blaisdell* recognized that laws intended to regulate existing contractual relationships must serve a legitimate public purpose. Legislation adjusting the rights and responsibilities of contracting parties must be upon reasonable conditions and of a character appropriate to the public purpose justifying its adoption. As is customary in reviewing economic and social regulation, however, courts properly defer to legislative judgment as to the necessity and reasonableness of a particular measure.

When a State impairs the obligation of its own contract, the reserved-powers doctrine has a different basis. The initial inquiry concerns the ability of the State to enter into an agreement that limits its power to act in the future. As early as *Fletcher v. Peck*, 10 U.S. (6 Cranch) 87 (1810), the Court considered the argument that "one legislature cannot abridge the powers of a succeeding legislature." It is often stated that "the legislature cannot bargain away the police power of a State." *Stone v. Mississippi*, 101 U.S. (11 Otto) 814 (1880). This doctrine requires a determination of the State's power to create irrevocable contract rights in the first place, rather than an inquiry into the purpose or reasonableness of the subsequent impairment. In short, the Contract Clause does not require a State to adhere to a contract that surrenders an essential attribute of its sovereignty.

In deciding whether a State's contract was invalid *ab initio* under the reserved-powers doctrine, earlier decisions relied on distinctions among the various powers of the State. Thus, the police power and the power of eminent domain were among those that could not be "contracted away," but the State could bind itself in the future exercise of the taxing and spending powers. Such formalistic distinctions perhaps cannot be dispositive, but they contain an important element of truth. Whatever the propriety of a State's binding itself to a future course of conduct in other contexts, the power to enter into effective financial contracts cannot be questioned. Any financial obligation could be regarded in theory as a relinquishment of the State's spending power, since money spent to repay debts is not available for other purposes. Similarly, the taxing power may have to be exercised if debts are to be repaid. Notwithstanding these effects, the Court has regularly held that the States are bound by their debt contracts.

The instant case involves a financial obligation and thus as a threshold matter may not be said automatically to fall within the reserved powers that cannot be contracted away. Not every security provision, however, is necessarily financial. For example, a revenue bond might be secured by the State's promise to continue operating the facility in question; yet such a promise surely could not validly be construed to bind the State never to close the facility for health or safety reasons. The security provision at issue here, however, is different: The States promised that revenues and reserves securing the bonds would not be depleted by the Port Authority's operation of deficit-producing passenger railroads. Such a promise is purely financial and thus not necessarily a compromise of the State's reserved powers.

Of course, to say that the financial restrictions of the 1962 covenant were valid when adopted does not finally resolve this case. The Contract Clause is not an absolute bar to subsequent modification of a State's own financial obligations. As with laws impairing the obligations of private contracts, an impairment may be constitutional if it is reasonable and necessary to serve an important public purpose. In applying this standard, however, complete deference to a legislative assessment of reasonableness and necessity is not appropriate because the State's self-interest is at stake. A governmental entity can always find a use for extra money, especially when taxes do not have to be raised. If a State could reduce its financial obligations whenever it wanted to spend the money for what it regarded as an important public purpose, the Contract Clause would provide no protection at all.

It is clear that the instant case involves a serious impairment. No one has suggested here that the States acted for the purpose of benefiting the bondholders, and there is no serious contention that the value of the bonds was enhanced by repeal of the 1962 covenant. Appellees recognized that it would have been impracticable to obtain consent of the bondholders for such a change in the 1962 covenant, even though only 60% approval would have been adequate.

V

Mass transportation, energy conservation, and environmental protection are goals that are important and of legitimate public concern. Appellees contend that these goals are so important that any harm to bondholders from repeal of the 1962 covenant is greatly outweighed by the public benefit. We do not accept this invitation to engage in a utilitarian comparison of public benefit and private loss. Thus a State cannot refuse to meet its legitimate financial obligations simply because it would prefer to spend the money to promote the public good rather than the private welfare of its creditors. We can only sustain the repeal of the 1962 covenant if that impairment was both reasonable and necessary to serve the admittedly important purposes claimed by the State.

The more specific justification offered for the repeal of the 1962 covenant was the States' plan for encouraging users of private automobiles to shift to public transportation. The States intended to discourage private automobile use by raising bridge and tunnel tolls and to use the extra revenue from those tolls to subsidize improved commuter railroad service. Appellees contend that repeal of the 1962 covenant was necessary to implement this plan because the new mass transit facilities could not possibly be self-supporting and the covenant's "permitted deficits" level had already been exceeded. We reject this justification because the repeal was neither necessary to achievement of the plan nor reasonable in light of the circumstances.

The determination of necessity can be considered on two levels. First, it cannot be said that total repeal of the covenant was essential; a less drastic modification would have permitted the contemplated plan without entirely removing the covenant's limitations on the use of Port Authority revenues and reserves to subsidize commuter railroads. Second, without modifying the covenant at all, the States could have adopted alternative means of achieving their twin goals of discouraging automobile use and improving mass transit. Appellees contend, however, that choosing among these alternatives is a matter for legislative discretion. But a State is not completely free to consider impairing the obligations of its own contracts on a par with other policy alternatives. Similarly, a State is not free to impose a drastic impairment when an evident and more moderate course would serve its purposes equally well. In the instant case the State has failed to demonstrate that repeal of the 1962 covenant was similarly necessary.

We also cannot conclude that repeal of the covenant was reasonable in light of the surrounding circumstances. [I]n the instant case the need for mass transportation in the New York metropolitan area was not a new development, and the likelihood that publicly owned commuter railroads would produce substantial deficits was well known. As early as 1922, over a half century ago, there were pressures to involve the Port Authority in mass transit. It was with full knowledge of these concerns that the 1962 covenant was adopted. Indeed, the covenant was specifically intended to protect the pledged revenues and reserves against the possibility that such concerns would lead the Port Authority into greater involvement in deficit mass transit.

During the 12-year period between adoption of the covenant and its repeal, public perception of the importance of mass transit undoubtedly grew because of increased general concern with environmental protection and energy conservation. But these concerns were not unknown in 1962, and the subsequent changes were of degree and not of kind. We cannot say that these changes caused the covenant to have a substantially different impact in 1974 than when it was adopted in 1962. And we cannot conclude that the repeal was reasonable in the light of changed circumstances.

We therefore hold that the Contract Clause of the United States Constitution prohibits the retroactive repeal of the 1962 covenant. The judgment of the Supreme Court of New Jersey is reversed.

It is so ordered.

Mr. Justice Stewart took no part in the decision of this case.

Mr. Justice Powell took no part in the consideration or decision of this case.

Mr. Chief Justice Burger, concurring. [omitted.]

Mr. Justice Brennan, with whom Mr. Justice White and Mr. Justice Marshall join, dissenting.

Decisions of this Court for at least a century have construed the Contract Clause largely to be powerless in binding a State to contracts limiting the authority of successor legislatures to enact laws in furtherance of the health, safety, and similar collective interests of the polity. In short, those decisions established the principle that lawful exercises of a State's police powers stand paramount to private rights held under contract. Today's decision, in invalidating the New Jersey Legislature's 1974 repeal of its predecessor's 1962 covenant, rejects this previous understanding and remolds the Contract Clause into a potent instrument for overseeing important policy determinations of the state legislature. At the same time, by creating a constitutional safe haven for property rights embodied in a contract, the decision substantially distorts modern constitutional jurisprudence governing regulation of private economic interests.

EXERCISE 6:

1. Why does the Court more rigorously scrutinize state statutes that impair contracts to which the state is a party?

2. What is the legal basis for this reason?

3. What precedents support the Supreme Court's conclusion that contracts to which a state is a party are subject to more rigorous scrutiny under the Contracts Clause?

4. Whose position is more faithful to *Blaisdell*, the majority's or dissent's? What about to the *West River Bridge* case?

5. Whose position is more faithful to the Contracts Clause's original meaning?

6. What "level of scrutiny" did the Court utilize?

The Supreme Court today utilizes a three part test to determine whether a statute affecting a private contract violates the Contracts Clause. First, the Court will ascertain whether there is a "substantial impairment of a contractual relationship." *Energy Reserves Group v. Kansas Power & Light*, 459 U.S. 400, 411 (1983). Second, the Court will decide, if the statute does substantially impair contracts, whether it serves a "significant and legitimate purpose." *Id.* Third, the Court will inquire whether the statute is reasonably related to its purpose. *Id.* at 412. In cases involving impairment of private contracts, deference to state judgment is the order of the day. *Id.* at 412–13.

ALLIED STRUCTURAL STEEL COMPANY v. WARREN SPANNAUS

438 U.S. 234 (1978)

Mr. Justice Stewart delivered the opinion of the Court.

The issue in this case is whether the application of Minnesota's Private Pension Benefits Protection Act to the appellant violates the Contract Clause of the United States Constitution.

I

In 1974 appellant Allied Structural Steel Co. (company), maintained an office in Minnesota with 30 employees. Under the company's general pension plan, adopted in 1963, salaried employees were covered as follows: At age 65 an employee was entitled to retire and receive a monthly pension. An employee could also become entitled to receive a pension, payable in full at age 65, if he met any one of [three] requirements. Those employees who quit or were discharged before age 65 without fulfilling one of the other three conditions did not acquire any pension rights.

The company was the sole contributor to the pension trust fund, and each year it made contributions to the fund based on actuarial predictions of eventual payout needs. Although those contributions once made were irrevocable, the plan neither required the company to make specific contributions nor imposed any sanction on it for failing to contribute adequately to the fund.

The company not only retained a virtually unrestricted right to amend the plan in whole or in part, but was also free to terminate the plan and distribute the trust assets at any time and for any reason. In the event of a termination, the assets of the fund were to go, first, to meet the plan's obligation to those employees already retired and receiving pensions; second, to those eligible for retirement; and finally, if any balance remained, to the other employees covered under the plan whose pension rights had not yet vested. Employees within each of these categories were assured payment only to the extent of the pension assets.

The plan expressly stated:

> "No employee shall have any right to, or interest in, any part of the Trust's assets upon termination of his employment or otherwise, except as provided from time to time under this Plan, and then only to the extent of the benefits payable to such employee out of the assets of the Trust. All payments of benefits as provided for in this Plan shall be made solely out of the assets of the Trust and neither the employer, the trustee, nor any member of the Committee shall be liable therefor in any manner."

The plan also specifically advised employees that neither its existence nor any of its terms were to be understood as implying any assurance that employees could not be dismissed from their employment with the company at any time.

In sum, an employee who did not die, did not quit, and was not discharged before meeting one of the requirements of the plan would receive a fixed pension at age 65 if the company remained in business and elected to continue the pension plan in essentially its existing form.

On April 9, 1974, Minnesota enacted the law here in question. Under the Act, a private employer of 100 employees or more—at least one of whom was a Minnesota resident—who provided pension benefits under a plan meeting the qualifications of [the Internal Revenue Code, which the company's plan did,] was subject to a "pension funding charge" if he either terminated the plan or closed a Minnesota office.[6] The charge was assessed if the pension funds were not sufficient to cover full pensions for all employees who had worked at least 10 years. The Act required the employer to satisfy the deficiency by purchasing deferred annuities, payable to the employees at their normal retirement age. A separate provision specified that periods of employment prior to the effective date of the Act were to be included in the 10-year employment criterion.

During the summer of 1974 the company began closing its Minnesota office. On July 31, it discharged 11 of its 30 Minnesota employees, and the following month it notified the Minnesota Commissioner of Labor and Industry, as required by the Act, that it was terminating an office in the State. At least nine of the discharged employees did not have any vested pension rights under the company's plan, but had worked for the company for 10 years or more and thus qualified as pension obligees of the company under the law that Minnesota had enacted. On August 18, the State notified the company that it owed a pension funding charge of approximately $185,000 under the Act.

The company brought suit in a Federal District Court asking for injunctive and declaratory relief. It claimed that the Act unconstitutionally impaired its contractual obligations to its employees under its pension agreement. The three-judge court upheld the constitutional validity of the Act as applied to the company, and an appeal was brought to this Court.

II

A

There can be no question of the impact of the Minnesota Private Pension Benefits Protection Act upon the company's contractual relationships with its employees. The Act substantially altered those relationships by superimposing pension obligations upon the company conspicuously beyond those that it had voluntarily agreed to undertake. But it does not inexorably follow that the Act, as applied to the company, violates the Contract Clause of the Constitution.

---

6. Although the company had only 30 employees in Minnesota, it was subject to the Act because it had over 100 employees altogether.

The language of the Contract Clause appears unambiguously absolute: "No State shall . . . pass any . . . Law impairing the Obligation of Contracts." U.S. Const., Art. I, § 10. The Clause is not, however, the Draconian provision that its words might seem to imply.

Although it was perhaps the strongest single constitutional check on state legislation during our early years as a Nation, the Contract Clause receded into comparative desuetude with the adoption of the Fourteenth Amendment, and particularly with the development of the large body of jurisprudence under the Due Process Clause of that Amendment in modern constitutional history. Nonetheless, the Contract Clause remains part of the Constitution. It is not a dead letter. And its basic contours are brought into focus by several of this Court's 20th-century decisions.

First of all, it is to be accepted as a commonplace that the Contract Clause does not operate to obliterate the police power of the States. It is the settled law of this court that the interdiction of statutes impairing the obligation of contracts does not prevent the State from exercising such powers as are vested in it for the promotion of the common weal, or are necessary for the general good of the public, though contracts previously entered into between individuals may thereby be affected. This power, which, in its various ramifications, is known as the police power, is an exercise of the sovereign right of the Government to protect the lives, health, morals, comfort and general welfare of the people, and is paramount to any rights under contracts between individuals.

B

If the Contract Clause is to retain any meaning at all, however, it must be understood to impose *some* limits upon the power of a State to abridge existing contractual relationships, even in the exercise of its otherwise legitimate police power. The existence and nature of those limits were clearly indicated in a series of cases in this Court arising from the efforts of the States to deal with the unprecedented emergencies brought on by the severe economic depression of the early 1930's.

In *Home Building & Loan Assn. v. Blaisdell*, 290 U.S. 398 (1934), the Court upheld against a Contract Clause attack a mortgage moratorium law that Minnesota had enacted to provide relief for homeowners threatened with foreclosure. Although the legislation conflicted directly with lenders' contractual foreclosure rights, the Court there acknowledged that, despite the Contract Clause, the States retain residual authority to enact laws "to safeguard the vital interests of [their] people." In upholding the state mortgage moratorium law, the Court found five factors significant.

The *Blaisdell* opinion thus clearly implied that if the Minnesota moratorium legislation had not possessed the characteristics attributed to it by the Court, it would have been invalid under the Contract Clause of the Constitution. These implications were given concrete force in cases that followed closely in *Blaisdell*'s wake.

The most recent Contract Clause case in this Court was *United States Trust Co. v. New Jersey*, 431 U.S. 1 (1977). In that case the Court again recognized that although the absolute language of the Clause must leave room for "the 'essential attributes of sovereign power,' . . . necessarily reserved by the States to safeguard the welfare of their citizens," that power has limits when its exercise effects substantial modifications of private contracts. Evaluating with particular scrutiny a modification of a contract to which the State itself was a party, the Court in that case held that legislative alteration of the rights and remedies of Port Authority bondholders violated the Contract Clause because the legislation was neither necessary nor reasonable.

III

In applying these principles to the present case, the first inquiry must be whether the state law has, in fact, operated as a substantial impairment of a contractual relationship.[16] The severity of the impairment measures the height of the hurdle the state legislation must clear. Minimal alteration of contractual obligations may end the inquiry at its first stage. Severe impairment, on the other hand, will push the inquiry to a careful examination of the nature and purpose of the state legislation.

The severity of an impairment of contractual obligations can be measured by the factors that reflect the high value the Framers placed on the protection of private contracts. Contracts enable individuals to order their personal and business affairs according to their particular needs and interests. Once arranged, those rights and obligations are binding under the law, and the parties are entitled to rely on them.

Here, the company's contracts of employment with its employees included as a fringe benefit or additional form of compensation, the pension plan. The company's maximum obligation was to set aside each year an amount based on the plan's requirements for vesting. The plan satisfied the current federal income tax code and was subject to no other legislative requirements. And, of course, the company was free to amend or terminate the pension plan at any time. The company thus had no reason to anticipate that its employees' pension rights could become vested except in accordance with the terms of the plan. It relied heavily, and reasonably, on this legitimate contractual expectation in calculating its annual contributions to the pension fund.

The effect of Minnesota's Act on this contractual obligation was severe. The company was required in 1974 to have made its contributions throughout the pre-1974 life of its plan as if employees' pension rights had vested after 10 years, instead of vesting in accord with the terms of the plan. Thus a basic term of the pension contract—one on which the company had relied for 10 years—was substantially modified. The result was that, although the company's past contributions were adequate when

---

16. The novel construction of the Contract Clause expressed in the dissenting opinion is wholly contrary to the decisions of this Court. The narrow view that the Clause forbids only state laws that diminish the duties of a contractual obligor and not laws that increase them, has been expressly repudiated.

Moreover, in any bilateral contract the diminution of duties on one side effectively increases the duties on the other. The even narrower view that the Clause is limited in its application to state laws relieving debtors of obligations to their creditors is, as the dissent recognizes, completely at odds with this Court's decisions. *Dartmouth College v. Woodward*, 17 U.S. (4 Wheat.) 518 (1819).

made, they were not adequate when computed under the 10-year statutory vesting requirement. The Act thus forced a current recalculation of the past 10 years' contributions based on the new, unanticipated 10-year vesting requirement.

Not only did the state law thus retroactively modify the compensation that the company had agreed to pay its employees from 1963 to 1974, but also it did so by changing the company's obligations in an area where the element of reliance was vital — the funding of a pension plan.

Moreover, the retroactive state-imposed vesting requirement was applied only to those employers who terminated their pension plans or who, like the company, closed their Minnesota offices. The company was thus forced to make all the retroactive changes in its contractual obligations at one time. By simply proceeding to close its office in Minnesota, a move that had been planned before the passage of the Act, the company was assessed an immediate pension funding charge of approximately $185,000.

Thus, the statute in question here nullifies express terms of the company's contractual obligations and imposes a completely unexpected liability in potentially disabling amounts. There is not even any provision for gradual applicability or grace periods.

Yet there is no showing in the record before us that this severe disruption of contractual expectations was necessary to meet an important general social problem. The presumption favoring "legislative judgment as to the necessity and reasonableness of a particular measure," simply cannot stand in this case.

The only indication of legislative intent in the record before us is to be found in a statement in the District Court's opinion: "It seems clear that the problem of plant closure and pension plan termination was brought to the attention of the Minnesota legislature when the Minneapolis-Moline Division of White Motor Corporation closed one of its Minnesota plants and attempted to terminate its pension plan."

[T]he legislation clearly has an extremely narrow focus. And it applies only when such an employer closes his Minnesota office or terminates his pension plan. Thus, this law can hardly be characterized, like the law at issue in the *Blaisdell* case, as one enacted to protect a broad societal interest rather than a narrow class.

Moreover, in at least one other important respect the Act does not resemble the mortgage moratorium legislation whose constitutionality was upheld in the *Blaisdell* case. This legislation, imposing a sudden, totally unanticipated, and substantial retroactive obligation upon the company to its employees, was not enacted to deal with a situation remotely approaching the broad and desperate emergency economic conditions of the early 1930's — conditions of which the Court in *Blaisdell* took judicial notice.

Entering a field it had never before sought to regulate, the Minnesota Legislature grossly distorted the company's existing contractual relationships with its employees by superimposing retroactive obligations upon the company substantially beyond the terms of its employment contracts. And that burden was imposed upon the company only because it closed its office in the State.

This Minnesota law simply does not possess the attributes of those state laws that in the past have survived challenge under the Contract Clause of the Constitution. The law was not even purportedly enacted to deal with a broad, generalized economic or social problem. *Cf. Home Building & Loan Assn. v. Blaisdell.* It did not operate in an area already subject to state regulation at the time the company's contractual obligations were originally undertaken, but invaded an area never before subject to regulation by the State. It did not effect simply a temporary alteration of the contractual relationships of those within its coverage, but worked a severe, permanent, and immediate change in those relationships — irrevocably and retroactively. *Cf. United States Trust Co. v. New Jersey*, 431 U.S. 1 (1977). And its narrow aim was leveled, not at every Minnesota employer, not even at every Minnesota employer who left the State, but only at those who had in the past been sufficiently enlightened as voluntarily to agree to establish pension plans for their employees.

[W]e hold that if the Contract Clause means anything at all, it means that Minnesota could not constitutionally do what it tried to do to the company in this case.

The judgment of the District Court is reversed.

It is so ordered.

MR. JUSTICE BLACKMUN took no part in the consideration or decision of this case.

MR. JUSTICE BRENNAN, with whom MR. JUSTICE WHITE and MR. JUSTICE MARSHALL join, dissenting.

Today's decision greatly expands the reach of the Clause. The Minnesota Private Pension Benefits Protection Act (Act) does not abrogate or dilute any obligation due a party to a private contract; rather, like all positive social legislation, the Act imposes new, additional obligations on a particular class of persons.

Decisions over the past 50 years have developed a coherent, unified interpretation of all the constitutional provisions that may protect economic expectations and these decisions have recognized a broad latitude in States to effect even severe interference with existing economic values when reasonably necessary to promote the general welfare. At the same time the prohibition of the Contract Clause, consistently with its wording and historic purposes, has been limited in application to state laws that diluted, with utter indifference to the legitimate interests of the beneficiary of a contract duty, the existing contract obligation, *see United States Trust Co. v. New Jersey*, [431 U.S. 1 (1977)]; *cf. Home Building & Loan Assn. v. Blaisdell*, [290 U.S. 398 (1934)].

Today's conversion of the Contract Clause into a limitation on the power of States to enact laws that impose duties additional to obligations assumed under private contracts must inevitably produce results difficult to square with any rational conception of a constitutional order. Under the Court's opinion, any law that may be characterized as "superimposing" new obligations on those provided for by contract is to be regarded as creating "sudden, substantial, and unanticipated burdens" and then to be subjected to the most exacting scrutiny. The validity of such a law will turn upon whether judges see it as a law that deals with a generalized social problem, whether it is temporary (as few will be) or permanent, whether it operates in an area previously subject to regulation, and, finally, whether its duties apply to a broad class of persons. The necessary consequence of the extreme malleability of these rather vague criteria is to vest judges with broad subjective discretion to protect property interests that happen to appeal to them.

EXERCISE 10:

1. The majority clearly wanted to ensure that the Contracts Clause remained a viable limitation on states. However, are the facts in *Spannaus* sufficiently different from those in *Blaisdell* to warrant a different result?

2. What other options were open to the state to pursue its goal of protecting pensions of workers in the state?

3. The rationale utilized in *United States Trust Company* to lessen the deference to the state statute in question does not apply to *Spannaus* because Minnesota did not impair one of its own contracts. Can you make an argument, based on the political landscape of Minnesota at the time, that a similar judicial skepticism should apply?

4. What limitations would apply to the federal government attempting the same law as Minnesota tried?

––––––––––

Following *United States Trust Company* and *Spannaus*—decided within a year of each other—many commentators, and some of the Justices on the Court, thought that the Supreme Court might resurrect the Contracts Clause as a robust limitation on state power. However, since *Spannaus*, the Court has not invalidated any state laws under the Contracts Clause, despite repeated cases offering the opportunity to do so. *See General Motors Corp. v. Romein*, 503 U.S. 181 (1992) (holding that a state statute which required employers to reimburse employees for monies previously received under an earlier workers compensation statute did not violate the Contracts Clause); *Keystone Bituminous Coal Ass'n v. DeBenedictis*, 480 U.S. 470 (1987) (ruling that a state statute which required coal companies to leave coal in mines to support surface owners, despite coal companies' purchase of the right to mine that coal, did not violate the Contracts Clause); *Exxon Corp. v. Eagerton*, 462 U.S. 176 (1983) (rejecting a Contracts Clause challenge to a state tax on oil and gas producers that prohibited the producers from passing along the tax, regardless of contractual provisions permitting pass-through). Instead, the Supreme Court has distinguished *Spannaus*. *Exxon*, 462 U.S. at 192.

Chapter 2

THE SUPREMACY CLAUSE

A. INTRODUCTION

The Supremacy Clause states: "This Constitution, and the Laws of the United States which shall be made in Pursuance thereof; and all Treaties made, or which shall be made, under the Authority of the United States, shall be the supreme Law of the Land." U.S. CONST. art. VI, cl. 2.

EXERCISE 1:

Apply the first four forms of argument to the Supremacy Clause.

1. Looking at the Supremacy Clause itself and the text of the rest of Article VI, what do you learn about the Supremacy Clause's meaning?

2. Looking at the Constitution's structure, and particularly at the federal system it creates, what do you learn about the Supremacy Clause's meaning?

3. Reviewing evidence of the Constitution's original meaning, what does it tell you about that meaning?

4. Do the materials following adoption of the Constitution offer any insight into the Supremacy Clause's meaning?

––––––––––

The Supremacy Clause creates a hierarchy of law. Whenever two legal norms in the hierarchy come into conflict—when they attempt to regulate the same person or activity in incompatible ways—the legal norm that is ranked higher "preempts" the other norm. *See Gade v. National Sold Waste Mgmt. Ass'n*, 505 U.S. 88, 108 (1992) ("But under the Supremacy Clause, from which our pre-emption doctrine is derived, any state law, however clearly within a State's acknowledged power, which interferes with or is contrary to federal law, must yield.") (internal quotations omitted). Preemption is different from the Contracts Clause and dormant Commerce Clause contexts because, for federal law to preempt or void state law, Congress must affirmatively act.

While preemption can occur between any two types of legal norms, this Chapter covers the preemption that occurs when federal law and state law[1] both seek to regulate

––––––––––

1. Laws created by local governments are part of "state law" for preemption purposes.

the same subject. Given our federal system of government, this Chapter therefore focuses on one of the major points of tension between the federal and state governments.

The Constitution contains the most authoritative legal norms in the Supremacy Clause's hierarchy. What comes next in the hierarchy is one of the questions that preemption doctrines seek to answer. While you might be tempted to answer that federal law ("Laws of the United States") is obviously second in the hierarchy, that is not necessarily true. Instead, federal law is second in the hierarchy and "trumps" contrary state law only when it is "made in Pursuance thereof." In other words, federal law preempts state law only if it is constitutional.

Also, federal law preempts state law only when the two, in some sense, conflict. Otherwise, in our constitutional system, states retain authority to legislate on any matter that their state constitutions permit them to regulate (and that is not prohibited by the federal Constitution). It is this aspect of preemption—conflict—that Chapter Two reviews.

In the Supreme Court's modern case law, there are two distinctions that play a crucial role. The first is the distinction between express and implied preemption; the second is the distinction between field and conflict preemption. This Chapter addresses each in turn.

As you read the materials below, some of the issues to consider include:

What tension—what two values pulling in divergent directions—does the Supreme Court's preemption case law attempt to navigate?

When, under the Supreme Court's current interpretation of the Supremacy Clause, may preemption occur?

After you identify the different types of preemption the Supreme Court has labeled, what distinguishes them? Are these distinctions of kind or degree?

What role does a textual statutory statement of preemption play? What role does legislative history play? What role does statutory structure play? What about a statute's purpose?

Why is state law preempted even when Congress has not explicitly preempted state law?

What rationale would support a broad interpretation of the Supremacy Clause, one that weights the scales in favor of preemption? Has the Supreme Court adopted this interpretation?

What presumption does the Supreme Court employ in determining whether preemption occurred? What reasons support this presumption?

B. ORIGINAL MEANING OF SUPREMACY CLAUSE

There was little discussion in the Philadelphia Convention on the Supremacy Clause's impact on state law. This indicates that the Supremacy Clause was not controversial, which, in turn, suggests that preemption was an understood part of the

Supremacy Clause because federal law trumping state law would have been the most important—and also likely the most controversial—aspect of the Clause. James Madison's *Notes* on the Federal Convention mentions without discussion the Supremacy Clause only three times, each of which was a unanimous approval.[2]

The primary discussion of the Clause concerned ensuring that federal law, and especially treaties made prior to the adoption of the Constitution, would continue in effect.[3] On Madison's motion, the words, "or which shall be made," were inserted after the words, "all treaties made," in order to "obviate all doubt concerning the force of treaties preexisting, by making the words 'all treaties made,' to refer to them, as the words inserted would refer to future treaties."[4]

The Supremacy Clause was a focus of the Anti-Federalists' challenge to the proposed Constitution.[5] It is common to see the Clause listed in Anti-Federalist literature as a reason against ratification.[6] Their concern was that the Supremacy Clause provided a means for excessive national power over the states. They argued that the Supremacy Clause set federal law above all others, and their concern was that this would lead to a marginalization of the states.[7] Regardless of the validity of their fear, the Anti-Federalists interpreted the Supremacy Clause as providing for federal preemption of state law.[8]

---

2. 5 The Debates in the Several State Conventions on the Adoption of the Federal Constitution as Recommended by the General Convention at Philadelphia in 1787, at 322, 467, 478 (Jonathan Elliott, ed., 1974) (hereinafter Elliot's Debates).

3. *Id*. at 467.

4. *Id*. at 478.

5. All Anti-Federalist material is taken from Herbert J. Storing, The Complete Anti-Federalist (1981) (hereinafter Storing); citations include pinpoints to the relevant portion found in Storing's collection.

6. *See A Review of the Constitution Proposed by the Late Convention by a Federal Republican* (1787) (Storing, *supra*, at 3.6.32); *Essays of Brutus*, I (18 October 1787) (Storing, *supra*, at 2.9.5); *Essays by Cincinnatus*, II (8 November 1787) (Storing, *supra*, at 6.1.16); *Essays by Vox Populi*, II (19 November 1787) (Storing, *supra*, at 4.4.34); *Letters of Centinel*, V (30 November 1787) (Storing, *supra*, at 2.7.97); *Essay by One of the Common People* (3 December 1787) (Storing, *supra*, at 4.8.1); *Letters of Agrippa*, V (11 December 1787) (Storing, *supra*, at 4.6.19); *Letters from a Countryman from Dutchess County*, IV (15 December 1787) (Storing, *supra*, at 6.6.25); *The Address and Reasons of Dissent of the Minority of the Convention of Pennsylvania to their Constituents* (18 December 1787) (Storing, *supra*, at 3.11.22); *The Government of Nature Delineated or An Exact Picture of the New Federal Constitution by Aristocrotis* (1788) (Storing, *supra*, at 3.16.16n); Letters from a Countryman, IV (10 January 1788) (Storing, *supra*, at 6.7.9); *Essay by Samuel* (10 January 1788) (Storing, *supra*, at 4.14.4); Letters of Agrippa, XII (11 January 1788) (Storing, *supra*, at 4.6.52); *Essays by The Impartial Examiner*, I (20 February 1788) (Storing, *supra*, at 5.14.4); *Essay by Deliberator* (20 February 1788) (Storing, *supra*, at 3.13.3); *Address of the Albany Antifederal Committee* (26 April 1788) (Storing, *supra*, at 6.10.4); *Address by Sydney* (13 and 14 June 1788) (Storing, *supra*, at 6.9.12).

7. *See, e.g., Address of the Albany Antifederal Committee* (26 April 1788) (Storing, *supra*, 6.10.4) ("Their laws are to be *the supreme law of the land*, and the judges in every state are to be bound thereby, notwithstanding *the constitution or laws* of any state to the contrary.—A sweeping clause, which subjects every thing to the controul of the new government.").

8. *See, e.g. Essays of Brutus*, I (18 October 1787) (Storing, *supra*, 2.9.5) ("[T]he constitution and laws of every state are nullified and declared void, so far as they are or shall be inconsistent with

The Federalists did not appear to contest this interpretation. For instance, James Madison, defending the Clause in FEDERALIST No. 44, wrote:

> The indiscreet zeal of the adversaries to the Constitution has betrayed them into an attack on this part of it also, without which it would have been evidently and radically defective. To be fully sensible of this, we need only suppose for a moment that the supremacy of the State constitutions had been left complete by a saving clause in their favor . . . . [T]he world would have seen, for the first time, a system of government founded on an inversion of the fundamental principles of all government; it would have seen the authority of the whole society every where subordinate to the authority of the parts; it would have seen a monster, in which the head was under the direction of the members.[9]

In FEDERALIST No. 27, Hamilton dismissed out of hand the assertion that the Clause would destroy state governments: "The sophistry which has been employed to show that this will tend to the destruction of the State governments, will, in its proper place, be fully detected."[10]

The earliest Supreme Court case to address the Supremacy Clause did so in a manner that suggests preemption was the accepted understanding of the Clause. The case was *Ware v. Hylton*[11] and involved a disputed Revolutionary War era debt. The issue was to what extent the treaty with Britain ending the war impacted that debt. It is the only instance that John Marshall argued before the Supreme Court, and he did not argue that treaties were not preemptive, even though doing so would have been to his client's benefit. Justice Chase made the power of the Supremacy Clause clear:

> Four things are apparent, on a view of this 6th article of the national constitution. 1st. That it is retrospective, and is to be considered in the same light as if the constitution had been established before the making of the treaty of 1783. 2d. That the constitution or laws of any of the states, so far as either of them shall be found contrary to that treaty, are, by force of the said article, prostrated before the treaty. 3d. That, consequently, the treaty of 1783 has superior power to the legislature of any state, because no legislature of any state has any kind of power over the constitution, which was its creator. 4th. That it is the declared duty of the state judges to determine any constitution or laws of any state, contrary to that treaty (or any other), made under the authority of the United States, null and void. National or federal judges are bound by duty and oath to the same conduct.[12]

---

this constitution, or the laws made in pursuance of it, or with treaties made under the authority of the United States.").

9. THE FEDERALIST No. 44 (James Madison).

10. THE FEDERALIST No. 27 (Alexander Hamilton).

11. *Ware v. Hylton*, 3 U.S. (3 Dallas) 199 (1796).

12. *Id.* at 237.

The Marshall Court continued to articulate what today we call the doctrine of preemption. For instance, in *Gibbons v. Ogden*, Chief Justice Marshall stated that:

> The appropriate application of that part of the clause which confers the . . . supremacy on laws . . . , is to such acts of the State Legislatures . . . but, though enacted in the execution of acknowledged State powers, interfere with, or are contrary to the laws of Congress, made in pursuance of the constitution, or some treaty made under the authority of the United States. In every such case, the act of Congress, or the treaty, is supreme; and the law of the State, though enacted in the exercise of powers not controverted, must yield to it.[13]

The next sections review the two central distinctions in modern preemption doctrine. First, covered in Section C, is the distinction between express and implied preemption. Second, in Section D, we will read cases applying the distinction between field and conflict preemption.

C. EXPRESS PREEMPTION AND IMPLIED PREEMPTION

The rule governing express preemption is simple to state (at least relative to discerning when implied preemption exists, as we will see below) though less simple in application. Express preemption occurs when Congress, via express statutory language, states that some class(es) of state law is(are) preempted by federal law. Of course, even when there is explicit statutory preemption language, the *scope* of preemption may not be clear. This fact has led the Supreme Court to repeatedly emphasize that the ultimate touchstone is Congress' intent: "Th[e] question of whether a certain state action is pre-empted by federal law is one of congressional intent." *Allis-Chalmers Corp. v. Lueck*, 471 U.S. 202, 208 (1985).

Implied preemption, by contrast, occurs when a statute's text, structure, history, and purpose require preemption, even though the statute did not explicitly state that it preempted state law. *Ingersoll-Rand Co. v. McClendon*, 498 U.S. 133, 138 (1990). Even more so than in the express preemption cases, the Supreme Court struggles to discern Congress' intent on the question of preemption, and then to effectuate that intent.

Given the federal nature of our system of government and the significant retained role of states, the Supreme Court utilizes a "clear statement" rule of construction. That is, before the Supreme Court will determine that federal law preempts state law, especially when the subject state law is in an area of traditional state governance, Congress must clearly manifest its intent to preempt state law. *Hillsborough County v. Automated Med. Labs., Inc.*, 471 U.S. 707, 715 (1985).

---

13. *Gibbons v. Ogden*, 22 U.S. (9 Wheat.) 1, 82 (1824).

The following case details the potential complexities that even express preemption can raise. The second case shows the interpretative tools the Supreme Court utilizes to ascertain congressional intent for implied preemption.

AMERICAN AIRLINES, INC. v. MYRON WOLENS
513 U.S. 219 (1995)

Justice Ginsburg delivered the opinion of the Court.

The Airline Deregulation Act of 1978 prohibits States from "enact[ing] or enforc[ing] any law . . . relating to [air carrier] rates, routes, or services." This case concerns the scope of that preemptive provision, specifically, its application to a state-court suit, brought by participants in an airline's frequent flyer program, challenging the airline's retroactive changes in terms and conditions of the program. We hold that the ADA's preemption prescription bars state-imposed regulation of air carriers, but allows room for court enforcement of contract terms set by the parties themselves.

I

A

Until 1978, the Federal Aviation Act of 1958 (FAA), empowered the Civil Aeronautics Board (CAB) to regulate the interstate airline industry. Although the FAA, pre-1978, authorized the Board both to regulate fares and to take administrative action against deceptive trade practices, the federal legislation originally contained no clause preempting state regulation. And from the start, the FAA has contained a "saving clause," stating: "Nothing . . . in this chapter shall in any way abridge or alter the remedies now existing at common law or by statute, but the provisions of this chapter are in addition to such remedies."

In 1978, Congress enacted the Airline Deregulation Act (ADA), which largely deregulated domestic air transport. "To ensure that the States would not undo federal deregulation with regulation of their own," *Morales v. Trans World Airlines, Inc.*, 504 U.S. 374, 378 (1992), the ADA included a preemption clause.

This case is our second encounter with the ADA's preemption clause. In 1992, in *Morales*, we confronted detailed Travel Industry Enforcement Guidelines, composed by the National Association of Attorneys General (NAAG). The NAAG guidelines purported to govern, *inter alia*, the content and format of airline fare advertising. Several States had endeavored to enforce the NAAG guidelines, under the States' general consumer protection laws, to stop allegedly deceptive airline advertisements. The States' initiative, we determined, "'relat[ed] to [airline] rates, routes, or services,'"; consequently, we held, the fare advertising provisions of the NAAG guidelines were preempted by the ADA.

For aid in construing the ADA words "relating to rates, routes, or services of any air carrier," the Court in *Morales* referred to the Employee Retirement Income Security Act of 1974 (ERISA), which provides for preemption of state laws "insofar as they . . . relate to any employee benefit plan." Under the ERISA, we had ruled, a state law "relates to" an employee benefit plan "if it has a connection with or reference to such a plan." *Shaw v. Delta Air Lines, Inc.*, 463 U.S. 85, 97 (1983). *Morales* analogously defined the "relating to" language in the ADA preemption clause as "having a connection with, or reference to, airline 'rates, routes, or services.'"

The *Morales* opinion presented much more, however, in accounting for the ADA's preemption of the state regulation in question. The opinion pointed out that the concerned federal agencies—the Department of Transportation (DOT)[2] and the Federal Trade Commission (FTC)—objected to the NAAG fare advertising guidelines as inconsistent with the ADA's deregulatory purpose; both agencies, *Morales* observed, regarded the guidelines as state regulatory measures preempted by the ADA. *Morales* emphasized that the challenged guidelines set "binding requirements as to how airline tickets may be marketed," and "imposed [obligations that] would have a significant impact upon . . . the fares [airlines] charge." The opinion further noted that the airlines would not have "*carte blanche* to lie and deceive consumers," for "the DOT retains the power to prohibit advertisements which in its opinion do not further competitive pricing." *Morales* also left room for state actions "too tenuous, remote, or peripheral . . . to have pre-emptive effect."

B

The litigation now before us, two consolidated state-court class actions brought in Illinois, was *sub judice* when we decided *Morales*. Plaintiffs in both actions (respondents here) are participants in American Airlines' frequent flyer program, AAdvantage. AAdvantage enrollees earn mileage credits when they fly on American. They can exchange those credits for flight tickets or class-of-service upgrades. Plaintiffs complained that AAdvantage program modifications, instituted by American in 1988, devalued credits AAdvantage members had already earned. Plaintiffs featured American's imposition of capacity controls (limits on seats available to passengers obtaining tickets with AAdvantage credits) and blackout dates (restrictions on dates credits could be used). Conceding that American had reserved the right to change AAdvantage terms and conditions, plaintiffs challenged only the retroactive application of modifications, *i.e.*, cutbacks on the utility of credits previously accumulated. These cutbacks, plaintiffs maintained, violated the Illinois Consumer Fraud and Deceptive Business Practices Act (Consumer Fraud Act or Act), and constituted a breach of contract. Plaintiffs currently seek only monetary relief.

In March 1992, the Illinois Supreme Court rejected plaintiffs' prayer for an injunction. Such a decree, the Illinois court reasoned, would involve regulation of an airline's current rendition of services, a matter preempted by the ADA. That court, however, allowed the breach-of-contract and Consumer Fraud Act monetary relief claims to survive. The ADA's preemption clause, the Illinois court said, ruled out

---

2. Deceptive trade practices regulatory authority formerly residing in the CAB was transferred to the DOT when the CAB was abolished in 1985.

"only those State laws and regulations that specifically relate to and have more than a tangential connection with an airline's rates, routes or services." After our decision in *Morales*, American petitioned for certiorari. The airline charged that the Illinois court, in a decision out of sync with *Morales*, had narrowly construed the ADA's broadly preemptive § 1305(a)(1). We granted the petition, vacated the judgment of the Supreme Court of Illinois, and remanded for further consideration in light of *Morales.*

On remand, the Illinois Supreme Court adhered to its prior judgment. Describing frequent flyer programs as not "essential," but merely "peripheral to the operation of an airline," the Illinois court typed plaintiffs' state-law claims for money damages as "relat[ed] to American's rates, routes, and services" only "tangential[ly]" or "tenuous[ly]."

We granted American's second petition for certiorari, and we now reverse the Illinois Supreme Court's judgment to the extent that it allowed survival of plaintiffs' Consumer Fraud Act claims; we affirm that judgment, however, to the extent that it permits plaintiffs' breach-of-contract action to proceed. In both respects, we adopt the position of the DOT, as advanced in this Court by the United States.

II

We need not dwell on the question whether plaintiffs' complaints state claims "relating to [air carrier] rates, routes, or services." *Morales*, we are satisfied, does not countenance the Illinois Supreme Court's separation of matters "essential" from matters unessential to airline operations. Plaintiffs' claims relate to "rates," *i.e.*, American's charges in the form of mileage credits for free tickets and upgrades, and to "services," *i.e.*, access to flights and class-of-service upgrades unlimited by retrospectively applied capacity controls and blackout dates. But the ADA's preemption clause contains other words in need of interpretation, specifically, the words "enact or enforce any law" in the instruction: "[N]o State . . . shall enact or enforce any law." Taking into account all the words Congress placed in § 1305(a)(1), we first consider whether plaintiffs' claims under the Consumer Fraud Act are preempted, and then turn to plaintiffs' breach-of-contract claims.

A

The Consumer Fraud Act declares unlawful "[u]nfair methods of competition and unfair or deceptive acts or practices . . . or the use or employment of any practice described in Section 2 of the 'Uniform Deceptive Trade Practices Act' . . . in the conduct of any trade or commerce . . . whether any person has in fact been misled, deceived or damaged thereby." Ill. Comp. Stat., ch. 815, § 505/2 (1992).

The Act is prescriptive; it controls the primary conduct of those falling within its governance. This Illinois law, in fact, is paradigmatic of the consumer protection legislation underpinning the NAAG guidelines. The NAAG Task Force on the Air Travel Industry, on which the Attorneys General of California, Illinois, Texas, and Washington served, reported that the guidelines created no "new laws or regulations regarding the advertising practices or other business practices of the airline industry. They merely explain in detail how existing state laws apply to air fare advertising and frequent flyer programs." *Morales*, 504 U.S., at 392.

The NAAG guidelines highlight the potential for intrusive regulation of airline business practices inherent in state consumer protection legislation typified by the Consumer Fraud Act. For example, the guidelines enforcing the legislation instruct airlines on language appropriate to reserve rights to alter frequent flyer programs, and they include transition rules for the fair institution of capacity controls.

As the NAAG guidelines illustrate, the Consumer Fraud Act serves as a means to guide and police the marketing practices of the airlines; the Act does not simply give effect to bargains offered by the airlines and accepted by airline customers. In light of the full text of the preemption clause, and of the ADA's purpose to leave largely to the airlines themselves, and not at all to States, the selection and design of marketing mechanisms appropriate to the furnishing of air transportation services, we conclude that § 1305(a)(1) preempts plaintiffs' claims under the Consumer Fraud Act.

B

American maintains, and we agree, that "Congress could hardly have intended to allow the States to hobble [competition for airline passengers] through the application of restrictive state laws." We do not read the ADA's preemption clause, however, to shelter airlines from suits alleging no violation of state-imposed obligations, but seeking recovery solely for the airline's alleged breach of its own, self-imposed undertakings. As persuasively argued by the United States, terms and conditions airlines offer and passengers accept are privately ordered obligations "and thus do not amount to a State's 'enact[ment] or enforce[ment] [of] any law, rule, regulation, standard, or other provision having the force and effect of law' within the meaning of [§] 1305(a) (1)."[5] Brief for United States as *Amicus Curiae* 9. A remedy confined to a contract's terms simply holds parties to their agreements — in this instance, to business judgments an airline made public about its rates and services.

The ADA, as we recognized in *Morales*, was designed to promote "maximum reliance on competitive market forces." Market efficiency requires effective means to enforce private agreements. *See* Farber, *Contract Law and Modern Economic Theory*, 78 Nw.U.L.Rev. 303, 315 (1983) (remedy for breach of contract "is necessary in order

---

5. The United States recognizes that § 1305(a)(1), because it contains the word "enforce" as well as "enact," "could perhaps be read to preempt even state-court enforcement of private contracts." Brief for United States as *Amicus Curiae* 17. But the word series "law, rule, regulation, standard, or other provision," as the United States suggests, "connotes official, government-imposed policies, not the terms of a private contract." Similarly, the phrase "having the force and effect of law" is most naturally read to "refe[r] to binding standards of conduct that operate irrespective of any private agreement." Finally, the ban on enacting or enforcing any law "relating to rates, routes, or services" is most sensibly read, in light of the ADA's overarching deregulatory purpose, to mean "States may not seek to impose their own public policies or theories of competition or regulation on the operations of an air carrier."

to ensure economic efficiency"); R. Posner, Economic Analysis of Law 90–91 (4th ed. 1992) (legal enforcement of contracts is more efficient than a purely voluntary system). That reality is key to sensible construction of the ADA.

The FAA's text, we note, presupposes the vitality of contracts governing transportation by air carriers. Section 411(b), 49 U.S.C.App. § 1381(b), thus authorizes airlines to "incorporate by reference in any ticket or other written instrument any of the terms of the contract of carriage" to the extent authorized by the DOT. And the DOT's regulations contemplate that, upon the January 1, 1983, termination of domestic tariffs, "ticket contracts" ordinarily would be enforceable under "the contract law of the States." 47 Fed. Reg. 52129 (1982). Correspondingly, the DOT requires carriers to give passengers written notice of the time period within which they may "bring an action against the carrier for its acts." 14 CFR § 253.5(b)(2) (1994).

American does not suggest that its contracts lack legal force. American sees the DOT, however, as the exclusively competent monitor of the airline's undertakings. American points to the Department's authority to require any airline, in conjunction with its certification, to file a performance bond conditioned on the airline's "making appropriate compensation . . . , as prescribed by the [Department], for failure . . . to perform air transportation services in accordance with agreements therefor." FAA § 401(q)(2), 49 U.S.C.App. § 1371(q)(2). But neither the DOT nor its predecessor, the CAB, has ever construed or applied this provision to displace courts as adjudicators in air carrier contract disputes. Instead, these agencies have read the provision to charge them with a less taxing task: In passing on air carrier fitness, the DOT and the CAB have used their performance bond authority to ensure that, when a carrier's financial fitness is marginal, funds will be available to compensate customers if the carrier goes under before providing already-paid-for services.

The United States maintains that the DOT has neither the authority nor the apparatus required to superintend a contract dispute resolution regime. Prior to airline deregulation, the CAB set rates, routes, and services through a cumbersome administrative process of applications and approvals. When Congress dismantled that regime, the United States emphasizes, the lawmakers indicated no intention to establish, simultaneously, a new administrative process for DOT adjudication of private contract disputes. We agree.

Nor is it plausible that Congress meant to channel into federal courts the business of resolving, pursuant to judicially fashioned federal common law, the range of contract claims relating to airline rates, routes, or services. The ADA contains no hint of such a role for the federal courts. In this regard, the ADA contrasts markedly with the ERISA, which does channel civil actions into federal courts, under a comprehensive scheme, detailed in the legislation, designed to promote "prompt and fair claims settlement."

The conclusion that the ADA permits state-law-based court adjudication of routine breach-of-contract claims also makes sense of Congress' retention of the FAA's saving clause, § 1106, 49 U.S.C.App. § 1506 (preserving "the remedies now existing at common law or by statute"). The ADA's preemption clause, § 1305(a)(1), read together with the FAA's saving clause, stops States from imposing their own substantive standards with respect to rates, routes, or services, but not from affording relief to a party who claims and proves that an airline dishonored a term the airline itself stipulated. This distinction between what the State dictates and what the airline itself undertakes confines courts, in breach-of-contract actions, to the parties' bargain, with no enlargement or enhancement based on state laws or policies external to the agreement.

III

Responding to our colleagues' diverse opinions dissenting in part, we add a final note. This case presents two issues that run all through the law. First, who decides (here, courts or the DOT, the latter lacking contract dispute resolution resources for the task)? On this question, all agree to this extent: None of the opinions in this case would foist on the DOT work Congress has neither instructed nor funded the Department to do. Second, where is it proper to draw the line (here, between what the ADA preempts, and what it leaves to private ordering, backed by judicial enforcement)? JUSTICE STEVENS reads our *Morales* decision to demand only minimal preemption; in contrast, JUSTICE O'CONNOR reads the same case to mandate total preemption. The middle course we adopt seems to us best calculated to carry out the congressional design; it also bears the approval of the statute's experienced administrator, the DOT. And while we adhere to our holding in *Morales*, we do not overlook that in our system of adjudication, principles seldom can be settled "on the basis of one or two cases, but require a closer working out." Pound, *Survey of the Conference Problems*, 14 U. Cin. L. Rev. 324, 339 (1940).

For the reasons stated, the judgment of the Illinois Supreme Court is affirmed in part and reversed in part, and the case is remanded for proceedings not inconsistent with this opinion.

It is so ordered.

JUSTICE SCALIA took no part in the decision of the case.

JUSTICE STEVENS, concurring in part and dissenting in part.

Although I agree with the majority that the Airline Deregulation Act of 1978 (ADA) does not pre-empt respondents' breach-of-contract claims, I do not agree with the Court's disposition of their consumer-fraud claims. In my opinion, private tort actions based on common-law negligence or fraud, or on a statutory prohibition against fraud, are not pre-empted. Under the broad (and in my opinion incorrect) interpretation of the words "law . . . relating to rates, routes, or services" that the Court adopted in *Morales v. Trans World Airlines, Inc.*, 504 U.S. 374 (1992), direct state regulation of airline advertising is pre-empted; but I would not extend the holding of that case to embrace the private claims that respondents assert in this case.

Unlike the National Association of Attorneys General (NAAG) guidelines reviewed in *Morales*, the Illinois Consumer Fraud and Deceptive Business Practices Act

(Consumer Fraud Act) does not instruct the airlines about how they can market their services. Instead, it merely requires all commercial enterprises—airlines included—to refrain from defrauding their customers. The *Morales* opinion said nothing about pre-empting general state laws prohibiting fraud. The majority's extension of the ADA's pre-emptive reach from airline-specific advertising standards to a general background rule of private conduct represents an alarming enlargement of *Morales'* holding.

I see no reason why a state law requiring an airline to honor its contractual commitments is any less a law relating to its rates and services than is a state law imposing a "duty not to make false statements of material fact or to conceal such facts." In this case, the two claims are grounded upon the exact same conduct and would presumably have an identical impact upon American's rates, routes, and services. The majority correctly finds that Congress did not intend to pre-empt a claim that an airline breached a private agreement. I see no reason why the ADA should pre-empt a claim that the airline defrauded its customers in the making and performance of that very same agreement.

I would analogize the Consumer Fraud Act to a codification of common-law negligence rules. Under ordinary tort principles, every person has a duty to exercise reasonable care toward all other persons with whom he comes into contact. Presumably, if an airline were negligent in a way that somehow affected its rates, routes, or services, and the victim of the airline's negligence were to sue in state court, the majority would not hold all common-law negligence rules to be pre-empted by the ADA. Like contract principles, the standard of ordinary care is a general background rule against which all individuals order their affairs. Surely Congress did not intend to give airlines free rein to commit negligent acts subject only to the supervision of the Department of Transportation, any more than it meant to allow airlines to breach contracts with impunity. And, if judge-made duties are not pre-empted, it would make little sense to find pre-emption of identical rules codified by the state legislature.

Accordingly, while I join the Court's disposition of the breach-of-contract claims, I would affirm the entire judgment of the Supreme Court of Illinois.

JUSTICE O'CONNOR, with whom JUSTICE THOMAS joins as to all but Part I-B, concurring in the judgment in part and dissenting in part.

In permitting respondents' contract action to go forward, the Court arrives at what might be a reasonable policy judgment as to when state law actions against airlines should be pre-empted if we were free to legislate it. It is not, however, consistent with our controlling precedents, and it requires some questionable assumptions about the nature of contract law. I would hold that none of respondents' actions may proceed.

I

A

The Airline Deregulation Act of 1978 (ADA) says that "no State . . . shall enact or enforce any law, rule, regulation, standard, or other provision having the force and effect of law relating to rates, routes, or services of any air carrier." 49 U.S.C.App. § 1305(a)(1). We considered the scope of that provision in *Morales v. Trans World Airlines, Inc.* We noted the similarity of § 1305's language to the pre-emption provision in ERISA, and said that, like ERISA's, § 1305's words "express a broad pre-emptive purpose." We concluded that "State enforcement actions having a connection with, or reference to, airline 'rates, routes, or services' are pre-empted."

Applying *Morales* to this case, I agree with the Court that respondents' consumer fraud and contract claims are "related to" airline "rates" and "services." The Court says, however, that judicial enforcement of a contract's terms, in accordance with state contract law, does not amount to a "State . . . enforc[ing] any law," § 1305, but instead is simply a State "hold[ing] parties to their agreemen[t]." It therefore concludes that § 1305 does not apply to respondents' contract actions. I cannot agree with that conclusion.

As I read § 1305 and *Morales*, respondents' contract claims must be preempted. The Court recognizes that the "guidelines" at issue in *Morales* did not "'create any new laws or regulations' applying to the airline industry; rather, they claim[ed] to 'explain in detail how existing state laws apply to air fare advertising and frequent flyer programs.'" Nonetheless, we stated our holding quite clearly: "We hold that the fare advertising provisions of the NAAG guidelines are pre-empted by [§ 1305]." How can it be that the guidelines, which did not themselves constitute "law," were nonetheless pre-empted by a statute whose coverage is limited to "laws" or other "provision[s] having the force and effect of law"? The answer is that in *Morales* we held that an action to invoke the State's coercive power against an airline, by means of a generally applicable law, when the subject matter of the action related to airline rates, would constitute "Stat[e] . . . enforce[ment]" of a "law . . . relating to rates, routes, or services." Accordingly, we held that § 1305 pre-empted the action. The only "laws" at issue in *Morales* were generally applicable consumer fraud statutes, not facially related to airlines, much like the law at issue in respondents' consumer fraud claims here.

The Court concludes, however, that § 1305 does *not* preempt enforcement, by means of generally applicable state law, of a private agreement relating to airline rates and services. I cannot distinguish this case from *Morales*. In both, the subject matter of the action (the guidelines in *Morales*, the contract here) relates to airline rates and services. In both, that subject matter has no legal force, except insofar as a generally applicable state law (a consumer fraud law in *Morales*, state contract law here) permits an aggrieved party to invoke the State's coercive power against someone refusing to comply with the subject matter's terms (the requirements of the guidelines in *Morales*, the terms of the contract here). *Morales'* conclusion that § 1305 pre-empts such an invocation is dispositive here, both of respondents' consumer fraud claims, and of their contract claims. The lower courts seem to agree; as far as I know, no court to have considered ADA pre-emption since we decided *Morales* has suggested that enforcement of state contract law does not fall within § 1305 if the necessary relation to airline rates, routes, or services exists.

[A] State is enforcing its "law" when it brings its coercive power to bear on a party who has violated a contractual obligation. [S]*ee Sturges v. Crowninshield*, 17 U.S. (4 Wheat.) 122 (1819) (Marshall, C.J.) ("A contract is an agreement, in which a party undertakes to do, or not to do, a particular thing. The law binds him to perform his undertaking, and this is, of course, the obligation of his contract"). I would give the words "any law" in § 1305 a similar reading.

B

Congress has recently revisited § 1305, and said that it "d[id] not intend to alter the broad pre-emption interpretation adopted by the United States Supreme Court in *Morales*," H.R.Conf.Rep. No. 103-677, p. 83 (1994). If the Court nonetheless believes that *Morales* misread § 1305, the proper course of action would be to overrule that case, despite Congress' apparent approval of it.

Stare decisis has "special force" in the area of statutory interpretation. It sometimes requires adherence to a wrongly decided precedent. Here, however, Congress apparently does not think that our decision in *Morales* was wrong, nor do I. If, at the end of the day, Congress believes we have erred in interpreting § 1305, it remains free to correct our mistake.

II

In addition, however, I disagree with the Court's view that courts can realistically be confined, "in breach-of-contract actions, to the parties' bargain, with no enlargement or enhancement based on state laws or policies external to the agreement." When they are so confined, the Court says, courts are "simply hold[ing] parties to their agreements," and are not "enforcing" any "law." The Court also says that "'[s]ome state-law principles of contract law ... might well be preempted to the extent they seek to effectuate the State's public policies, rather than the intent of the parties.'" *Ante* (quoting Brief for United States as *Amicus Curiae*).

The doctrinal underpinnings of the notion that judicial enforcement of the "intent of the parties" can be divorced from a State's "public policy" have been in serious question for many years. Contract law is a set of policy judgments concerning how to decide the meaning of private agreements, which private agreements should be legally enforceable, and what remedy to afford for their breach. The Court fails to recognize that when a State decides to force parties to comply with a contract, it does so only because it is satisfied that state policy, as expressed in its contract law, will be advanced by that decision.

For these reasons, I would reverse the judgment of the Illinois Supreme Court.

EXERCISE 2:

1. What role did the Supremacy Clause itself play in this case?

2. What tools of analysis did the Supreme Court utilize to determine that Congress expressly preempted Illinois' fraud act?

3. What role did the Court's citation to Daniel Farber's and Richard Posner's scholarship play? Is it appropriate for the Supreme Court to cite scholarly writings?

4. The majority distinguishes between the plaintiffs' claims brought under the Illinois Fraud Act and their breach of contract claims. Did the majority or Justice O'Connor have the better argument regarding whether the ADA preempted the plaintiffs' contract claims?

5. Why did the Court stress the fact that the DOT has the authority to act against unfair and deceptive trade practices?

6. The majority does not directly respond to Justice Stevens' argument that the ADA's preemption clause failed to overcome the presumption against preemption. Articulate a response on the majority's behalf. Is it persuasive?

7. What role did the ADA's savings clause play?

8. Why did Justice O'Connor refer to what lower courts have decided when faced with the question of whether the ADA preempted state breach of contract actions?

9. Why does stare decisis have special force in the context of precedents that interpret statutes? Does this make sense?

––––––––––

Implied preemption occurs when federal law displaces state law without the federal law expressly stating that the federal law does so. The Supreme Court has found implied preemption in a number of more-or-less similar situations. First, the Court has held that state law is preempted if regulated persons or entities cannot comply with the requirements of both the federal and state law. *See McDermott v. Wisconsin*, 228 U.S. 115 (1913) (holding that a state law was preempted when it prohibited labeling of maple syrup in a manner required by federal law). Second, state law is preempted when it impedes the attainment of the federal law's objective. *See Perez v. Campbell*, 402 U.S. 637 (1971) (ruling that a state law, which suspended drivers licenses for those who failed to pay judgments from auto accidents, was preempted by federal bankruptcy law because the state law punished persons whose judgments had been discharged in bankruptcy). Below is a case where the Supreme Court found implied preemption of the second kind.

GEIER v. AMERICAN HONDA MOTOR COMPANY, INC.

529 U.S. 861 (2000)

Justice Breyer delivered the opinion of the Court.

This case focuses on the 1984 version of a Federal Motor Vehicle Safety Standard promulgated by the Department of Transportation under the authority of the National Traffic and Motor Vehicle Safety Act of 1966. The standard, FMVSS 208, required auto manufacturers to equip some but not all of their 1987 vehicles with passive restraints. We ask whether the Act pre-empts a state common-law tort action in which the plaintiff claims that the defendant auto manufacturer, who was in compliance with the standard, should nonetheless have equipped a 1987 automobile with airbags. We conclude that the Act, taken together with FMVSS 208, pre-empts the lawsuit.

I

In 1992, petitioner Alexis Geier, driving a 1987 Honda Accord, collided with a tree and was seriously injured. The car was equipped with manual shoulder and lap belts which Geier had buckled up at the time. The car was not equipped with airbags or other passive restraint devices.

Geier and her parents, also petitioners, sued the car's manufacturer, American Honda Motor Company, Inc., under District of Columbia tort law. They claimed, among other things, that American Honda had designed its car negligently and defectively because it lacked a driver's side airbag. The District Court dismissed the lawsuit. The court noted that FMVSS 208 gave car manufacturers a choice as to whether to install airbags. And the court concluded that petitioners' lawsuit, because it sought to establish a different safety standard — i.e., an airbag requirement — was expressly pre-empted by a provision of the Act which pre-empts "any safety standard" that is not identical to a federal safety standard applicable to the same aspect of performance, 15 U.S.C. § 1392(d) (1988 ed.).

The Court of Appeals agreed with the District Court's conclusion but on somewhat different reasoning. It had doubts, given the existence of the Act's "saving" clause, 15 U.S.C. § 1397(k) (1988 ed.), that petitioners' lawsuit involved the potential creation of the kind of "safety standard" to which the Safety Act's express pre-emption provision refers. But it declined to resolve that question because it found that petitioners' state-law tort claims posed an obstacle to the accomplishment of FMVSS 208's objectives. For that reason, it found that those claims conflicted with FMVSS 208, and that, under ordinary pre-emption principles, the Act consequently pre-empted the lawsuit. The Court of Appeals thus affirmed the District Court's dismissal.

We now hold that this kind of "no airbag" lawsuit conflicts with the objectives of FMVSS 208, a standard authorized by the Act, and is therefore pre-empted by the Act. In reaching our conclusion, we consider three subsidiary questions. First, does the Act's express pre-emption provision pre-empt this lawsuit? We think not. Second, do ordinary pre-emption principles nonetheless apply? We hold that they do. Third, does this lawsuit actually conflict with FMVSS 208, hence with the Act itself? We hold that it does.

II

We first ask whether the Safety Act's express pre-emption provision pre-empts this tort action. The provision reads as follows:

> "Whenever a Federal motor vehicle safety standard established under this subchapter is in effect, no State or political subdivision of a State shall have any authority either to establish, or to continue in effect, with respect to any motor

vehicle or item of motor vehicle equipment[,] any safety standard applicable to the same aspect of performance of such vehicle or item of equipment which is not identical to the Federal standard." 15 U.S.C. § 1392(d) (1988 ed.).

American Honda points out that a majority of this Court has said that a somewhat similar statutory provision in a different federal statute — a provision that uses the word "requirements" — may well expressly pre-empt similar tort actions. *See, e.g., Medtronic, Inc. v. Lohr*, 518 U.S. 470 (1996). Petitioners reply that this statute speaks of pre-empting a state-law "safety *standard*," not a "requirement," and that a tort action does not involve a safety *standard*. Hence, they conclude, the express pre-emption provision does not apply.

We need not determine the precise significance of the use of the word "standard," rather than "requirement," however, for the Act contains another provision, which resolves the disagreement. That provision, a "saving" clause, says that "[c]ompliance with" a federal safety standard "does not exempt any person from any liability under common law." 15 U.S.C. § 1397(k) (1988 ed.). The saving clause assumes that there are some significant number of common-law liability cases to save. And a reading of the express pre-emption provision that excludes common-law tort actions gives actual meaning to the saving clause's literal language, while leaving adequate room for state tort law to operate — for example, where federal law creates only a floor, *i.e.*, a minimum safety standard. Without the saving clause, a broad reading of the express pre-emption provision arguably might pre-empt those actions, for, as we have just mentioned, it is possible to read the pre-emption provision, standing alone, as applying to standards imposed in common-law tort actions, as well as standards contained in state legislation or regulations. And if so, it would pre-empt all nonidentical state standards established in tort actions covering the same aspect of performance as an applicable federal standard, even if the federal standard merely established a minimum standard. On that broad reading of the pre-emption clause little, if any, potential "liability at common law" would remain. And few, if any, state tort actions would remain for the saving clause to save. We have found no convincing indication that Congress wanted to pre-empt, not only state statutes and regulations, but also common-law tort actions, in such circumstances. Hence the broad reading cannot be correct. The language of the pre-emption provision permits a narrow reading that excludes common-law actions. Given the presence of the saving clause, we conclude that the pre-emption clause must be so read.

III

We have just said that the saving clause *at least* removes tort actions from the scope of the express pre-emption clause. Does it do more? In particular, does it foreclose or limit the operation of ordinary pre-emption principles insofar as those principles instruct us to read statutes as pre-empting state laws (including common-law rules) that "actually conflict" with the statute or federal standards promulgated thereunder? Petitioners concede, as they must in light of *Freightliner Corp. v. Myrick*, 514 U.S. 280 (1995), that the pre-emption provision, by itself, does not foreclose (through negative implication) "any possibility of implied [conflict] pre-emption." But they argue that the saving clause has that very effect.

We conclude that the saving clause (like the express pre-emption provision) does *not* bar the ordinary working of conflict pre-emption principles.

Nothing in the language of the saving clause suggests an intent to save state-law tort actions that conflict with federal regulations. The words "[c]ompliance" and "does not exempt," 15 U.S.C. § 1397(k) (1988 ed.), sound as if they simply bar a special kind of defense, namely, a defense that compliance with a federal standard automatically exempts a defendant from state law, whether the Federal Government meant that standard to be an absolute requirement or only a minimum one. *See* Restatement (Third) of Torts: Products Liability § 4(b), Comment *e* (1997) (distinguishing between state-law compliance defense and a federal claim of pre-emption). It is difficult to understand why Congress would have insisted on a compliance-with-federal-regulation precondition to the provision's applicability had it wished the Act to "save" all state-law tort actions, regardless of their potential threat to the objectives of federal safety standards promulgated under that Act. Nor does our interpretation conflict with the purpose of the saving provision, say, by rendering it ineffectual. As we have previously explained, the saving provision still makes clear that the express pre-emption provision does not of its own force pre-empt common-law tort actions. And it thereby preserves those actions that seek to establish greater safety than the minimum safety achieved by a federal regulation intended to provide a floor.

Moreover, this Court has repeatedly "decline[d] to give broad effect to saving clauses where doing so would upset the careful regulatory scheme established by federal law." We find this concern applicable in the present case. And we conclude that the saving clause foresees — it does not foreclose — the possibility that a federal safety standard will pre-empt a state common-law tort action with which it conflicts.

Why, in any event, would Congress not have wanted ordinary pre-emption principles to apply where an actual conflict with a federal objective is at stake? Some such principle is needed. In its absence, state law could impose legal duties that would conflict directly with federal regulatory mandates. Insofar as petitioners' argument would permit common-law actions that "actually conflict" with federal regulations, it would take from those who would enforce a federal law the very ability to achieve the law's congressionally mandated objectives that the Constitution, through the operation of ordinary pre-emption principles, seeks to protect. To the extent that such an interpretation of the saving provision reads into a particular federal law toleration of a conflict that those principles would otherwise forbid, it permits that law to defeat its own objectives. We do not claim that Congress lacks the constitutional power to write a statute that mandates such a complex type of state/federal relationship. But there is no reason to believe Congress has done so here.

IV

The basic question, then, is whether a common-law "no airbag" action like the one before us actually conflicts with FMVSS 208. We hold that it does.

In petitioners' and the dissent's view, FMVSS 208 sets a minimum airbag standard. As far as FMVSS 208 is concerned, the more airbags, and the sooner, the better. But that was not the Secretary's view. The Department of Transportation's (DOT's) comments, which accompanied the promulgation of FMVSS 208, make clear that the standard deliberately provided the manufacturer with a range of choices among different passive restraint devices. Those choices would bring about a mix of different devices introduced gradually over time; and FMVSS 208 would thereby lower costs, overcome technical safety problems, encourage technological development, and win widespread consumer acceptance—all of which would promote FMVSS 208's safety objectives.

A

The history of FMVSS 208 helps explain why and how DOT sought these objectives. In 1967, DOT, understanding that seatbelts would save many lives, required manufacturers to install manual seatbelts in all automobiles. It became apparent, however, that most occupants simply would not buckle up their belts. DOT then began to investigate the feasibility of requiring "passive restraints," such as airbags and automatic seatbelts. In 1970, it amended FMVSS 208 to include some passive protection requirements, while making clear that airbags were one of several "equally acceptable" devices and that it neither "'favored' [n]or expected the introduction of airbag systems." In 1971, it added an express provision permitting compliance through the use of nondetachable passive belts, and in 1972, it mandated full passive protection for all front seat occupants for vehicles manufactured after August 15, 1975. Although the agency's focus was originally on airbags, at no point did FMVSS 208 formally require the use of airbags. From the start, as in 1984, it permitted passive restraint options.

DOT gave manufacturers a further choice for new vehicles manufactured between 1972 and August 1975. Manufacturers could either install a passive restraint device such as automatic seatbelts or airbags or retain manual belts and add an "ignition interlock" device that in effect forced occupants to buckle up by preventing the ignition otherwise from turning on. The interlock soon became popular with manufacturers. And in 1974, when the agency approved the use of detachable automatic seatbelts, it conditioned that approval by providing that such systems must include an interlock system *and* a continuous warning buzzer to encourage reattachment of the belt. But the interlock and buzzer devices were most unpopular with the public. And Congress, responding to public pressure, passed a law that forbade DOT from requiring, or permitting compliance by means of, such devices.

That experience influenced DOT's subsequent passive restraint initiatives. In 1976, DOT Secretary William T. Coleman, Jr., fearing continued public resistance, suspended the passive restraint requirements. He sought to win public acceptance for a variety of passive restraint devices through a demonstration project that would involve about half a million new automobiles. But his successor, Brock Adams, canceled the project, instead amending FMVSS 208 to require passive restraints, principally either airbags or passive seatbelts.

Andrew Lewis, a new DOT Secretary in a new administration, rescinded the Adams requirements, primarily because DOT learned that the industry planned to satisfy those requirements almost exclusively through the installation of detachable automatic seatbelts. This Court held the rescission unlawful. And the stage was set for then-DOT Secretary, Elizabeth Dole, to amend FMVSS 208 once again, promulgating the version that is now before us. 49 Fed.Reg. 28962 (1984).

B

Read in light of this history, DOT's own contemporaneous explanation of FMVSS 208 makes clear that the 1984 version of FMVSS 208 reflected [numerous] significant considerations.

FMVSS 208 reflected these considerations in several ways. Most importantly, that standard deliberately sought variety—a mix of several different passive restraint systems. It did so by setting a performance requirement for passive restraint devices and allowing manufacturers to choose among different passive restraint mechanisms, such as airbags, automatic belts, or other passive restraint technologies to satisfy that requirement. DOT wrote that it had *rejected* a proposed FMVSS 208 "all airbag" standard because of safety concerns (perceived or real) associated with airbags, which concerns threatened a "backlash" more easily overcome "if airbags" were "not the only way of complying." It added that a mix of devices would help develop data on comparative effectiveness, would allow the industry time to overcome the safety problems and the high production costs associated with airbags, and would facilitate the development of alternative, cheaper, and safer passive restraint systems. And it would thereby build public confidence, necessary to avoid another interlock-type fiasco.

The 1984 FMVSS 208 standard also deliberately sought a *gradual* phase-in of passive restraints. It required the manufacturers to equip only 10% of their car fleet manufactured after September 1, 1986, with passive restraints. It then increased the percentage in three annual stages, up to 100% of the new car fleet for cars manufactured after September 1, 1989.

Finally, FMVSS 208's passive restraint requirement was conditional. DOT believed that ordinary manual lap and shoulder belts would produce about the same amount of safety as passive restraints, and at significantly lower costs—*if only auto occupants would buckle up.* Thus, FMVSS 208 provided for rescission of its passive restraint requirement if, by September 1, 1989, two-thirds of the States had laws in place that, like those of many other nations, required auto occupants to buckle up. In the end, two-thirds of the States did not enact mandatory buckle-up laws, and the passive restraint requirement remained in effect.

In sum, as DOT now tells us through the Solicitor General, the 1984 version of FMVSS 208 "embodies the Secretary's policy judgment that safety would best be promoted if manufacturers installed *alternative* protection systems in their fleets rather than one particular system in every car." Brief for United States as *Amicus Curiae.* Petitioners' tort suit claims that the manufacturers of the 1987 Honda Accord "had a duty to design, manufacture, distribute and sell a motor vehicle with an effective and safe passive restraint system, including, but not limited to, airbags." Complaint, ¶ 11.

In effect, petitioners' tort action depends upon its claim that manufacturers had a duty to install an airbag when they manufactured the 1987 Honda Accord. Such a state law—*i.e.*, a rule of state tort law imposing such a duty—by its terms would have required manufacturers of all similar cars to install airbags rather than other passive restraint systems, such as automatic belts or passive interiors. It thereby would have presented an obstacle to the variety and mix of devices that the federal regulation sought. It would have required all manufacturers to have installed airbags in respect to the entire District-of-Columbia-related portion of their 1987 new car fleet, even though FMVSS 208 at that time required only that 10% of a manufacturer's nationwide fleet be equipped with any passive restraint device at all. It thereby also would have stood as an obstacle to the gradual passive restraint phase-in that the federal regulation deliberately imposed. In addition, it could have made less likely the adoption of a state mandatory buckle-up law. Because the rule of law for which petitioners contend would have stood "as an obstacle to the accomplishment and execution of" the important means-related federal objectives that we have just discussed, it is pre-empted.

One final point: We place some weight upon DOT's interpretation of FMVSS 208's objectives and its conclusion, as set forth in the Government's brief, that a tort suit such as this one would "'stan[d] as an obstacle to the accomplishment and execution'" of those objectives. Brief for United States as *Amicus Curiae.* Congress has delegated to DOT authority to implement the statute; the subject matter is technical; and the relevant history and background are complex and extensive. The agency is likely to have a thorough understanding of its own regulation and its objectives and is "uniquely qualified" to comprehend the likely impact of state requirements. And DOT has explained FMVSS 208's objectives, and the interference that "no airbag" suits pose thereto, consistently over time. In these circumstances, the agency's own views should make a difference.

The judgment of the Court of Appeals is affirmed.

It is so ordered.

JUSTICE STEVENS, with whom JUSTICE SOUTER, JUSTICE THOMAS, and JUSTICE GINSBURG join, dissenting.

Airbag technology has been available to automobile manufacturers for over 30 years. There is now general agreement on the proposition "that, to be safe, a car must have an airbag." Indeed, current federal law imposes that requirement on all automobile manufacturers. The question raised by petitioners' common-law tort action is whether that proposition was sufficiently obvious when Honda's 1987 Accord was manufactured to make the failure to install such a safety feature actionable under theories of negligence or defective design.

"This is a case about federalism," *Coleman v. Thompson*, 501 U.S. 722, 726 (1991), that is, about respect for "the constitutional role of the States as sovereign entities." *Alden v. Maine*, 527 U.S. 706, 713 (1999). It raises important questions concerning the way in which the Federal Government may exercise its undoubted power to oust state courts of their traditional jurisdiction over common-law tort actions. The rule the Court enforces today was not enacted by Congress and is not to be found in the text of any Executive Order or regulation. It has a unique origin: It is the product of the Court's interpretation of the final commentary accompanying an interim administrative regulation and the history of airbag regulation generally. Like many other judge-made rules, its contours are not precisely defined.

Perhaps such a rule would be a wise component of a legislative reform of our tort system. I express no opinion about that possibility. It is, however, quite clear to me that Congress neither enacted any such rule itself nor authorized the Secretary of Transportation to do so. It is equally clear to me that the objectives that the Secretary intended to achieve through the adoption of Federal Motor Vehicle Safety Standard 208 would not be frustrated one whit by allowing state courts to determine whether in 1987 the lifesaving advantages of airbags had become sufficiently obvious that their omission might constitute a design defect in some new cars. Finally, I submit that the Court is quite wrong to characterize its rejection of the presumption against pre-emption, and its reliance on history and regulatory commentary rather than either statutory or regulatory text, as "ordinary experience-proved principles of conflict pre-emption."

I

The question presented is whether either the National Traffic and Motor Vehicle Safety Act of 1966 (Safety Act or Act), or the version of Standard 208 promulgated by the Secretary of Transportation in 1984, pre-empts common-law tort claims that an automobile manufactured in 1987 was negligently and defectively designed because it lacked "an effective and safe passive restraint system, including, but not limited to, airbags."

The 1984 [version of Standard 208] provided for a phase-in of passive restraint requirements beginning with the 1987 model year. Although the standard did not require airbags in all cars, it is clear that the Secretary did intend to encourage wider use of airbags. The Secretary therefore included a phase-in period in order to encourage manufacturers to comply with the standard by installing airbags and other (perhaps more effective) nonbelt technologies that they might develop, rather than by installing less expensive automatic seatbelts. [T]here is no mention, either in the text of the final standard or in the accompanying comments, of the possibility that the risk of potential tort liability would provide an incentive for manufacturers to install airbags. Nor is there any other specific evidence of an intent to preclude common-law tort actions.

III

When a state statute, administrative rule, or common-law cause of action conflicts with a federal statute, it is axiomatic that the state law is without effect. U.S.

Const., Art. VI, cl. 2. On the other hand, it is equally clear that the Supremacy Clause does not give unelected federal judges *carte blanche* to use federal law as a means of imposing their own ideas of tort reform on the States. Because of the role of States as separate sovereigns in our federal system, we have long presumed that state laws— particularly those, such as the provision of tort remedies to compensate for personal injuries, that are within the scope of the States' historic police powers—are not to be pre-empted by a federal statute unless it is the clear and manifest purpose of Congress to do so.

When a federal statute contains an express pre-emption provision, "the task of statutory construction must in the first instance focus on the plain wording of [that provision], which necessarily contains the best evidence of Congress' pre-emptive intent." The Safety Act contains both an express pre-emption provision, and a saving clause that expressly preserves common-law claims.

Relying on § 1392(d) and legislative history discussing Congress' desire for uniform national safety standards, Honda argues that petitioners' common-law no-airbag claims are expressly pre-empted because success on those claims would necessarily establish a state "safety standard" not identical to Standard 208. It is perfectly clear, however, that the term "safety standard" as used in these two sections refers to an objective rule prescribed by a legislature or an administrative agency and does not encompass case-specific decisions by judges and juries that resolve common-law claims. In addition, when the two sections are read together, they provide compelling evidence of an intent to distinguish between legislative and administrative rulemaking, on the one hand, and common-law liability, on the other. This distinction was certainly a rational one for Congress to draw in the Safety Act given that common-law liability—unlike most legislative or administrative rulemaking— necessarily performs an important remedial role in compensating accident victims.

The saving clause in the Safety Act unambiguously expresses a decision by Congress that compliance with a federal safety standard does not exempt a manufacturer from *any* common-law liability. In light of this reference to common-law liability in the saving clause, Congress surely would have included a similar reference in § 1392(d) if it had intended to pre-empt such liability.

The Court does not disagree with this interpretation of the term "safety standard." Because the meaning of that term as used by Congress in this statute is clear, the text of § 1392(d) is itself sufficient to establish that the Safety Act does not expressly pre-empt common-law claims. In order to avoid the conclusion that the saving clause is superfluous, therefore, it must follow that it has a different purpose: to limit, or possibly to foreclose entirely, the possible pre-emptive effect of safety standards promulgated by the Secretary. The Court's approach to the case has the practical effect of reading the saving clause out of the statute altogether.

Given the cumulative force of the fact that § 1392(d) does not expressly pre-empt common-law claims and the fact that § 1397(k) was obviously intended to limit the pre-emptive effect of the Secretary's safety standards, it is quite wrong for the Court to assume that a possible implicit conflict with the purposes to be achieved by such a standard should have the same pre-emptive effect "'as an obstacle to the accomplishment and execution of the full purposes and objectives of Congress.'" Properly construed, the Safety Act imposes a special burden on a party relying on an arguable, implicit conflict with a temporary regulatory policy—rather than a conflict with congressional policy or with the text of any regulation—to demonstrate that a common-law claim has been pre-empted.

IV

Even though the Safety Act does not expressly pre-empt common-law claims, Honda contends that Standard 208—of its own force—implicitly pre-empts the claims in this case. Both the text of the statute and the text of the standard provide persuasive reasons for rejecting this argument. The saving clause of the Safety Act arguably denies the Secretary the authority to promulgate standards that would pre-empt common-law remedies.[16] Moreover, the text of Standard 208 says nothing about pre-emption, and I am not persuaded that Honda has overcome our traditional presumption that it lacks any implicit pre-emptive effect.

Honda argues, and the Court now agrees, that the risk of liability presented by common-law claims that vehicles without airbags are negligently and defectively designed would frustrate the policy decision that the Secretary made in promulgating Standard 208. There are at least three flaws in this argument that provide sufficient grounds for rejecting it. First, the entire argument is based on an unrealistic factual predicate. Whatever the risk of liability on a no-airbag claim may have been prior to the promulgation of the 1984 version of Standard 208, that risk did not lead any manufacturer to install airbags in even a substantial portion of its cars. If there had been a realistic likelihood that the risk of tort liability would have that consequence, there would have been no need for Standard 208. The promulgation of that standard certainly did not *increase* the pre-existing risk of liability. Even if the standard did not create a previously unavailable pre-emption defense, it likely *reduced* the manufacturers' risk of liability by enabling them to point to the regulation and their compliance therewith as evidence tending to negate charges of negligent and defective design.

---

16. The Court contends, in essence, that a saving clause cannot foreclose *implied* conflict pre-emption. The cases it cites to support that point, however, merely interpreted the language of the particular saving clauses at issue and concluded that those clauses did not foreclose implied pre-emption; they do not establish that a saving clause in a given statute cannot foreclose implied pre-emption based on frustration of that statute's purposes, or even (more importantly for our present purposes) that a saving clause in a given statute cannot deprive a *regulation* issued pursuant to that statute of any implicit pre-emptive effect.

As stated in the text, I believe the language of this particular saving clause unquestionably limits, and possibly forecloses entirely, the pre-emptive effect that safety standards promulgated by the Secretary have on common-law remedies. Under that interpretation, there is by definition no frustration of federal purposes—that is, no "tolerat[ion of] actual conflict"—when tort suits are allowed to go forward.

Second, even if the manufacturers' assessment of their risk of liability ultimately proved to be wrong, the purposes of Standard 208 would not be frustrated. In light of the inevitable time interval between the eventual filing of a tort action alleging that the failure to install an airbag is a design defect and the possible resolution of such a claim against a manufacturer, as well as the additional interval between such a resolution (if any) and manufacturers' "compliance with the state-law duty in question," by modifying their designs to avoid such liability in the future, it is obvious that the phase-in period would have ended long before its purposes could have been frustrated by the specter of tort liability. Thus, even without pre-emption, the public would have been given the time that the Secretary deemed necessary to gradually adjust to the increasing use of airbag technology and allay their unfounded concerns about it.

Third, despite its acknowledgment that the saving clause "preserves those actions that seek to establish greater safety than the minimum safety achieved by a federal regulation intended to provide a floor," the Court completely ignores the important fact that by definition all of the standards established under the Safety Act impose minimum, rather than fixed or maximum, requirements. The possibility that exposure to potential tort liability might accelerate the rate of increase would actually further the only goal explicitly mentioned in the standard itself: reducing the number of deaths and severity of injuries of vehicle occupants. Had gradualism been independently important as a method of achieving the Secretary's safety goals, presumably the Secretary would have put a ceiling as well as a floor on each annual increase in the required percentage of new passive restraint installations.

V

Our presumption against pre-emption is rooted in the concept of federalism. The signal virtues of this presumption are its placement of the power of pre-emption squarely in the hands of Congress, which is far more suited than the Judiciary to strike the appropriate state/federal balance (particularly in areas of traditional state regulation), and its requirement that Congress speak clearly when exercising that power. In this way, the structural safeguards inherent in the normal operation of the legislative process operate to defend state interests from undue infringement. In addition, the presumption serves as a limiting principle that prevents federal judges from running amok with our potentially boundless (and perhaps inadequately considered) doctrine of implied conflict pre-emption based on frustration of purposes

While the presumption is important in assessing the pre-emptive reach of federal statutes, it becomes crucial when the pre-emptive effect of an administrative regulation is at issue. Unlike Congress, administrative agencies are clearly not designed to represent the interests of States, yet with relative ease they can promulgate comprehensive and detailed regulations that have broad pre-emption ramifications for state law. We have addressed the heightened federalism and nondelegation concerns that agency pre-emption raises by using the presumption to build a procedural bridge across the political accountability gap between States and administrative agencies. Thus, even in cases where implied regulatory pre-emption is at issue, we generally "expect an administrative regulation to declare any intention to pre-empt state law with some specificity." This expectation, which is shared by the Executive Branch,[24] serves to ensure that States will be able to have a dialog with agencies regarding pre-emption decisions *ex ante* through the normal notice-and-comment procedures of the Administrative Procedure Act (APA).

When the presumption and its underpinnings are properly understood, it is plain that Honda has not overcome the presumption in this case. Neither Standard 208 nor its accompanying commentary includes the slightest specific indication of an intent to pre-empt common-law no-airbag suits.

Given the Secretary's contention that he has the authority to promulgate safety standards that pre-empt state law and the fact that he could promulgate a standard with relative ease, we should be quite reluctant to find pre-emption based only on the Secretary's informal effort to recast the 1984 version of Standard 208 into a pre-emptive mold. Requiring the Secretary to put his pre-emptive position through formal notice-and-comment rulemaking — whether contemporaneously with the promulgation of the allegedly pre-emptive regulation or at any later time that the need for pre-emption becomes apparent — respects both the federalism and nondelegation principles that underlie the presumption against pre-emption in the regulatory context and the APA's requirement of new rulemaking when an agency substantially modifies its interpretation of a regulation.

Because neither the text of the statute nor the text of the regulation contains any indication of an intent to pre-empt petitioners' cause of action, and because I cannot agree with the Court's unprecedented use of inferences from regulatory history and commentary as a basis for implied pre-emption, I am convinced that Honda has not overcome the presumption against pre-emption in this case. I therefore respectfully dissent.

EXERCISE 3:

1. What difference is there between express and implied preemption? Is it a difference in kind or of degree?

2. What is the basis for the Supreme Court's conclusion that implied preemption principles may apply even though an express preemption provision did not preempt the relevant state law? Is that a sufficient argument?

3. What is the basis for the Supreme Court's conclusion that implied preemption principles may apply despite the existence of a savings clause? Is that a sufficient argument?

4. When does a state law impede federal objectives?

---

24. *See* Exec. Order No. 12612, §4(e), 3 C.F.R. §252, 255 (1988) ("When an Executive department or agency proposes to act through adjudication or rule-making to preempt State law, the department or agency shall provide all affected States notice and an opportunity for appropriate participation in the proceedings"); Exec. Order No. 13132, §4(e), 64 Fed.Reg. 43255, 43257 (1999) (same).

5. What interpretive tools did the Supreme Court use to ascertain FMV 208's objectives?

6. Do you agree that FMV 208's objectives would have been thwarted by permitting tort claims like the plaintiff's to go forward? Why or why not?

7. Did a presumption play a role in the majority's opinion? In Justice Stevens' opinion, what principles underlay the presumption?

8. What form of implied preemption did the Court apply in this case?

9. How is the savings clause in *Geier* different from the savings clause in *Wolens*?

10. Is it legitimate to "impliedly" apply the Supremacy Clause via implied preemption?

11. In some ways, implied preemption is akin to the dormant Commerce Clause, and in some ways it is different. Describe the similarities and differences.

12. Should the reasoning underlying implied preemption apply to federal regulations promulgated by administrative agencies? What answer does the Court give? Should the Court require an agency to engage in express preemption using notice and comment rulemaking, as Justice Stevens suggests?

13. This case offers a good example of the detailed statutory and regulatory analysis the Supreme Court goes through in preemption cases. The goal of this analysis is to best effectuate Congress' intent. In *Geier*, did the majority or the dissent do the better job determining congressional intent? Why?

D. FIELD PREEMPTION AND CONFLICT PREEMPTION

In the Section above, we reviewed the distinction between express and implied preemption. This Section reviews the distinction between field and conflict preemption.

Field preemption occurs when Congress precludes state regulation of an entire "area" or "field" of law.[14] There are two analytically distinct questions that determine whether Congress has preempted a field: (1) is there express or implied preemption? and (2) does that preemption cover an entire field?

Perhaps the most prominent example of express field preemption is found in the Employee Retirement Income Security Act of 1974. 29 U.S.C. § 1001 *et seq.* ERISA, as the Act is popularly known, "supersede[s] any and all state laws insofar as they may now or hereafter relate to any employee benefit plan." *Id.* § 1144(a). The Supreme Court has held that ERISA "occupied the field" of employee retirement plans.

---

14. It is possible to think of field preemption as a subset of conflict preemption. The relevant conflict is between a broadly worded express statutory statement and state law, or between a pervasive regulatory scheme and state law. *See English v. Generl Elec. Co.*, 496 U.S. 72, 79–80 n.5 (1990) (identifying this possibility).

As you may have already surmised, defining the pertinent "field" is not, in many situations, an easy task. Even with express preemption, like ERISA, the extent of preemption is heavily litigated. *See* ERWIN CHEMERINSKY, CONSTITUTIONAL LAW: PRINCIPLES AND POLICIES 421–22 (5th ed. 2015) (noting that the Supreme Court has issued dozens of opinions and that there are thousands of lower court opinions on the scope of ERISA preemption).

Conflict preemption, on the other hand, occurs when Congress precludes state regulation that "conflicts" with Congress' regulation of the same subject(s). As noted above in the discussion of implied preemption, the Supreme Court has articulated two forms of conflict preemption: (1) state regulation makes it impossible to comply with federal law; and (2) state law impedes attainment of the federal law's objective.

Field preemption can be either express or implied, while conflict preemption is usually understood as occurring in the form of implied preemption.[15] *Freightliner Corp. v. Myrick*, 514 U.S. 280, 287 (1995). Below are two cases. The first is a modern case applying the Court's field preemption analysis, and the second is a recent example of conflict preemption.

In *Rice v. Santa Fe Elevator Corp.*, 331 U.S. 218 (1947), a classic case examining field preemption, the Supreme Court articulated the general contours of field preemption:

> The question in each case is what the purpose of Congress was. Congress legislated here in a field[, grain warehouse operation and storage,] which the States have traditionally occupied. So we start with the assumption that the historic police powers of the States were not to be superseded by the Federal [United States Warehouse] Act unless that was the clear and manifest purpose of Congress. Such a purpose may be evidenced in several ways. The scheme of federal regulation may be so pervasive as to make reasonable the inference that Congress left no room for the States to supplement it. Or the Act of Congress may touch a field in which the federal interest is so dominant that the federal system will be assumed to preclude enforcement of state laws on the same subject. Or the state policy may produce a result inconsistent with the objective of the federal statute.

Id. at 230. The majority noted, however, that "[i]t is often a perplexing question whether Congress has precluded state action or by the choice of selective regulatory measures has left the police power of the States undisturbed except as the state and federal regulation collide." *Id.* at 230–31.

Although the *Rice* majority noted that a "forceful argument" was made that the state statute merely supplemented the United States Warehouse Act, the Court ultimately concluded that through the 1931 amendments to the Act, which stated that "the power, jurisdiction, and authority conferred upon the Secretary of Agriculture

---

15. There is no reason, however, why Congress could not expressly state that a given federal law preempts only state law that actually conflicts with the federal law.

under this act shall be exclusive with respect to all persons securing a license here-under," Congress "act[ed] so unequivocally as to make clear that it intend[ed] no regu-lation except its own." *Id.* at 236. As you read the following case, consider whether the federal statute demonstrated Congress' "clear and manifest purpose" to preempt one or both of the plaintiffs' claims.

KURNS v. RAILROAD FRICTION PRODUCTS CORPORATION
565 U.S. 625 (2012)

Justice Thomas delivered the opinion of the Court.

This case requires us to determine whether petitioners' state-law tort claims for defective design and failure to warn are pre-empted by the Locomotive Inspection Act (LIA), 49 U.S.C. § 20701 *et seq.* The United States Court of Appeals for the Third Circuit determined that petitioners' claims fall within the field pre-empted by that Act, as that field was defined by this Court's decision in *Napier v. Atlantic Coast Line R. Co.,* 272 U.S. 605 (1926). We agree.

I

George Corson was employed as a welder and machinist by the Chicago, Milwau-kee, St. Paul & Pacific Railroad from 1947 until 1974. Corson worked in locomotive repair and maintenance facilities, where his duties included installing brakeshoes on locomotives and stripping insulation from locomotive boilers. In 2005, Corson was diagnosed with malignant mesothelioma.

In 2007, Corson and his wife filed suit in Pennsylvania state court against 59 defendants, including respondents Railroad Friction Products Corporation (RFPC) and Viad Corp (Viad). According to the complaint, RFPC distributed locomotive brakeshoes containing asbestos, and Viad was the successor-in-interest to a company that manufactured and sold locomotives and locomotive engine valves containing asbestos. Corson alleged that he handled this equipment and that he was injured by exposure to asbestos. The complaint asserted state-law claims that the equipment was defectively designed because it contained asbestos, and that respondents failed to warn of the dangers of asbestos or to provide instructions regarding its safe use. After the complaint was filed, Corson passed away, and the executrix of his estate, Gloria Kurns, was substituted as a party. Corson's widow and the executrix are petitioners here.

II

Congress enacted the predecessor to the LIA, the Boiler Inspection Act (BIA), in 1911. The BIA made it unlawful to use a steam locomotive "unless the boiler of said locomotive and appurtenances thereof are in proper condition and safe to operate . . . without unnecessary peril to life or limb." In 1915, Congress amended the BIA to apply to "the entire locomotive and tender and all parts and appurtenances thereof." The BIA as amended became commonly known as the Locomotive Inspection Act. As relevant here, the LIA provides:

"A railroad carrier may use or allow to be used a locomotive or tender on its railroad line only when the locomotive or tender and its parts and appurtenances —

"(1) are in proper condition and safe to operate without unnecessary danger of personal injury;

"(2) have been inspected as required under this chapter and regulations prescribed by the Secretary of Transportation under this chapter; and

"(3) can withstand every test prescribed by the Secretary under this chapter." 49 U.S.C. § 20701.

The issue presented in this case is whether the LIA pre-empts petitioners' state-law claims that respondents defectively designed locomotive parts and failed to warn Corson of dangers associated with those parts. In light of this Court's prior decision in *Napier, supra,* we conclude that petitioners' claims are pre-empted

III

A

The Supremacy Clause provides that federal law "shall be the supreme Law of the Land . . . any Thing in the Constitution or Laws of any State to the Contrary not-withstanding." U.S. Const., Art. VI, cl. 2. Pre-emption of state law thus occurs through the "direct operation of the Supremacy Clause." Congress may, of course, expressly pre-empt state law, but "[e]ven without an express provision for preemption, we have found that state law must yield to a congressional Act in at least two circumstances." *Crosby v. National Foreign Trade Council,* 530 U.S. 363, 372 (2000). First, "state law is naturally preempted to the extent of any conflict with a federal statute." *Ibid.* Second, we have deemed state law pre-empted "when the scope of a [federal] statute indicates that Congress intended federal law to occupy a field exclusively." *Freightliner Corp. v. Myrick,* 514 U.S. 280, 287 (1995). We deal here only with the latter, so-called field pre-emption.

B

We do not, however, address the LIA's pre-emptive effect on a clean slate, because this Court addressed that issue 85 years ago in *Napier.* In that case, railroads challenged two state laws that "prohibit[ed] use within the State of locomotives not equipped with" certain prescribed devices, on the ground that the Interstate Commerce Commission (ICC), the agency then vested with the authority to carry out the LIA's requirements, had not required the devices in question. 272 U.S., at 607, 609. In response, the States argued that their requirements were not pre-empted because they were directed at a different objective than the LIA. According to the States, their regulations were intended to protect railroad workers from sickness and disease, whereas "the federal regulation endeavors solely to prevent accidental injury in the operation of trains."

To determine whether the state requirements were pre-empted, this Court asked whether the LIA "manifest[s] the intention to occupy the entire field of regulating locomotive equipment[.]" *Id.*, at 611. The Court answered that question in the affirmative, stating that "[t]he broad scope of the authority conferred upon the [ICC]" by Congress in the LIA led to that conclusion. The power delegated to the ICC, the Court explained, was a "general one" that "extends to the design, the construction and the material of every part of the locomotive and tender and of all appurtenances."

The Court rejected the States' contention that the scope of the pre-empted field was to "be determined by the object sought through the legislation, rather than the physical elements affected by it." *Id.*, at 612. The Court found it dispositive that "[t]he federal and the state statutes are directed to the same subject—the equipment of locomotives." Because the States' requirements operated upon the same physical elements as the LIA, the Court held that the state laws, "however commendable or however different their purpose," fell within the LIA's pre-empted field.

IV

Against the backdrop of *Napier*, petitioners advance two arguments in support of their position that their state-law claims related to the use of asbestos in locomotive equipment do not fall within the LIA's pre-empted field. Petitioners first contend that *Napier* no longer defines the scope of the LIA's pre-empted field because that field has been narrowed by a subsequently enacted federal statute. Alternatively, petitioners argue that their claims do not fall within the LIA's pre-empted field, even as that field was defined by *Napier*. We address each of petitioners' arguments in turn.

A

First, petitioners suggest that the Federal Railroad Safety Act of 1970 (FRSA), 84 Stat. 971 (codified at 49 U.S.C. §20102 *et seq.*), altered the LIA's pre-emptive scope. The FRSA grants the Secretary of Transportation broad regulatory authority over railroad safety. Petitioners point to the FRSA's pre-emption provision, which provides in part that "[a] State may adopt or continue in force a law, regulation, or order related to railroad safety... until the Secretary of Transportation... prescribes a regulation or issues an order covering the subject matter of the State requirement." §20106(a)(2) (2006 ed., Supp. III). According to petitioners, the FRSA's pre-emption provision supplanted the LIA's pre-emption of the field, with the result that petitioners' claims are not pre-empted because the Secretary has not issued a regulation or order addressing the use of asbestos in locomotives or locomotive parts.

Petitioners' reliance on the FRSA is misplaced. The FRSA instructs that "[t]he Secretary of Transportation, as necessary, shall prescribe regulations and issue orders for every area of railroad safety *supplementing laws and regulations in effect on October 16, 1970.*" §20103(a) (2006 ed.) (emphasis added). By its terms, the FRSA does not alter pre-existing federal statutes on railroad safety. "Rather, it leaves existing statutes intact,... and authorizes the Secretary to fill interstitial areas of railroad safety with supplemental regulation." *Marshall v. Burlington Northern, Inc.*, 720 F.2d 1149, 1152–1153 (9th Cir. 1983) (Kennedy, J.). Because the LIA was already in effect when the FRSA was enacted, we conclude that the FRSA left the LIA, and its pre-emptive scope as defined by *Napier*, intact.

B

Since the LIA's pre-emptive scope remains unaltered, petitioners must contend with *Napier*. Petitioners do not ask us to overrule *Napier* and thus do not seek to overcome the presumption of *stare decisis* that attaches to this 85–year–old precedent. See *Global–Tech Appliances, Inc. v. SEB S.A.*, 131 S.Ct. 2060, 2068 (2011) (noting the "special force of the doctrine of *stare decisis* with regard to questions of statutory interpretation" (internal quotation marks omitted)). Instead, petitioners advance several arguments aimed at demonstrating that their claims fall outside of the field pre-empted by the LIA, as it was defined in *Napier*. Each is unpersuasive.

1

Petitioners, along with the Solicitor General as *amicus curiae*, first argue that petitioners' claims do not fall within the LIA's pre-empted field because the claims arise out of the repair and maintenance of locomotives, rather than the use of locomotives on a railroad line. Specifically, they contend that the scope of the field pre-empted by the LIA is coextensive with the scope of the Federal Government's regulatory authority under the LIA, which, they argue, does not extend to the regulation of hazards arising from the repair or maintenance of locomotives. Therefore, the argument goes, state-law claims arising from repair or maintenance—as opposed to claims arising from use on the line—do not fall within the pre-empted field.

We reject this attempt to redefine the pre-empted field. In *Napier*, the Court held that Congress, in enacting the LIA, "manifest[ed] the intention to occupy the entire field of regulating locomotive equipment," and the Court did not distinguish between hazards arising from repair and maintenance as opposed to those arising from use on the line. 272 U.S., at 611. The pre-empted field as defined by *Napier* plainly encompasses the claims at issue here. Petitioners' common-law claims for defective design and failure to warn are aimed at the equipment of locomotives. Because those claims "are directed to the same subject" as the LIA, *Napier* dictates that they fall within the pre-empted field. *Id.*, at 612.

2

Petitioners further argue that, even if their design-defect claims are pre-empted, their failure-to-warn claims do not suffer the same fate. According to petitioners, these claims do not fall within the LIA's pre-empted field because "[t]he basis of liability for failure to warn . . . is not the 'design' or 'manufacture' of a product," but is instead "the failure to provide adequate warnings regarding the product's risks."

We disagree. A failure-to-warn claim alleges that the product itself is unlawfully dangerous unless accompanied by sufficient warnings or instructions. Restatement (Third) of Torts: Products Liability § 2(c) (1997) (A failure-to-warn claim alleges that a product is defective "when the foreseeable risks of harm posed by the product could have been reduced or avoided by the provision of reasonable instructions or warnings by the seller or other distributor, . . . and the omission of the instructions or warnings renders the product not reasonably safe"). Thus, the "gravamen" of petitioners' failure-to-warn claims "is still that [Corson] suffered harmful consequences as a result of his exposure to asbestos contained in locomotive parts and appurtenances." 620 F.3d, at 398, n. 8. Because petitioners' failure-to-warn claims are therefore directed at the equipment of locomotives, they fall within the pre-empted field defined by *Napier*, 272 U.S., at 612.[4]

3

Petitioners also contend that their state-law claims against manufacturers of locomotives and locomotive parts fall outside of the LIA's pre-empted field because manufacturers were not regulated under the LIA at the time that Corson was allegedly exposed to asbestos. Petitioners point out that the LIA, as originally enacted in the BIA, subjected only common carriers to civil penalties. Act of Feb. 17, 1911, § 9, 36 Stat. 916. It was not until 1988, well after the events of this case, that the LIA's penalty provision was revised to apply to "[a]ny person" violating the LIA. Rail Safety Improvement Act of 1988, § 14(7)(A), 102 Stat. 633.

This argument fails for the same reason as the two preceding arguments: It is inconsistent with *Napier. Napier* defined the field pre-empted by the LIA on the basis of the physical elements regulated—"the equipment of locomotives"—not on the basis of the entity directly subject to regulation. 272 U.S., at 612. Because petitioners' claims are directed at the equipment of locomotives, they fall within the pre-empted field.

4

Finally, petitioners contend that the LIA's pre-emptive scope does not extend to state common-law claims, as opposed to state legislation or regulation. Petitioners note that "a preempted field does not necessarily include state common law." *Napier,* however, held that the LIA "occup[ied] the entire field of regulating locomotive equipment" to the exclusion of state regulation. That categorical conclusion admits of no exception for state common-law duties and standards of care. As we have recognized, state "regulation can be . . . effectively exerted through an award of damages," and "[t]he obligation to pay compensation can be, indeed is designed to be, a potent method of governing conduct and controlling policy." *San Diego Building Trades Council v. Garmon*, 359 U.S. 236, 247 (1959). We therefore conclude that state common-law duties and standards of care directed to the subject of locomotive equipment are pre-empted by the LIA.

* * *

---

4. JUSTICE SOTOMAYOR apparently agrees that petitioners' failure-to-warn claims are directed at the equipment of locomotives. Yet, she argues, those claims affect locomotive equipment only "'tangentially.'" Not so. A failure-to-warn claim imposes liability on a particular design of locomotive equipment unless warnings deemed sufficient under state law are given. This duty to warn and the accompanying threat of liability will inevitably influence a manufacturer's choice whether to use that particular design. By influencing design decisions in that manner, failure-to-warn liability has a "'direct and substantial effect'" on the "physical elements" of a locomotive.

For the foregoing reasons, we hold that petitioners' state-law design-defect and failure-to-warn claims fall within the field of locomotive equipment regulation preempted by the LIA, as that field was defined in *Napier*. Accordingly, the judgment of the Court of Appeals is affirmed.

It is so ordered.

Justice Kagan, concurring.

Like Justice Sotomoayor, I doubt this Court would decide *Napier v. Atlantic Coast Line R. Co.*, 272 U.S. 605 (1926), in the same way today. The *Napier* Court concluded that Congress had "manifest[ed] the intention to occupy the entire field of regulating locomotive equipment," based on nothing more than a statute granting regulatory authority over that subject matter to a federal agency. *Id.*, at 611. Under our more recent cases, Congress must do much more to oust all of state law from a field. Viewed through the lens of modern preemption law, *Napier* is an anachronism.

But *Napier* governs so long as Congress lets it—and that decision provides a straightforward way to determine whether state laws relating to locomotive equipment are preempted. According to *Napier*, the scope of the agency's power under the Locomotive Inspection Act (LIA) determines the boundaries of the preempted field. And under that test, none of the state-law claims at issue here can survive.

All of us agree that the petitioners' defective-design claims are preempted. *Napier* recognized the federal agency's delegated authority over "the design, the construction and the material of every part of the locomotive." 272 U.S., at 611. In doing so, *Napier* did not distinguish between "hazards arising from repair and maintenance" of the parts and hazards stemming from their "use on the line." The agency thus has authority to regulate the design of locomotive equipment—like the asbestos-containing brakeshoes here—to prevent either danger. And that fact resolves the preemption question. Because the agency could have banned use of the brakeshoes as designed, the petitioners' defective-design claims—which would effectively accomplish the identical result—fall within the preempted field.

So too the petitioners' failure-to-warn claims, and for the same reason. *Napier* did not specifically address warnings, because the case in no way involved them. But if an agency has the power to prohibit the use of locomotive equipment, it also has the power to condition the use of that equipment on proper warnings. And because the agency could have required warnings about the equipment's use, the petitioners' failure-to-warn claims, no less than their defective-design claims, are preempted under *Napier*.

I understand these views to comport with the Court's opinion in this case, and I accordingly join it in full.

Justice Sotomayor, with whom Justice Ginsburg and Justice Breyer join, concurring in part and dissenting in part.

I concur in the Court's holding that the Locomotive Inspection Act (LIA), 49 U.S.C. §20701 *et seq.*, pre-empts petitioners' tort claims for defective design, but I respectfully dissent from the Court's holding that the same is true of petitioners' claims for failure to warn. In my view, the latter escape pre-emption because they impose no state-law requirements in the field reserved for federal regulation: "the equipment of locomotives." *Napier v. Atlantic Coast Line R. Co.,* 272 U.S. 605, 612 (1926).

I

Statutory *stare decisis* compels me to agree that the LIA occupies "the field of regulating locomotive equipment used on a highway of interstate commerce." *Id.,* at 607. Perhaps this Court might decide *Napier* differently today. The LIA lacks an express pre-emption clause, and "our recent cases have frequently rejected field pre-emption in the absence of statutory language expressly requiring it." *Camps Newfound/Owatonna, Inc. v. Town of Harrison,* 520 U.S. 564, 617 (1997) (THOMAS, J., dissenting). The LIA contains no substantive regulations, let alone a "scheme of federal regulation . . . so pervasive as to make reasonable the inference that Congress left no room for the States to supplement it." *Rice v. Santa Fe Elevator Corp.,* 331 U.S. 218, 230 (1947). Nonetheless, *Napier*'s construction of the LIA has been settled law for 85 years, and " '[c]onsiderations of *stare decisis* have special force in the area of statutory interpretation.' " *Hilton v. South Carolina Public Railways Comm'n,* 502 U.S. 197, 202 (1991).

Consistent with the values served by statutory *stare decisis,* however, it is important to be precise about what *Napier* held: *Napier* defined the pre-empted field as the physical composition of locomotive equipment. Petitioners' defective-design claims fall within the pre-empted field because they would impose state-law requirements on a locomotive's physical makeup.

II

Petitioners' failure-to-warn claims, by contrast, proceed on a fundamentally different theory of tort liability that does not implicate a product's physical composition at all. A failure-to-warn claim asks nothing of a product's design, but requires instead that a manufacturer caution of nonobvious dangers and provide instructions for safe use. Indeed, a product may be flawlessly designed and still subject its manufacturer or seller to liability for lack of adequate instructions or warnings.

In the jurisdictions relevant to this suit, failure to warn is "a distinct cause of action under the theory of strict products liability." Thus, " 'a failure to warn of an injury[-]causing risk associated with the use of a technically pure and fit product can render such product unreasonably dangerous.' " Similarly, this Court has explained that a failure-to-warn claim is "narrower" than a claim that alleges a defect in the underlying product. *Wyeth v. Levine,* 555 U.S. 555, 565 (2009).

The majority treats defective-design and failure-to-warn claims as congruent, reasoning that each asserts a product defect. That may be true at a high level of generality, but "[d]esign and failure-to-warn claims . . . rest on different factual allegations and distinct legal concepts." Restatement § 2, at 35, Comment *n.* For example, a manufacturer or seller cannot escape liability for an unreasonably unsafe design merely by issuing a warning. See *id.,* at 33, Comment *l* ("Warnings are not . . . a substitute for the provision of a reasonably safe design"). In a fundamental sense, therefore, a failure-to-warn claim proceeds by taking a product's physical design as a given. A failure-to-warn claim alleges a "defect" by asserting that a product, as designed, is safe for use only when accompanied by a warning—not that a product must be designed differently.

Respondents could have complied with state-law duties to warn by providing instructions for the safe maintenance of asbestos-containing locomotive parts in equipment manuals. Or respondents could have ensured that repair shops posted signs. Neither step would encroach on the pre-empted field of locomotives' "physical elements." *Napier,* 272 U.S., at 612. The majority is therefore wrong to say that "the 'gravamen' of petitioners' failure-to-warn claims 'is still that [Corson] suffered harmful consequences as a result of his exposure to asbestos contained in locomotive parts and appurtenances.'" Rather, the "gravamen" of these claims is that petitioners' decedent George Corson could have avoided the harmful consequences of exposure to asbestos while repairing precisely the same locomotive parts had respondents cautioned him, for example, to wear a mask.

Finally, preserving petitioners' failure-to-warn claims coheres with the LIA's regulatory regime. Neither the Interstate Commerce Commission, to which Congress first delegated authority under the LIA, nor the Federal Railroad Administration (FRA), to whom that authority now belongs, has ever regulated locomotive repair and maintenance. To the contrary, the FRA takes the position that it lacks power under the LIA to regulate within locomotive maintenance and repair facilities. And the FRA has not promulgated regulations that address warnings specific to maintenance and repair. Because the pre-empted field is congruent with the regulated field, the majority's decision sweeps far too broadly.

In short, the majority affords the LIA field-pre-emptive effect well beyond what *Napier* requires, leaving petitioners without a remedy for what they allege was fatal exposure to asbestos in repair facilities. "It is difficult to believe that Congress would, without comment, remove all means of judicial recourse for those injured by illegal conduct." *Silkwood,* 464 U.S., at 251. That is doubly true in light of the LIA's "purpose . . . of facilitating employee recovery, not of restricting such recovery or making it impossible." *Urie v. Thompson,* 337 U.S. 163, 189 (1949).

I therefore concur in part and dissent in part.

EXERCISE 4:

1. What is the governing rule that determines whether and to what extent federal law preempts state law?

2. What is the basis for the presumption that the Court employs in *Rice*? Is that a sufficient justification for the practical result, which is to deny preemption in cases where the Court reasonably thinks Congress intended preemption but did not do so sufficiently clearly?

3. In what ways may Congress overcome the presumption?

4. What is the scope of the "area" or "field" that federal law preempted in *Kurns*? How did the Court arrive at its conclusion?

5. What is the reason to preempt an entire field of state law when, as the majority concedes is the case, much state law in the field could operate consistently with federal law, at least most of the time?

6. The Supreme Court's use of legislative history has ebbed and waned over the years. *Rice* provides an example of the period during which the Court was moving toward greater reliance on legislative history. One of the most interesting impacts of Justice Scalia's and others' advocacy of "textualism" and related theories has been the Court's movement away from resort to legislative history in statutory interpretation cases. Does the majority rely on legislative history in *Kurns*? On what does the *Kurns* majority primarily rely? Should courts ever rely on legislative history when interpreting statutes? If so, when?

7. Justice Frankfurter was a well-known proponent of abstention doctrines, the purpose of which is to allow states to resolve issues before federal courts become involved. In a portion of his *Rice* dissent, Justice Frankfurter again advocated this approach. He argued that the Court should have abstained from ruling until the Illinois Supreme Court had a chance to rule on whether Illinois law actually conflicted with federal law. What are the benefits and detriments of following Justice Frankfurter's prescription? What is the source of federal court authority to abstain from deciding a case until state processes are completed?

8. How does the majority in *Kurns* rely on *stare decisis* to reach its conclusion? Does the majority or the dissent have the better interpretation of *Napier v. Atlantic Coast Line R. Co.*, 272 U.S. 605 (1926)?

9. In *Kurns*, should the majority have concluded that the Locomotive Inspection Act pre-empted the petitioners' failure-to-warn claims? Does Congress's intent to pre-empt claims relating to "the equipment of locomotives" include claims alleging a failure-to-warn?

MARY GADE, DIRECTOR, ILLINOIS ENVIRONMENTAL PROTECTION AGENCY v. NATIONAL SOLID WASTES MANAGEMENT ASSOCIATION

505 U.S. 88 (1992)

JUSTICE O'CONNOR announced the judgment of the Court and delivered the opinion of the Court with respect to Parts I, III, and IV, and an opinion with respect to Part II in which THE CHIEF JUSTICE, JUSTICE WHITE, and JUSTICE SCALIA join.

In 1988, the Illinois General Assembly enacted the Hazardous Waste Crane and Hoisting Equipment Operators Licensing Act, and the Hazardous Waste Laborers Licensing Act (together, licensing acts). The stated purpose of the licensing acts is both "to promote job safety" and "to protect life, limb and property." In this case, we consider whether these "dual impact" statutes, which protect both workers and the general public, are pre-empted by the federal Occupational Safety and Health Act of 1970 (OSH Act), and the standards promulgated thereunder by the Occupational Safety and Health Administration (OSHA).

I

The OSH Act authorizes the Secretary of Labor to promulgate federal occupational safety and health standards. In the Superfund Amendments and Reauthorization Act of 1986 (SARA), Congress directed the Secretary of Labor to "promulgate standards for the health and safety protection of employees engaged in hazardous waste operations" pursuant to her authority under the OSH Act. In relevant part, SARA requires the Secretary to establish standards for the initial and routine training of workers who handle hazardous wastes.

In response to this congressional directive, OSHA, to which the Secretary has delegated certain of her statutory responsibilities, promulgated regulations on "Hazardous Waste Operations and Emergency Response," including detailed regulations on worker training requirements. The OSHA regulations require, among other things, that workers engaged in an activity that may expose them to hazardous wastes receive a minimum of 40 hours of instruction off the site, and a minimum of three days actual field experience under the supervision of a trained supervisor. Workers who are on the site only occasionally or who are working in areas that have been determined to be under the permissible exposure limits must complete at least 24 hours of off-site instruction and one day of actual field experience. On-site managers and supervisors directly responsible for hazardous waste operations must receive the same initial training as general employees, plus at least eight additional hours of specialized training on various health and safety programs. Employees and supervisors are required to receive eight hours of refresher training annually. Those who have satisfied the training and field experience requirement receive a written certification; uncertified workers are prohibited from engaging in hazardous waste operations.

In 1988, while OSHA's interim hazardous waste regulations were in effect, the State of Illinois enacted the licensing acts at issue here. The laws are designated as acts "in relation to environmental protection," and their stated aim is to protect both employees and the general public by licensing hazardous waste equipment operators and laborers working at certain facilities. Both licensing acts require a license applicant to provide a certified record of at least 40 hours of training under an approved program conducted within Illinois, to pass a written examination, and to complete an annual refresher course of at least eight hours of instruction. In addition, applicants for a hazardous waste crane operator's license must submit "a certified record showing operation of equipment used in hazardous waste handling for a minimum of 4,000 hours." Employees who work without the proper license, and employers who knowingly permit an unlicensed employee to work, are subject to escalating fines for each offense.

The respondent in this case, National Solid Wastes Management Association (Association), is a national trade association of businesses that remove, transport, dispose, and handle waste material, including hazardous waste. The Association's members are subject to the OSH Act and OSHA regulations, and are therefore required to train, qualify, and certify their hazardous waste remediation workers. For hazardous waste operations conducted in Illinois, certain of the workers employed by the Association's members are also required to obtain licenses pursuant to the Illinois licensing acts. Thus, for example, some of the Association's members must ensure that their employees receive not only the 3 days of field experience required for certification under the OSHA regulations, but also the 500 days of experience (4,000 hours) required for licensing under the state statutes.

Shortly before the state licensing acts were due to go into effect, the Association brought a declaratory judgment action in United States District Court against the Director of the Illinois Environmental Protection Agency (IEPA). The Association sought to enjoin IEPA from enforcing the Illinois licensing acts, claiming that the acts were pre-empted by the OSH Act and OSHA regulations. [T]he District Court held that the Illinois licensing acts were not pre-empted because each protected public safety in addition to promoting job safety.

On appeal, the United States Court of Appeals for the Seventh Circuit affirmed in part and reversed in part.

We granted certiorari to resolve a conflict between the decision below and decisions in which other Courts of Appeals have found the OSH Act to have a much narrower pre-emptive effect on "dual impact" state regulations.

II

Before addressing the scope of the OSH Act's pre-emption of dual impact state regulations, we consider petitioner's threshold argument, drawn from Judge Easterbrook's separate opinion below, that the Act does not pre-empt nonconflicting state regulations at all. "[T]he question whether a certain state action is pre-empted by federal law is one of congressional intent. '"The purpose of Congress is the ultimate touchstone."'" *Allis-Chalmers Corp. v. Lueck*, 471 U.S. 202, 208 (1985). "To discern Congress' intent we examine the explicit statutory language and the structure and purpose of the statute."

In the OSH Act, Congress endeavored "to assure so far as possible every working man and woman in the Nation safe and healthful working conditions." 29 U.S.C. §651(b). To that end, Congress authorized the Secretary of Labor to set mandatory occupational safety and health standards applicable to all businesses affecting interstate commerce, and thereby brought the Federal Government into a field that traditionally had been occupied by the States. Federal regulation of the workplace was not intended to be all encompassing, however. First, Congress expressly saved two areas from federal pre-emption. Section 4(b)(4) of the OSH Act states that the Act does not "supersede or in any manner affect any workmen's compensation law or . . . enlarge or diminish or affect in any other manner the common law or statutory rights, duties, or liabilities of employers and employees under any law with respect to injuries, diseases, or death of employees arising out of, or in the course of, employment." 29 U.S.C. §653(b)(4). Section 18(a) provides that the Act does not "prevent any State agency or court from asserting jurisdiction under State law over any occupational safety or health issue with respect to which no [federal] standard is in effect." 29 U.S.C. §667(a).

Congress not only reserved certain areas to state regulation, but it also, in §18(b) of the Act, gave the States the option of pre-empting federal regulation entirely. That section provides:

> "Submission of State plan for development and enforcement of State standards to preempt applicable Federal standards.

> "Any State which, at any time, desires to assume responsibility for development and enforcement therein of occupational safety and health standards relating to any occupational safety or health issue with respect to which a Federal standard has been promulgated [by the Secretary under the OSH Act] shall submit a State plan for the development of such standards and their enforcement." 29 U.S.C. §667(b).

About half the States have received the Secretary's approval for their own state plans as described in this provision. Illinois is not among them.

In the decision below, the Court of Appeals held that §18(b) "unquestionably" pre-empts any state law or regulation that establishes an occupational health and safety standard on an issue for which OSHA has already promulgated a standard, unless the State has obtained the Secretary's approval for its own plan. Every other federal and state court confronted with an OSH Act pre-emption challenge has reached the same conclusion, and so do we.

Pre-emption may be either expressed or implied, and "is compelled whether Congress' command is explicitly stated in the statute's language or implicitly contained in its structure and purpose." *Jones v. Rath Packing Co.*, 430 U.S. 519, 525 (1977). Absent explicit pre-emptive language, we have recognized at least two types of implied pre-emption: field pre-emption, where the scheme of federal regulation is "'so pervasive as to make reasonable the inference that Congress left no room for the States to supplement it,'" *id.*, at 98 (quoting *Rice v. Santa Fe Elevator Corp.*, 331 U.S. 218, 230 (1947)), and conflict pre-emption, where "compliance with both federal and state regulations is a physical impossibility," *Florida Lime & Avocado Growers, Inc. v. Paul*, 373 U.S. 132, 142–143 (1963), or where state law "stands as an obstacle to the accomplishment and execution of the full purposes and objectives of Congress," *Hines v. Davidowitz*, 312 U.S. 52, 67 (1941).

Our ultimate task in any pre-emption case is to determine whether state regulation is consistent with the structure and purpose of the statute as a whole. Looking to the provisions of the whole law, and to its object and policy, we hold that non-approved state regulation of occupational safety and health issues for which a federal standard is in effect is impliedly pre-empted as in conflict with the full purposes and objectives of the OSH Act. The design of the statute persuades us that Congress intended to subject employers and employees to only one set of regulations, be it federal or state, and that the only way a State may regulate an OSHA-regulated occupational safety and health issue is pursuant to an approved state plan that displaces the federal standards.

The principal indication that Congress intended to pre-empt state law is § 18(b)'s statement that a State "shall" submit a plan if it wishes to "assume responsibility" for "development and enforcement . . . of occupational safety and health standards relating to any occupational safety or health issue with respect to which a Federal standard has been promulgated." The unavoidable implication of this provision is that a State may not enforce its own occupational safety and health standards without obtaining the Secretary's approval, and petitioner concedes that § 18(b) would require an approved plan if Illinois wanted to "assume responsibility" for the regulation of occupational safety and health within the State. Petitioner contends, however, that an approved plan is necessary only if the State wishes completely to replace the federal regulations, not merely to supplement them. She argues that the correct interpretation of § 18(b) is that posited by Judge Easterbrook below: i.e., a State may either "oust" the federal standard by submitting a state plan to the Secretary for approval or "add to" the federal standard without seeking the Secretary's approval.

Petitioner's interpretation of § 18(b) might be plausible were we to interpret that provision in isolation, but it simply is not tenable in light of the OSH Act's surrounding provisions. The OSH Act as a whole evidences Congress' intent to avoid subjecting workers and employers to duplicative regulation; a State may develop an occupational safety and health program tailored to its own needs, but only if it is willing completely to displace the applicable federal regulations.

Cutting against petitioner's interpretation of § 18(b) is the language of § 18(a), which saves from pre-emption any state law regulating an occupational safety and health issue with respect to which no federal standard is in effect. Although this is a saving clause, not a pre-emption clause, the natural implication of this provision is that state laws regulating the same issue as federal laws are not saved, even if they merely supplement the federal standard. Moreover, if petitioner's reading of § 18(b) were correct, and if a State were free to enact nonconflicting safety and health regulations, then § 18(a) would be superfluous: There is no possibility of conflict where there is no federal regulation. Because "[i]t is our duty 'to give effect, if possible, to every clause and word of a statute,'" we conclude that § 18(a)'s preservation of state authority in the absence of a federal standard presupposes a background pre-emption of all state occupational safety and health standards whenever a federal standard governing the same issue is in effect.

Our understanding of the implications of § 18(b) is likewise bolstered by § 18(c) of the Act, which sets forth the conditions that must be satisfied before the Secretary can approve a plan submitted by a State under subsection (b). State standards that affect interstate commerce will be approved only if they "are required by compelling local conditions" and "do not unduly burden interstate commerce." If a State could supplement federal regulations without undergoing the § 18(b) approval process, then the protections that § 18(c) offers to interstate commerce would easily be undercut. It would make little sense to impose such a condition on state programs intended to supplant federal regulation and not those that merely supplement it: The burden on interstate commerce remains the same.

Section 18(f) also confirms our view that States are not permitted to assume an enforcement role without the Secretary's approval, unless no federal standard is in effect. That provision gives the Secretary the authority to withdraw her approval of a state plan. Once approval is withdrawn, the plan "cease[s] to be in effect" and the State is permitted to assert jurisdiction under its occupational health and safety law only for those cases "commenced before the withdrawal of the plan." Under petitioner's reading of § 18(b), § 18(f) should permit the continued exercise of state jurisdiction over purely "supplemental" and nonconflicting standards. Instead, § 18(f) assumes that the State loses the power to enforce all of its occupational safety and health standards once approval is withdrawn.

Looking at the provisions of § 18 as a whole, we conclude that the OSH Act precludes any state regulation of an occupational safety or health issue with respect to which a federal standard has been established, unless a state plan has been submitted and approved pursuant to § 18(b). Our review of the Act persuades us that Congress sought to promote occupational safety and health while at the same time avoiding duplicative, and possibly counterproductive, regulation. It thus established a system of uniform federal occupational health and safety standards, but gave States the option of pre-empting federal regulations by developing their own occupational safety and health programs. To allow a State selectively to "supplement" certain federal regulations with ostensibly nonconflicting standards would be inconsistent with this federal scheme of establishing uniform federal standards, on the one hand, and encouraging States to assume full responsibility for development and enforcement of their own OSH programs, on the other.[2]

---

2. JUSTICE KENNEDY, while agreeing on the pre-emptive scope of the OSH Act, finds that its pre-emption is express rather than implied. The Court's previous observation that our pre-emption categories are not "rigidly distinct," is proved true by this case. We, too, are persuaded that the text of the Act provides the strongest indication that Congress intended the promulgation of a federal safety and health standard to pre-empt all nonapproved state regulation of the same issue, but we cannot say that it rises to the level of express pre-emption. In the end, even JUSTICE KENNEDY finds express pre-emption by relying on the negative "inference" of § 18(b), which governs when *state* law will pre-empt *federal* law. We cannot agree that the negative implications of the text, although ultimately dispositive to our own analysis, *expressly* address the issue of federal pre-emption of state law. We therefore prefer to place this case in the category of implied pre-emption. Although we have chosen to use the term "conflict" pre-emption, we could as easily have stated that the promulgation of a federal safety and health standard "pre-empts the field" for any nonapproved state law regulating the same safety and health issue. Frequently, the pre-emptive "label" we choose will carry with it substantive implications for the scope of pre-emption. In this case, however, it does not. Our disagreement with JUSTICE KENNEDY as to whether the OSH Act's pre-emptive effect is labeled "express" or "implied" is less important than our agreement that the implications of the text of the statute evince a congressional intent to pre-empt nonapproved state regulations when a federal standard is in effect.

III

Petitioner next argues that, even if Congress intended to pre-empt all nonapproved state occupational safety and health regulations whenever a federal standard is in effect, the OSH Act's pre-emptive effect should not be extended to state laws that address public safety as well as occupational safety concerns. We now consider whether a dual impact law can be an "occupational safety and health standard" subject to pre-emption under the Act.

The OSH Act defines an "occupational safety and health standard" as "a standard which requires conditions, or the adoption or use of one or more practices, means, methods, operations, or processes, reasonably necessary or appropriate to provide safe or healthful employment and places of employment." 29 U.S.C. §652(8). Any state law requirement designed to promote health and safety in the workplace falls neatly within the Act's definition of an "occupational safety and health standard." Clearly, under this definition, a state law that expressly declares a legislative purpose of regulating occupational health and safety would, in the absence of an approved state plan, be pre-empted by an OSHA standard regulating the same subject matter. But petitioner asserts that if the state legislature articulates a purpose other than (or in addition to) workplace health and safety, then the OSH Act loses its pre-emptive force. We disagree.

Although "part of the pre-empted field is defined by reference to the purpose of the state law in question, . . . another part of the field is defined by the state law's actual effect." In assessing the impact of a state law on the federal scheme, we have refused to rely solely on the legislature's professed purpose and have looked as well to the effects of the law.

Our precedents leave no doubt that a dual impact state regulation cannot avoid OSH Act pre-emption simply because the regulation serves several objectives rather than one. Whatever the purpose or purposes of the state law, pre-emption analysis cannot ignore the effect of the challenged state action on the pre-empted field. The key question is thus at what point the state regulation sufficiently interferes with federal regulation that it should be deemed pre-empted under the Act.

In the decision below, the Court of Appeals [held] that, in the absence of the approval of the Secretary, the OSH Act pre-empts all state law that "constitutes, in a direct, clear and substantial way, regulation of worker health and safety." We agree that this is the appropriate standard for determining OSH Act pre-emption. On the other hand, state laws of general applicability (such as laws regarding traffic safety or fire safety) that do not conflict with OSHA standards and that regulate the conduct of workers and nonworkers alike would generally not be pre-empted. Although some laws of general applicability may have a "direct and substantial" effect on worker safety, they cannot fairly be characterized as "occupational" standards, because they regulate workers simply as members of the general public. In this case, we agree with the court below that a law directed at workplace safety is not saved from pre-emption simply because the State can demonstrate some additional effect outside of the workplace.

In sum, a state law requirement that directly, substantially, and specifically regulates occupational safety and health is an occupational safety and health standard within the meaning of the Act. That such a law may also have a nonoccupational impact does not render it any less of an occupational standard for purposes of pre-emption analysis. If the State wishes to enact a dual impact law that regulates an occupational safety or health issue for which a federal standard is in effect, § 18 of the Act requires that the State submit a plan for the approval of the Secretary.

IV

We recognize that "the States have a compelling interest in the practice of professions within their boundaries, and that as part of their power to protect the public health, safety, and other valid interests they have broad power to establish standards for licensing practitioners and regulating the practice of professions." But under the Supremacy Clause, from which our pre-emption doctrine is derived, " 'any state law, however clearly within a State's acknowledged power, which interferes with or is contrary to federal law, must yield.' " We therefore reject petitioner's argument that the State's interest in licensing various occupations can save from OSH Act pre-emption those provisions that directly and substantially affect workplace safety.

The judgment of the Court of Appeals is hereby

Affirmed.

JUSTICE KENNEDY, concurring in part and concurring in the judgment.

Though I concur in the Court's judgment and with the ultimate conclusion that the state law is pre-empted, I would find express pre-emption from the terms of the federal statute. I cannot agree that we should denominate this case as one of implied pre-emption. The contrary view of the plurality is based on an undue expansion of our implied pre-emption jurisprudence which, in my view, is neither wise nor necessary.

As both the majority and dissent acknowledge, we have identified three circumstances in which a federal statute pre-empts state law: First, Congress can adopt express language defining the existence and scope of pre-emption. Second, state law is pre-empted where Congress creates a scheme of federal regulation so pervasive as to leave no room for supplementary state regulation. And third, "state law is pre-empted to the extent that it actually conflicts with federal law." *English v. General Electric Co.*, 496 U.S. 72, 78–79 (1990). This third form of pre-emption, so-called actual conflict pre-emption, occurs either "where it is impossible for a private party to comply with both state and federal requirements . . . or where state law 'stands as an obstacle to the accomplishment and execution of the full purposes and objectives of Congress.' " *English, supra*, at 79. The plurality would hold today that state occupational safety and health standards regulating an issue on which a federal standard exists conflict with Congress' purpose to "subject employers and employees to only one set of regulations."

Our decisions establish that a high threshold must be met if a state law is to be pre-empted for conflicting with the purposes of a federal Act. Any conflict must be "irreconcilable. The existence of a hypothetical or potential conflict is insufficient to warrant the pre-emption of the state statute." *Rice v. Norman Williams Co.*, 458 U.S. 654, 659 (1982). In my view, this type of pre-emption should be limited to state laws which impose prohibitions or obligations which are in direct contradiction to Congress' primary objectives, as conveyed with clarity in the federal legislation.

I do not believe that supplementary state regulation of an occupational safety and health issue can be said to create the sort of actual conflict required by our decisions. The purpose of state supplementary regulation, like the federal standards promulgated by the Occupational Safety and Health Administration (OSHA), is to protect worker safety and health.

The plurality's broad view of actual conflict pre-emption is contrary to two basic principles of our pre-emption jurisprudence. First, we begin "with the assumption that the historic police powers of the States [are] not to be superseded . . . unless that was the clear and manifest purpose of Congress." *Rice v. Santa Fe Elevator Corp.*, 331 U.S. 218, 230 (1947). Second, "'[t]he purpose of Congress is the ultimate touchstone'" in all pre-emption cases. A free wheeling judicial inquiry into whether a state statute is in tension with federal objectives would undercut the principle that it is Congress rather than the courts that pre-empts state law.

Nonetheless, I agree with the Court. I believe, however, that this result is mandated by the express terms of § 18(b) of the OSH Act. It follows from this that the pre-emptive scope of the Act is also limited to the language of the statute. When the existence of pre-emption is evident from the statutory text, our inquiry must begin and end with the statutory framework itself.

Justice Souter, with whom Justice Blackmun, Justice Stevens, and Justice Thomas join, dissenting.

The Court holds today that § 18 of the Occupational Safety and Health Act of 1970 (Act), pre-empts state regulation of any occupational safety or health issue as to which there is a federal standard, whether or not the state regulation conflicts with the federal standard in the sense that enforcement of one would preclude application of the other. With respect, I dissent. In light of our rule that federal pre-emption of state law is only to be found in a clear congressional purpose to supplant exercises of the States' traditional police powers, the text of the Act fails to support the Court's conclusion.

I

Our cases recognize federal pre-emption of state law in three variants: express pre-emption, field pre-emption, and conflict pre-emption. Express pre-emption requires "explicit pre-emptive language." Field pre-emption is wrought by a manifestation of congressional intent to occupy an entire field such that even without a federal rule on some particular matter within the field, state regulation on that matter is pre-empted, leaving it untouched by either state or federal law. Finally, there is conflict pre-emption in either of two senses. The first is found when compliance with both state and federal law is impossible, the second when a state law "stands as an obstacle to the accomplishment and execution of the full purposes and objectives of Congress." *Hines v. Davidowitz*, 312 U.S. 52, 67 (1941).

II

Analysis begins with the presumption that "Congress did not intend to displace state law." Where, as here, the field which Congress is said to have pre-empted has been traditionally occupied by the States, *see, e.g.*, U.S. Const., Art. I, § 10, 'we start with the assumption that the historic police powers of the States were not to be superseded by the Federal Act unless that was the clear and manifest purpose of Congress.' *Rice v. Santa Fe Elevator Corp.*, 331 U.S. 218, 230 (1947). [T]he enquiry into the possibly pre-emptive effect of federal legislation is an exercise of statutory construction. If the statute's terms can be read sensibly not to have a pre-emptive effect, the presumption controls and no pre-emption may be inferred.

III

At first blush, respondent's strongest argument might seem to rest on § 18(a) of the Act, the full text of which is this:

"(a) Assertion of State standards in absence of applicable Federal standards

"Nothing in this chapter shall prevent any State agency or court from asserting jurisdiction under State law over any occupational safety or health issue with respect to which no standard is in effect under section 655 of this title."

That is to say, where there is no federal standard in effect, there is no pre-emption. The plurality reasons that there must be pre-emption, however, when there is a federal standard in effect, else § 18(a) would be rendered superfluous because "[t]here is no possibility of conflict where there is no federal regulation."

The plurality errs doubly. First, its premise is incorrect. In the sense in which the plurality uses the term, there is the possibility of "conflict" even absent federal regulation since the mere enactment of a federal law like the Act may amount to an occupation of an entire field, preventing state regulation. Second, the necessary implication of § 18(a) is not that every federal regulation pre-empts all state law on the issue in question, but only that some federal regulations may pre-empt some state law. The plurality ignores the possibility that the provision simply rules out field pre-emption and is otherwise entirely compatible with the possibility that pre-emption will occur only when actual conflict between a federal regulation and a state rule renders compliance with both impossible. Indeed, if Congress had meant to say that any state rule should be pre-empted if it deals with an issue as to which there is a federal regulation in effect, the text of subsection (a) would have been a very inept way of trying to make the point. It was not, however, an inept way to make the different point that Congress intended no field pre-emption of the sphere of health and safety subject to regulation, but not necessarily regulated, under the Act. Unlike the case where field pre-emption occurs, the provision tells us, absence of a federal standard leaves a State free to do as it will on the issue. Beyond this, subsection (a) does not necessarily mean anything, and the provision is perfectly consistent with the

conclusion that as long as compliance with both a federal standard and a state regulation is not physically impossible, each standard shall be enforceable. If, indeed,
the presumption against pre-emption means anything, § 18(a) must be read in just
this way.

Respondent also relies on § 18(b):

"(b) Submission of State plan for development and enforcement of State
standards to preempt applicable Federal standards

"Any State which, at any time, desires to assume responsibility for development and enforcement therein of occupational safety and health standards
relating to any occupational safety or health issue with respect to which a
Federal standard has been promulgated under section 655 of this title shall
submit a State plan for the development of such standards and their
enforcement."

Respondent argues that the necessary implication of this provision is clear: the
only way that a state rule on a particular occupational safety and health issue may
be enforced once a federal standard on the issue is also in place is by incorporating
the state rule in a plan approved by the Secretary.

The subsection simply does not say that unless a plan is approved, state law on an
issue is pre-empted by the promulgation of a federal standard. In fact it tugs the other
way, and in actually providing a mechanism for a State to "assume responsibility"
for an issue with respect to which a federal standard has been promulgated (that is,
to pre-empt federal law), § 18(b) is far from pre-emptive of anything adopted by the
States. Its heading, enacted as part of the statute and properly considered under our
canons of construction for whatever light it may shed, speaks expressly of the "development and enforcement of State standards to preempt applicable Federal standards."
The provision does not in any way provide that absent such state pre-emption of
federal rules, the State may not even supplement the federal standards with consistent regulations of its own. Once again, nothing in the provision's language speaks
one way or the other to the question whether promulgation of a federal standard pre-
empts state regulation, or whether, in the absence of a plan, consistent federal and
state regulations may coexist. The provision thus makes perfect sense on the assumption that a dual regulatory scheme is permissible but subject to state pre-emption if
the State wishes to shoulder enough of the federal mandate to gain approval of a plan.

Nor does the provision setting out conditions for the Secretary's approval of a plan
indicate that a state regulation on an issue federally addressed is never enforceable
unless incorporated in a plan so approved. Subsection (c)(2) requires the Secretary
to approve a plan when in her judgment, among other things, it will not "unduly
burden interstate commerce." Respondent argues, and the plurality concludes, that
if state regulations were not pre-empted, this provision would somehow suggest that
States acting independently could enforce regulations that did burden interstate
commerce unduly. But this simply does not follow. The subsection puts a limit on the
Secretary's authority to approve a plan that burdens interstate commerce, thus capping

the discretion that might otherwise have been read into the congressional delegation of authority to the Secretary to approve state plans. From this restriction applying only to the Secretary's federal authority it is clearly a non sequitur to conclude that pre-emption must have been intended to avoid the equally objectionable undue burden that independent state regulation might otherwise impose. Quite the contrary; the dormant Commerce Clause can take care of that, without any need to assume pre-emption.

IV

In sum, our rule is that the traditional police powers of the State survive unless Congress has made a purpose to pre-empt them clear. Each provision [of the Act is] in fact just as consistent with a purpose and objective to permit overlapping state and federal regulation as with one to guarantee that employers and employees would be subjected to only one regulatory regime. Restriction to one such regime by precluding supplemental state regulation might or might not be desirable. But in the absence of any clear expression of congressional intent to pre-empt, I can only conclude that, as long as compliance with federally promulgated standards does not render obedience to Illinois' regulations impossible, the enforcement of the state law is not prohibited by the Supremacy Clause. I respectfully dissent.

EXERCISE 5:

1. According to the respective opinions in this case, what is the difference between express and implied preemption? What is the difference between field and conflict preemption? What are the advantages and disadvantages of the different approaches taken by the different opinions? Explain whether, in your view, this case involved express or implied preemption.

2. What role, if any, does a presumption against preemption of state law play in the analyses utilized by the different opinions?

3. What sources did the plurality consult to determine Congress' intent regarding preemption?

4. Why were the Illinois laws, the purpose of which was to protect the environment, preempted by federal worker safety laws?

Chapter 3

THE "DORMANT" OR "NEGATIVE" COMMERCE CLAUSE

A. INTRODUCTION

What the Supreme Court labels the "dormant" or "negative" Commerce Clause does not appear—at least not explicitly—in the Constitution. Instead, it is a series of legal doctrines, elucidated in the Supreme Court's opinions, that limit the ability of states to burden interstate (and foreign) commerce. The Court has justified its dormant Commerce Clause doctrine by reference to the Commerce Clause in Article I, § 8, cl. 3, and its implied exclusion of state regulation through its grant of commerce power to Congress.

EXERCISE 1:

Apply the first four forms of argument to the dormant Commerce Clause.

1. Looking at the Commerce Clause itself, and the text of the rest of Article I, § 8, what do you learn about the dormant Commerce Clause's meaning?

2. Looking at the Constitution's structure, and particularly at the federal system it preserves, what do you learn about the dormant Commerce Clause's meaning?

3. Reviewing evidence of the Constitution's original meaning, what does it tell you about that meaning?

4. What insight do the materials following adoption of the Constitution offer into the dormant Commerce Clause's meaning?

In this Chapter, we will review the origin of the dormant Commerce Clause and the Supreme Court's struggle with defining its scope. We also will cover the transformation of the Clause during the New Deal and the current doctrine governing it.

Like much of the Supreme Court's case law and of its interpretation of the Constitution, the scope of the dormant Commerce Clause has waxed and waned. Today, the Clause is a relatively robust limitation on the power of states to limit or burden interstate commerce. In fact, of the structural limits in Article I that you will review in law school, the negative implications of the Commerce Clause is one of the few with modern "bite."

As you read the materials below, some of the issues to consider include:

Is the dormant Commerce Clause a legitimate interpretation of the Constitution?

If so, which of the Supreme Court's different conceptions of the dormant Commerce Clause is the most appropriate?

What has caused the Supreme Court to utilize so many different interpretations of the dormant Commerce Clause?

How does the Supreme Court's current interpretation of the dormant Commerce Clause differ from its previous interpretations?

To what extent, if any, do the Supreme Court's previous interpretations of the dormant Commerce Clause influence the Court's current interpretation?

Why not allow Congress alone—to the exclusion of the courts—to determine when state regulation too greatly burdens interstate or foreign commerce?

Why does the Supreme Court currently distinguish between state regulation that discriminates against interstate commerce and regulation that does not?

What is the basis for the Supreme Court's modern interpretation of the dormant Commerce Clause?

Are there—or should there be—any exceptions to the dormant Commerce Clause?

B. ORIGINAL MEANING

Given the tenuous textual basis for the Supreme Court's dormant Commerce Clause doctrine, the Court regularly refers to the doctrine's historical roots and uses the Commerce Clause's history to guide its decisions. For instance, in one of the Court's most recent dormant Commerce Clause cases, *Granholm v. Heald*, 544 U.S. 460 (2005), the Court focused on history. It noted that commercial infighting was one of the main causes of the Constitutional Convention. *Id.* at 472. The Court also reflected on the positive economic impact occasioned by the elimination of trade barriers between states and the creation of a free trade union. *Id.*

The history surrounding the drafting and ratification of the Commerce Clause indicates that states would retain regulatory authority over matters that Congress *could* regulate under its Commerce Clause authority.[1] In other words, the Founders envisioned some overlap of jurisdiction between the federal and state governments.

---

1. The writings detailing the history and origin of the dormant aspects of the Commerce Clause are voluminous. *See, e.g.*, FELIX FRANKFURTER, THE COMMERCE CLAUSE UNDER MARSHALL, TANEY AND WHITE (1937); BERNARD C. GAVIT, THE COMMERCE CLAUSE OF THE UNITED STATES

There are at least four reasons for believing that the grant of power over inter-state commerce to Congress is not exclusive. First, unlike many of the powers dele-gated to Congress, there is no corresponding denial of authority to states to regulate interstate commerce. For example, Article I, § 8 gives Congress the "Power To lay and collect Taxes, Duties, Imposts and Excises."[2] Correspondingly, Article I, § 10 states that "No State shall, without the Consent of the Congress, lay any Imposts or Duties on Imports or Exports."[3] There is no similar limitation on state jurisdiction over commerce. As Alexander Hamilton pointed out in FEDERALIST No. 32, some powers vested in the national government admit of "concurrent" exercise by the states, while others are of their nature "exclusive," rendering the notion of a like power in the states "contradictory and repugnant."[4] Hamilton gave Congress' power to pass uniform naturalization laws as an example of an exclusive power of Congress.[5]

Second, there is nothing in the nature of state regulation having an impact on interstate commerce that requires the elimination of all such state regulation. States regulating in the interests of their citizens' health, in a manner that has some impact on interstate commerce, is not necessarily inconsistent with Congress' power to regulate interstate commerce.

Third, the background of Article I, § 10, supports this conclusion. On Septem-ber 15, 1787, in the Federal Convention at Philadelphia, the Framers debated whether the states should have the ability to lay duties of tonnage, without interference by Congress, to finance the clearing of harbors and the building of lighthouses.[6] In James Madison's view, the existence of the Commerce Clause would bar states from imposing any duty on tonnage, thereby obviating the need for an explicit prohibition on state regulation.[7] Roger Sherman, the progenitor of Article I, § 10, disagreed,

---

CONSTITUTION (1932); John B. Sholleys, *The Negative Implications of the Commerce Clause*, 3 U. CHI. L. REV. 556 (1936); *see also* Brannon P. Denning, *Reconstructing the Dormant Commerce Clause Doctrine*, 50 WM. & MARY L. REV. 417 (2008); Robert A. Sedler, *The Negative Commerce Clause as a Restriction on State Regulation and Taxation: An Analysis in Terms of Constitutional Structure*, 31 WAYNE L. REV. 885 (1985); Thomas A. Anson & P.M. Schenkkan, *Federalism, The Dormant Com-merce Clause, and State-Owned Resources*, 59 TEX. L. REV. 71 (1980); James F. Blumstein, *Some Interactions of the Negative Commerce Clause and the New Federalism: The Case of Discriminatory Income Tax Treatment of Out-of-State Tax-Exempt Bonds*, 31 VAND. L. REV. 473 (1978); Julian N. Eule, *Laying the Dormant Commerce Clause to Rest*, 91 YALE L.J. 425 (1982); Walter Hellerstein, Hughes v. Oklahoma: *The Court, The Commerce Clause, and State Control of Natural Resources*, 1979 SUP. CT. REV. 51. For a fuller discussion, see W. CROSSKEY, POLITICS AND THE CONSTITUTION IN THE HISTORY OF THE UNITED STATES 295–323 (1953).

   2. U.S. CONST. art. 1, § 8, cl. 1.

   3. U.S. CONST. art. 1, § 10, cl. 2.

   4. THE FEDERALIST No. 32 (A. Hamilton).

   5. *Id.*

   6. 2 THE RECORDS OF THE FEDERAL CONVENTION OF 1787, at 625 (Max Farrand ed., 1966).

   7. *See id.* ("He was more and more convinced that the regulation of Commerce was in its nature indivisible and ought to be wholly under one authority."); *id.* ("Whether the States are now restrained from laying tonnage duties depends on the extent of the power 'to regulate commerce.' These terms are vague but seem to exclude this power of the States.").

stating that a concurrent jurisdiction of the federal and state governments on Commerce is more appropriate.[8]

Ultimately, the Convention adopted Article I, § 10 prohibiting states, "without the consent of Congress, [to] lay any duty of tonnage."[9] This indicates that the Convention believed that states retained some authority over commerce and hence an explicit restriction on that residual authority must be placed in the Constitution.

Fourth, one of the overarching purposes of the Commerce Clause was the elimination of interstate trade barriers. This purpose can be accomplished without completely eliminating state ability to impact interstate commerce in pursuance of other objectives, such as health.

The Framers anticipated great advantages from the grant to Congress of power over commerce because state interference with trade had become a source of sharp discontent under the Articles of Confederation.[10] Thus, the Commerce Clause received support in the Constitutional Convention mainly to protect the national market from the oppressive power of individual states acting to stifle or curb commerce.[11] Numerous references in the Convention's records to the Commerce Clause were directed to the dangers of interstate rivalry and retaliation.[12]

---

8. *See id.* ("The power of the United States to regulate trade being supreme can controul interferences of the State regulations when such interferences happen; so that there is no danger to be apprehended from a concurrent jurisdiction.").

9. U.S. Const. art. 1, § 10, cl. 3.

10. Albert Abel, *The Commerce Clause in the Constitutional Convention and in Contemporary Comment*, 25 Minn. L. Rev. 432, 432 (1941) ("[T]he general government as constituted—or reconstituted—by the convention was to possess *a* power of regulating commerce. It was by no means so universally agreed that there should be a clause granting to it *the* power 'to regulate commerce.'").

11. This statement has support in *Federalist Nos.* 7 (Hamilton), 11 (Hamilton) ("An unrestrained intercourse between the states themselves will advance the trade of each by an interchange of their respective productions, not only for the supply of reciprocal wants at home, but for exportation to foreign markets."), 22 (Hamilton), 42 (Madison) ("The defect of power in the existing confederacy to regulate the commerce between its several members is in the number of those which have been clearly pointed out by experience. To the proofs and remarks which former papers have brought into view on this subject, it may be added that, without this supplemental provision, the great and essential power of regulating foreign commerce, would have been incomplete and ineffectual. A very material object of this power was the relief of the states which import and export through other states from the improper contributions levied on them by the latter. Were these at liberty to regulate the trade between state and state, it must be foreseen that ways would be found out to load the articles of import and export, during the passage through their jurisdiction, with duties which would fall on the makers of the latter and the consumers of the former. We may be assured by past experience that such a practise would be introduced by future contrivances; and both by that and a common knowledge of human affairs, that it would nourish unceasing animosities and not improbably terminate in serious interruptions of the public tranquillity."), and 53 (Madison).

12. Abel, *supra*, at 470–71; *see also* 2 The Records of the Federal Convention of 1787, 360 ("Mr. Govr. Morris . . . there is great weight in the argument, that the exporting states will tax the produce of their uncommercial neighbours. The power of regulating the trade between Pa. & N. Jersey will never prevent the former from taxing the latter. Nor will such a tax force a direct exportation from N. Jersey—the advantages possessed by a large trading city outweigh the disadvantages of a moderate duty; and will retain the trade in that channel."); *id.* at 361 ("Mr. M[adison] . . . the

Further, the notion that the Commerce Clause, without implementation by congressional legislation, took away from the states all power over interstate commerce, was counter-intuitive considering the extent of state regulation that existed before the Constitution. If, at the time of the Framing and Ratification, the public understood the Commerce Clause to broadly exclude all state regulation that impacted interstate commerce, there likely would have been significant opposition and the Anti-Federalists would have trumpeted this prospect. The lack of criticism premised on the "dormant" aspect of the Commerce Clause arguably shows that it was not controversial because the Framers and Ratifiers did not anticipate a very broad "dormant" category of Commerce Clause law.

C. EARLY CASES AND LATER STRUGGLES WITH DEFINITION

1. Foundation

The origin of the dormant Commerce Clause, in its explicit judicial articulation, is found in a passage from Chief Justice Marshall's opinion in *Gibbons v. Ogden*, 22 U.S. (9 Wheat.) 1 (1824). You previously encountered *Gibbons* in Volume 3 where you covered the Interstate Commerce Clause.

GIBBONS v. OGDEN

22 U.S. (9 Wheat.) 1 (1824)

[New York, by statute, granted a license to Robert R. Livingston and Robert Fulton for "the exclusive navigation of all the waters within the jurisdiction of that State, with boats moved by fire or steam." Ogden, who was the assignee of Livingston and Fulton, sued Gibbons because Gibbons operated two boats in violation of the

---

regulation of trade between state and state cannot effect more than indirectly to hinder a state from taxing its own exports: by authorizing its citizens to carry their commodities freely into a neighbouring state which might decline taxing exports in order to draw into its channel the trade of its neighbours."); *id.* at 441 ("Col. Mason observed that particular states might wish to encourage by impost duties certain manufactures for which they enjoyed natural advantages, as Virginia the manufacture of hemp &c. Mr. Madison—The encouragement of manufacture in that mode requires duties not only on imports directly from foreign countries, but from the other states in the Union, which would revive all the mischiefs experienced from the want of a genl. government over commerce."); *id.* at 504 ("Is it proper to declare all the navigable waters or rivers and within the United States common high ways? Perhaps a power to restrain any state from demanding tribute of another state in such cases is comprehended in the power to regulate trade between state and state. This to be further considered."); *id.* at 588–89 ("Mason had moved the insertion of the clause permitting state inspection fees to pay expenses of inspection. Mr. Madison 2ded the motion—It would at least be harmless; and might have the good effect of restraining the states to bona fide duties for the purpose, as well as of authorizing explicitly such duties; tho' perhaps the best guard against an abuse of the power of the states on this subject, was the right in the genl. government to regulate trade between state and state.").

exclusive license. Gibbons argued in defense that, since he was operating and licensed pursuant to a federal statute, the New York statute violated the Commerce Clause.]

MR. CHIEF JUSTICE MARSHALL delivered the opinion of the Court, and, after stating the case, proceeded as follows:

The appellant contends that this decree is erroneous, because the laws which purport to give the exclusive privilege it sustains, are repugnant to the constitution and laws of the United States.

They are said to be repugnant — 1st. To that clause in the constitution which authorizes Congress to regulate commerce.

[The Supreme Court first explained the meaning of the Commerce Clause's component parts. Then, Chief Justice Marshall stated:]

But it has been urged with great earnestness, that, although the power of Congress to regulate commerce with foreign nations, and among the several States, be co-extensive with the subject itself, and have no other limits than are prescribed in the constitution, yet the States may severally exercise the same power, within their respective jurisdictions. In support of this argument, it is said, that they possessed it as an inseparable attribute of sovereignty, before the formation of the constitution, and still retain it, except so far as they have surrendered it by that instrument; that this principle results from the nature of the government, and is secured by the tenth amendment; that an affirmative grant of power is not exclusive, unless in its own nature it be such that the continued exercise of it by the former possessor is inconsistent with the grant, and that this is not of that description.

The appellant, conceding these postulates, except the last, contends, that full power to regulate a particular subject, implies the whole power, and leaves no residuum; that a grant of the whole is incompatible with the existence of a right in another to any part of it.

The grant of the power to lay and collect taxes is, like the power to regulate commerce, made in general terms, and has never been understood to interfere with the exercise of the same power by the State; and hence has been drawn an argument which has been applied to the question under consideration. But the two grants are not, it is conceived, similar in their terms or their nature. Although many of the powers formerly exercised by the States, are transferred to the government of the Union, yet the State governments remain, and constitute a most important part of our system. The power of taxation is indispensable to their existence, and is a power which, in its own nature, is capable of residing in, and being exercised by, different authorities at the same time. We are accustomed to see it placed, for different purposes, in different hands. Taxation is the simple operation of taking small portions from a perpetually accumulating mass, susceptible of almost infinite division; and a power in one to take what is necessary for certain purposes, is not, in its nature, incompatible with a power in another to take what is necessary for other purposes. Congress is authorized to lay and collect taxes, &c. to pay the debts, and provide for the common defence and general welfare of the United States. This does not interfere with the power of the States to tax for the support of their own governments; nor is the exercise of that power by the States, an exercise of any portion of the power that is granted to the United States. In imposing taxes for State purposes, they are not doing what Congress is empowered to do. Congress is not empowered to tax for those purposes which are within the exclusive province of the States. When, then, each government exercises the power of taxation, neither is exercising the power of the other. But, when a State proceeds to regulate commerce with foreign nations, or among the several States, it is exercising the very power that is granted to Congress, and is doing the very thing which Congress is authorized to do. There is no analogy, then, between the power of taxation and the power of regulating commerce.

In discussing the question, whether this power is still in the States, in the case under consideration, we may dismiss from it the inquiry, whether it is surrendered by the mere grant to Congress, or is retained until Congress shall exercise the power. We may dismiss that inquiry, because it has been exercised, and the regulations which Congress deemed it proper to make, are now in full operation. The sole question is, can a State regulate commerce with foreign nations and among the States, while Congress is regulating it?

But, the inspection laws are said to be regulations of commerce, and are certainly recognised in the constitution, as being passed in the exercise of a power remaining with the States.

That inspection laws may have a remote and considerable influence on commerce, will not be denied; but that a power to regulate commerce is the source from which the right to pass them is derived, cannot be admitted. The object of inspection laws, is to improve the quality of articles produced by the labour of a country; to fit them for exportation; or, it may be, for domestic use. They act upon the subject before it becomes an article of foreign commerce, or of commerce among the States, and prepare it for that purpose. They form a portion of that immense mass of legislation, which embraces every thing within the territory of a State, not surrendered to the general government: all which can be most advantageously exercised by the States themselves. Inspection laws, quarantine laws, health laws of every description, as well as laws for regulating the internal commerce of a State, and those which respect turnpike roads, ferries, &c., are component parts of this mass.

Since in exercising the power of regulating their own purely internal affairs, whether of trading or police, the States may sometimes enact laws, the validity of which depends on their interfering with, and being contrary to, an act of Congress passed in pursuance of the constitution, the Court will enter upon the inquiry, whether the laws of New-York, as expounded by the highest tribunal of that State, have, in their application to this case, come into collision with an act of Congress, and deprived a citizen of a right to which that act entitles him. Should this collision exist, it will be immaterial whether those laws were passed in virtue of a concurrent power 'to regulate commerce with foreign nations and among the several States,' or, in virtue of a power to regulate their domestic trade and police. In one case and the other, the acts of New-York must yield to the law of Congress; and the decision sustaining the privilege they confer, against a right given by a law of the Union, must be erroneous.

[After reviewing the federal and state laws at issue in this case, the Court held that the state statutes conflicted with federal law and where therefore void.]

MR. JUSTICE JOHNSON.

The judgment entered by the Court in this cause, has my entire approbation.

[I]

The history of the times [surrounding the framing and ratification of the Commerce Clause] sustain the opinion, that the grant of power over commerce, if intended to be commensurate with the evils existing, and the purpose of remedying those evils, could be only commensurate with the power of the States over the subject.

There was not a State in the Union, in which there did not, at that time, exist a variety of commercial regulations; concerning which it is too much to suppose, that the whole ground covered by those regulations was immediately assumed by actual legislation, under the authority of the Union. By common consent, those [state] laws dropped lifeless from their statute books, for want of the sustaining power, that had been relinquished to Congress.

[II]

And the plain and direct import of the words of the grant, is consistent with this general understanding. The words of the constitution are, 'Congress shall have power to regulate commerce with foreign nations, and among the several States, and with the Indian tribes.'

My opinion is founded on the application of the words of the grant to the subject of it. The 'power to regulate commerce,' here meant to be granted, was that power to regulate commerce which previously existed in the States. But what was that power? The States were, unquestionably, supreme; and each possessed that power over commerce, which is acknowledged to reside in every sovereign State. The definition and limits of that power are to be sought among the features of international law. The law of nations, regarding man as a social animal, pronounces all commerce legitimate in a state of peace, until prohibited by positive law. The power of a sovereign state over commerce, therefore, amounts to nothing more than a power to limit and restrain it at pleasure. And since the power to prescribe the limits to its freedom, necessarily implies the power to determine what shall remain unrestrained, it follows, that the power must be exclusive; it can reside but in one potentate; and hence, the grant of this power carries with it the whole subject, leaving nothing for the State to act upon.

[III]

When speaking of the power of Congress over navigation, I do not regard it as a power incidental to that of regulating commerce; I consider it as the thing itself; inseparable from it as vital motion is from vital existence.

It is impossible, with the views which I entertain of the principle on which the commercial privileges of the people of United States, among themselves, rests, to concur in the view which this Court takes of the effect of the coasting license in this cause. I do not regard it as the foundation of the right set up in behalf of the appellant. If there was any one object riding over every other in the adoption of the constitution, it was to keep the commercial intercourse among the States free from all invidious and partial restraints. And I cannot overcome the conviction, that if the licensing act was repealed to-morrow, the rights of the appellant to a reversal of the decision complained of, would be as strong as it is under this license. The act, in this instance, forms part of an extensive system, the object of which is to encourage American shipping, and place them on an equal footing with the shipping of other nations. Almost every commercial nation reserves to its own subjects a monopoly of its coasting trade; and a countervailing privilege in favour of American shipping is contemplated, in the whole legislation of the United States on this subject. I consider the license, therefore, as nothing more than what it purports to be, according to the 1st section of this act, conferring on the licensed vessel certain privileges in that trade, not conferred on other vessels; but the abstract right of commercial intercourse, stripped of those privileges, is common to all.

[IV]

It is no objection to the existence of distinct, substantive powers, that, in their application, they bear upon the same subject. The same bale of goods, the same cask of provisions, or the same ship, that may be the subject of commercial regulation, may also be the vehicle of disease. And the health laws that require them to be stopped and ventilated, are no more intended as regulations on commerce, than the laws which permit their importation, are intended to innoculate the community with disease. Their different purposes mark the distinction between the powers brought into action; and while frankly exercised, they can produce no serious collision. As to laws affecting ferries, turnpike roads, and other subjects of the same class, so far from meriting the epithet of commercial regulations, they are, in fact, commercial facilities, for which, by the consent of mankind, a compensation is paid. Inspection laws are of a more equivocal nature, and it is obvious, that the constitution has viewed that subject with much solicitude. But so far from sustaining an inference in favour of the power of the States over commerce, I cannot but think that the guarded provisions of the 10th section, on this subject, furnish a strong argument against that inference. It was obvious, that inspection laws must combine municipal with commercial regulations; and, while the power over the subject is yielded to the States, for obvious reasons, an absolute control is given over State legislation on the subject, as far as that legislation may be exercised, so as to affect the commerce of the country. The inferences, to be correctly drawn, from this whole article, appear to me to be altogether in favour of the exclusive grants to Congress of power over commerce, and the reverse of that which the appellee contends for.

It would be in vain to deny the possibility of a clashing and collision between the measures of the two governments. The line cannot be drawn with sufficient distinctness between the municipal powers of the one, and the commercial powers of the other. In some points they meet and blend so as scarcely to admit of separation. Hitherto the only remedy has been applied which the case admits of; that of a frank and candid co-operation for the general good. Witness the laws of Congress requiring its officers to respect the inspection laws of the States, and to aid in enforcing their health laws; that which surrenders to the States the superintendence of pilotage, and the many laws passed to permit a tonnage duty to be levied for the use of their ports. Other instances could be cited, abundantly to prove that collision must be sought to be produced; and when it does arise, the question must be decided how far the powers of Congress are adequate to put it down. Wherever the powers of the respective governments are frankly exercised, with a distinct view to the ends of such powers, they may act upon the same object, or use the same means, and yet the powers be kept perfectly distinct. A resort to the same means, therefore, is no argument to prove the identity of their respective powers.

EXERCISE 2:

1. Why is the power to regulate commerce exclusively Congress'?

2. What is the distinction that Chief Justice Marshall articulates to resolve this case?

3. From where did he derive that distinction?

4. Are the bases upon which Marshall drew the dormant Commerce Clause sufficient to support it?

5. Is the distinction tenable?

6. If you believe that the Constitution permits states to regulate with some effect on interstate and foreign commerce, where would you draw the line and why?

7. If you were an attorney representing a state in a later case, how might you narrow the potential scope of the dormant Commerce Clause by narrowly reading *Gibbons*?

8. Why did Justice Johnson conclude that states could regulate in a manner that impacted interstate commerce? Where did he draw the line between permissible and impermissible regulations?

9. In his famous *Commentaries on the Constitution*, Justice Story described the dormant Commerce Clause this way:

> Nor do the acknowledged powers of the states over certain subjects, having a connexion with commerce, in any degree impugn this reasoning. These powers are entirely distinct in their nature from that to regulate commerce; and though the same means may be resorted to, for the purpose of carrying each of these powers into effect, this by no just reasoning furnishes any ground to assert, that they are identical. Among these, are inspection laws, health laws, laws regulating turnpikes, roads, and ferries, all of which, when exercised by a state, are legitimate, arising from the general powers belonging to it, unless so far as they conflict with the powers delegated to congress. They are not so much regulations of commerce, as of police; and may truly be said

to belong, if at all to commerce, to that which is purely internal. The pilotage laws of the states may fall under the same description. But they have been adopted by congress, and without question are controllable by it.

2 JOSEPH STORY, COMMENTARIES ON THE CONSTITUTION OF THE UNITED STATES § 1066 (1833). Describe the line Justice Story drew between permissible state laws that effect interstate commerce and impermissible state laws.

2. Struggles with Definition

Following Chief Justice Marshall's suggestion in *Gibbons* that states may, consistent with the Commerce Clause, regulate activity even when it impacts interstate and foreign commerce, the Supreme Court struggled to describe the line between legitimate state regulation under their reserved "police" powers, and illegitimate state regulation of "commerce." In the next case, the Court rejected a dormant Commerce Clause challenge to state regulation of navigable waters based on the police powers rationale articulated in *Gibbons*.

THOMPSON WILLSON v. THE BLACK BIRD CREEK MARSH COMPANY

27 U.S. (2 Pet.) 245 (1829)

MR. CHIEF JUSTICE MARSHALL delivered the opinion of the Court.

[Delaware passed a statute that created and authorized the Black Bird Creek Company to construct a dam across Black Bird Creek. The Creek emptied into the Delaware river and was used for boat traffic, including by Willson. The Company erected a dam that blocked the Creek.]

The act of assembly by which the plaintiffs were authorized to construct their dam, shows plainly that this is one of those many creeks, passing through a deep level marsh adjoining the Delaware, up which the tide flows for some distance. The value of the property on its banks must be enhanced by excluding the water from the marsh, and the health of the inhabitants probably improved. Measures calculated to produce these objects, provided they do not come into collision with the powers of the general government, are undoubtedly within those which are reserved to the states. But the measure authorised by this act stops a navigable creek, and must be supposed to abridge the rights of those who have been accustomed to use it. But this abridgement, unless it comes in conflict with the constitution or a law of the United States, is an affair between the government of Delaware and its citizens, of which this Court can take no cognizance.

The counsel for the plaintiffs in error insist that it comes in conflict with the power of the United States 'to regulate commerce with foreign nations and among the several states.' If congress had passed any act which bore upon the case we should feel not much difficulty in saying that a state law coming in conflict with such act would be void. But congress has passed no such act. The repugnancy of the law of Delaware to the constitution is placed entirely on its repugnancy to the power to regulate commerce with foreign nations and among the several states; a power which has not been so exercised as to affect the question.

We do not think that the act empowering the Black Bird Creek Marsh Company to place a dam across the creek, can, under all the circumstances of the case, be considered as repugnant to the power to regulate commerce in its dormant state, or as being in conflict with any law passed on the subject.

There is no error, and the judgment is affirmed.

EXERCISE 3:

1. On what basis did the Supreme Court uphold the challenged Delaware law?

2. *Black Bird Creek Marsh Co.* was the only case in which Chief Justice Marshall applied his police powers rationale from *Gibbons v. Ogden.*

3. Does *Black Bird Creek Marsh Co.* clarify the scope of Chief Justice Marshall's dicta in *Gibbons v. Ogden* regarding the scope of state police power regulatory authority?

———————

The Supreme Court also used another dormant Commerce Clause analysis that distinguished between those subjects that were "national" in nature and those that were "local" in nature. States could regulate the latter, but not the former. The Court articulated this distinction below.

AARON B. COOLEY v. THE BOARD OF WARDENS OF THE PORT OF PHILADELPHIA

53 U.S. (12 How.) 299 (1851)

Mr. Justice Curtis delivered the opinion of the court.

These cases are brought here by writs of error to the Supreme Court of the Commonwealth of Pennsylvania.

[I]

They are actions to recover half pilotage fees under the 29th section of the act of the Legislature of Pennsylvania, passed on the second day of March, 1803. The plaintiff in error alleges that the highest court of the state has decided against a right claimed by him under the Constitution of the United States. That right is to be exempted from the payment of the sums of money demanded, pursuant to the State law above referred to, because that law contravenes several provisions of the Constitution of the United States.

The particular section of the state law drawn in question is as follows:

> 'That every ship or vessel arriving from or bound to any foreign port or place, and every ship or vessel of the burden of seventy-five tons or more, sailing from or bound to any port not within the river Delaware, shall be obliged to

receive a pilot. . . . And if the master of any ship or vessel shall neglect to make such report, he shall forfeit and pay the sum of sixty dollars. And if the master of any such ship or vessel shall refuse or neglect to take a pilot, the master, owner or consignee of such vessel shall forfeit and pay to the warden aforesaid, a sum equal to the half-pilotage of such ship or vessel, to the use of the Society for the Relief, &c., to be recovered as pilotage in the manner hereinafter directed.'

We think this particular regulation concerning half-pilotage fees, is an appropriate part of a general system of regulations of this subject. Testing it by the practice of commercial states and countries legislating on this subject, we find it has usually been deemed necessary to make similar provisions. Numerous laws of this kind are cited in the learned argument of the counsel for the defendant in error; and their fitness, as a part of the system of pilotage, in many places, may be inferred from their existence in so many different states and countries. Like other laws they are framed to meet the most usual cases *quae frequentius accidunt;* they rest upon the propriety of securing lives and property exposed to the perils of a dangerous navigation, by taking on board a person peculiarly skilled to encounter or avoid them; upon the policy of discouraging the commanders of vessels from refusing to receive such persons on board at the proper times and places; and upon the expediency, and even intrinsic justice, of not suffering those who have incurred labor, and expense, and danger, to place themselves in a position to render important service generally necessary, to go unrewarded, because the master of a particular vessel either rashly refuses their proffered assistance, or, contrary to the general experience, does not need it. The laws of commercial states and countries have made an offer of pilotage-service one of those cases; and we cannot pronounce a law which does this, to be so far removed from the usual and fit scope of laws for the regulation of pilots and pilotage, as to be deemed, for this cause, a covert attempt to legislate upon another subject under the appearance of legislating on this one.

[II]

[After rejecting other constitutional challenges, the Court stated:] It remains to consider the objection, that [the statute] is repugnant to the third clause of the eighth section of the first article. 'The Congress shall have power to regulate commerce with foreign nations and among the several states, and with the Indian tribes.'

That the power to regulate commerce includes the regulation of navigation, we consider settled. And when we look to [the piloting activities that the Pennsylvania statute regulates we find that it does] constitute regulations of navigation, and consequently of commerce, within the just meaning of this clause of the Constitution.

The power to regulate navigation is the power to prescribe rules in conformity with which navigation must be carried on. It extends to the persons who conduct it, as well as to the instruments used. Accordingly, the first Congress assembled under the Constitution passed laws, requiring the masters of ships and vessels of the United States to be citizens of the United States, and established many rules for the government and regulation of officers and seamen. 1 Stat. at L., 55, 131 [1789]. These have been from time to time added to and changed.

Now, a pilot, so far as respects the navigation of the vessel in that part of the voyage which is his pilotage-ground, is the temporary master charged with the safety of the vessel and cargo, and of the lives of those on board, and intrusted with the command of the crew. He is not only one of the persons engaged in navigation, but he occupies a most important and responsible place among those thus engaged. And if Congress has power to regulate the seamen who assist the pilot in the management of the vessel, a power never denied, we can perceive no valid reason why the pilot should be beyond the reach of the same power.

Nor should it be lost sight of, that this subject of the regulation of pilots and pilotage has an intimate connection with, and an important relation to, the general subject of commerce with foreign nations and among the several states, over which it was one main object of the Constitution to create a national control. Conflicts between the laws of neighboring states, and discriminations favorable or adverse to commerce with particular foreign nations, might be created by state laws regulating pilotage, deeply affecting that equality of commercial rights, and that freedom from state interference, which those who formed the Constitution were so anxious to secure, and which the experience of more than half a century has taught us to value so highly. The apprehension of this danger is not speculative merely. For, in 1837, Congress actually interposed to relieve the commerce of the country from serious embarrassment, arising from the laws of different states, situate upon waters which are the boundary between them. This was done by an enactment of the 2d of March, 1837, in the following words:

> 'Be it enacted, that it shall and may be lawful for the master or commander of any vessel coming into or going out of any port situate upon waters which are the boundary between two states, to employ any pilot duly licensed or authorized by the laws of either of the states bounded on the said waters, to pilot said vessel to or from said port, any law, usage, or custom, to the contrary, notwithstanding.'

The act of 1789, already referred to, contains a clear legislative exposition of the Constitution by the first Congress, to the effect that the power to regulate pilots was conferred on Congress by the Constitution; as does also the act of March the 2d, 1837, the terms of which have just been given. The weight to be allowed to this contemporaneous construction, and the practice of Congress under it, has, in another connection, been adverted to. And a majority of the court are of opinion, that a regulation of pilots is a regulation of commerce, within the grant to Congress of the commercial power, contained in the third clause of the eighth section of the first article of the Constitution.

[III]

[A]

It becomes necessary, therefore, to consider whether this law of Pennsylvania, being a regulation of commerce, is valid.

The act of Congress of the 7th of August, 1789, sect. 4, is as follows:

> 'That all pilots in the bays, inlets, rivers, harbors, and ports of the United States shall continue to be regulated in conformity with the existing laws of the states, respectively, wherein such pilots may be, or with such laws as the states may respectively hereafter enact for the purpose, until further legislative provision shall be made by Congress.'

If the law of Pennsylvania, now in question, had been in existence at the date of this act of Congress, we might hold it to have been adopted by Congress, and thus made a law of the United States, and so valid. Because this act does, in effect, give the force of an act of Congress, to the then existing state laws on this subject, so long as they should continue unrepealed by the state which enacted them.

But the law on which these actions are founded was not enacted till 1803. What effect then can be attributed to so much of the act of 1789, as declares, that pilots shall continue to be regulated in conformity, 'with such laws as the states may respectively hereafter enact for the purpose, until further legislative provision shall be made by Congress?'

If the states were divested of the power to legislate on this subject by the grant of the commercial power to Congress, it is plain this act could not confer upon them power thus to legislate. If the Constitution excluded the states from making any law regulating commerce, certainly Congress cannot re-grant, or in any manner re-convey to the states that power. And yet this act of 1789 gives its sanction only to laws enacted by the states. This necessarily implies a constitutional power to legislate; for only a rule created by the sovereign power of a state acting in its legislative capacity, can be deemed a law, enacted by a state; and if the state has so limited its sovereign power that it no longer extends to a particular subject, manifestly it cannot, in any proper sense, be said to enact laws thereon.

[B]

Entertaining these views we are brought directly and unavoidably to the consideration of the question, whether the grant of the commercial power to Congress, did *per se* deprive the states of all power to regulate pilots. This question has never been decided by this court, nor, in our judgment, has any case depending upon all the considerations which must govern this one, come before this court. The grant of commercial power to Congress does not contain any terms which expressly exclude the states from exercising an authority over its subject-matter. If they are excluded it must be because the nature of the power, thus granted to Congress, requires that a similar authority should not exist in the states.

The diversities of opinion, therefore, which have existed on this subject, have arisen from the different views taken of the nature of this power. But when the nature of a power like this is spoken of, when it is said that the nature of the power requires that it should be exercised exclusively by Congress, it must be intended to refer to the subjects of that power, and to say they are of such a nature as to require exclusive legislation by Congress. Now the power to regulate commerce, embraces a vast field, containing not only many, but exceedingly various subjects, quite unlike in their nature; some imperatively demanding a single uniform rule, operating equally on the commerce of the United States in every port; and some, like the subject now in question, as imperatively demanding that diversity, which alone can meet the local necessities of navigation.

[C]

Either absolutely to affirm, or deny that the nature of this power requires exclusive legislation by Congress, is to lose sight of the nature of the subjects of this power, and to assert concerning all of them, what is really applicable but to a part. Whatever subjects of this power are in their nature national, or admit only of one uniform system, or plan of regulation, may justly be said to be of such a nature as to require exclusive legislation by Congress. That this cannot be affirmed of laws for the regulation of pilots and pilotage is plain. The act of 1789 contains a clear and authoritative declaration by the first Congress, that the nature of this subject is such, that until Congress should find it necessary to exert its power, it should be left to the legislation of the states; that it is local and not national; that it is likely to be the best provided for, not by one system, or plan of regulations, but by as many as the legislative discretion of the several states should deem applicable to the local peculiarities of the ports within their limits.

[The] act of 1789 manifests the understanding of Congress, at the outset of the government, that the nature of this subject is not such as to require its exclusive legislation. The practice of the states, and of the national government, has been in conformity with this declaration, from the origin of the national government to this time; and the nature of the subject when examined, is such as to leave no doubt of the superior fitness and propriety, not to say the absolute necessity, of different systems of regulation, drawn from local knowledge and experience, and conformed to local wants. How then can we say, that by the mere grant of power to regulate commerce, the states are deprived of all the power to legislate on this subject, because from the nature of the power the legislation of Congress must be exclusive. This would be to affirm that the nature of the power is in any case, something different from the nature of the subject to which, in such case, the power extends, and that the nature of the power necessarily demands, in all cases, exclusive legislation by Congress, while the nature of one of the subjects of that power, not only does not require such exclusive legislation, but may be best provided for by many different systems enacted by the states, in conformity with the circumstances of the ports within their limits. In construing an instrument designed for the formation of a government, and in determining the extent of one of its important grants of power to legislate, we can make no such distinction between the nature of the power and the nature of the subject on which that power was intended practically to operate, nor consider the grant more extensive by affirming of the power, what is not true of its subject now in question.

It is the opinion of a majority of the court that the mere grant to Congress of the power to regulate commerce, did not deprive the states of power to regulate pilots, and that although Congress has legislated on this subject, its legislation manifests an intention not to regulate this subject, but to leave its regulation to the several states.

[D]

We have not adverted to the practical consequences of holding that the states possess no power to legislate for the regulation of pilots, though in our apprehension these would be of the most serious importance. For more than sixty years this subject has been acted on by the states, and the systems of some of them created and of others essentially modified during that period. To hold that pilotage fees and penalties demanded and received during that time, have been illegally exacted, under color of void laws, would work an amount of mischief which a clear conviction of constitutional duty, if entertained, must force us to occasion, but which could be viewed by no just mind without deep regret. Nor would the mischief be limited to the past. If Congress were now to pass a law adopting the existing state laws, if enacted without authority, and in violation of the Constitution, it would seem to us to be a new and questionable mode of legislation.

We are of opinion that this state law was enacted by virtue of a power, residing in the state to legislate; that it is not in conflict with any law of Congress; that it does not interfere with any system which Congress has established by making regulations, or by intentionally leaving individuals to their own unrestricted action; that this law is therefore valid, and the judgment of the Supreme Court of Pennsylvania in each case must be affirmed.

MR. JUSTICE MCLEAN and MR. JUSTICE WAYNE dissented; and MR. JUSTICE DANIEL, although he concurred in the judgment of the court, yet dissented from its reasoning.

MR. JUSTICE MCLEAN.

It is with regret that I feel myself obliged to dissent from the opinion of a majority of my brethren in this case.

Why did Congress pass the act of 1789, adopting the pilot-laws of the respective states? Laws they unquestionably were, having been enacted by the states before the adoption of the Constitution. But were they laws under the Constitution? If they had been so considered by Congress, they would not have been adopted by a special act.

Congress adopted the pilot-laws of the states, because it was well understood, they could have had no force, as regulations of foreign commerce or of commerce among the states, if not so adopted. By their adoption they were made acts of Congress, and ever since they have been so considered and enforced.

Each state regulates the commerce within its limits; which is not within the range of federal powers. So far, and no farther could effect have been given to the pilot laws of the states, under the Constitution. But those laws were only adopted 'until further legislative provisions shall be made by Congress.'

This shows that Congress claimed the whole commercial power on this subject, by adopting the pilot laws of the states, making them acts of Congress; and also by declaring that the adoption was only until some further legislative provision could be made by Congress.

That a state may regulate foreign commerce, or commerce among the states, is a doctrine which has been advanced by individual judges of this court; but never before, I believe, has such a power been sanctioned by the decision of this court. In this case, the power to regulate pilots is admitted to belong to the commercial power of Congress; and yet it is held, that a state, by virtue of its inherent power, may regulate the subject, until such regulation shall be annulled by Congress. This is the principle established by this decision. Its language is guarded, in order to apply the decision only to the case before the court. But such restriction can never operate, so as to render the principle inapplicable to other cases. And it is in this light that the decision is chiefly to be regretted. The power is recognised in the state, because the subject is more appropriate for state than federal action; and consequently, it must be presumed the Constitution cannot have intended to inhibit state action. This is not a rule by which the Constitution is to be construed. It can receive but little support from the discussions which took place on the adoption of the Constitution, and none at all from the earlier decisions of this court.

It will be found that the principle in this case, if carried out, will deeply affect the commercial prosperity of the country. If a state has power to regulate foreign commerce, such regulation must be held valid, until Congress shall repeal or annul it. How can the unconstitutional acts of Louisiana, or of any other state which has ports on the Mississippi, or the Ohio, or on any of our other rivers, be corrected, without the action of Congress? And when Congress shall act, the state has only to change its ground, in order to enact and enforce its regulations.

From this race of legislation between Congress and the states, and between the states, if this principle be maintained, will arise a conflict similar to that which existed before the adoption of the Constitution. The states favorably situated, as Louisiana, may levy a contribution upon the commerce of other states which shall be sufficient to meet the expenditures of the states.

Mr. Justice Daniel [Opinion omitted].

EXERCISE 4:

1. Are you persuaded that pilotage is "commerce" within the meaning of the Commerce Clause?

2. If you are, are there portions of "commerce" that are national in scope, as the majority finds, and portions that are local? Is your answer different for 1851 than today?

3. If you agree that some "commerce" is local and some is national, does it follow that Congress does not have exclusive legislative authority over the portion of "commerce" that is local?

4. Is the Court's distinction between national and local commerce one that courts can apply in a principled manner?

6. What argument from political theory may support the Court's rule?

7. What role do the *FEDERALIST PAPERS* play in the Court's reasoning? Is that a proper role?

8. Is the majority correct that exclusive congressional control of commerce would lead to disastrous results? What role did these policy considerations play in the Supreme Court's decision? Was the majority or Justice McLean (more) correct?

9. Are you persuaded by Justice McLean's argument that the Act passed by Congress in 1789, 1 Stat. 55 (1789), showed that states did *not* retain the authority to regulate matters that affected interstate commerce? Is there another way to characterize Congress' action? Which characterization is most accurate? How do you know?

10. What forms of argument does Justice McLean muster to support his position?

11. Justice McLean argues that the majority's ruling, which allows states to regulate commerce, cannot be cabined. "The noted *Blackbird Creek* case shows what little influence the facts and circumstances of a case can have in restraining the principle it is supposed to embody." Do you agree?

———————

A further distinction the Supreme Court articulated to distinguish activities states could regulate from those they could not regulate, consistent with the Commerce Clause, was the direct-indirect effects dichotomy discussed in the next case. You saw a version of this in Volume 3 when you covered the Interstate Commerce Clause.

DI SANTO v. COMMONWEALTH OF PENNSYLVANIA
273 U.S. 34 (1927)

MR. JUSTICE BUTLER delivered the opinion of the Court.

Plaintiff in error was indicted in Pennsylvania for a violation of an Act of the Legislature of May 20, 1921, requiring licenses to sell steamship tickets or orders for transportation to or from foreign countries. The indictment alleged that, without having obtained a license so to do, plaintiff in error held himself out as authorized to sell tickets and orders for transportation as agent of certain steamship companies, and that he engaged in the sale of such tickets. There was no controversy as to the facts, and, by direction of the court, the jury returned to verdict of guilty. Plaintiff in error, by motion in arrest of judgment, challenged the validity of the act on the ground that it contravenes the commerce clause of the federal Constitution. The court held the statute, valid, and sentenced him to pay a fine.

The state Supreme Court declared that the act is one to prevent fraud. [Di Santo brought a writ of error to the U.S. Supreme Court.]

The soliciting of passengers and the sale of steamship tickets and orders for passage between the United States and Europe constitute a well-recognized part of foreign commerce. A state statute which by its necessary operation directly interferes with or burdens foreign commerce is a prohibited regulation and invalid, regardless of the purpose with which it was passed. Such legislation cannot be sustained as an exertion of the police power of the state to prevent possible fraud. The Congress has complete and paramount authority to regulate foreign commerce and, by appropriate measures, to protect the public against the frauds of those who sell these tickets and orders.

The sales here in question are related to foreign commerce as directly as are sales made in ticket offices maintained by the carriers and operated by their servants and employees. The license fee and other things imposed by the act on plaintiff in error, who initiates for his principals a transaction in foreign commerce, constitute a direct burden on that commerce.

Judgment reversed.

MR. JUSTICE BRANDEIS, with whom MR. JUSTICE HOLMES concurs, dissenting.

The statute is an exertion of the police power of the state. Its evident purpose is to prevent a particular species of fraud and imposition found to have been practiced in Pennsylvania upon persons of small means, unfamiliar with our language and institutions.

Although the purchase made is of an ocean steamship ticket, the transaction regulated is wholly intrastate. There is no purpose on the part of the state to regulate foreign commerce. The statute is not an obstruction to foreign commerce. It does not discriminate against foreign commerce. It places no direct burden upon such commerce. It does not affect the commerce except indirectly. Congress could, of course, deal with the subject, because it is connected with foreign commerce. But it has not done so. Nor has it legislated on any allied subject. Thus, there can be no contention that Congress has occupied the field. And obviously, also, this is not a case in which the silence of Congress can be interpreted as a prohibition of state action. If Pennsylvania must submit to seeing its citizens defrauded, it is not because Congress has so willed, but because the Constitution so commands. I cannot believe that it does.

While the question whether a particular statute has the effect of burdening interstate or foreign commerce directly presents always a question of law, the determination upon which the validity or invalidity of the statute depends is largely or wholly one of fact. The rule of law which governs is that a State may not obstruct, discriminate against or directly burden interstate or foreign commerce. The question at bar is whether as applied to existing facts this particular statute is a direct burden. The decision as to state regulations of this character, depends often, 'upon their effect upon interstate commerce.' Each case require[s] the decision of the question of law. Each involve[s] merely an appreciation of the facts. [None] involved the declaration of a [new] rule of law.

MR. JUSTICE STONE, dissenting.

I agree with all that MR. JUSTICE BRANDEIS has said, but I would add a word with respect to one phase of the matter which seems to me of some importance.

In this case the traditional test of the limit of state action by inquiring whether the interference with commerce is direct or indirect seems to me too mechanical, too uncertain in its application, and too remote from actualities, to be of value. In thus making use of the expressions, 'direct' and 'indirect interference' with commerce, we are doing little more than using labels to describe a result rather than any trustworthy formula by which it is reached.

Interferences not deemed forbidden are to be sustained, not because the effect on commerce is nominally indirect, but because a consideration of all the facts and circumstances, such as the nature of the regulation, its function, the character of the business involved and the actual effect on the flow of commerce, lead to the conclusion that the regulation concerns interests peculiarly local and does not infringe the national interest in maintaining the freedom of commerce across state lines.

I am not persuaded that the regulation here is more than local in character or that it interposes any barrier to commerce. Until Congress undertakes the protection of local communities from the dishonesty of the sellers of steamship tickets, it would seem that there is no adequate ground for holding that the regulation here involved is a prohibited interference with commerce.

Mr. Justice Holmes and Mr. Justice Brandeis concur in this opinion.

EXERCISE 5:

1. What dichotomy does the Supreme Court utilize to distinguish those aspects of commerce subject to state regulation from those not subject to such regulation?

2. What is the source of this dichotomy?

3. On what basis does the Court determine whether the regulation is direct or indirect?

4. The three dissenters, Justices Holmes, Brandeis, and Stone, were well-known legal realists and progressives. One of the tenets of Legal Realism was that categories like "direct" and "indirect" were matters of degree and not of kind. As a result, legislatures have an institutional competence greater than courts in deciding where the line between intrastate and interstate commerce should be drawn. What in the dissenting opinions fits this proposition?

5. Do you agree that courts can draw a line between direct and indirect effects on interstate commerce in a principled manner? Does the division of the Court itself show that the Court cannot consistently apply the dichotomy?

6. When you read *Southern Pacific Co. v. Arizona*, 325 U.S. 761 (1945), below, consider how the dissenting Justices' concern in *Di Santo* impacts the Supreme Court's dormant Commerce Clause doctrine.

D. NEW DEAL REVISIONS

During the New Deal, this area of constitutional law, like many others, changed. In its dormant Commerce Clause jurisprudence, the Supreme Court rejected the distinctions drawn in its prior case law between those areas of social life subject to state regulation and those areas subject to federal regulation. For example, in *Cooley v. Board of Wardens*, 53 U.S. (12 How.) 299 (1851), reprinted above, the Supreme Court distinguished subjects that were local in nature, which states could regulate, and subjects that were national in nature, which only the federal government could regulate.

In place of this and other similar distinctions, the Court articulated a balancing approach to determine when state regulation violated the dormant Commerce Clause. This balancing analysis continues to play a prominent role today. Below, in *Southern Pacific Co. v. Arizona*, 325 U.S. 761 (1945), the Supreme Court built on the balancing test it had used earlier, though implicitly, in *South Carolina State Highway Dep't v. Barnwell Bros.*, 303 U.S. 177 (1938).

The changes in constitutional law during the New Deal were the result of many factors. In the academic realm, the movement in American legal thought known as Legal Realism found on the Supreme Court a sympathetic majority. One of the central claims of legal realists was that tests like those utilized by the Court over the nineteenth century in its dormant Commerce Clause jurisprudence—police power vs. commerce, local vs. national, and direct vs. indirect—were masks for the inevitable balancing the justices were doing when they decided these cases. The realists argued that the justices balanced the costs and benefits of their decision and then, based on that balancing, chose the category into which the challenged activity fell. For instance, if the justices believed that the challenged state regulation resulted in more benefits than costs, they would find that the regulation was a "police power" regulation, or that it was regulating "local" activity, or that it had only an "indirect" effect on interstate commerce. By explicitly balancing the costs and benefits of a regulation, realists asserted, Supreme Court decisions would be more transparent and, therefore, better.

SOUTHERN PACIFIC CO. v. STATE OF ARIZONA EX REL. SULLIVAN, ATTORNEY GENERAL OF ARIZONA
325 U.S. 761 (1945)

Mr. Chief Justice Stone delivered the opinion of the Court.

The Arizona Train Limit Law of May 16, 1912, makes it unlawful for any person or corporation to operate within the state a railroad train of more than fourteen passenger or seventy freight cars . The question[] for decision [is] whether the statute contravenes the commerce clause of the federal Constitution.

In 1940 the State of Arizona brought suit in the Arizona Superior Court against appellant, the Southern Pacific Company, to recover the statutory penalties for operating within the state two interstate trains, one a passenger train of more than fourteen cars, and one a freight train of more than seventy cars. Appellant answered, admitting the train operations, but defended on the ground that the statute offends against the commerce clause. After an extended trial, without a jury, the court made detailed findings of fact on the basis of which it gave judgment for the railroad company. The Supreme Court of Arizona reversed and directed judgment for the state. The case comes here on appeal.

The Supreme Court sustained the Act as a safety measure to reduce the number of accidents attributed to the operation of trains of more than the statutory maximum length, enacted by the state legislature in the exercise of its 'police power'. It thought that a state statute, enacted in the exercise of the police power, and bearing some reasonable relation to the health, safety and well-being of the people of the state, of which the state legislature is the judge, was not to be judicially overturned, notwithstanding its admittedly adverse effect on the operation of interstate trains.

Although the commerce clause conferred on the national government power to regulate commerce, its possession of the power does not exclude all state power of regulation. Ever since *Willson v. Black-Bird Creek Marsh Co.*, [27 U.S.] (2 Pet.) 245, and *Cooley v. Board of Wardens*, 53 U.S. [(12 How.)] 299 (1852), it has been recognized that, in the absence of conflicting legislation by Congress, there is a residuum of power in the state to make laws governing matters of local concern which nevertheless in some measure affect interstate commerce or even, to some extent, regulate it. *South Carolina State Highway Department v. Barnwell Bros.*, 303 U.S. 177 (1938). Thus the states may regulate matters which, because of their number and diversity, may never be adequately dealt with by Congress. *Cooley v. Board of Wardens*; *South Carolina State Highway Department v. Barnwell Bros.* When the regulation of matters of local concern is local in character and effect, and its impact on the national commerce does not seriously interfere with its operation, and the consequent incentive to deal with them nationally is slight, such regulation has been generally held to be within state authority. *South Carolina Highway Dept. v. Barnwell Bros.*

But ever since *Gibbons v. Ogden*, 22 U.S. [(9 Wheat.)] 1 (1824), the states have not been deemed to have authority to impede substantially the free flow of commerce from state to state, or to regulate those phases of the national commerce which, because of the need of national uniformity, demand that their regulation, if any, be prescribed by a single authority.[2] *Cooley v. Board of Wardens*. Whether or not this long recognized distribution of power between the national and the state governments is predicated upon the implications of the commerce clause itself, *Brown v. State of Maryland*, 25 U.S. [(12 Wheat.)] 419 (1827); *South Carolina State Highway Department v. Barnwell Bros.*, or upon the presumed intention of Congress, where Congress has not spoken, the result is the same.

In the application of these principles some enactments may be found to be plainly within and others plainly without state power. But between these extremes lies the infinite variety of cases in which regulation of local matters may also operate as a regulation of commerce, in which reconciliation of the conflicting claims of state and

---

2. In applying this rule the Court has often recognized that to the extent that the burden of state regulation falls on interests outside the state, it is unlikely to be alleviated by the operation of those political restraints normally exerted when interests within the state are affected. *Cooley v. Board of Wardens*; *South Carolina State Highway Department v. Barnwell Bros.*

national power is to be attained only by some appraisal and accommodation of the competing demands of the state and national interests involved. *Di Santo v. Commonwealth of Pennsylvania*, 273 U.S. 34 (1927).

For a hundred years it has been accepted constitutional doctrine that the commerce clause, without the aid of Congressional legislation, thus affords some protection from state legislation inimical to the national commerce, and that in such cases, where Congress has not acted, this Court, and not the state legislature, is under the commerce clause the final arbiter of the competing demands of state and national interests. *Cooley v. Board of Wardens.*

Congress has undoubted power to redefine the distribution of power over interstate commerce. It may either permit the states to regulate the commerce in a manner which would otherwise not be permissible, or exclude state regulation even of matters of peculiarly local concern which nevertheless affect interstate commerce.

But in general Congress has left it to the courts to formulate the rules thus interpreting the commerce clause in its application, doubtless because it has appreciated the destructive consequences to the commerce of the nation if their protection were withdrawn, and has been aware that in their application state laws will not be invalidated without the support of relevant factual material which will 'afford a sure basis' for an informed judgment. Meanwhile, Congress has accommodated its legislation, as have the states, to these rules as an established feature of our constitutional system. There has thus been left to the states wide scope for the regulation of matters of local state concern, even though it in some measure affects the commerce, provided it does not materially restrict the free flow of commerce across state lines, or interfere with it in matters with respect to which uniformity of regulation is of predominant national concern.

Hence the matters for ultimate determination here are the nature and extent of the burden which the state regulation of interstate trains, adopted as a safety measure, imposes on interstate commerce, and whether the relative weights of the state and national interests involved are such as to make inapplicable the rule, generally observed, that the free flow of interstate commerce and its freedom from local restraints in matters requiring uniformity of regulation are interests safeguarded by the commerce clause from state interference.

The findings [of the trial court] show that the operation of long trains, that is trains of more than fourteen passenger and more than seventy freight cars, is standard practice over the main lines of the railroads of the United States, and that, if the length of trains is to be regulated at all, national uniformity in the regulation adopted, such as only Congress can prescribe, is practically indispensable to the operation of an efficient and economical national railway system. On many railroads passenger trains of more than fourteen cars and freight trains of more than seventy cars are operated, and on some systems freight trains are run ranging from one hundred and twenty-five to one hundred and sixty cars in length.

In Arizona, approximately 93% of the freight traffic and 95% of the passenger traffic is interstate. Because of the Train Limit Law appellant is required to haul over 30% more trains in Arizona than would otherwise have been necessary. The record shows a definite relationship between operating costs and the length of trains, the increase in length resulting in a reduction of operating costs per car. The additional cost of operation of trains complying with the Train Limit Law in Arizona amounts for the two railroads traversing that state to about $1,000,000 a year. The reduction in train lengths also impedes efficient operation. More locomotives and more manpower are required; the necessary conversion and reconversion of train lengths at terminals and the delay caused by breaking up and remaking long trains upon entering and leaving the state in order to comply with the law, delays the traffic and diminishes its volume moved in a given time, especially when traffic is heavy.

The unchallenged findings leave no doubt that the Arizona Train Limit Law imposes a serious burden on the interstate commerce conducted by appellant. It materially impedes the movement of appellant's interstate trains through that state and interposes a substantial obstruction to the national policy proclaimed by Congress, to promote adequate, economical and efficient railway transportation service.

Although the seventy car maximum for freight trains is the limitation which has been most commonly proposed, various bills introduced in the state legislatures provided for maximum freight train lengths of from fifty to one hundred and twenty-five cars, and maximum passenger train lengths of from ten to eighteen cars. With such laws in force in states which are interspersed with those having no limit on train lengths, the confusion and difficulty with which interstate operations would be burdened under the varied system of state regulation and the unsatisfied need for uniformity in such regulation, if any, are evident.

At present the seventy freight car laws are enforced only in Arizona and Oklahoma, with a fourteen car passenger car limit in Arizona. The record here shows that the enforcement of the Arizona statute results in freight trains being broken up and reformed at the California border and in New Mexico, some distance from the Arizona line. Frequently it is not feasible to operate a newly assembled train from the New Mexico yard nearest to Arizona, with the result that the Arizona limitation governs the flow of traffic as far east as El Paso, Texas. For similar reasons the Arizona law often controls the length of passenger trains all the way from Los Angeles to El Paso.

The trial court found that such increased danger of accident and personal injury as may result from the greater length of trains is more than offset by the increase in the number of accidents resulting from the larger number of trains when train lengths are reduced. In considering the effect of the statute as a safety measure, therefore, the factor of controlling significance for present purposes is not whether there is basis for the conclusion of the Arizona Supreme Court that the increase in length of trains beyond the statutory maximum has an adverse effect upon safety of operation. The decisive question is whether in the circumstances the total effect of the law as a safety measure in reducing accidents and casualties is so slight or problematical as not to outweigh the national interest in keeping interstate commerce free from interferences which seriously impede it and subject it to local regulation which does not have a uniform effect on the interstate train journey which it interrupts.

The principal source of danger of accident from increased length of trains is the resulting increase of 'slack action' of the train. Slack action is the amount of free movement of one car before it transmits its motion to an adjoining coupled car. The length of the train increases the slack since the slack action of a train is the total of the free movement between its several cars. The amount of slack action has some effect on the severity of the shock of train movements, and on freight trains some-times results in injuries to operatives, which most frequently occur to occupants of the caboose. On comparison of the number of slack action accidents in Arizona with those in Nevada, where the length of trains is now unregulated, the trial court found that with substantially the same amount of traffic in each state the number of accidents was relatively the same in long as in short train operations. While accidents from slack action do occur in the operation of passenger trains, it does not appear that they are more frequent or the resulting shocks more severe on long than on short passenger trains. Nor does it appear that slack action accidents occurring on pas-senger trains, whatever their length, are of sufficient severity to cause serious injury or damage.

As the trial court found, reduction of the length of trains also tends to increase the number of accidents because of the increase in the number of trains. The appli-cation of the Arizona law compelled appellant to operate 30.08%, or 4,304, more freight trains in 1938 than would otherwise have been necessary. And the record amply supports the trial court's conclusion that the frequency of accidents is closely related to the number of trains run. The number of accidents due to grade crossing collisions between trains and motor vehicles and pedestrians, and to collisions between trains, which are usually far more serious than those due to slack action and accidents due to locomotive failures, in general vary with the number of trains. Increase in the number of trains results in more starts and stops, more 'meets' and 'passes', and more switching movements, all tending to increase the number of acci-dents not only to train operatives and other railroad employees, but to passengers and members of the public exposed to danger by train operations.

The principle that, without controlling Congressional action, a state may not regulate interstate commerce so as substantially to affect its flow or deprive it of needed uniformity in its regulation is not to be avoided by 'simply invoking the con-venient apologetics of the police power.' Here we conclude that the state does go too far. Its regulation of train lengths, admittedly obstructive to interstate train operation, and having a seriously adverse effect on transportation efficiency and economy, passes beyond what is plainly essential for safety since it does not appear that it will lessen rather than increase the danger of accident. Its attempted regulation of the operation of interstate trains cannot establish nation-wide control such as is essential to the maintenance of an efficient transportation system, which Congress alone can prescribe. The state interest cannot be preserved at the expense of the national inter-est by an enactment which regulates interstate train lengths without securing such control, which is a matter of national concern. To this the interest of the state here asserted is subordinate.

[Under the dormant commerce clause, courts must] enter into a determination of the relative weights of state and national interests where state regulation affecting interstate commerce is attempted. Here examination of all the relevant factors makes it plain that the state interest is outweighed by the interest of the nation in an ade-quate, economical and efficient railway transportation service, which must prevail.

Reversed.

MR. JUSTICE RUTLEDGE concurs in the result.

MR. JUSTICE BLACK, dissenting.

Under circumstances [where there is conflicting evidence], the determination of whether it is in the interest of society for the length of trains to be governmentally regulated is a matter of public policy. Someone must fix that policy—either the Con-gress, or the state, or the courts. A century and a half of constitutional history and government admonishes this Court to leave that choice to the elected legislative rep-resentatives of the people themselves, where it properly belongs both on democratic principles and the requirements of efficient government.

[Justice Black reviewed the extensive controversy on both the state and federal lev-els over whether to regulate train length and, if so, what regulation(s) to adopt. Justice Black emphasized the substantial evidence supporting the respective positions.]

I think that legislatures, to the exclusion of courts, have the constitutional power to enact laws limiting train lengths, for the purpose of reducing injuries. Their power is not less because a requirement of short trains might increase grade crossing acci-dents. This latter fact raises an entirely different element of danger which is itself sub-ject to legislative regulation. For legislatures may, if necessary, require railroads to take appropriate steps to reduce the likelihood of injuries at grade crossings.

The Supreme Court of Arizona properly designated the Arizona statute as a safety measure, and finding that it bore a reasonable relation to its purpose declined to review the judgment of the legislature as to the necessity for the passage of the act. In so doing it was well fortified by a long line of decisions of this Court. Today's deci-sion marks an abrupt departure from that line of cases.

There have been many sharp divisions of this Court concerning its authority, in the absence of congressional enactment, to invalidate state laws as violating the Com-merce Clause. That discussion need not be renewed here, because even the broadest exponents of judicial power in this field have not heretofore expressed doubt as to a state's power, absent a paramount congressional declaration, to regulate interstate trains in the interest of safety.

In [none of the Court's] cases was it more appropriate than here to call attention to the fact that Congress could when it pleased establish a uniform rule as to the length of trains. Congress knew about the Arizona law. It is common knowledge that the Interstate Commerce Committees of the House and the Senate keep in close and intimate touch with the affairs of railroads and other national means of transportation. The attention of the members of Congress and of the Senate have been focused on the particular problem of the length of railroad trains. We cannot assume that they were ignorant of the commonly known fact that a long train might be more dangerous in some territories and on some particular types of railroad. The history of congressional consideration of this problem leaves little if any room to doubt that the choice of Congress to leave the state free in this field was a deliberate choice, which was taken with a full knowledge of the complexities of the problems and the probable need for diverse regulations in different localities. I am therefore compelled to reach the conclusion that today's decision is the result of the belief of a majority of this Court that both the legislature of Arizona and the Congress made wrong policy decisions in permitting a law to stand which limits the length of railroad trains. I should at least give the Arizona statute the benefit of the same rule which this Court said should be applied in connection with state legislation under attack for violating the Fourteenth Amendment, that is, that legislative bodies have 'a wide range of legislative discretion, and their conclusions respecting the wisdom of their legislative acts are not reviewable by the courts.'

When we finally get down to the gist of what the Court today actually decides, it is this: Even though more railroad employees will be injured by 'slack action' movements on long trains than on short trains, there must be no regulation of this danger in the absence of 'uniform regulations.' That means that no one can legislate against this danger except the Congress; and even though the Congress is perfectly content to leave the matter to the different state legislatures, this Court, on the ground of 'lack of uniformity', will require it to make an express avowal of that fact before it will permit a state to guard against that admitted danger.

This record in its entirety leaves me with no doubt whatever that many employees have been seriously injured and killed in the past, and that many more are likely to be so in the future, because of 'slack movement' in trains. Everyday knowledge as well as direct evidence presented at the various hearings, substantiates the report of the Senate Committee that the danger from slack movement is greater in long trains than in short trains. It may be that offsetting dangers are possible in the operation of short trains. The balancing of these probabilities, however, is not in my judgment a matter for judicial determination, but one which calls for legislative consideration. Representatives elected by the people to make their laws, rather than judges appointed to interpret those laws, can best determine the policies which govern the people. That at least is the basic principle on which our democratic society rests. I would affirm the judgment of the Supreme Court of Arizona.

MR. JUSTICE DOUGLAS, dissenting.

I have expressed my doubts whether the courts should intervene in situations like the present and strike down state legislation on the grounds that it burdens interstate commerce. My view has been that the courts should intervene only where the state legislation discriminated against interstate commerce or was out of harmony with laws which Congress had enacted. It seems to me particularly appropriate that that course be followed here.

EXERCISE 6:

1. What analysis did the Supreme Court utilize to arrive at its conclusion? Describe the components of that analysis along with how the Court analyzed those components.

2. Some have questioned whether there was any difference between *Southern Pacific Co.* and *Barnwell* that could account for the different outcomes (the Supreme Court upheld the state regulation in *Barnwell*). Of what importance is the fact that the Interstate Commerce Commission had issued a ruling that Arizona's requirements violated the national policy of efficient train transportation? *In re Matter of Service Order No. 85,* 256 I.C.C. 523, 534.

3. How would this case have come out under the Court's previous case law?

4. How did the Supreme Court address its prior case law?

5. Was Justice Black right that state regulations, such as Arizona's, that substantially affect interstate commerce, should receive the deference due state economic regulations under the Due Process Clause?

6. Was Justice Black right that Congress had looked at the issue of train length and decided to permit the states to regulate as they saw fit?

7. Was Justice Black correct when he argued that Arizona's decision to regulate train length, and the substantive decision it made, were "policy" decisions about which reasonable persons could disagree and, hence, the Supreme Court should refrain from second-guessing Arizona?

8. Was the Supreme Court right and/or wise to utilize a balancing test in place of its previous rationales?

9. Keep Justice Douglas' argument—that the dormant Commerce Clause should forbid discriminatory state laws—in mind as we read the cases below.

E. TODAY

The key factor in application of the dormant Commerce Clause today is whether the state regulation at issue discriminates against out-of-state commerce. This determination is not as easy as it might seem, and the Supreme Court has struggled to provide workable standards to make this determination.

Below, we first review the case law on what constitutes discrimination against out-of-state commerce. Then, we cover the standards used if the state law does not discriminate and the standards if the law does discriminate, respectively. Much hinges on this characterization. If a law is found to discriminate against out-of-state commerce, it is almost always struck down. By contrast, if a law does not so discriminate, a state has a lower burden to justify the law. Next is a case where the Supreme Court articulated this analytical structure.

CITY OF PHILADELPHIA v. STATE OF NEW JERSEY
437 U.S. 617 (1978)

Mr. Justice Stewart delivered the opinion of the Court.

A New Jersey law[, ch. 363,] prohibits the importation of most "solid or liquid waste which originated or was collected outside the territorial limits of the State." In this case we are required to decide whether this statutory prohibition violates the Commerce Clause of the United States Constitution.

I

Apart from narrow exceptions [not at issue here], New Jersey closed its borders to all waste from other States.

Immediately affected by these developments were the operators of private landfills in New Jersey, and several cities in other States that had agreements with these operators for waste disposal. They brought suit against New Jersey and its Department of Environmental Protection in state court, attacking the statute. In an oral opinion granting the plaintiffs' motion for summary judgment, the trial court declared the law unconstitutional because it discriminated against interstate commerce. The New Jersey Supreme Court found that ch. 363 advanced vital health and environmental objectives with no economic discrimination against, and with little burden upon, interstate commerce, and that the law was therefore permissible under the Commerce Clause of the Constitution.

The plaintiffs then appealed to this Court.

II

Before it addressed the merits of the appellants' claim, the New Jersey Supreme Court questioned whether the interstate movement of those wastes banned by ch. 363 is "commerce" at all within the meaning of the Commerce Clause. Any doubts on that score should be laid to rest at the outset.

The state court expressed the view that there may be two definitions of "commerce" for constitutional purposes. When relied on "to support some exertion of federal control or regulation," the Commerce Clause permits "a very sweeping concept" of commerce. But when relied on "to strike down or restrict state legislation," that Clause and the term "commerce" have a "much more confined . . . reach."

The state court reached this conclusion in an attempt to reconcile modern Commerce Clause concepts with several old cases of this Court holding that States can prohibit the importation of some objects because they "are not legitimate subjects of trade and commerce." *Bowman v. Chicago & Northwestern R. Co.*, 125 U.S. 465 [(1888)]. These articles include items "which, on account of their existing condition, would bring in and spread disease, pestilence, and death, such as rags or other substances infected with the germs of yellow fever or the virus of small-pox, or cattle or meat or other provisions that are diseased or decayed, or otherwise, from their condition and quality, unfit for human use or consumption." *Ibid.*

We think the state court misread our cases, and thus erred in assuming that they require a two-tiered definition of commerce. In saying that innately harmful articles "are not legitimate subjects of trade and commerce," the *Bowman* Court was stating its conclusion, not the starting point of its reasoning. All objects of interstate trade merit Commerce Clause protection; none is excluded by definition at the outset. In *Bowman* and similar cases, the Court held simply that because the articles' worth in interstate commerce was far outweighed by the dangers inhering in their very movement, States could prohibit their transportation across state lines. Hence, we reject the state court's suggestion that the banning of "valueless" out-of-state wastes by ch. 363 implicates no constitutional protection. Just as Congress has power to regulate the interstate movement of these wastes, States are not free from constitutional scrutiny when they restrict that movement.

III

A

Although the Constitution gives Congress the power to regulate commerce among the States, many subjects of potential federal regulation under that power inevitably escape congressional attention "because of their local character and their number and diversity." *South Carolina State Highway Dep't v. Barnwell Bros., Inc.*, 303 U.S. 177 [(1938)]. In the absence of federal legislation, these subjects are open to control by the States so long as they act within the restraints imposed by the Commerce Clause itself. The bounds of these restraints appear nowhere in the words of the Commerce Clause, but have emerged gradually in the decisions of this Court giving effect to its basic purpose. That broad purpose was well expressed by Mr. Justice Jackson in his opinion for the Court in *H.P. Hood & Sons, Inc. v. Du Mond*, 336 U.S. 525 [(1949)]:

> "This principle that our economic unit is the Nation, which alone has the gamut of powers necessary to control of the economy, including the vital power of erecting customs barriers against foreign competition, has as its corollary that the states are not separable economic units."

The opinions of the Court through the years have reflected an alertness to the evils of "economic isolation" and protectionism, while at the same time recognizing that incidental burdens on interstate commerce may be unavoidable when a State legislates to safeguard the health and safety of its people. Thus, where simple economic protectionism is effected by state legislation, a virtually *per se* rule of invalidity has been erected. *See, e.g., H.P. Hood & Sons, Inc. v. Du Mond, supra.* The clearest example of such legislation is a law that overtly blocks the flow of interstate commerce at a State's borders. But where other legislative objectives are credibly advanced and there is no patent discrimination against interstate trade, the Court has adopted a much more flexible approach, the general contours of which were outlined in *Pike v. Bruce Church, Inc.*, 397 U.S. 137, 142 [(1970)]:

> "Where the statute regulates evenhandedly to effectuate a legitimate local public interest, and its effects on interstate commerce are only incidental, it will be upheld unless the burden imposed on such commerce is clearly excessive in relation to the putative local benefits. If a legitimate local purpose is found, then the question becomes one of degree. And the extent of the burden that will be tolerated will of course depend on the nature of the local interest involved, and on whether it could be promoted as well with a lesser impact on interstate activities."

See also Hunt v. Washington Apple Advertising Comm'n, 432 U.S. 333 [(1977)].

The crucial inquiry, therefore, must be directed to determining whether ch. 363 is basically a protectionist measure, or whether it can fairly be viewed as a law directed to legitimate local concerns, with effects upon interstate commerce that are only incidental.

B

The purpose of ch. 363 is set out in the statute itself as follows:

> "The Legislature finds and determines that . . . the volume of solid and liquid waste continues to rapidly increase, that the treatment and disposal of these wastes continues to pose an even greater threat to the quality of the environment of New Jersey, that the available and appropriate land fill sites within the State are being diminished, that the environment continues to be threatened by the treatment and disposal of waste which originated or was collected outside the State, and that the public health, safety and welfare require that the treatment and disposal within this State of all wastes generated outside of the State be prohibited."

Th[e parties'] dispute about ultimate legislative purpose need not be resolved, because its resolution would not be relevant to the constitutional issue to be decided in this case. Contrary to the evident assumption of the state court and the parties, the evil of protectionism can reside in legislative means as well as legislative ends. Thus, it does not matter whether the ultimate aim of ch. 363 is to reduce the waste disposal costs of New Jersey residents or to save remaining open lands from pollution, for we assume New Jersey has every right to protect its residents' pocketbooks as well as their environment. And it may be assumed as well that New Jersey may pursue those ends by slowing the flow of *all* waste into the State's remaining landfills, even though interstate commerce may incidentally be affected. But whatever New Jersey's ultimate purpose, it may not be accomplished by discriminating against articles of commerce coming from outside the State unless there is some reason, apart from their origin, to treat them differently. Both on its face and in its plain effect, ch. 363 violates this principle of nondiscrimination.

The Court has consistently found parochial legislation of this kind to be constitutionally invalid, whether the ultimate aim of the legislation was to assure a steady supply of milk by erecting barriers to allegedly ruinous outside competition, or to create jobs by keeping industry within the State, or to preserve the State's financial resources from depletion by fencing out indigent immigrants. In each of these cases, a presumably legitimate goal was sought to be achieved by the illegitimate means of isolating the State from the national economy. Also relevant here are the Court's decisions holding that a State may not accord its own inhabitants a preferred right of access over consumers in other States to natural resources located within its borders. These cases stand for the basic principle that a "State is without power to prevent privately owned articles of trade from being shipped and sold in interstate commerce on the ground that they are required to satisfy local demands or because they are needed by the people of the State."

The New Jersey law at issue in this case falls squarely within the area that the Commerce Clause puts off limits to state regulation. On its face, it imposes on out-of-state commercial interests the full burden of conserving the State's remaining landfill space. It is true that in our previous cases the scarce natural resource was itself the article of commerce, whereas here the scarce resource and the article of commerce are distinct. But that difference is without consequence. In both instances, the State has overtly moved to slow or freeze the flow of commerce for protectionist reasons. It does not matter that the State has shut the article of commerce inside the State in one case and outside the State in the other. What is crucial is the attempt by one State to isolate itself from a problem common to many by erecting a barrier against the movement of interstate trade.

The appellees argue that not all laws which facially discriminate against out-of-state commerce are forbidden protectionist regulations. In particular, they point to quarantine laws, which this Court has repeatedly upheld even though they appear to single out interstate commerce for special treatment. In the appellees' view, ch. 363 is analogous to such health-protective measures, since it reduces the exposure of New Jersey residents to the allegedly harmful effects of landfill sites.

It is true that certain quarantine laws have not been considered forbidden protectionist measures, even though they were directed against out-of-state commerce. But those quarantine laws banned the importation of articles such as diseased livestock that required destruction as soon as possible because their very movement risked contagion and other evils. Those laws thus did not discriminate against interstate commerce as such, but simply prevented traffic in noxious articles, whatever their origin.

The New Jersey statute is not such a quarantine law. There has been no claim here that the very movement of waste into or through New Jersey endangers health, or that waste must be disposed of as soon and as close to its point of generation as possible. The harms caused by waste are said to arise after its disposal in landfill sites, and at that point, as New Jersey concedes, there is no basis to distinguish out-of-state waste from domestic waste. If one is inherently harmful, so is the other. Yet New Jersey has banned the former while leaving its landfill sites open to the latter. The New Jersey law blocks the importation of waste in an obvious effort to saddle those outside the State with the entire burden of slowing the flow of refuse into New Jersey's remaining landfill sites. That legislative effort is clearly impermissible under the Commerce Clause of the Constitution.

Today, cities in Pennsylvania and New York find it expedient or necessary to send their waste into New Jersey for disposal, and New Jersey claims the right to close its borders to such traffic. Tomorrow, cities in New Jersey may find it expedient or necessary to send their waste into Pennsylvania or New York for disposal, and those States might then claim the right to close their borders. The Commerce Clause will protect New Jersey in the future, just as it protects her neighbors now, from efforts by one State to isolate itself in the stream of interstate commerce from a problem shared by all. The judgment is

Reversed.

MR. JUSTICE REHNQUIST, with whom THE CHIEF JUSTICE joins, dissenting.

A growing problem in our Nation is the sanitary treatment and disposal of solid waste. For many years, solid waste was incinerated. Because of the significant environmental problems attendant on incineration, however, this method of solid waste disposal has declined in use in many localities, including New Jersey. "Sanitary" landfills have replaced incineration as the principal method of disposing of solid waste. In ch. 363 the State of New Jersey legislatively recognized the unfortunate fact that landfills also present extremely serious health and safety problems. First, in New Jersey, "virtually all sanitary landfills can be expected to produce leachate, a noxious and highly polluted liquid which is seldom visible and frequently pollutes . . . ground and surface waters." The natural decomposition process which occurs in landfills also produces large quantities of methane and thereby presents a significant explosion hazard. Landfills can also generate "health hazards caused by rodents, fires and scavenger birds" and, "needless to say, do not help New Jersey's aesthetic appearance nor New Jersey's noise or water or air pollution problems."

The health and safety hazards associated with landfills present appellees with a currently unsolvable dilemma. Other, hopefully safer, methods of disposing of solid wastes are still in the development stage and cannot presently be used. But appellees obviously cannot completely stop the tide of solid waste that its citizens will produce in the interim. For the moment, therefore, appellees must continue to use sanitary landfills to dispose of New Jersey's own solid waste despite the critical environmental problems thereby created.

The question presented in this case is whether New Jersey must also continue to receive and dispose of solid waste from neighboring States, even though these will inexorably increase the health problems discussed above. The Court answers this question in the affirmative. New Jersey must either prohibit *all* landfill operations, leaving itself to cast about for a presently nonexistent solution to the serious problem of disposing of the waste generated within its own borders, or it must accept waste from every portion of the United States, thereby multiplying the health and safety problems which would result if it dealt only with such wastes generated within the State. Because past precedents establish that the Commerce Clause does not present appellees with such a Hobson's choice, I dissent.

The Court recognizes that States can prohibit the importation of items " 'which, on account of their existing condition, would bring in and spread disease, pestilence, and death.' " As the Court points out, such "quarantine laws have not been considered forbidden protectionist measures, *even though they were directed against out-of-state commerce.*"

In my opinion, these cases are dispositive of the present one. Under them, New Jersey may require germ-infected rags or diseased meat to be disposed of as best as possible within the State, but at the same time prohibit the *importation* of such items for disposal at the facilities that are set up within New Jersey for disposal of such material generated *within* the State. The physical fact of life that New Jersey must somehow dispose of its own noxious items does not mean that it must serve as a depository for those of every other State. Similarly, New Jersey should be free under our past precedents to prohibit the importation of solid waste because of the health and safety problems that such waste poses to its citizens. The fact that New Jersey continues to, and indeed must continue to, dispose of its own solid waste does not mean that New Jersey may not prohibit the importation of even more solid waste into the State. I simply see no way to distinguish solid waste, on the record of this case, from germ-infected rags, diseased meat, and other noxious items.

EXERCISE 7:

1. Who had the better argument over whether waste is an article of commerce, the majority or dissent? Despite the majority's conclusion, some of the Court's precedents seemed to support the contrary conclusion that waste was not an article of commerce. We will see one such instance in *Pike v. Bruce Church*, 397 U.S. 137 (1970), discussed below.

2. How did the majority determine that the New Jersey statute at issue discriminated against out-of-state commerce?

3. How did the Court distinguish quarantine laws which it had repeatedly upheld? Articulate a counter-argument.

4. Once the Court determined that New Jersey discriminated against interstate commerce, what analysis did the Court use to determine if the statute violated the dormant Commerce Clause?

5. What policies would be served by utilizing, as the lower state court suggested, two different definitions of commerce, one for when Congress is regulating commerce, and a second when states are regulating it?

1. Does the State Regulation Discriminate against Out-of-State Commerce

We first review how the Supreme Court determines whether a state statute discriminates against out-of-state commerce.

a. Facially Discriminatory Statutes

Often, the distinction between in- and out-of-state commerce is clear on the statute's face. For example, in *Granholm v. Heald*, 544 U.S. 460 (2005), the New York and Michigan statutes at issue textually differentiated between in-state and out-of-state wineries, and imposed onerous restrictions on the latter. This was also the case in *City of Philadelphia v. New Jersey*, above. These statutes are facially discriminatory.

The Supreme Court has repeatedly stated that state laws that facially discriminate against out-of-state commerce are subject to "the strictest scrutiny" and will be upheld only if they serve a weighty state interest more effectively than any alterative. *See Hughes v. Oklahoma*, 441 U.S. 322, 336–37 (1979) (noting that where a state statute discriminates against interstate commerce "either on its face or in practical effect . . . the burden falls on the State to justify it both in terms of the local benefits flowing from the statute and the unavailability of nondiscriminatory alternatives adequate to preserve the local interests at stake"). Indeed, the Court rarely has approved a facially discriminatory law, holding repeatedly that laws discriminating against out-of-state commerce are subject to "a virtually *per se* rule of invalidity." *Philadelphia*, 437 U.S. at 624.

One of the few instances where the Supreme Court has upheld a discriminatory law is *Maine v. Taylor*, 477 U.S. 131 (1986). In *Maine v. Taylor*, Maine passed a statute that forbid the importation of live baitfish into the state. *Id.* at 133. Thus, the statute facially discriminated against interstate commerce and did so without congressional authorization. *See id* at 138 (stating that "Congress may authorize the States to engage in regulation that the Commerce Clause would otherwise forbid"). The Supreme Court ruled, however, that the statute did not violate the dormant Commerce Clause because the importation ban protected Maine's native fish species and aquatic ecology in a manner that no other mechanism could as effectively serve. *Id.* at 151. Although "[a] State must make reasonable efforts to avoid restraining the free flow of commerce across its borders," Maine was "not required to develop new and unproven means of protection at an uncertain cost." *Id.* at 147.

As you read the following case, consider whether the facially discriminatory laws advanced legitimate local interests that could not be served adequately by reasonable nondiscriminatory alternatives.

GRANHOLM v. HEALD

544 U.S. 460 (2005)

JUSTICE KENNEDY delivered the opinion of the Court.

These consolidated cases present challenges to state laws regulating the sale of wine from out-of-state wineries to consumers in Michigan and New York. The details and mechanics of the two regulatory schemes differ, but the object and effect of the laws are the same: to allow in-state wineries to sell wine directly to consumers in that State but to prohibit out-of-state wineries from doing so, or, at the least, to make direct sales impractical from an economic standpoint. It is evident that the object and design of the Michigan and New York statutes is to grant in-state wineries a competitive advantage over wineries located beyond the States' borders.

We hold that the laws in both States discriminate against interstate commerce in violation of the Commerce Clause, Art. I, § 8, cl. 3, and that the discrimination is neither authorized nor permitted by the Twenty-first Amendment. Accordingly, we affirm the judgment of the Court of Appeals for the Sixth Circuit, which invalidated the Michigan laws; and we reverse the judgment of the Court of Appeals for the Second Circuit, which upheld the New York laws.

I

Like many other States, Michigan and New York regulate the sale and importation of alcoholic beverages, including wine, through a three-tier distribution system. Separate licenses are required for producers, wholesalers, and retailers. The three-tier scheme is preserved by a complex set of overlapping state and federal regulations. For example, both state and federal laws limit vertical integration between tiers. We have held previously that States can mandate a three-tier distribution scheme in the exercise of their authority under the Twenty-first Amendment. *North Dakota v. United States*, 495 U.S. 423, 432 (1990). As relevant to today's cases, though, the three-tier system is, in broad terms and with refinements to be discussed, mandated by Michigan and New York only for sales from out-of-state wineries. In-state wineries, by contrast, can obtain a license for direct sales to consumers. The differential treatment between in-state and out-of-state wineries constitutes explicit discrimination against interstate commerce. This discrimination substantially limits the direct sale of wine to consumers, an otherwise emerging and significant business.

Approximately 26 States allow some direct shipping of wine, with various restrictions. Thirteen of these States have reciprocity laws, which allow direct shipment from wineries outside the State, provided the State of origin affords similar nondiscriminatory treatment. In many parts of the country, however, state laws that prohibit or severely restrict direct shipments deprive consumers of access to the direct market. According to the Federal Trade Commission (FTC), "[s]tate bans on interstate direct shipping represent the single largest regulatory barrier to expanded e-commerce in wine."

The wine producers in the cases before us are small wineries that rely on direct consumer sales as an important part of their businesses.

A

The plaintiffs contended that Michigan's direct-shipment laws discriminated against interstate commerce in violation of the Commerce Clause. The trade association Michigan Beer & Wine Wholesalers intervened as a defendant. Both the State and the wholesalers argued that the ban on direct shipment from out-of-state wineries is a valid exercise of Michigan's power under § 2 of the Twenty-first Amendment.

On cross-motions for summary judgment the District Court sustained the Michigan scheme. The Court of Appeals for the Sixth Circuit reversed.

C

We granted certiorari on the following question: " 'Does a State's regulatory scheme that permits in-state wineries directly to ship alcohol to consumers but restricts the ability of out-of-state wineries to do so violate the dormant Commerce Clause in light of § 2 of the Twenty-first Amendment?' "

II

A

Time and again this Court has held that, in all but the narrowest circumstances, state laws violate the Commerce Clause if they mandate "differential treatment of in-state and out-of-state economic interests that benefits the former and burdens the latter." This rule is essential to the foundations of the Union. The mere fact of non-residence should not foreclose a producer in one State from access to markets in other States. *H.P. Hood & Sons, Inc. v. Du Mond,* 336 U.S. 525, 539 (1949). States may not enact laws that burden out-of-state producers or shippers simply to give a competitive advantage to in-state businesses. This mandate "reflect[s] a central concern of the Framers that was an immediate reason for calling the Constitutional Convention: the conviction that in order to succeed, the new Union would have to avoid the tendencies toward economic Balkanization that had plagued relations among the Colonies and later among the States under the Articles of Confederation." *Hughes v. Oklahoma,* 441 U.S. 322, 325–326 (1979).

The rule prohibiting state discrimination against interstate commerce follows also from the principle that States should not be compelled to negotiate with each other regarding favored or disfavored status for their own citizens. States do not need, and may not attempt, to negotiate with other States regarding their mutual economic interests. Cf. U.S. Const., Art. I, § 10, cl. 3. Rivalries among the States are thus kept to a minimum, and a proliferation of trade zones is prevented. The Federalist No. 22, pp. 143–145 (C. Rossiter ed. 1961) (A. Hamilton).

Laws of the type at issue in the instant case contradict these principles. They deprive citizens of their right to have access to the markets of other States on equal terms. The perceived necessity for reciprocal sale privileges risks generating the trade rivalries and animosities, the alliances and exclusivity, that the Constitution and, in particular, the Commerce Clause were designed to avoid. State laws that protect local wineries have led to the enactment of statutes under which some States condition the right of out-of-state wineries to make direct wine sales to in-state consumers on a reciprocal right in the shipping State . . . . The current patchwork of laws—with some States banning direct shipments altogether, others doing so only for out-of-state wines, and still others requiring reciprocity — is essentially the product of an ongoing, low-level trade war. Allowing States to discriminate against out-of-state wine "invite[s] a multiplication of preferential trade areas destructive of the very purpose of the Commerce Clause." *Dean Milk Co. v. Madison*, 340 U.S. 349, 356 (1951).

B

The discriminatory character of the Michigan system is obvious. Michigan allows in-state wineries to ship directly to consumers, subject only to a licensing requirement. Out-of-state wineries, whether licensed or not, face a complete ban on direct shipment. The differential treatment requires all out-of-state wine, but not all in-state wine, to pass through an in-state wholesaler and retailer before reaching consumers. These two extra layers of overhead increase the cost of out-of-state wines to Michigan consumers. The cost differential, and in some cases the inability to secure a wholesaler for small shipments, can effectively bar small wineries from the Michigan market.

III

State laws that discriminate against interstate commerce face "a virtually *per se* rule of invalidity." *Philadelphia v. New Jersey*, 437 U.S. 617, 624 (1978). The Michigan and New York laws by their own terms violate this proscription.

IV

We must consider whether either state regime "advances a legitimate local purpose that cannot be adequately served by reasonable nondiscriminatory alternatives." The States offer two primary justifications for restricting direct shipments from out-of-state wineries: keeping alcohol out of the hands of minors and facilitating tax collection. We consider each in turn.

The States, aided by several *amici*, claim that allowing direct shipment from out-of-state wineries undermines their ability to police underage drinking. Minors, the States argue, have easy access to credit cards and the Internet and are likely to take advantage of direct wine shipments as a means of obtaining alcohol illegally.

The States provide little evidence that the purchase of wine over the Internet by minors is a problem. Indeed, there is some evidence to the contrary. A recent study by the staff of the FTC found that the 26 States currently allowing direct shipments report no problems with minors' increased access to wine . . . . Without concrete evidence that direct shipping of wine is likely to increase alcohol consumption by minors, we are left with the States' unsupported assertions. Under our precedents, which require the "clearest showing" to justify discriminatory state regulation, this is not enough.

Even were we to credit the States' largely unsupported claim that direct shipping of wine increases the risk of underage drinking, this would not justify regulations limiting only out-of-state direct shipments. As the wineries point out, minors are just as likely to order wine from in-state producers as from out-of-state ones . . . . In addition, the States can take less restrictive steps to minimize the risk that minors will order wine by mail. For example, the Model Direct Shipping Bill developed by the National Conference of State Legislatures requires an adult signature on delivery and a label so instructing on each package.

The States' tax-collection justification is also insufficient. Increased direct shipping, whether originating in state or out of state, brings with it the potential for tax evasion. With regard to Michigan, however, the tax-collection argument is a diversion. That is because Michigan, unlike many other States, does not rely on wholesalers to collect taxes on wines imported from out of state. Instead, Michigan collects taxes directly from out-of-state wineries on all wine shipped to in-state wholesalers. Mich. Admin. Code Rule 436.1725(2) (1989). If licensing and self-reporting provide adequate safeguards for wine distributed through the three-tier system, there is no reason to believe they will not suffice for direct shipments.

Michigan and New York benefit, furthermore, from provisions of federal law that supply incentives for wineries to comply with state regulations. The Tax and Trade Bureau (formerly the Bureau of Alcohol, Tobacco and Firearms) has authority to revoke a winery's federal license if it violates state law. BATF Industry Circular 96–3 (1997). Without a federal license, a winery cannot operate in any State. In addition the Twenty-first Amendment Enforcement Act gives state attorneys general the power to sue wineries in federal court to enjoin violations of state law. § 122a(b).

These federal remedies, when combined with state licensing regimes, adequately protect States from lost tax revenue. The States have not shown that tax evasion from out-of-state wineries poses such a unique threat that it justifies their discriminatory regimes.

In summary, the States provide little concrete evidence for the sweeping assertion that they cannot police direct shipments by out-of-state wineries. Our Commerce Clause cases demand more than mere speculation to support discrimination against out-of-state goods. The "burden is on the State to show that 'the *discrimination* is demonstrably justified,'" *Chemical Waste Management, Inc. v. Hunt,* 504 U.S. 334 (1992) (emphasis in original). The Court has upheld state regulations that discriminate against interstate commerce only after finding, based on concrete record evidence, that a State's nondiscriminatory alternatives will prove unworkable. See, *e.g., Maine v. Taylor,* 477 U.S. 131, 141–144 (1986). Michigan and New York have not satisfied this exacting standard.

V

If a State chooses to allow direct shipment of wine, it must do so on evenhanded terms. Without demonstrating the need for discrimination, New York and Michigan have enacted regulations that disadvantage out-of-state wine producers. Under our Commerce Clause jurisprudence, these regulations cannot stand.

We affirm the judgment of the Court of Appeals for the Sixth Circuit and remand the case for further proceedings consistent with our opinion.

It is so ordered.

Justice Stevens, with whom Justice O'Connor joins, dissenting. [Opinion omitted]

Justice Thomas, with whom The Chief Justice, Justice Stevens, and Justice O'Connor join, dissenting. [Opinion omitted]

EXERCISE 8:

1. In *Granhom v. Heald*, what interests did Michigan and New York claim justified their discriminatory laws? Did the majority strike down the statutes because these interests were not legitimate? Because they could be served adequately by reasonable nondiscriminatory alternatives? Or both?

2. In *Maine v. Taylor*, the Supreme Court permitted the State of Maine to ban the importation of live out-of-state baitfish to protect Maine's fish ecology from parasites and nonnative species. In *Hughes v. Taylor*, the State of Oklahoma prohibited any person from "transport[ing] or ship[ping] any minnows for sale outside the state which were seined or procured within the waters of this state." 441 U.S. 322, 323 (1979). Oklahoma claimed that its statute was a "conservation method" that was intended to "maintain[] the ecological balance in state waters" by prohibiting the removal of too many minnows. *Id*. at 337. If Maine can keep baitfish out to protect its local environment, should Oklahoma be allowed to keep its natural resources in-state to protect its local ecology? What is the proper outcome in *Hughes* under the Court's analysis in *Maine v. Taylor* and *Granholm v. Heald*?

b. Facially Neutral Statutes

When a discriminatory distinction is not patent on the statute's face, the Court will determine whether the challenged law has a discriminatory impact on out-of-state commerce. If it does, the Court will subject the law to the same scrutiny facially discriminatory laws face. We already saw an early version of this in *Southern Pacific Co.*, where the Supreme Court held unconstitutional a facially neutral Arizona statute because its significant adverse effects on interstate commerce outweighed the minor benefits of the statute. Below is one of the cases where the Supreme Court determined that a facially neutral state statute in fact had a substantial discriminatory impact.

HUNT v. WASHINGTON STATE APPLE ADVERTISING COMMISSION

432 U.S. 333 (1977)

Mr. Chief Justice Burger delivered the opinion of the Court.

In 1973, North Carolina enacted a statute which required all closed containers of apples sold, offered for sale, or shipped into the State to bear "no grade other than the applicable U.S. grade or standard." In an action brought by the Washington State Apple Advertising Commission, a three-judge Federal District Court invalidated the statute insofar as it prohibited the display of Washington State apple grades on the ground that it unconstitutionally discriminated against interstate commerce.

The specific question[] presented on appeal [is] whether the challenged North Carolina statute constitutes an unconstitutional burden on interstate commerce.

(1)

Washington State is the Nation's largest producer of apples, its crops accounting for approximately 30% of all apples grown domestically and nearly half of all apples shipped in closed containers in interstate commerce. As might be expected, the production and sale of apples on this scale is a multimillion dollar enterprise which plays a significant role in Washington's economy. Because of the importance of the apple industry to the State, its legislature has undertaken to protect and enhance the reputation of Washington apples by establishing a stringent, mandatory inspection program, administered by the State's Department of Agriculture, which requires all apples shipped in interstate commerce to be tested under strict quality standards and graded accordingly. In all cases, the Washington State grades, which have gained substantial acceptance in the trade, are the equivalent of, or superior to, the comparable grades and standards adopted by the United States Department of Agriculture (USDA). Compliance with the Washington inspection scheme costs the State's growers approximately $1 million each year.

In addition to the inspection program, the state legislature has sought to enhance the market for Washington apples through the creation of a state agency, the Washington State Apple Advertising Commission, charged with the statutory duty of promoting and protecting the State's apple industry. The Commission itself is composed of 13 Washington apple growers and dealers who are nominated and elected within electoral districts by their fellow growers and dealers. Among its activities are the promotion of Washington apples in both domestic and foreign markets through advertising, market research and analysis, and public education, as well as scientific research into the uses, development, and improvement of apples. Its activities are financed entirely by assessments levied upon the apple industry; in the year during which this litigation began, these assessments totaled approximately $1.75 million.

In 1972, the North Carolina Board of Agriculture adopted an administrative regulation, unique in the 50 States, which in effect required all closed containers of apples shipped into or sold in the State to display either the applicable USDA grade or none at all. State grades were expressly prohibited. In addition to its obvious consequence prohibiting the display of Washington State apple grades on containers of apples shipped into North Carolina, the regulation presented the Washington apple industry with a marketing problem of potentially nationwide significance. Washington apple growers annually ship in commerce approximately 40 million closed containers of apples, nearly 500,000 of which eventually find their way into North Carolina, stamped with the applicable Washington State variety and grade. It is the industry's practice to purchase these containers preprinted with the various apple varieties and grades, prior to harvest. After these containers are filled with apples of the appropriate type and grade, a substantial portion of them are placed in cold-storage warehouses where the grade labels identify the product and facilitate its handling. These apples are then shipped as needed throughout the year; after February 1 of each year, they constitute approximately two-thirds of all apples sold in fresh markets in this country. Since the ultimate destination of these apples is unknown at the time they are placed in storage, compliance with North Carolina's unique regulation would have required Washington growers to obliterate the printed labels on containers shipped to North Carolina, thus giving their product a damaged appearance. Alternatively, they could have changed their marketing practices to accommodate the needs of the North Carolina market, i.e., repack apples to be shipped to North Carolina in containers bearing only the USDA grade, and/or store the estimated portion of the harvest destined for that market in such special containers. As a last resort, they could discontinue the use of the preprinted containers entirely. None of these costly and less efficient options was very attractive to the industry. Moreover, in the event a number of other States followed North Carolina's lead, the resultant inability to display the Washington grades could force the Washington growers to abandon the State's expensive inspection and grading system which their customers had come to know and rely on over the 60-odd years of its existence.

With these problems confronting the industry, the Washington State Apple Advertising Commission petitioned the North Carolina Board of Agriculture to amend its regulation to permit the display of state grades. An administrative hearing was held on the question but no relief was granted. Indeed, North Carolina hardened its position shortly thereafter by enacting the regulation into law [which is challenged in this litigation]. Nonetheless, the Commission once again requested an exemption which would have permitted the Washington apple growers to display both the United States and the Washington State grades on their shipments to North Carolina. This request, too, was denied.

Unsuccessful in its attempts to secure administrative relief, the Commission instituted this action challenging the constitutionality of the statute in the United States District Court for the Eastern District of North Carolina. Its complaint sought a declaration that the statute violated the Commerce Clause of the United States Constitution, Art. I, § 8, cl. 3, insofar as it prohibited the display of Washington State grades, and prayed for a permanent injunction against its enforcement in this manner.

The court held that the statute unconstitutionally discriminated against commerce, insofar as it affected the interstate shipment of Washington apples,[5] and enjoined its application. This appeal followed.

---

5. As an alternative ground for its holding, the District Court found that the statute would have constituted an undue burden on commerce even if it had been neutral and nondiscriminatory in its impact. *Pike v. Bruce Church, Inc.*, 397 U.S. 137 [(1970)].

(4)

[Appellants] maintain that any burdens on the interstate sale of Washington apples were far outweighed by the local benefits flowing from what they contend was a valid exercise of North Carolina's inherent police powers designed to protect its citizenry from fraud and deception in the marketing of apples.

Prior to the statute's enactment, appellants point out, apples from 13 different States were shipped into North Carolina for sale. Seven of those States, including the State of Washington, had their own grading systems which, while differing in their standards, used similar descriptive labels (e.g., fancy, extra fancy, etc.). This multiplicity of inconsistent state grades, as the District Court itself found, posed dangers of deception and confusion not only in the North Carolina market, but in the Nation as a whole. The North Carolina statute, appellants claim, was enacted to eliminate this source of deception and confusion by replacing the numerous state grades with a single uniform standard. Moreover, it is contended that North Carolina sought to accomplish this goal of uniformity in an evenhanded manner as evidenced by the fact that its statute applies to all apples sold in closed containers in the State without regard to their point of origin. Nonetheless, appellants argue that the District Court gave "scant attention" to the obvious benefits flowing from the challenged legislation and to the long line of decisions from this Court holding that the States possess "broad powers" to protect local purchasers from fraud and deception in the marketing of foodstuffs.

As the appellants properly point out, not every exercise of state authority imposing some burden on the free flow of commerce is invalid. Although the Commerce Clause acts as a limitation upon state power even without congressional implementation, e.g., *Cooley v. Board of Wardens*, [53 U.S.] (12 How.) 299 (1852), our opinions have long recognized that,

> "in the absence of conflicting legislation by Congress, there is a residuum of power in the state to make laws governing matters of local concern which nevertheless in some measure affect interstate commerce or even, to some extent, regulate it." *Southern Pacific Co. v. Arizona*, 325 U.S. 761 (1945).

Moreover, as appellants correctly note, that "residuum" is particularly strong when the State acts to protect its citizenry in matters pertaining to the sale of foodstuffs. By the same token, however, a finding that state legislation furthers matters of legitimate local concern, even in the health and consumer protection areas, does not end the inquiry. Rather, when such state legislation comes into conflict with the Commerce Clause's overriding requirement of a national "common market," we are confronted with the task of effecting an accommodation of the competing national and local interests. *Pike v. Bruce Church, Inc.*, 397 U.S. 137 (1970). We turn to that task.

As the District Court correctly found, the challenged statute has the practical effect of not only burdening interstate sales of Washington apples, but also discriminating against them. This discrimination takes various forms. The first, and most obvious, is the statute's consequence of raising the costs of doing business in the North

Carolina market for Washington apple growers and dealers, while leaving those of their North Carolina counterparts unaffected. As previously noted, this disparate effect results from the fact that North Carolina apple producers, unlike their Washington competitors, were not forced to alter their marketing practices in order to comply with the statute. They were still free to market their wares under the USDA grade or none at all as they had done prior to the statute's enactment. Obviously, the increased costs imposed by the statute would tend to shield the local apple industry from the competition of Washington apple growers and dealers who are already at a competitive disadvantage because of their great distance from the North Carolina market.

Second, the statute has the effect of stripping away from the Washington apple industry the competitive and economic advantages it has earned for itself through its expensive inspection and grading system.

Third, by prohibiting Washington growers and dealers from marketing apples under their State's grades, the statute has a leveling effect which insidiously operates to the advantage of local apple producers. As noted earlier, the Washington State grades are equal or superior to the USDA grades in all corresponding categories. Hence, with free market forces at work, Washington sellers would normally enjoy a distinct market advantage vis-a-vis local producers in those categories where the Washington grade is superior. However, because of the statute's operation, Washington apples which would otherwise qualify for and be sold under the superior Washington grades will now have to be marketed under their inferior USDA counterparts.

Despite the statute's facial neutrality, the Commission suggests that its discriminatory impact on interstate commerce was not an unintended byproduct and there are some indications in the record to that effect. The most glaring is the response of the North Carolina Agriculture Commissioner to the Commission's request for an exemption following the statue's passage in which he indicated that before he could support such an exemption, he would "want to have the sentiment from our apple producers since they were mainly responsible for this legislation being passed." Moreover, we find it somewhat suspect that North Carolina singled out only closed containers of apples, the very means by which apples are transported in commerce, to effectuate the statute's ostensible consumer protection purpose when apples are not generally sold at retail in their shipping containers. However, we need not ascribe an economic protection motive to the North Carolina Legislature to resolve this case; we conclude that the challenged statute cannot stand insofar as it prohibits the display of Washington State grades even if enacted for the declared purpose of protecting consumers from deception and fraud in the marketplace.

When discrimination against commerce of the type we have found is demonstrated, the burden falls on the State to justify it both in terms of the local benefits flowing from the statute and the unavailability of nondiscriminatory alternatives adequate to preserve the local interests at stake. *Dean Milk Co. v. Madison*, 340 U.S. [349 (1950)]. *See also Pike v. Bruce Church, Inc.*, 397 U.S., at 142. North Carolina has failed to sustain that burden on both scores.

The several States unquestionably possess a substantial interest in protecting their citizens from confusion and deception in the marketing of foodstuffs, but the challenged statute does remarkably little to further that laudable goal at least with respect to Washington apples and grades. The statute permits the marketing of closed containers of apples under no grades at all. Such a result can hardly be thought to eliminate the problems of deception and confusion created by the multiplicity of differing state grades; indeed, it magnifies them by depriving purchasers of all information concerning the quality of the contents of closed apple containers. Moreover, although the statute is ostensibly a consumer protection measure, it directs its primary efforts, not at the consuming public at large, but at apple wholesalers and brokers who are the principal purchasers of closed containers of apples. And those individuals are presumably the most knowledgeable individuals in this area. Since the statute does nothing at all to purify the flow of information at the retail level, it does little to protect consumers against the problems it was designed to eliminate. Finally, we note that any potential for confusion and deception created by the Washington grades was not of the type that led to the statute's enactment. Since Washington grades are in all cases equal or superior to their USDA counterparts, they could only "deceive" or "confuse" a consumer to his benefit, hardly a harmful result.

In addition, it appears that nondiscrimnatory alternatives to the outright ban of Washington State grades are readily available. For example, North Carolina could effectuate its goal by permitting out-of-state growers to utilize state grades only if they also marked their shipments with the applicable USDA label. If this alternative was for some reason inadequate to eradicate problems caused by state grades inferior to those adopted by the USDA, North Carolina might consider banning those state grades which, unlike Washington's could not be demonstrated to be equal or superior to the corresponding USDA categories.

The judgment of the District Court is

Affirmed.

EXERCISE 9:

1. What caused the Supreme Court to find that the North Carolina statute discriminated against out-of-state commerce?

2. How rigorous would you characterize the level of scrutiny utilized by the Court once it determined that the North Carolina law discriminated against out-of-state commerce?

3. Suppose that the State of New York, in an effort to stabilize milk prices, passes a law setting the minimum prices that New York milk dealers must pay to any and all milk producers. Is the New York law facially discriminatory? If not, does it nonetheless have a discriminatory purpose or effect? How so? Applying the Court's analysis in *Hunt*, does the New York statute violate the dormant Commerce Clause? *See Baldwin v. G.A.F. Seelig, Inc.*, 294 U.S. 511 (1935).

4. Suppose Minnesota law bans the sale of milk in plastic disposable containers but allows cardboard containers. Suppose further that Minnesota has a paper

industry that will benefit and no plastic industry that would suffer. Also assume that the stated purpose of the legislation is to minimize energy waste and to reduce the depletion of natural resources. Does the statute violate the dormant Commerce Clause? Is this case like *Hunt*? Or can you fashion an argument to distinguish the two cases? Articulate the possible differences, and explain why those differences might lead a court to uphold the statute. *See Minnesota v. Clover Leaf Creamery Co.*, 449 U.S. 456 (1981).

5. Suppose that Richmond, Virginia passes an ordinance barring the sale of pasteurized milk within its city limits unless it is processed and bottled at an approved pasteurization plant within fifteen miles of the city center of Richmond. Does the ordinance discriminate against interstate commerce? Does it matter that the ordinance discriminates against milk pasteurized in other parts of Virginia? The Court has been particularly wary of state regulations that require certain operations to be performed within that state, so-called "home" or "local" processing requirements. *See, e.g., C & A Carbone, Inc. v. Clarkstown*, 511 U.S. 383 (1994).

The Supreme Court has not been clear on what role a discriminatory purpose plays in its dormant Commerce Clause analysis. The *Hunt* Court briefly touched on discriminatory purpose, noting that there was some evidence that North Carolina enacted its discriminatory statute to protect in-state apple growers at the expense of out-of-state growers. The Court, however, declined to rest its conclusion on those facts. Thus, some cases, including *Hunt*, suggest that a purpose to discriminate against interstate commerce is not necessary to find that the statute discriminates against out-of-state commerce. Other cases, such as *H.P. Hood & Sons v. Du Mond*, indicate that the Court does take the presence or absence of discriminatory purpose into account.

H.P. HOOD & SONS, INC. v. DU MOND

336 U.S. 525 (1949)

MR. JUSTICE JACKSON delivered the opinion of the Court.

[I]

This case concerns the power of the State of New York to deny additional facilities to acquire and ship milk in interstate commerce where the grounds of denial are that such limitation upon interstate business will protect and advance local economic interests.

H.P. Hood & Sons, Inc., a Massachusetts corporation, has long distributed milk and its products to inhabitants of Boston. That city obtains about 90% of its fluid milk from states other than Massachusetts. Dairies located in New York State since about 1900 have been among the sources of Boston's supply. The area in which Hood has been denied an additional license to make interstate purchases has been developed as a part of the Boston milkshed from which both the Hood Company and a competitor have shipped to Boston.

The state courts have held and it is conceded here that Hood's entire business in New York is interstate commerce. This Hood has conducted for some time by means of three receiving depots, where it takes raw milk from farmers. The milk is not processed in New York but is weighed, tested and, if necessary, cooled and on the same day shipped as fluid milk to Boston. These existing plants have been operated under license from the State and are not in question here as the State has licensed Hood to continue them. The controversy concerns a proposed additional plant for the same kind of operation at Greenwich, New York.

Article 21 of the Agriculture and Markets Law of New York, forbids a dealer to buy milk from producers unless licensed to do so by the Commissioner of Agriculture and Markets. For the license he must pay a substantial fee and furnish a bond to assure prompt payment to producers for milk. Under § 258, the Commissioner may not grant a license unless satisfied 'that the applicant is qualified by character, experience, financial responsibility and equipment to properly conduct the proposed business.' The Hood Company concededly has met all the foregoing tests and license for an additional plant was not denied for any failure to comply with these requirements.

The Commissioner's denial was based on further provisions of this section which require him to be satisfied 'that the issuance of the license will not tend to a destructive competition in a market already adequately served, and that the issuance of the license will be in the public interest.'

In denying the application for expanded facilities, the Commissioner states his grounds as follows:

> 'If applicant is permitted to equip and operate another milk plant in this territory, and to take on producers now delivering to plants other than those which it operates, it will tend to reduce the volume of milk received at the plants which lose those producers, and will tend to increase the cost of handling milk in those plants.

> 'If applicant takes producers now delivering milk to local markets such as Troy, it will have a tendency to deprive such markets of a supply needed during the short season.

> 'There is no evidence that any producer is without a market for his milk. There is no evidence that any producers not now delivering milk to applicant would receive any higher price, were they to deliver their milk to applicant's proposed plant.

> 'The issuance of a license to applicant which would permit it to operate an additional plant, would tend to a destructive competition in a market already adequately served, and would not be in the public interest.'

[II]

Production and distribution of milk are so intimately related to public health and welfare that the need for regulation to protect those interests has long been recognized and is, from a constitutional standpoint, hardly controversial. Also, the economy of the industry is so eccentric that economic controls have been found at once necessary and difficult. These have evolved detailed, intricate and comprehensive regulations, including price-fixing. They have been much litigated but were generally sustained by this Court as within the powers of the State over its internal commerce. As the states extended their efforts to control various phases of export and import also, questions were raised as to limitations on state power under the Commerce Clause of the Constitution.

Our decision in a milk litigation most relevant to the present controversy deals with the converse of the present situation. *Baldwin v. G.A.F. Seelig, Inc.*, 294 U.S. 511 (1935). In that case, New York placed conditions and limitations on the local sale of milk imported from Vermont designed in practical effect to exclude it, while here its order proposes to limit the local facilities for purchase of additional milk so as to withhold milk from export. The State agreed then, as now, that the Commerce Clause prohibits it from directly curtailing movement of milk into or out of the State. But in the earlier case, it contended that the same result could be accomplished by controlling delivery, bottling and sale after arrival, while here it says it can do so by curtailing facilities for its purchase and receipt before it is shipped out. In neither case is the measure supported by health or safety considerations but solely by protection of local economic interests, such as supply for local consumption and limitation of competition. This Court unanimously rejected the State's contention in the *Seelig* case and held that the Commerce Clause prohibits such regulations for such ends.

The opinion was by Mr. Justice Cardozo, experienced in the milk problems of New York and favorably disposed toward the efforts of the State to control the industry. It recognized, as do we, broad power in the State to protect its inhabitants against perils to health or safety, fraudulent traders and highway hazards even by use of measures which bear adversely upon interstate commerce. But it laid repeated emphasis upon the principle that the State may not promote its own economic advantages by curtailment or burdening of interstate commerce.

This distinction between the power of the State to shelter its people from menaces to their health or safety and from fraud, even when those dangers emanate from interstate commerce, and its lack of power to retard, burden or constrict the flow of such commerce for their economic advantage, is one deeply rooted in both our history and our law.

This Court consistently has rebuffed attempts of states to advance their own commercial interests by curtailing the movement of articles of commerce, either into or out of the state, while generally supporting their right to impose even burdensome regulations in the interest of local health and safety.

Th[e] principle that our economic unit is the Nation, which alone has the gamut of powers necessary to control of the economy, including the vital power of erecting customs barriers against foreign competition, has as its corollary that the states are not separable economic units. As the Court said in *Baldwin v. G.A.F. Seelig, Inc.*, 'What is ultimate is the principle that one state in its dealings with another may not place itself in a position of economic isolation.' In so speaking it but followed the principle that the state may not use its admitted powers to protect the health and safety of its people as a basis for suppressing competition. The same argument here advanced, that limitation of competition would itself contribute to safety and conservation, and therefore indirectly serve an end permissible to the state. This Court has not only recognized this disability of the state to isolate its own economy as a basis for striking down parochial legislative policies designed to do so, but it has recognized the incapacity of the state to protect its own inhabitants from competition as a reason for sustaining particular exercises of the commerce power of Congress to reach matters in which states were so disabled.

The material success that has come to inhabitants of the states which make up this federal free trade unit has been the most impressive in the history of commerce, but the established interdependence of the states only emphasizes the necessity of protecting interstate movement of goods against local burdens and repressions. We need only consider the consequences if each of the few states that produce copper, lead, high-grade iron ore, timber, cotton, oil or gas should decree that industries located in that state shall have priority. What fantastic rivalries and dislocations and reprisals would ensue if such practices were begun! Or suppose that the field of discrimination and retaliation be industry. May Michigan provide that automobiles cannot be taken out of that State until local dealers' demands are fully met? Would she not have every argument in the favor of such a statute that can be offered in support of New York's limiting sales of milk for out-of-state shipment to protect the economic interests of her competing dealers and local consumers? Could Ohio then pounce upon the rubber-tire industry, on which she has a substantial grip, to retaliate for Michigan's auto monopoly?

Our system, fostered by the Commerce Clause, is that every farmer and every craftsman shall be encouraged to produce by the certainty that he will have free access to every market in the Nation, that no home embargoes will withhold his export, and no foreign state will by customs duties or regulations exclude them. Likewise, every consumer may look to the free competition from every producing area in the Nation to protect him from exploitation by any. Such was the vision of the Founders; such has been the doctrine of this Court which has given it reality.

[III]

The State, however, contends that such restraint or obstruction as its order imposes on interstate commerce does not violate the Commerce Clause because the State regulation coincides with, supplements and is part of the federal regulatory scheme. This contention that Congress has taken possession of 'the field' but shared it with the State, it is to be noted, reverses the contention usually made in comparable cases, which is that Congress has not fully occupied the field and hence the State may fill the void.

Congress, as a part of its Agricultural Marketing Agreement Act, authorizes the Secretary of Agriculture to issue orders regulating the handling of several agricultural products, including milk, when they are within the reach of its commerce power. As to milk, it sets up a rather complicated system of fixing prices to be paid to producers through equalization pools which distribute the total value of all milk sold in a specified market among the producers supplying that market.

The Congressional regulation contemplates and permits a wide latitude in which the State may exercise its police power over the local facilities for handling milk. We assume, though it is not necessary to decide, that the Federal Act does not preclude a state from placing restrictions and obstructions in the way of interstate commerce for the ends and purposes always held permissible under the Commerce Clause. But here the challenge is only to a denial of facilities for interstate commerce upon the sole and specific grounds that it will subject others to competition and take supplies needed locally, an end, as we have shown, always held to be precluded by the Commerce Clause. We have no doubt that Congress in the national interest could prohibit or curtail shipments of milk in interstate commerce, unless and until local demands are met.

When it is considered that the Federal Act was passed expressly to overcome 'disruption of the orderly exchange of commodities in interstate commerce' and conditions found to 'burden and obstruct the normal channels of interstate commerce,' 7 U.S.C. §601, it seems clear that we can not sustain the State's argument that its restrictions here involved supplement and further the federal scheme.

Moreover, we can hardly assume that the challenged provisions of this order advance the federal scheme of regulation because Congress forbids inclusion of such a policy in a federal milk order. Section 8c(5)(G) of the Act provides:

> 'No marketing agreement or order applicable to milk and its products in any marketing area shall prohibit or in any manner limit, in the case of the products of milk, the marketing in that area of any milk or product thereof produced in any production area in the United States.'

[I]t is clear that the policy of the provision is inconsistent with the State's contention that it may, in its own interest, impose such a limitation as a coincident or supplement to federal regulation.

[IV]

Since the statute as applied violates the Commerce Clause and is not authorized by federal legislation pursuant to that Clause, it cannot stand. The judgment is reversed and the cause remanded for proceedings not inconsistent with this opinion. It is so ordered.

Reversed and remanded.

MR. JUSTICE FRANKFURTER, with whom MR. JUSTICE RUTLEDGE joins, dissenting.

If the Court's opinion has meaning beyond deciding this case in isolation, its effect is to hold that no matter how important to the internal economy of a State may be the prevention of destructive competition, and no matter how unimportant the interstate commerce affected, a State cannot as a means of preventing such competition deny an applicant access to a market within the State if that applicant happens to intend the out-of-state shipment of the product that he buys. I feel constrained to dissent because I cannot agree in treating what is essentially a problem of striking a balance between competing interests as an exercise in absolutes. Nor does it seem to me that such a problem should be disposed of on a record from which we cannot tell what weights to put in which side of the scales.

Some of the principles relevant to decision of this case are settled beyond dispute. One of these is that the prevention of destructive competition is a permissible exercise of the police power. As matters now stand . . . it is impossible to say whether or not the restriction of competition among dealers in milk does in fact contribute to their economic well-being and, through them, to that of the entire industry. And if we assume that some contribution is made, we cannot guess how much. Why, when the State has fixed a minimum price for producers, does it take steps to keep competing dealers from increasing the price by bidding against each other for the existing supply? Is it concerned with protecting consumers from excessive prices? Or is it concerned with seeing that marginal dealers, forced by competition to pay more and charge less, are not driven either to cut corners in the maintenance of their plants or to close them down entirely? Might these consequences follow from operation at less than capacity? What proportion of capacity is necessary to enable the marginal dealer to stay in business? Could Hood's potential competitors in the Greenwich area maintain efficient and sanitary standards of operation on a lower margin of profit? How would their closing down affect producers? Would the competition of Hood affect dealers other than those in that area? How many of those dealers are also engaged in interstate commerce? How much of a strain would be put on the price structure maintained by the State by a holding that it cannot regulate the competition of dealers buying for an out-of-state market? Is this a situation in which State regulation, by supplementing federal regulation, is of benefit to interstate as well as to intrastate commerce?

We should, I submit, have answers at least to some of these questions before we can say either how seriously interstate commerce is burdened by New York's licensing power or how necessary to New York is that power. Since the needed information is neither accessible to judicial notice nor within its proper scope, I believe we should seek further light by remanding the case to the courts of the State.

Mr. Justice Black, dissenting.

In this case the Court sets up a new constitutional formula for invalidation of state laws regulating local phases of interstate commerce. I believe the New York law is invulnerable to constitutional attack under constitutional rules which the majority of this Court have long accepted.

Gibbons v. Ogden, decided in 1824, held invalid a New York statute regulating commerce which conflicted with an Act of Congress. The Court there left undecided the question strongly urged that the Commerce Clause of itself forbade New York to regulate commerce. In 1847 this undecided question was discussed by Chief Justice

Taney.[1] His view was that the Commerce Clause of itself did no more than grant power to Congress to regulate commerce among the states; that until Congress acted states could regulate the commerce; and that this Court was without power to strike down state regulations unless they conflicted with a valid federal law. This the Chief Justice thought was the intention of the Constitution's framers, drawing his inference of their intent from his belief that they knew 'a multitude of minor regulations must be necessary, which Congress amid its great concerns could never find time to consider and provide.'[2]

In 1852 this Court rejected in part the Taney interpretation of the Commerce Clause. *Cooley v. Board of Wardens*, [53 U.S. (12 How.) 299 (1851)]. The opinion there stated that the commerce clause per se forbade states to regulate commerce under some circumstances but left them free to do so under other circumstances. It decided no more than that this Court in passing upon state regulations of commerce would always weigh the conflicting interests of state and nation. Moreover, implicit in the rule, as shown by what the Court said, was a determined purpose not to leave areas in which interstate activities could be insulated from any regulation at all.

The basic principles of the *Cooley* rule have been entangled and sometimes obscured with much language. In the main, however, those principles have been the asserted grounds for determination of all commerce cases decided by this Court from 1852 until today. Many of the cases have used the words 'restraints,' 'obstructions,' 'in commerce,' 'on commerce,' 'burdens,' 'direct burdens,' 'undue burdens,' 'unreasonable burdens,' 'unfair burdens,' 'incidental burdens,' etc., but such words have almost always been used, as the opinions reveal, to aid in application of the *Cooley* balance-of-interests rule.[3]

In this Court, challenges to the *Cooley* rule on the ground that the rule was an ineffective protector of interstate commerce from state regulations have been confined to dissents and concurring opinions.[4]

---

1. *The License Cases*, [36 U.S.] 5 How. 504, 578–579 (1847). And see [Felix] Frankfurter, The Commerce Clause[: Under Marshall, Taney and Waite], 50–58 (1937).

2. State legislation which patently discriminates against interstate commerce has long been held to conflict with the commerce clause itself. The writer has acquiesced in this interpretation, although agreeing with the views of Chief Justice Taney that the commerce clause was not intended to grant courts power to regulate commerce even to this extent.

3. [Noel T.] Dowling, *Interstate Commerce and State Power*, 27 Va.L.Rev. 1 (1940); and see for illustration *Southern Pacific Co. v. State of Arizona*, 325 U.S. 761, 768–769 [(1945)]; *Cloverleaf Butter Co. v. Patterson*, 315 U.S. 148, 154–155 [(1942)]; *Milk Control Board v. Eisenberg Farm Products*; 306 U.S. 346 [(1939)]; *South Carolina State Highway Dep't v. Barnwell Bros., Inc.*, 303 U.S. 177, 184–191 [(1938)]. And see cases collected by Mr. Justice Brandeis, in his dissenting opinion in *Di Santo v. Commonwealth of Pennsylvania*, 273 U.S. 34, 39–40 [(1927) (Brandeis, J., dissenting)].

4. The writer's view has been that the *Cooley* rule resulted in this Court's invalidating state statutes that should be left operative unless Congress should strike them down. See dissenting opinion in *Southern Pac. Co. v. State of Arizona*, [325 U.S. 761 (1945) (Black, J., dissenting)]. But since my views were rejected, I joined in disposition of [a later case] by application of the *Cooley* rule.

The philosophy [that *Cooley* is ineffective in limiting state overregulation] can alone support the holding and opinion today. The *Cooley* balancing-of-interests principle is today supplanted by th[at] philosophy.[8] For the New York statute is killed by a mere automatic application of a new mechanistic formula. The Court appraises nothing, unless its stretching of the old commerce clause interpretation results from a reappraisal of the power and duty of this Court under the commerce clause. Numerous cases, which made judicial appraisals under the *Cooley* rule, are gently laid to rest. Their interment is tactfully accomplished, without ceremony, eulogy, or report of their demise. The ground beneath them has been deftly excavated by a soothing process which limits them to their facts, their precise facts, their 'plain requirements.' The vacancy left by the *Cooley* principle will be more than filled, however, by the new formula which without balancing interests, automatically will relieve many businesses from state regulations. This Court will thereby be relieved of much trouble in attempting to reconcile state and federal interests. State regulatory agencies too will be relieved of a large share of their traditional duties when they discover that bad local business practices are now judicially immunized from state regulation. But it is doubtful if the relief accorded will promote the welfare of the state or nation since Congress cannot possibly undertake the monumental task of suppressing all pernicious local business practices.

The sole immediate result of today's holding is that petitioner will be allowed to operate a new milk plant in New York. This consequence standing alone is of no great importance. But there are other consequences of importance. It is always a serious thing for this Court to strike down a statewide law. It is more serious when the state law falls under a new rule which will inescapably narrow the area in which states can regulate and control local business practices found inimical to the public welfare. The gravity of striking down state regulations is immeasurably increased when it results as here in leaving a no-man's land immune from any effective regulation whatever. It is dangerous to assume that the aggressive cupidity of some need never be checked by government in the interest of all.

Both the commerce and due process clauses serve high purposes when confined within their proper scope. But a stretching of either outside its sphere can paralyze the legislative process, rendering the people's legislative representatives impotent to perform their duty of providing appropriate rules to govern this dynamic civilization. Both clauses easily lend themselves to inordinate expansions of this Court's power at the expense of legislative power. For under the prevailing due process rule, appeals can be made to the 'fundamental principles of liberty and justice' which our 'fathers' wished to preserve. In commerce clause cases reference can appropriately be made to the far-seeing wisdom of the 'fathers' in guarding against commercial and even shooting wars among the states. Such arguments have strong emotional appeals and when skillfully utilized they sometimes obscure the vision.

---

8. Barnett, *Interstate Commerce—State Control*, 21 Ore.L.Rev. 385, 391–392 (1942); Note, 26 Minn.L.Rev. 654, 655 (1942).

I would leave New York's law alone.

Mr. Justice Murphy joins in this opinion.

EXERCISE 10:

1. Why was New York's refusal to permit H.P. Hood & Sons, Inc., to build another milk processing facility unconstitutional? Was the Court's analysis consistent with *Southern Pacific Railroad v. Arizona*?

2. What role does the fact that a law has a discriminatory effect on out-of-state commerce play in the Court's ascertainment of discriminatory purpose? Should it play a role?

3. Should the Supreme Court use "purpose" in its dormant Commerce Clause analysis?

4. Is the Court good at making such an inquiry? Is there such a thing as legislative purpose?

5. Note that the Supreme Court rejected the state's argument that its statutory scheme received congressional approval and hence was protected from invalidation under the dormant Commerce Clause.

6. The Supreme Court articulated a number of rationales for the dormant Commerce Clause. What are they? Are they persuasive?

7. How did Justice Frankfurter differ from the majority in his analysis?

8. Justice Black's dissent attempts to synthesize the Supreme Court's dormant Commerce Clause jurisprudence. It is very common for judges — and, of course, for attorneys making arguments to judges — to synthesize prior case law as standing for a particular legal principle. Legal philosopher Ronald Dworkin's theory of adjudication explains how this works. Ronald Dworkin, Law's Empire (1986). Professor Dworkin argued that the law is the best explanation of the relevant authoritative text, precedents interpreting that text, legal principles, and legal practices. Judges will first, in the context of cases they decide, determine which legal principle fits the legal materials. However, for Dworkin, since there will often be more than one legal principle that fits the applicable legal materials, he argued that judges should choose the morally best principle.

9. It appears that Justice Black may have employed Professor Dworkin's methodology. Could you articulate, using Dworkin's methodology, Justice Black's argument?

10. Justice Black states, in footnote four of his dissent, that even though the Court rejected his view in one case, he later followed that precedent. Is that what judges should do? Justice Black had a considered view on the Constitution's meaning which was rejected by a majority of his fellow Justices. Should Justice Black thereafter follow — what in his view is a — mistaken constitutional interpretation? Does it depend?

11. Does Justice Black have a presumption in how the Supreme Court should balance a state's interest in regulating against the national interest in the free flow of goods and services?

12. Justice Black argued that the rule employed by the majority is wrong, in part because it is a return to the Court's earlier due process jurisprudence that eliminated the ability of states to regulate in the public's interest. Are you persuaded that he is right?

13. What did the Supreme Court mean when it stated: "Perhaps even more than by interpretation of its written word, this Court has advanced the solidarity and prosperity of this Nation by the meaning it has given to these great silences of the Constitution." When the Court strikes down state laws on the basis of the analysis proposed in the quoted sentence, upon what basis does it do so? Is that an adequate basis?

14. Why does the majority refer to one of its precedents as being authored by Justice Cardozo? Why note the precedent's primary author?

2. Neutral State Laws

When a state law does not discriminate against interstate commerce, facially or in its purpose or effect, the Supreme Court utilizes a balancing test to evaluate the law's constitutionality. The Court will not strike it down under the dormant Commerce Clause so long as, first, the statute is supported by a legitimate state interest and, second, the local benefit outweighs the statute's burden on interstate commerce. *Pike v. Bruce Church*, below, is the Supreme Court's most prominent articulation of this analysis.

LOREN J. PIKE v. BRUCE CHURCH, INC.
397 U.S. 137 (1970)

MR. JUSTICE STEWART delivered the opinion of the Court.

[I]

The appellee is a company engaged in extensive commercial farming operations in Arizona and California. The appellant is the official charged with enforcing the Arizona Fruit and Vegetable Standardization Act. A provision of the Act requires that, with certain exceptions, all cantaloupes grown in Arizona and offered for sale must "be packed in regular compact arrangement in closed standard containers approved by the supervisor." Invoking his authority under that provision, the appellant issued an order prohibiting the appellee company from transporting uncrated cantaloupes from its Parker, Arizona, ranch to nearby Blythe, California, for packing and processing. The company then brought this action in a federal court to enjoin the order as unconstitutional. A three-judge court was convened. [T]he court issued a permanent injunction upon the ground that the challenged order constituted an unlawful burden upon interstate commerce. This appeal followed.

The facts are not in dispute, having been stipulated by the parties. The appellee company has for many years been engaged in the business of growing, harvesting, processing, and packing fruits and vegetables at numerous locations in Arizona and

California for interstate shipment to markets throughout the Nation. One of the company's newest operations is at Parker, Arizona, where it undertook to develop approximately 6,400 acres of uncultivated, arid land for agricultural use. The company has spent more than $3,000,000 in developing this land. The company began growing cantaloupes on part of the land in 1966, and has harvested a large cantaloupe crop there in each subsequent year. Because they are highly perishable, cantaloupes must upon maturity be immediately harvested, processed, packed, and shipped in order to prevent spoliage. The processing and packing operations can be performed only in packing sheds. Because the company had no such facilities at Parker, it transported its 1966 Parker cantaloupe harvest in bulk loads to Blythe, California, 31 miles away, where it operated centralized and efficient packing shed facilities. In 1967 the company again sent its Parker cantaloupe crop to Blythe for sorting, packing, and shipping. In 1968, however, the appellant entered the order here in issue, prohibiting the company from shipping its cantaloupes out of the State unless they were packed in containers in a manner and of a kind approved by the appellant. [A]n agreed statement of facts contained a stipulation that the practical effect of the appellant's order would be to compel the company to build packing facilities in or near Parker, Arizona, that would take many months to construct and would cost approximately $200,000.

[II]

[A]

The appellant's threshold contention here is that even though the challenged order expressly forbids the interstate bulk shipment of the company's cantaloupes, it imposes no burden upon interstate commerce. If the Arizona Act is complied with, he argues, all that will be regulated will be the intrastate packing of goods destined for interstate commerce. Articles being made ready for interstate movement are not necessarily yet in interstate commerce, which, he says, begins only when the articles are delivered to the interstate shipper.

[Contrary to appellant's argument,] the order in the present case does affect interstate commerce. In the first place, the perishable cantaloupes were destined to be shipped to an ascertainable location in California immediately upon harvest. Even more to the point, the application of the statute at issue here would require that an operation now carried on outside the State must be performed instead within the State so that it can be regulated there. If the appellant's theory were correct, then statutes expressly requiring that certain kinds of processing be done in the home State before shipment to a sister State would be immune from constitutional challenge. Yet such statutes have been consistently invalidated by this Court under the commerce clause. Thus it is clear that the appellant's order does affect and burden interstate commerce, and the question then becomes whether it does so unconstitutionally.

[B]

Although the criteria for determining the validity of state statutes affecting interstate commerce have been variously stated, the general rule that emerges can be phrased as follows: Where the statute regulates even-handedly to effectuate a legitimate local public interest, and its effects on interstate commerce are only incidental, it will be upheld unless the burden imposed on such commerce is clearly excessive in relation to the putative local benefits. If a legitimate local purpose is found, then the question becomes one of degree. And the extent of the burden that will be tolerated will of course depend on the nature of the local interest involved, and on whether it could be promoted as well with a lesser impact on interstate activities. Occasionally the Court has candidly undertaken a balancing approach in resolving these issues, *Southern Pacific Co. v. Arizona*, 325 U.S. 761 (1945), but more frequently it has spoken in terms of "direct" and "indirect" effects and burdens.

[C]

At the core of the Arizona Fruit and Vegetable Standardization Act are the requirements that fruits and vegetables shipped from Arizona meet certain standards of wholesomeness and quality, and that they be packed in standard containers in such a way that the pack does not "materially misrepresent" the quality of the lot as a whole. The State has stipulated that its primary purpose is to promote and preserve the reputation of Arizona growers by prohibiting deceptive packaging.

[The Act's] purpose and design are simply to protect and enhance the reputation of growers within the State. These are surely legitimate state interests. We have upheld a State's power to require that produce packaged in the State be packaged in a particular kind of receptacle. And we have recognized the legitimate interest of a State in maximizing the financial return to an industry within it. Therefore, as applied to Arizona growers who package their produce in Arizona, we may assume the constitutional validity of the Act. We may further assume that Arizona has full constitutional power to forbid the misleading use of its name on produce that was grown or packed elsewhere. And, to the extent the Act forbids the shipment of contaminated or unfit produce, it clearly rests on sure footing. For, as the Court has said, such produce is "not the legitimate subject of trade or commerce, nor within the protection of the commerce clause of the Constitution."

But application of the Act through the appellant's order to the appellee company has a far different impact, and quite a different purpose. The cantaloupes grown by the company at Parker are of exceptionally high quality. The company does not pack them in Arizona and cannot do so without making a capital expenditure of approximately $200,000. It transports them in bulk to nearby Blythe, California, where they are sorted, inspected, packed, and shipped in containers that do not identify them as Arizona cantaloupes, but bear the name of their California packer. The appellant's order would forbid the company to pack its cantaloupes outside Arizona, not for the purpose of keeping the reputation of its growers unsullied, but to enhance their reputation through the reflected good will of the company's superior produce. The appellant, in other words, is not complaining because the company is putting the good name of Arizona on an inferior or deceptively packaged product, but because it is not putting that name on a product that is superior and well packaged.

Although it is not easy to see why the other growers of Arizona are entitled to benefit at the company's expense from the fact that it produces superior crops, we may assume that the asserted state interest is a legitimate one. But the State's tenuous interest in having the company's cantaloupes identified as originating in Arizona cannot constitutionally justify the requirement that the company build and operate an unneeded $200,000 packing plant in the State. The nature of that burden is, constitutionally, more significant than its extent. For the Court has viewed with particular suspicion state statutes requiring business operations to be performed in the home State that could more efficiently be performed elsewhere. Even where the State is pursuing a clearly legitimate local interest, this particular burden on commerce has been declared to be virtually per se illegal.

While the order issued under the Arizona statute does not impose rigidity on an entire industry, it does impose just such a straitjacket on the appellee company with respect to the allocation of its interstate resources. Such an incidental consequence of a regulatory scheme could perhaps be tolerated if a more compelling state interest were involved. But here the State's interest is minimal at best.

The judgment is affirmed.

EXERCISE 11:

1. Describe the analysis used by the Court to find that the Arizona statute violated the dormant Commerce Clause.

2. How did the Court determine that the Arizona statute in question was neutral?

3. The Supreme Court explicitly adopted a balancing test to determine when non-discriminatory laws violate the dormant Commerce Clause. Are there problems associated with the Court balancing in the manner required by the *Pike* test? Are there benefits?

4. The Court describes at length the many ways in which states may regulate without unconstitutionally impeding interstate commerce. One aspect of state regulatory authority is the authority of states to regulate "contaminated or unfit produce." What about the manner in which the Court referenced this doctrine undermines the Court's conclusion in *Philadelphia v. New Jersey*, discussed above, that waste is an object of commerce?

5. Recall the problem in Exercise 9 involving the Minnesota law banning the sale of milk in plastic disposable containers but allowing it in cardboard containers. Does this statute survive the *Pike* balancing test?

6. Suppose Iowa passes a statute prohibiting the use of 65-foot double-trailer trucks within its borders, while allowing 55-foot single-trailer trucks and 60-foot double-trailer trucks. The statute provides exceptions for trucks transporting farm equipment, livestock, and mobile homes and permits border cities to adopt the length limitations of an adjoining state. Iowa claims that the statute is designed to increase safety and reduce road wear. Is the statute constitutional? If not, what is the constitutional problem? Does it have a discriminatory purpose? Does it fail the *Pike* balancing test? *See Kassel v. Consolidated Freightways Corp.*, 450 U.S. 662 (1981).

3. Exceptions

There are two primary situations in which the dormant Commerce Clause does not prohibit states from burdening interstate commerce. The first is where Congress has authorized the challenged state regulation, and the second is where the state is itself a participant in interstate commerce.

a. Congressional Approval

Since the dormant Commerce Clause's restrictions on state regulation are based on the Article I grant of power to Congress to regulate interstate commerce, Congress may authorize state regulation that the dormant Commerce Clause would otherwise prohibit. This has, in fact, occurred in many fields of law and in discrete circumstances. Congress may by statute authorize a particular form of state regulation explicitly or implicitly. This "exception" was recognized in *Gibbons v. Ogden*, 22 U.S. (9 Wheat.) 1, 207 (1824), where Chief Justice Marshall stated that Congress "may adopt the provisions of a state on any subject."

Examples of the latter, *implicit* congressional authorization, are fairly difficult to identify for the same reasons that we discussed above in the context of preemption. To find an implied authorization of state regulation of interstate commerce, the Supreme Court must first determine that Congress has authorized state regulation and, second, that the challenged state action fits within this implied congressional approval.

Examples of the former, such as where Congress explicitly authorized state regulation of insurance even when the state regulation burdened interstate commerce, are easier to identify. McCarren-Ferguson Act, 59 Stat. 33 (1945), *codified at* 15 U.S.C. § 101 (2011). This is because there is a textual statement of exemption. However, the issue of determining whether a particular state law falls within that exemption remains.

b. Market Participant

The market participant "exception" to the dormant Commerce Clause relies on the distinction between states acting as regulators of commerce and states acting as participants in commerce. The dormant Commerce Clause, as the Supreme Court articulated in *Hughes v. Alexandria Scrap Corp.*, 426 U.S. 794 (1976), reprinted below, does not forbid states from favoring its own citizens when the state itself is a participant in the market.

HUGHES v. ALEXANDRIA SCRAP CORPORATION
426 U.S. 794 (1976)

Mr. Justice Powell delivered the opinion of the Court.

This case involves a constitutional attack on a recent amendment to one part of a complex Maryland plan for ridding that State of abandoned automobiles.

I

The 1967 session of the Maryland Legislature commissioned a study to suggest some way to deal with the growing aesthetic problem of abandoned automobiles. The study concluded that the root of the problem was the existence of bottlenecks in the "scrap cycle," the course that a vehicle follows from abandonment to processing into scrap metal for ultimate re-use by steel mills. At its 1969 session, the legislature responded by enacting a comprehensive statute designed to speed up the scrap cycle by using state money both as a carrot and as a stick.

The legislative study had found that one of the bottlenecks occurred in the junk-yards of wrecking companies, which tended to accumulate vehicles for the resale value of their spare parts. The statute's stick designed to clear this bottleneck is a require-ment that a Maryland wrecker desiring to keep abandoned vehicles on its premises must obtain a license and pay a recurring fine for any vehicle of a specified age retained for more than a year. The study had identified as another cause of sluggishness in the scrap cycle the low profits earned by wreckers and others for delivering vehicles to scrap processors. The carrot written into the statute to remedy this problem is a "bounty" paid by the State for the destruction, by a processor licensed under the stat-ute, of any vehicle formerly titled in Maryland. When a wrecker licensed under the statute to stockpile vehicles delivers one of them for scrapping it[] shares the bounty equally with the processor. The processor receives the entire bounty when it destroys a vehicle supplied by someone other than a licensed wrecker.

These penalty and bounty provisions work with elementary laws of economics to speed up the scrap cycle. The penalty for retention of vehicles, plus the prospect of sharing the bounty, work in tandem to encourage licensed wreckers to move vehicles to processors. The bounties to processors on vehicles from unlicensed suppliers also encourage those suppliers to deliver to the processors, because the processors are able to pay higher than normal market prices by sharing the bounties with them.

The penalty and bounty provisions, however, did not remove another impediment to the smooth functioning of the scrap cycle that was legal rather than economic in origin. This was the possibility of suits for conversion against a processor by owners who might claim that they had not abandoned their vehicles. To meet this problem the statute specified several documents with which a processor could prove clear title to a vehicle, and required that a processor obtain one of these documents from its supplier and submit it to the State as a condition of receiving the bounty. One of the documents, called a "Wrecker's Certificate," can be given only by a wrecker licensed under the statute. It is essentially a clear title that the wrecker secures by following statutory notice procedures at the time it first obtains a vehicle. Suppliers other than licensed wreckers must provide some other document either a properly endorsed cer-tificate of title, a certificate from a police department vesting title in the supplier after statutory notices, or a bill of sale from a police auction.

These documentation requirements, although vital for the protection of pro-cessors, are themselves some slight encumbrance upon the free transfer of abandoned vehicles to processors. Apparently in recognition of this fact, and the reduced potential for owners' claims in the case of ancient automobiles, the statute placed vehicles over eight years old and inoperable ("hulks") into a special category. [T]he statute, as enacted, provided in substance that anyone in possession of a hulk could transfer it to a scrap processor, and the processor could claim a bounty for its destruction, without delivery to the processor or subsequent submission to the State of *any* documentation of title.

A

The statute extends its burdens of fines, and its benefits in the form of a share in bounties, only to wreckers that maintain junkyards located in Maryland, and requires a license only of those wreckers. There is no similar residency requirement for scrap processors that wish to obtain a license and participate in the bounty program, and in fact seven of the 16 scrap processors that have participated are located in either Pennsylvania or Virginia. Appellee, a Virginia corporation, was an original licensee under the Maryland statute. Presumably because of its proximity to the southern Maryland and Washington, D.C., areas, appellee attracted enough Maryland-titled vehicles to its plant to rank third among licensed processors in receipt of bounties through the summer of 1974.

As is apparently the case with most of the licensed processors, virtually all (96%) of the bounty-eligible vehicles processed by appellee during that period were hulks, upon which appellee did not have to demand title documentation from its suppliers in order later to receive the bounty. In the summer of 1974, however, Maryland changed significantly the treatment of hulks by amending [its statute]. Under the law as amended it is no longer possible for a licensed scrap processor to receive a bounty on a hulk without submitting title documentation to the State. But the documentation required of a processor whose plant is in Maryland differs from that required of a processor, like appellee, whose plant is not in Maryland. The former need only submit a simple document in which the person who delivered the hulk certified his own right to it and agreed to indemnify the processor for any third-party claims arising from its destruction. Hulk processors long had required such "indemnity agreements" from their hulk suppliers as a matter of industry practice. The effect of the 1974 amendment is to give these agreements legal recognition and to require one when a Maryland processor applies for a bounty on a hulk. The non-Maryland processor, however, cannot submit a simple indemnity agreement. For it, receipt of a bounty on a hulk now depends upon the same documentation specified for abandoned vehicles in general: a certificate of title, a police certificate vesting title, a bill of sale from a police auction, or in the case of licensed wreckers only a Wrecker's Certificate.

B

The complaint in this case was filed shortly after the effective date of the amendment. Papers submitted to the three-judge District Court on summary judgment indicated that enactment of the amendment had been followed by a precipitate decline in the number of bounty-eligible hulks supplied to appellee's plant from Maryland sources. Appellee attributed the decline primarily to the effect of the amendment upon the decision of unlicensed suppliers as to where to dispose of their hulks. It is easier for an unlicensed supplier to sign an indemnity agreement upon delivering a hulk to a processor than it is for it to secure some form of title documentation. Because only a Maryland processor can use an indemnity agreement to obtain a bounty, the amendment gave Maryland processors an advantage over appellee and other non-Maryland processors in the competition for bounty-eligible hulks from unlicensed suppliers. Such hulks therefore now tend to remain in State instead of moving to licensed processors outside Maryland.

II

In this Court appellee relies on the Commerce Clause argument that was adopted by the District Court. The argument starts from the premise, well established by the history of the Commerce Clause, that this Nation is a common market in which state lines cannot be made barriers to the free flow of both raw materials and finished goods in response to the economic laws of supply and demand.

The practical effect of the amendment, however, was to limit the enhanced price available to unlicensed suppliers to hulks that stayed inside Maryland, thus discouraging such suppliers from taking their hulks out of State for processing. The result was that the movement of hulks in interstate commerce was reduced. Appellee contends that this effect of the 1974 amendment is a "burden" on interstate commerce, the permissibility of which must be determined under the test of *Pike v. Bruce Church, Inc.*, 397 U.S. 137 (1970).

[W]e are not persuaded that Maryland's action in amending its statute was the kind of action with which the Commerce Clause is concerned.

The situation presented by the 1974 amendment is quite unlike that found in the cases upon which appellee relies. In the most recent of those cases, *Pike v. Bruce Church, supra*, a burden was found to be imposed by an Arizona requirement that fresh fruit grown in the State be packed there before shipment interstate. The requirement prohibited the interstate shipment of fruit in bulk, no matter what the market demand for such shipments. In *H.P. Hood & Sons v. Du Mond*, 336 U.S. 525 (1949), a New York official denied a license to a milk distributor who wanted to open a new plant at which to receive raw milk from New York farmers for immediate shipment to Boston. The denial blocked a potential increase in the interstate movement of raw milk. [The Supreme Court reviewed five other cases relied on by appellee.]

The common thread of all these cases is that the State interfered with the natural functioning of the interstate market either through prohibition or through burdensome regulation. By contrast, Maryland has not sought to prohibit the flow of hulks, or to regulate the conditions under which it may occur. Instead, it has entered into the market itself to bid up their price. There has been an impact upon the interstate flow of hulks only because, since the 1974 amendment, Maryland effectively has made it more lucrative for unlicensed suppliers to dispose of their hulks in Maryland rather than take them outside the State.[15]

We believe that the novelty of this case is not its presentation of a new form of "burden" upon commerce, but that appellee should characterize Maryland's action as a burden which the Commerce Clause was intended to make suspect. The Clause was designed in part to prevent trade barriers that had undermined efforts of the fledgling States to form a cohesive whole following their victory in the Revolution.

In realizing the Founders' vision this Court has adhered strictly to the principle "that the right to engage in interstate commerce is not the gift of a state, and that a state cannot regulate or restrain it." But until today the Court has not been asked to hold that the entry by the State itself into the market as a purchaser, in effect, of a potential article of interstate commerce creates a burden upon that commerce if the State restricts its trade to its own citizens or businesses within the State.

We do not believe the Commerce Clause was intended to require independent justification for such action. Maryland entered the market for the purpose, agreed by all to be commendable as well as legitimate, of protecting the State's environment. As the means of furthering this purpose, it elected the payment of state funds in the form of bounties to encourage the removal of automobile hulks from Maryland streets and junkyards. [N]o trade barrier of the type forbidden by the Commerce Clause, and involved in previous cases, impedes their movement out of State. They remain within Maryland in response to market forces, including that exerted by money from the State. Nothing in the purposes animating the Commerce Clause prohibits a State, in the absence of congressional action, from participating in the market and exercising the right to favor its own citizens over others.

We hold that the District Court erred in finding the 1974 amendment invalid under the Commerce Clause. Accordingly, its judgment is reversed.

So ordered.

Mr. Justice Stevens, concurring.

The dissent creates the impression that the Court's opinion, which I join without reservation, represents a significant retreat from its settled practice in adjudicating claims that a state program places an unconstitutional burden on interstate commerce. This is not the fact. There is no prior decision of this Court even addressing the critical Commerce Clause issue presented by this case.

It is important to differentiate between commerce which flourishes in a free market and commerce which owes its existence to a state subsidy program. Our cases finding that a state regulation constitutes an impermissible burden on interstate commerce all dealt with restrictions that adversely affected the operation of a free

---

15. Again, we emphasize that the 1974 amendment, by its terms, does not require unlicensed suppliers to deliver hulks in State to receive enhanced prices. This is simply its effect in practice.

market. This case is unique because the commerce which Maryland has "burdened" is commerce which would not exist if Maryland had not decided to subsidize a portion of the automobile scrap-processing business.

MR. JUSTICE BRENNAN, with whom MR. JUSTICE WHITE and MR. JUSTICE MARSHALL join, dissenting.

The Court continues its reinterpretation of the Commerce Clause and its repudiation of established principles guiding judicial analysis thereunder in this case shifting its focus from congressional power arising under the Commerce Clause, to the role of this Court in considering the constitutionality of state action claimed impermissibly to burden interstate commerce. I cannot agree that well-established principles for analyzing claims arising under the Commerce Clause are inapplicable merely because of the "kind of [state] action" involved, or that it is defensible that legal analysis should cease, irrespective of the impact on commerce or the other facts and circumstances of the case, merely because the Court somehow categorically determines that the instant case involves "a burden which the Commerce Clause was [not] intended to make suspect."

II

I first address the question that the Court answers: the question whether a State may restrict its purchases of items of interstate commerce to items produced, manufactured, or processed within its own boundaries. When a State so restricts purchases for its own use, it does not affect the total flow of interstate commerce, but rather precludes only that quantum that would otherwise occur if the State were to behave as a private and disinterested purchaser. Nevertheless, it cannot be gainsaid that a State's refusal for purposes of economic protectionism to purchase for end use items produced elsewhere is a facial and obvious "discrimination against interstate commerce" that we have often said "[t]he commerce clause, by its own force, prohibits, whatever its form or method." *South Carolina Hwy. Dept. v. Barnwell Bros. See H.P. Hood & Sons, Inc. v. Du Mond.* Clearly the "aim and effect" of such a discrimination is "establishing an economic barrier against competition with the products of another state or the labor of its residents." Certainly the Court's naked assertion today that "[n]othing in the purposes animating the Commerce Clause prohibits a State . . . from participating in the market and exercising the right to favor its own citizens over others," stands in stark contrast to our "repeated emphasis upon the principle that the State may not promote its own economic advantages by curtailment or burdening of interstate commerce." *H.P. Hood & Sons, Inc. v. Du Mond.*

Moreover, the particular form of discrimination arising when the State restricts its purchases for use to items produced in its own State is of a kind particularly suspect under our precedents, as it is aimed directly at requiring the relocation of labor and industry within the bounds of the State, thus tending "to neutralize advantages belonging to" other States. We have "viewed with particular suspicion state statutes requiring business operations to be performed in the home State that could more efficiently be performed elsewhere. Even where the State is pursuing a clearly legitimate local interest, this particular burden on commerce has been declared to be virtually per se illegal." *Pike v. Bruce Church, Inc.*

I would hold, consistent with accepted Commerce Clause principles, that state statutes that facially or in practical effect restrict state purchases of items in interstate commerce to those produced within the State are invalid unless justified by asserted state interests other than economic protectionism in regulating matters of local concern for which "reasonable nondiscriminatory alternatives, adequate to conserve legitimate local interests, are [not] available." *Dean Milk Co. v. Madison*, 340 U.S. 349 (1951).

III

Second, the Court's insistence on viewing this case as qualitatively different under the Commerce Clause merely because the State is in some sense acting as a "purchaser" of the affected items of commerce leads it completely to forgo analysis of another equally vital question. Even if, as the Court concludes, state economic protectionism in "purchasing" items of interstate commerce is not a suspect motive under the Commerce Clause, analysis in this case cannot cease at that point, for by the instant regulation Maryland is allegedly affecting a larger area of commerce by diverting processing of scrap metal in interstate commerce to within its own boundaries.

Rather, once a legitimate state regulation of an object of local concern is found to burden interstate commerce, [e]stablished principles dictate that in such a situation analysis proceed[s under *Pike v. Bruce Church, Inc.*]

EXERCISE 12:

1. Are you persuaded by the Supreme Court that Maryland's actions, even though they burden interstate commerce, are not subject to analysis under the *Pike* balancing test?

2. Does the majority respond to the dissent's argument that Maryland's bounty scheme is simply protectionism and hence is subject to invalidation under cases like *H.P. Hood*?

3. Is there any reason to be less suspicious of state intervention in interstate commerce like Maryland's?

4. Suppose Oregon sells timber cut on land that it owns to Oregon residents at a discount. Nonresidents are not eligible for the discount. Is this form of discrimination constitutional? Should it be? Suppose Oregon imposes an additional restriction — all state-owned timber must be processed in Oregon before being used in or shipped out of state. Is this additional requirement constitutional?

Chapter 4

FEDERALISM LIMITS ON THE FEDERAL GOVERNMENT

A. INTRODUCTION

The Tenth Amendment states that the "powers not delegated to the United States by the Constitution, nor prohibited by it to the States, are reserved to the States respectively, or to the people." U.S. Const., amend. X. The Tenth Amendment is and has been cited as the textual home for limits on the federal government that exist because of our federal system, one in which states play an enduring and important role.

The Supreme Court's interpretation of—and conventional wisdom regarding—the Amendment has oscillated on two distinct, though related, axes. The first axis concerns whether the Tenth Amendment is judicially enforceable. One interpretation is that the Amendment carves out a judicially enforceable zone of state immunity from federal regulation. The other pole is that there are no judicially enforceable federalism limits on the federal government only politically enforceable limits.

The second axis concerns what limits, if any, the Tenth Amendment places on federal power. One view is that the Tenth Amendment, of its own authority, preserves a sphere of state autonomy from federal regulation. On the other end of the spectrum is the claim that the Amendment has no substantive content; instead, it merely repeats that the federal government is one of limited and enumerated powers. The Amendment, on this view, does no legal "work" because the enumeration of powers pre-exists the Amendment.

This Chapter first reviews the Tenth Amendment's origin. Then, it covers the evolution of the Supreme Court's interpretation of the Amendment.

EXERCISE 1:

Volume 1 in this series introduced five commonly accepted forms of argument in constitutional interpretation. They include: (1) the Constitution's text; (2) the structure of the government created and contemplated by the Constitution; (3) the historical setting from which the Constitution emerged and the text's meaning as articulated in that setting; (4) the traditional understanding of the Constitution on a particular matter; and (5) judicial precedent.

Apply the first four forms of argument to the Tenth Amendment:

1. Looking at the Tenth Amendment itself, the Ninth Amendment's text, the text of the rest of the Bill of Rights, and the text of the Necessary and Proper Clause in Article I, §8, what do you learn about the Tenth Amendment's meaning?

2. Looking at the Constitution's structure, and particularly at the enumeration of powers and the existence of the Bill of Rights, what do you learn about the Tenth Amendment's meaning?

3. Reviewing materials from the framing and ratification debates for both the original Constitution and the Tenth Amendment, what do they tell you about that meaning?

4. What insight do the materials following ratification of the Tenth Amendment (including early treatises) offer into the Tenth Amendment's meaning?

As you read the materials throughout the rest of this Chapter, some of the issues to consider include:

Does the Tenth Amendment have independent substantive content, or does it merely reiterate the enumeration of powers? If the Amendment does have independent content, what is it?

Is the Tenth Amendment judicially enforceable? Should it be?

What function has the Tenth Amendment played in the Supreme Court's case law?

What is the Tenth Amendment's relationship to the Necessary and Proper Clause? The Ninth Amendment?

What legal doctrines have and have had their roots in the Tenth Amendment?

What is the Supreme Court's current interpretation of the Tenth Amendment?

How does the Supreme Court's current interpretation of the Tenth Amendment differ from its previous interpretation(s)?

What is the basis for the Supreme Court's modern interpretation of the Tenth Amendment?

Is that interpretation faithful to the Amendment's original meaning? If not, how do you account for the divergence?

Which of the Supreme Court's interpretations of the Tenth Amendment has the most support from the five forms of argument?

B. ORIGINS

The original Constitution that the Framers at the Philadelphia Convention sent to the states for ratification did not contain what today is known as the Bill of Rights.[1]

---

1. For a broader description of the background and events leading up to the Bill of Rights, see LEONARD W. LEVY, ORIGINS OF THE BILL OF RIGHTS (1999). For discussions of the meanings of the

It did contain *some* restrictions on both the federal and state governments, found primarily[2] in Article I, Sections 9 and 10.[3] The Framers did not include a comprehensive bill of rights for two primary[4] reasons: first, it was unnecessary because the federal government was one of limited and enumerated powers that did not have the authority to trench on individual rights;[5] and second, a bill of rights would lead to the perverse conclusion that the Constitution authorized the federal government to infringe individual rights, both enumerated and unenumerated.[6]

During the subsequent state ratification debates, the Anti-Federalists utilized the lack of a comprehensive bill of rights as their primary — and most effective — argument against ratification. They controverted both of the Federalists' claims.[7] Pointing especially to the Necessary and Proper Clause,[8] Anti-Federalists claimed, for instance, that Congress could utilize unenumerated means that violated individual rights to achieve enumerated ends.[9]

Second, and more important to the ultimate development of the Tenth Amendment, Anti-Federalists raised two arguments against the Federalists' (legitimate) concern that the enumeration of rights would imply federal power to infringe on those and other, *un*enumerated rights. First, Anti-Federalists claimed that the enumeration of some rights in Sections 9 and 10 undermined the Federalists' concern that the enumeration of rights would imply federal power to violate rights.[10] Second, Anti-Federalists pointed to the ubiquitous practice in England and the new United States of utilizing bills of rights, and contended that the Federalists' concern did not fit this experience.[11]

---

amendments, see AKHIL REED AMAR, THE BILL OF RIGHTS: CREATION AND RECONSTRUCTION (1998); THE BILL OF RIGHTS: ORIGINAL MEANING AND CURRENT UNDERSTANDING (Eugene W. Hickok, Jr., ed., 1991). For a discussion of the Tenth Amendment's original meaning, see Gary Lawson, *A Truism with Attitude: The Tenth Amendment in Constitutional Context*, 83 NOTRE DAME L. REV. 469 (2008). For a discussion of the relationship between the Ninth and Tenth Amendments see Kurt T. Lash, *The Original Meaning of an Omission: The Tenth Amendment, Popular Sovereignty, and "Expressly" Delegated Power*, 83 NOTRE DAME L. REV. 1889 (2008).

2. Additional limits are scattered throughout the original Constitution. For example, Article III, §2, cl. 3, contains the requirement that the "Trial of all Crimes . . . shall be by Jury."

3. Some scholars have labeled Sections 9 and 10 a "mini bill of rights" or the "original" Bill of Rights.

4. Other reasons also caused the Framers not to adopt a bill of rights, including weariness from the long, hot summer during which the convention was held. LEVY, *supra*, at 12–13.

5. *Id.* at 20; Lash, *supra*, at 1913.

6. LEVY, *supra*, at 12–13.

7. *See* Lash, *supra*, at 1904 ("The omission of a provision like Article II [from the Articles of Confederation], however, left the proposed Constitution without any express limitation on the construction of federal authority.").

8. U.S. CONST., art. I, §8, cl. 18; *see also* LEVY, *supra*, at 28 ("The necessary and proper clause particularly enraged advocates of a bill of rights."); Lawson, *supra*, at 479–80 (describing the Anti-Federalists' use of the Necessary and Proper Clause).

9. LEVY, *supra*, at 27.

10. *Id.* at 28–29.

11. *Id.* at 22–25.

Ultimately recognizing that the Anti-Federalists' arguments had significant traction, and that the issue threatened ratification, the Federalists in the various state ratification conventions prudently agreed to introduce a bill of rights when the federal government was organized. In reliance on this explicit Federalist promise, states ratified the Constitution.

It fell to James Madison to draft and introduce into the House what became the Bill of Rights. However, Madison wished to avoid the inference that the Federalists feared would arise if the Constitution included an enumeration of rights. To do so, while still fulfilling the Federalists' promise to enact a bill of rights, Madison devised what became the Ninth and Tenth Amendments.

The Ninth and Tenth Amendments were Madison's complimentary, two-pronged solution to the basic Federalist concerns. Both Amendments protected federalism by limiting the federal government's powers.

The Tenth Amendment textually reaffirmed that the new federal government was one of limited and enumerated powers.[12] It reiterated[13] that all governmental power not delegated via the Constitution to the federal government remained with the states or the People.[14] The Tenth Amendment, therefore, had a close relationship to the Necessary and Proper Clause.[15]

The Tenth Amendment's explicit limitation of the federal government to enumerated powers left open the possibility, however, that the federal government might over-broadly construe its enumerated powers or utilize overbroad means to achieve enumerated powers. The Ninth Amendment introduced a rule of construction to rebut these possibilities.[16] "The enumeration . . . of certain rights, shall not be construed to deny or disparage others retained by the people."[17] This rule of construction required interpreters to narrowly construe federal power.

Madison's initial draft of the Tenth Amendment was drawn primarily from an amendment proposed by Virginia,[18] although a number of other states also submitted similar proposals. It stated: "The powers not delegated by this Constitution, nor prohibited by it to the States, are reserved to the States respectively."[19]

---

12. Eugene W. Hickok, Jr., *The Original Understanding of the Tenth Amendment, in* THE BILL OF RIGHTS: ORIGINAL MEANING AND CURRENT UNDERSTANDING, *supra*, at 461.

13. The Tenth Amendment was a restatement of Article I, § 1, cl. 1, which likewise provided that the federal government could only exercise the powers "herein granted," and the Necessary and Proper Clause, which prohibited "[im]proper" federal legislation that, for example, violated the structural principle of federalism.

14. AMAR, *supra*, at 123; Hickok, *supra*, at 462.

15. *See* Lawson, *supra*, at 472 ("The Bill of Rights, including the Tenth Amendment, in large measure simply reformulates the restrictions on federal power built into the Sweeping Clause."); *id.* at 483 ("'[P]roper' laws must respect background norms of . . . federalism.").

16. AMAR, *supra*, at 124; LEVY *supra*, at 247.

17. U.S. CONST., amend. IX.

18. Lash, *supra*, at 1918.

19. Hickok, *supra*, at 462.

The Tenth Amendment did not engender significant debate. The most significant event that occurred was a proposal by Representative Thomas Tudor Tucker for two modifications to Madison's proffered Tenth Amendment. Tucker proposed adding "all powers being derived from the people" and "expressly," so that the amendment would read: "*All powers being derived from the people,* the powers not *expressly* delegated by this Constitution, nor prohibited by it to the States, are reserved to the States respectively."[20] The House accepted only Tucker's first proposal because it agreed with Madison's argument that the addition of "expressly" would lead to the problems faced by Congress under the Articles of Confederation and disable the new federal government from performing necessary tasks.[21]

Over time, courts and scholars lost sight of the Ninth and Tenth Amendments' complementarity. The received wisdom today is that the Ninth Amendment is a potential source of (judicially enforceable) protection for unenumerated constitutional rights.[22] The Tenth Amendment, by contrast, is perceived as a repository for protection of states from federal regulation.[23] This can put the Amendments at cross-purposes.[24]

The cases and text below describe the Supreme Court's interpretation of the Tenth Amendment. We will see that the Court's interpretations have varied on both axes described above. In some cases, the Court held that the Amendment is judicially enforceable; and in others, that it is not. Similarly, in some cases the Court concluded that the Tenth Amendment was an independent limit on Congress' power; while in other cases, it described the Amendment as lacking its own substantive content.

C. FEDERALISM'S APOTHEOSIS PRIOR TO THE NEW DEAL

Beginning in the late-nineteenth century, the Supreme Court explicitly utilized the Tenth Amendment in a number of ways. The two most prominent roles that the Tenth Amendment played during this period, and up to the New Deal,

---

20. 1 ANNALS OF CONG. 761 (Joseph Gales ed., 1834) (emphases added).

21. *Id.*

22. *See Griswold v. Connecticut*, 381 U.S. 479, 486–98 (1965) (utilizing the Ninth Amendment as a repository for the unenumerated, judicially enforceable right to use artificial birth control); LEVY, *supra*, at 241–56 (making this claim); RANDY E. BARNETT, RESTORING THE LOST CONSTITUTION: THE PRESUMPTION OF LIBERTY 54–60, 224–69 (2004) (arguing that the Ninth Amendment protects judicially enforceable unenumerated natural rights).

23. *See National League of Cities v. Usery*, 426 U.S. 833, 842 (1976), *overruled by San Antonio v. Garcia*, 469 U.S. 528 (1985) ("The Amendment expressly declares the constitutional policy that Congress may not exercise power in a fashion that impairs the States' integrity or their ability to function effectively in a federal system.").

24. *See* AMAR, *supra*, at 121 ("[C]onventional wisdom today misses the close triangular interrelation among the Preamble and the Ninth and Tenth Amendments. The Ninth is said to be about unenumerated individual rights . . . ; the Tenth about federalism.").

included: (1) a rule of construction for Congress' enumerated powers—especially the Commerce Clause; and (2) an independent check on federal authority.

United States v. E.C. Knight Co., 156 U.S. 1 (1895), for instance, exemplified the Supreme Court's use of the Tenth Amendment as an aid in interpreting Congress' Commerce Clause power. (*E.C. Knight* was covered in detail in Volume 3.) There, the federal government prosecuted sugar manufacturers for illegally monopolizing the sugar market. The defendants argued that Congress' Commerce Clause authority did not reach their alleged activity—manufacturing—and the Supreme Court agreed. In reaching its conclusion, the Court gave, as one of its reasons, the need to limit federal power in order to preserve state authority:

> It is vital that the independence of the commercial power and of the police power, and the delimitation between them, however sometimes perplexing, should always be recognized and observed, for, while the one furnishes the strongest bond of union, the other is essential to the preservation of the autonomy of the states as required by our dual form of government; and acknowledged evils, however grave and urgent they may appear to be, had better be borne, than the risk be run, in the effort to suppress them, of more serious consequences by resort to expedients of even doubtful constitutionality.

Id. at 13. The Court repeatedly employed this argument to bolster its narrow Commerce Clause interpretations. *See, e.g., Carter v. Carter Coal Co.*, 298 U.S. 238, 295–96 (1936) ("[T]he danger of such a step by the federal government in the direction of taking over the powers of the states is that the end of the journey may find the states so despoiled of their powers, or—what may amount to the same thing—so relieved of the responsibilities which possession of the powers necessarily enjoins, as to reduce them to little more than geographical subdivisions of the national domain."); *A.L.A. Schechter Poultry Corp. v. United States*, 295 U.S. 495, 546 (1935) ("If the commerce clause were construed to reach all enterprises and transactions which could be said to have an indirect effect upon interstate commerce, the federal authority would embrace practically all the activities of the people, and the authority of the state over its domestic concerns would exist only by sufferance of the federal government. Indeed, on such a theory, even the development of the state's commercial facilities would be subject to federal control.").

In the *Hammer v. Dagenhart*, below, the Supreme Court utilized the Tenth Amendment in the second way, as an independent limitation on federal power.

HAMMER v. DAGENHART
247 U.S. 251 (1918)

Mr. Justice Day delivered the opinion of the Court.

A bill was filed in the United States District Court for the Western District of North Carolina by a father in his own behalf and as next friend of his two minor sons, one under the age of fourteen years and the other between the ages of fourteen and sixteen years, employees in a cotton mill at Charlotte, North Carolina, to enjoin the enforcement of the act of Congress intended to prevent interstate commerce in the products of child labor.

The attack upon the act rests upon [two] propositions: First: It is not a regulation of interstate and foreign commerce; second: It contravenes the Tenth Amendment to the Constitution.

The controlling question for decision is: Is it within the authority of Congress in regulating commerce among the states to prohibit the transportation in interstate commerce of manufactured goods, the product of a factory in which, within thirty days prior to their removal therefrom, children under the age of fourteen have been employed or permitted to work, or children between the ages of fourteen and sixteen years have been employed or permitted to work more than eight hours in any day, or more than six days in any week, or after the hour of 7 o'clock p.m., or before the hour of 6 o'clock a.m.?

The power essential to the passage of this act, the government contends, is found in the commerce clause of the Constitution. [T]he [commerce] power is one to control the means by which commerce is carried on, which is directly the contrary of the assumed right to forbid commerce from moving and thus destroying it as to particular commodities.

The thing intended to be accomplished by this statute is the denial of the facilities of interstate commerce to those manufacturers in the states who employ children within the prohibited ages. The act in its effect does not regulate transportation among the states, but aims to standardize the ages at which children may be employed in mining and manufacturing within the states. The goods shipped are of themselves harmless.

Over interstate transportation, or its incidents, the regulatory power of Congress is ample, but the production of articles, intended for interstate commerce, is a matter of local regulation. If it were otherwise, all manufacture intended for interstate shipment would be brought under federal control to the practical exclusion of the authority of the states, a result certainly not contemplated by the framers of the Constitution when they vested in Congress the authority to regulate commerce among the States.

It is further contended that the authority of Congress may be exerted to control interstate commerce in the shipment of childmade goods because of the effect of the circulation of such goods in other states where the evil of this class of labor has been recognized by local legislation, and the right to thus employ child labor has been more rigorously restrained than in the state of production. In other words, that the unfair competition, thus engendered, may be controlled by closing the channels of interstate commerce to manufacturers in those states where the local laws do not meet what Congress deems to be the more just standard of other states.

The grant of power of Congress over the subject of interstate commerce was to enable it to regulate commerce, and not to give it authority to control the states in their exercise of the police power over local trade and manufacture.

The grant of authority over a purely federal matter was not intended to destroy the local power always existing and carefully reserved to the states in the Tenth Amendment to the Constitution. It may be desirable that [child labor] laws be uniform, but our federal government is one of enumerated powers.

In interpreting the Constitution it must never be forgotten that the nation is made up of states to which are entrusted the powers of local government. And to them and to the people the powers not expressly delegated to the national government are reserved. The power of the states to regulate their purely internal affairs by such laws as seem wise to the local authority is inherent and has never been surrendered to the general government. To sustain this statute would not be in our judgment a recognition of the lawful exertion of congressional authority over interstate commerce, but would sanction an invasion by the federal power of the control of a matter purely local in its character, and over which no authority has been delegated to Congress in conferring the power to regulate commerce among the states.

We have neither authority nor disposition to question the motives of Congress in enacting this legislation. The purposes intended must be attained consistently with constitutional limitations and not by an invasion of the powers of the states. This court has no more important function than that which devolves upon it the obligation to preserve inviolate the constitutional limitations upon the exercise of authority federal and state to the end that each may continue to discharge, harmoniously with the other, the duties entrusted to it by the Constitution.

In our view the necessary effect of this act is, by means of a prohibition against the movement in interstate commerce of ordinary commercial commodities to regulate the hours of labor of children in factories and mines within the states, a purely state authority. Thus the act in a two-fold sense is repugnant to the Constitution. It not only transcends the authority delegated to Congress over commerce but also exerts a power as to a purely local matter to which the federal authority does not extend. The far reaching result of upholding the act cannot be more plainly indicated than by pointing out that if Congress can thus regulate matters entrusted to local authority by prohibition of the movement of commodities in interstate commerce, all freedom of commerce will be at an end, and the power of the states over local matters may be eliminated, and thus our system of government be practically destroyed.

For these reasons we hold that this law exceeds the constitutional authority of Congress. It follows that the decree of the District Court must be

Affirmed.

Mr. Justice Holmes, dissenting.

The Act does not meddle with anything belonging to the States. They may regulate their internal affairs and their domestic commerce as they like. But when they seek to send their products across the State line they are no longer within their rights. If there were no Constitution and no Congress their power to cross the line would depend upon their neighbors. Under the Constitution such commerce belongs not to the States but to Congress to regulate. It may carry out its views of public policy whatever indirect effect they may have upon the activities of the States. Instead of being encountered by a prohibitive tariff at her boundaries the State encounters the public policy of the United States which it is for Congress to express. The public policy of the United States is shaped with a view to the benefit of the nation as a whole. The national welfare as understood by Congress may require a different attitude within its sphere from that of some self-seeking State. It seems to me entirely constitutional for Congress to enforce its understanding by all the means at its command.

MR. JUSTICE MCKENNA, MR. JUSTICE BRANDEIS, and MR. JUSTICE CLARKE concur in this opinion.

EXERCISE 2:

1. Is the *Hammer v Dagenhart* case faithful to the Tenth Amendment's original meaning?

2. What arguments did the Court give to support its use of the Amendment?

3. Is it an attractive interpretation of the Tenth Amendment? What would be bad about adopting Justice Holmes' interpretation of the Commerce Clause which lacked the Tenth Amendment limit identified by the majority?

4. The Supreme Court's reasoning would require it to draw principled lines protecting "local matter[s]" from federal regulation; is that something courts can do?

5. A prominent reason motivating the Court's narrow reading of the Commerce Clause and broad reading of the Tenth Amendment was its "slippery slope" concern that alternative interpretations would lead to the end of federalism. How does one evaluate that claim? Is it true?

D. NEW DEAL TRANSFORMATION

One of the many changes made during the New Deal was that the Supreme Court ceased enforcing many federalism limits on the federal government. The key case that made this transition in the Tenth Amendment context is below.

UNITED STATES v. DARBY
312 U.S. 100 (1941)

MR. JUSTICE STONE delivered the opinion of the Court.

The two principal questions raised by the record in this case are, first, whether Congress has constitutional power to prohibit the shipment in interstate commerce of lumber manufactured by employees whose wages are less than a prescribed minimum or whose weekly hours of labor at that wage are greater than a prescribed maximum, and, second, whether it has power to prohibit the employment of workmen in the production of goods "for interstate commerce" at other than prescribed wages and hours.

Appellee demurred to an indictment found in the district court for southern Georgia charging him with violation of the Fair Labor Standards Act of 1938. The demurrer challenged the validity of the Fair Labor Standards Act under the Commerce Clause, and the Fifth and Tenth Amendments.

[I]

Section 15(a)(1) prohibits the shipment in interstate commerce, of goods produced for interstate commerce by employees whose wages and hours of employment do not conform to the requirements of the Act.

While manufacture is not of itself interstate commerce the shipment of manufactured goods interstate is such commerce and the prohibition of such shipment by Congress is indubitably a regulation of commerce. The power to regulate commerce is the power "to prescribe the rule by which commerce is to be governed." *Gibbons v. Ogden*, [22 U.S.] (9 Wheat.) 1, 196 [(1824)]. It extends not only to those regulations which aid, foster and protect the commerce, but embraces those which prohibit it. *Lottery Case*, 188 U.S. 321 [(1903)].

But it is said that while the prohibition is nominally a regulation of commerce its motive or purpose is regulation of wages and hours of persons engaged in manufacture, the control of which has been reserved to the states and upon which Georgia and some of the states of destination have placed no restriction. The power of Congress over interstate commerce "is complete in itself, may be exercised to its utmost extent, and acknowledges no limitations, other than are prescribed by the constitution." *Gibbons v. Ogden*. Congress, following its own conception of public policy concerning the restrictions which may appropriately be imposed on interstate commerce, is free to exclude from the commerce articles whose use in the states for which they are destined it may conceive to be injurious to the public health, morals or welfare, even though the state has not sought to regulate their use. *Lottery Case*.

In the more than a century which has elapsed since the decision of *Gibbons v. Ogden*, these principles of constitutional interpretation have been so long and repeatedly recognized by this Court as applicable to the Commerce Clause, that there would be little occasion for repeating them now were it not for the decision of this Court twenty-two years ago in *Hammer v. Dagenhart*, 247 U.S. 251 [(1918)]. In that case it was held by a bare majority of the Court over the powerful and now classic dissent of Mr. Justice Holmes setting forth the fundamental issues involved, that Congress was without power to exclude the products of child labor from interstate commerce. The reasoning and conclusion of the Court's opinion there cannot be reconciled with the conclusion which we have reached.

Hammer v. Dagenhart has not been followed. The distinction on which the decision was rested that Congressional power to prohibit interstate commerce is limited to articles which in themselves have some harmful or deleterious property—a distinction which was novel when made and unsupported by any provision of the Constitution—has long since been abandoned. The thesis of the opinion that the motive of the prohibition or its effect to control in some measure the use or production within the states of the article thus excluded from the commerce can operate to deprive the regulation of its constitutional authority has long since ceased to have force. *Lottery Case.*

Hammer v. Dagenhart should be and now is overruled.

[II]

There remains the question whether [the] restriction on the production of goods for commerce is a permissible exercise of the commerce power. The power of Congress over interstate commerce is not confined to the regulation of commerce among the states. It extends to those activities intrastate which so affect interstate commerce or the exercise of the power of Congress over it as to make regulation of them appropriate means to the attainment of a legitimate end, the exercise of the granted power of Congress to regulate interstate commerce. *See McCulloch v. Maryland*, [17 U.S.] (4 Wheat.) 316 [(1819)].

Congress, having by the present Act adopted the policy of excluding from interstate commerce all goods produced for the commerce which do not conform to the specified labor standards, it may choose the means reasonably adapted to the attainment of the permitted end, even though they involve control of intrastate activities.

The means adopted by § 15(a)(2) for the protection of interstate commerce by the suppression of the production of the condemned goods for interstate commerce is so related to the commerce and so affects it as to be within the reach of the commerce power.

[III]

Our conclusion is unaffected by the Tenth Amendment. The amendment states but a truism that all is retained which has not been surrendered. There is nothing in the history of its adoption to suggest that it was more than declaratory of the relationship between the national and state governments as it had been established by the Constitution before the amendment or that its purpose was other than to allay fears that the new national government might seek to exercise powers not granted, and that the states might not be able to exercise fully their reserved powers. *See e.g.*, II Elliot's Debates, 123, 131; III *id.* 450, 464, 600; IV *id.* 140, 149; I Annals of Congress, 432, 761, 767–768; Story, Commentaries on the Constitution, secs. 1907, 1908.

From the beginning and for many years the amendment has been construed as not depriving the national government of authority to resort to all means for the exercise of a granted power which are appropriate and plainly adapted to the permitted end. *McCulloch v. Maryland, Lottery Case.*

Reversed.

EXERCISE 3:

1. What arguments does the *Darby* Court provide to support its conclusion that the Tenth Amendment is "but a truism"?

2. Is *Darby* faithful to the Tenth Amendment's original meaning?

3. Is it a normatively attractive interpretation of the Tenth Amendment?

4. Did the *Darby* Court adequately justify overruling *Hammer*?

5. One reading of the Supreme Court's reasoning in Part II of *Darby* (upholding Section 15(a)(2)'s regulation of manufacturing) that has recently gained some prominence, is that the Court relied on Congress' Necessary and Proper Clause powers. Assuming this reading is right, make an argument that, in light of the Tenth Amendment, the Court's reasoning was unsound.

E. ABORTIVE REVIVAL

Darby's interpretation of the Tenth Amendment dominated the post-New Deal era. In the mid-1970s, across a number of doctrinal areas, the Supreme Court appeared poised to reinvigorate constitutional doctrines that had languished since the New Deal. For example, in Chapter 1, we saw that the Contracts Clause experienced a brief reinvigoration. And the same thing happened in the Tenth Amendment context in *National League of Cities v. Usery*, 426 U.S. 833 (1976), where a 5–4 majority of the Court held that the Tenth Amendment precluded Congress' extending the federal minimum wage and maximum hour provisions of the Fair Labor Standards Act ("FLSA") to state and municipal employees.

Writing for the majority in *National League of Cities*, Justice Rehnquist held that, even though the FLSA was a valid exercise of Congress' commerce power, the Tenth Amendment limited Congress' ability to extend FLSA's minimum wage and overtime provisions to the States: "[W]hen Congress seeks to regulate directly the activities of States as public employers, it transgresses an affirmative limitation on the exercise of its power akin to other commerce power affirmative limitations contained in the Constitution." *Id.* at 841. Just as other legislation duly enacted under the Commerce Clause cannot "offend against the right to trial by jury ... or the Due Process Clause[,] ... the 1974 Amendments to the Act, while undoubtedly within the scope of the Commerce Clause, encounter a similar constitutional barrier because they are to be applied directly to the States and subdivisions of States as employers." *Id.*

The *National League of Cities* majority concluded that the FLSA impermissibly infringed on the autonomy of the states in two ways. First, the "substantial costs" imposed on state and local governments would have "a significant impact on the functioning of the governmental bodies involved." *Id.* at 846–47. Second, Justice Rehnquist emphasized that the 1974 amendments "will impermissibly interfere with the integral governmental functions of these bodies .... [T]heir application will significantly alter or displace the States' abilities to structure employer-employee relationships in such areas as fire prevention, police protection, sanitation, public health, and parks and recreation .... Indeed, it is functions such as these which governments are created to provide, services such as these which the States have traditionally afforded their citizens. If Congress may withdraw from the States the authority to make those fundamental employment decisions ... , we think there would be little left of the States' 'separate and independent existence.'" *Id.* at 851. As a result, the majority concluded "that insofar as the challenged amendments operate to directly displace the States' freedom to structure integral operations in areas of traditional governmental functions, they are not within the authority granted Congress by Art. I, § 8, cl. 3." *Id.* at 852.

Support for the majority's Tenth Amendment analysis was tenuous from the start. Justice Blackmun concurred but made clear that he was "not untroubled by certain possible implications of the Court's opinion." *Id.* at 856 (Blackmun, J., concurring). According to Justice Blackmun, the majority adopted a "balancing approach" that did "not outlaw federal power in areas such as environmental protection, where the federal interest is demonstrably greater and where state facility compliance with imposed federal standards would be essential." *Id.* In a dissent joined by Justices White and Marshall, Justice Brennan argued that the majority opinion "repudiate[d] principles governing judicial interpretation of our Constitution settled since the time of Mr. Chief Justice John Marshall, discarding his postulate that the Constitution contemplates that restraints upon exercise by Congress of its plenary commerce power lie in the political process and not in the judicial process." *Id.* at 857 (Brennan, J., dissenting). For Justice Brennan, "nothing in the Tenth Amendment constitutes a limitation on congressional exercise of powers delegated by the Constitution to Congress. Rather, as the Tenth Amendment's significance was more recently summarized: 'The amendment states but a truism that all is retained which has not been surrendered.'" *Id.* at 862 (quoting *United States v. Darby*, 312 U.S. 100, 124 (1941)). Justice Brennan lobbied for "[j]udicial restraint" and deference to Congress because "the political branches of our Government are structured to protect the interests of States, as well as the Nation as a whole, and that States are fully able to protect their own interests." *Id.* at 876.

Ultimately, the Tenth Amendment revival, like that under the Contracts Clause, floundered. Following *National League of Cities*, states and others brought many challenges to federal statutory regulations claiming that the regulations, as applied to states, violated the Tenth Amendment. In each of these cases, the Supreme Court rejected the Tenth Amendment claim. Each decision purported to follow and apply *National League of Cities*. For example, in *Hodel v. Virginia Surface Mining and Reclamation Ass'n, Inc.*, 452 U.S. 264 (1981), the Supreme Court turned back a Tenth Amendment challenge and, in doing so, it refined the analysis it used to evaluate Tenth Amendment claims: "First, there must be a showing that the challenged statute regulates the States as States. Second, the federal regulation must address matters that are indisputably attribute[s] of state sovereignty. And, third, it must be apparent that the States' compliance with the federal law would directly impair their ability to structure integral operations in areas of traditional governmental functions." *Id.* at 287–88 (internal citations and quotations omitted). However, only nine years later, in *Garcia v. San Antonio*, the Supreme Court reversed course completely, overruling *National League of Cities*.

GARCIA v. SAN ANTONIO

469 U.S. 528 (1985)

JUSTICE BLACKMUN delivered the opinion of the Court.

We revisit in these cases an issue raised in *National League of Cities v. Usery*, 426 U.S. 833 (1976). In that litigation, this Court, by a sharply divided vote, ruled that the Commerce Clause does not empower Congress to enforce the minimum-wage and overtime provisions of the Fair Labor Standards Act (FLSA) against the States "in areas of traditional governmental functions." Since then, federal and state courts have struggled with the task, thus imposed, of identifying a traditional function for purposes of state immunity under the Commerce Clause.

Our examination of this "function" standard applied in these and other cases over the last eight years now persuades us that the attempt to draw the boundaries of state regulatory immunity in terms of "traditional governmental function" is not only unworkable but is also inconsistent with established principles of federalism and, indeed, with those very federalism principles on which *National League of Cities* purported to rest. That case, accordingly, is overruled.

I

The present controversy concerns the extent to which SAMTA [San Antonio Metropolitan Transit Authority] may be subjected to the minimum-wage and overtime requirements of the FLSA.

II

Appellees have not argued that SAMTA is immune from regulation under the FLSA on the ground that it is a local transit system engaged in intrastate commercial activity. In a practical sense, SAMTA's operations might well be characterized as "local." Nonetheless, it long has been settled that Congress' authority under the Commerce Clause extends to intrastate economic activities that affect interstate commerce. *See, e.g., Heart of Atlanta Motel, Inc. v. United States*, 379 U.S. 241, 258 (1964); *Wickard v. Filburn* [317 U.S. 111 (1942)]; *United States v. Darby*, 312 U.S. 100 (1941). Were SAMTA a privately owned and operated enterprise, it could not credibly argue that Congress exceeded the bounds of its Commerce Clause powers in prescribing minimum wages and overtime rates for SAMTA's employees. Any constitutional exemption from the requirements of the FLSA therefore must rest on SAMTA's status as a governmental entity rather than on the "local" nature of its operations.

The prerequisites for governmental immunity under *National League of Cities* were summarized by this Court in *Hodel* [*v. Virginia Surface Mining & Reclamation Ass'n, Inc.*, 452 U.S. 264 (1981)]. The controversy in the present cases has focused on the third *Hodel* requirement—that the challenged federal statute trench on "traditional governmental functions." Just how troublesome the task has been is revealed by the results reached in other federal cases. Thus, courts have held that regulating ambulance services; licensing automobile drivers; operating a municipal airport; performing solid waste disposal; and operating a highway authority, are functions *protected* under *National League of Cities.* At the same time, courts have held that issuance of industrial development bonds; regulation of intrastate natural gas sales; regulation of traffic on public roads; regulation of air transportation; operation of a telephone system; leasing and sale of natural gas; operation of a mental health facility; and provision of in-house domestic services for the aged and handicapped, are *not* entitled to immunity. We find it difficult, if not impossible, to identify an organizing principle that places each of the cases in the first group on one side of a line and each of the cases in the second group on the other side. The constitutional distinction between licensing drivers and regulating traffic, for example, or between operating a highway authority and operating a mental health facility, is elusive at best.

Many constitutional standards involve "undoubte[d] . . . gray areas," and, despite the difficulties that this Court and other courts have encountered so far, it normally might be fair to venture the assumption that case-by-case development would lead to a workable standard for determining whether a particular governmental function should be immune from federal regulation under the Commerce Clause.

[None] of the alternative standards that might be employed to distinguish between protected and unprotected governmental functions appear manageable. We rejected the possibility of making immunity turn on a purely historical standard of "tradition[,]" and properly so. The most obvious defect of a historical approach to state immunity is that it prevents a court from accommodating changes in the historical functions of States, changes that have resulted in a number of once-private functions like education being assumed by the States and their subdivisions. At the same time, the only apparent virtue of a rigorous historical standard, namely, its promise of a reasonably objective measure for state immunity, is illusory. Reliance on history as an organizing principle results in line-drawing of the most arbitrary sort; the genesis of state governmental functions stretches over a historical continuum from before the Revolution to the present, and courts would have to decide by fiat precisely how longstanding a pattern of state involvement had to be for federal regulatory authority to be defeated.

A nonhistorical standard for selecting immune governmental functions is likely to be just as unworkable as is a historical standard. The goal of identifying "uniquely" governmental functions is unmanageable. Another possibility would be to confine immunity to "necessary" governmental services, that is, services that would be provided inadequately or not at all unless the government provided them. The set of services that fits into this category, however, may well be negligible.

We believe, however, that there is a more fundamental problem at work here. The problem is that any [distinction] that purports to separate out important governmental functions can[not] be faithful to the role of federalism in a democratic society. The essence of our federal system is that within the realm of authority left open to them under the Constitution, the States must be equally free to engage in any activity that their citizens choose for the common weal, no matter how unorthodox or unnecessary anyone else—including the judiciary—deems state involvement to be. Any rule of state immunity that looks to the "traditional," "integral," or "necessary" nature of governmental functions inevitably invites an unelected federal judiciary to make decisions about which state policies it favors and which ones it dislikes. [T]he States cannot serve as laboratories for social and economic experiment if they must pay an added price when they meet the changing needs of their citizenry by taking up functions that an earlier day and a different society left in private hands.

We therefore now reject, as unsound in principle and unworkable in practice, a rule of state immunity from federal regulation that turns on a judicial appraisal of whether a particular governmental function is "integral" or "traditional." If there are to be limits on the Federal Government's power to interfere with state functions — as undoubtedly there are — we must look elsewhere to find them. We accordingly return to the underlying issue that confronted this Court in *National League of Cities* — the manner in which the Constitution insulates States from the reach of Congress' power under the Commerce Clause.

III

The central theme of *National League of Cities* was that the States occupy a special position in our constitutional system and that the scope of Congress' authority under the Commerce Clause must reflect that position. Of course, the Commerce Clause by its specific language does not provide any special limitation on Congress' actions with respect to the States. It is equally true, however, that the text of the Constitution provides the beginning rather than the final answer to every inquiry into questions of federalism, for "[b]ehind the words of the constitutional provisions are postulates which limit and control." *Monaco v. Mississippi*, 292 U.S. 313, 322 (1934).

What has proved problematic is not the perception that the Constitution's federal structure imposes limitations on the Commerce Clause, but rather the nature and content of those limitations. We doubt that courts ultimately can identify principled constitutional limitations on the scope of Congress' Commerce Clause powers over the States merely by relying on *a priori* definitions of state sovereignty. In part, this is because of the elusiveness of objective criteria for "fundamental" elements of state sovereignty, a problem we have witnessed in the search for "traditional governmental functions." There is, however, a more fundamental reason: the sovereignty of the States is limited by the Constitution itself.

As a result, to say that the Constitution assumes the continued role of the States is to say little about the nature of that role. With rare exceptions, like the guarantee, in Article IV, § 3, of state territorial integrity, the Constitution does not carve out express elements of state sovereignty that Congress may not employ its delegated powers to displace. The power of the Federal Government is a "power to be respected" as well, and the fact that the States remain sovereign as to all powers not vested in Congress or denied them by the Constitution offers no guidance about where the frontier between state and federal power lies.

When we look for the States' "residuary and inviolable sovereignty," The Federalist No. 39 (J. Madison), in the shape of the constitutional scheme rather than in predetermined notions of sovereign power, a different measure of state sovereignty emerges. Apart from the limitation on federal authority inherent in the delegated nature of Congress' Article I powers, the principal means chosen by the Framers to ensure the role of the States in the federal system lies in the structure of the Federal Government itself. It is no novelty to observe that the composition of the Federal Government was designed in large part to protect the States from overreaching by Congress. The Framers thus gave the States a role in the selection both of the Executive and the Legislative Branches of the Federal Government. The States were vested with indirect influence over the House of Representatives and the Presidency by their control of electoral qualifications and their role in Presidential elections. U.S. Const., Art. I, § 2, and Art. II, § 1. They were given more direct influence in the Senate, where each State received equal representation and each Senator was to be selected by the legislature of his State. Art. I, § 3. The significance attached to the States' equal representation in the Senate is underscored by the prohibition of any constitutional amendment divesting a State of equal representation without the State's consent. Art. V.

The extent to which the structure of the Federal Government itself was relied on to insulate the interests of the States is evident in the views of the Framers. James Madison explained that the Federal Government "will partake sufficiently of the spirit [of the States], to be disinclined to invade the rights of the individual States, or the prerogatives of their governments." The Federalist No. 46. [T]he Framers chose to rely on a federal system in which special restraints on federal power over the States inhered principally in the workings of the National Government itself, rather than in discrete limitations on the objects of federal authority. State sovereign interests, then, are more properly protected by procedural safeguards inherent in the structure of the federal system than by judicially created limitations on federal power.

The effectiveness of the federal political process in preserving the States' interests is apparent even today in the course of federal legislation. On the one hand, the States have been able to direct a substantial proportion of federal revenues into their own treasuries in the form of general and program-specific grants in aid. Moreover, at the same time that the States have exercised their influence to obtain federal support, they have been able to exempt themselves from a wide variety of obligations imposed by Congress under the Commerce Clause. The fact that some federal statutes such as the FLSA extend general obligations to the States cannot obscure the extent to which the political position of the States in the federal system has served to minimize the burdens that the States bear under the Commerce Clause.[17]

We realize that changes in the structure of the Federal Government have taken place since 1789, not the least of which has been the substitution of popular election of Senators by the adoption of the Seventeenth Amendment in 1913, and that these changes may work to alter the influence of the States in the federal political process.

---

17. Even as regards the FLSA, Congress incorporated special provisions concerning overtime pay for law enforcement and firefighting personnel when it amended the FLSA in 1974 in order to take account of the special concerns of States and localities with respect to these positions. Congress also declined to impose any obligations on state and local governments with respect to policymaking personnel who are not subject to civil service laws.

Nonetheless, against this background, we are convinced that the fundamental limitation that the constitutional scheme imposes on the Commerce Clause to protect the "States as States" is one of process rather than one of result. Any substantive restraint on the exercise of Commerce Clause powers must find its justification in the procedural nature of this basic limitation, and it must be tailored to compensate for possible failings in the national political process rather than to dictate a "sacred province of state autonomy."

Insofar as the present cases are concerned, then, we need go no further than to state that we perceive nothing in the overtime and minimum-wage requirements of the FLSA, as applied to SAMTA, that is destructive of state sovereignty or violative of any constitutional provision. SAMTA faces nothing more than the same minimum-wage and overtime obligations that hundreds of thousands of other employers, public as well as private, have to meet.

IV

We do not lightly overrule recent precedent. We have not hesitated, however, when it has become apparent that a prior decision has departed from a proper understanding of congressional power under the Commerce Clause. Due respect for the reach of congressional power within the federal system mandates that we do so now.

National League of Cities v. Usery is overruled. The judgment of the District Court is reversed, and these cases are remanded to that court for further proceedings consistent with this opinion.

It is so ordered.

JUSTICE POWELL, with whom THE CHIEF JUSTICE, JUSTICE REHNQUIST, and JUSTICE O'CONNOR join, dissenting.

The Court today, in its 5–4 decision, overrules *National League of Cities v. Usery*, a case in which we held that Congress lacked authority to impose the requirements of the Fair Labor Standards Act on state and local governments. Because I believe this decision substantially alters the federal system embodied in the Constitution, I dissent.

I

Whatever effect the Court's decision may have in weakening the application of *stare decisis*, it is likely to be less important than what the Court has done to the Constitution itself. A unique feature of the United States is the *federal* system of government guaranteed by the Constitution and implicit in the very name of our country. Despite some genuflecting in the Court's opinion to the concept of federalism, today's decision effectively reduces the Tenth Amendment to meaningless rhetoric when Congress acts pursuant to the Commerce Clause.

II

The Court finds that the test of state immunity approved in *National League of Cities* and its progeny is unworkable and unsound in principle.

B

Today's opinion does not explain how the States' role in the electoral process guarantees that particular exercises of the Commerce Clause power will not infringe on residual state sovereignty. Members of Congress are elected from the various States, but once in office they are Members of the Federal Government. Although the States participate in the Electoral College, this is hardly a reason to view the President as a representative of the States' interest against federal encroachment.[9]

The Court apparently thinks that the States' success at obtaining federal funds for various projects and exemptions from the obligations of some federal statutes is indicative of the "effectiveness of the federal political process in preserving the States' interests." But such political success is not relevant to the question whether the political *processes* are the proper means of enforcing constitutional limitations. The fact that Congress generally does not transgress constitutional limits on its power to reach state activities does not make judicial review any less necessary to rectify the cases in which it does do so. The States' role in our system of government is a matter of constitutional law, not of legislative grace. "The powers not delegated to the United States by the Constitution, nor prohibited by it to the States, are reserved to the States, respectively, or to the people." U.S. Const., Amdt. 10.

More troubling than the logical infirmities in the Court's reasoning is the result of its holding, *i.e.*, that federal political officials, invoking the Commerce Clause, are the sole judges of the limits of their own power. This result is inconsistent with the fundamental principles of our constitutional system. *See, e.g.*, The Federalist No. 78 (Hamilton). At least since *Marbury v. Madison*, [5 U.S. (]1 Cranch[)] 137 (1803), it has been the settled province of the federal judiciary "to say what the law is" with respect to the constitutionality of Acts of Congress. In rejecting the role of the judiciary in protecting the States from federal overreaching, the Court's opinion offers no explanation for ignoring the teaching of the most famous case in our history.

---

9. At one time in our history, the view that the structure of the Federal Government sufficed to protect the States might have had a somewhat more practical, although not a more logical, basis. Professor Wechsler, whose seminal article in 1954 proposed the view adopted by the Court today, predicated his argument on assumptions that simply do not accord with current reality. Professor Wechsler wrote: "National action has . . . always been regarded as exceptional in our polity, an intrusion to be justified by some necessity, the special rather than the ordinary case." [Herbert] Wechsler, *The Political Safeguards of Federalism: The Role of the States in the Composition and Selection of the National Government*, 54 Colum. L. Rev. 543, 544 (1954). Not only is the premise of this view clearly at odds with the proliferation of national legislation over the past 30 years, but "a variety of structural and political changes occurring in this century have combined to make Congress particularly *insensitive* to state and local values." The adoption of the Seventeenth Amendment (providing for direct election of Senators), the weakening of political parties on the local level, and the rise of national media, among other things, have made Congress increasingly less representative of state and local interests, and more likely to be responsive to the demands of various national constituencies.

III

A

In our federal system, the States have a major role that cannot be pre-empted by the National Government. As contemporaneous writings and the debates at the ratifying conventions make clear, the States' ratification of the Constitution was predicated on this understanding of federalism. Indeed, the Tenth Amendment was adopted specifically to ensure that the important role promised the States by the proponents of the Constitution was realized.

Much of the initial opposition to the Constitution was rooted in the fear that the National Government would be too powerful and eventually would eliminate the States as viable political entities. This concern was voiced repeatedly until proponents of the Constitution made assurances that a Bill of Rights, including a provision explicitly reserving powers in the States, would be among the first business of the new Congress. As a result, eight States voted for the Constitution only after proposing amendments to be adopted after ratification. All eight of these included among their recommendations some version of what later became the Tenth Amendment.

This history, which the Court simply ignores, documents the integral role of the Tenth Amendment in our constitutional theory. It exposes as well, I believe, the fundamental character of the Court's error today. Far from being "unsound in principle," judicial enforcement of the Tenth Amendment is essential to maintaining the federal system so carefully designed by the Framers and adopted in the Constitution.

B

The Framers had definite ideas about the nature of the Constitution's division of authority between the Federal and State Governments. In The Federalist No. 39, for example, Madison explained this division by drawing a series of contrasts between the attributes of a "national" government and those of the government to be established by the Constitution. While a national form of government would possess an "indefinite supremacy over all persons and things," the form of government contemplated by the Constitution instead consisted of "local or municipal authorities [which] form distinct and independent portions of the supremacy, no more subject within their respective spheres to the general authority, than the general authority is subject to them, within its own sphere." Under the Constitution, the sphere of the proposed government extended to jurisdiction of "certain enumerated objects only . . . leav[ing] to the several States a residuary and inviolable sovereignty over all other objects."

The Framers believed that the separate sphere of sovereignty reserved to the States would ensure that the States would serve as an effective "counterpoise" to the power of the Federal Government. The States would serve this essential role because they would attract and retain the loyalty of their citizens.

Thus, the harm to the States that results from federal overreaching under the Commerce Clause is not simply a matter of dollars and cents. Nor is it a matter of the wisdom or folly of certain policy choices. Rather, by usurping functions traditionally performed by the States, federal overreaching under the Commerce Clause undermines the constitutionally mandated balance of power between the States and the Federal Government, a balance designed to protect our fundamental liberties.

IV

I return now to the state interest [that] is compelling. The financial impact on States and localities of displacing their control over wages, hours, overtime regulations, pensions, and labor relations with their employees could have serious, as well as unanticipated, effects on state and local planning, budgeting, and the levying of taxes. As we said in *National League of Cities*, federal control of the terms and conditions of employment of state employees also inevitably "displaces state policies regarding the manner in which [States] will structure delivery of those governmental services that citizens require."

The Court emphasizes that municipal operation of an intracity mass transit system is relatively new in the life of our country. It nevertheless is a classic example of the type of service traditionally provided by local government. It is *local* by definition. It is indistinguishable in principle from the traditional services of providing and maintaining streets, public lighting, traffic control, water, and sewerage systems. State and local officials of course must be intimately familiar with these services and sensitive to their quality as well as cost. It is this kind of state and local control and accountability that the Framers understood would insure the vitality and preservation of the federal system that the Constitution explicitly requires.

V

Although the Court's opinion purports to recognize that the States retain some sovereign power, it does not identify even a single aspect of state authority that would remain when the Commerce Clause is invoked to justify federal regulation.

As I view the Court's decision today as rejecting the basic precepts of our federal system and limiting the constitutional role of judicial review, I dissent.

JUSTICE REHNQUIST, dissenting.

I join both JUSTICE POWELL's and JUSTICE O'CONNOR's thoughtful dissents. [J]udicial protection for state sovereignty is] a principle that will, I am confident, in time again command the support of a majority of this Court.

JUSTICE O'CONNOR, with whom JUSTICE POWELL and JUSTICE REHNQUIST join, dissenting. [Opinion omitted]

EXERCISE 4:

1. Was it appropriate for the Supreme Court to overrule *National League of Cities*? What is the standard for *stare decisis* articulated by the majority? What arguments and factors did the majority use to bolster its conclusion? Are those the correct

factors of *stare decisis*? What arguments did the primary dissent provide for its conclusion to preserve *National League of Cities*?

2. The majority argued that one reason to overrule the *National League of Cities* test was its indeterminacy. Describe the majority's claim.

3. The majority distinguished the indeterminacy to which the *National League of Cities* test was subject from the "gray areas" of other standards, such as those found in the Court's "fundamental rights" case law. Was the majority successful?

4. The Court claimed that an analysis that sought to distinguish "unique" or "necessary" governmental functions was unworkable. What arguments did the Court provide to support this conclusion? Are they persuasive?

5. The Supreme Court claimed that *National League of Cities* attempted to define a set of attributes that constituted the essential core of state sovereignty and then judicially protect those facets of sovereignty. The *Garcia* Court argued that this was an "elusive" goal. Is the Court right? Is there a judicially enforceable concept of state sovereignty? Why does the test articulated in *Hodel v. Virginia Surface Mining & Reclamation Ass'n, Inc.*, 452 U.S. 264 (1981), provide insufficient guidance?

6. Arguably the central reason given by the Court to overrule *National League of Cities* was that state sovereignty is not judicially enforceable. What reasons did the Court rely on to support this conclusion?

7. The majority argued that political federalism safeguards have worked well. What evidence did the majority provide to support that claim? Is it persuasive? In her dissent, Justice O'Connor stated that "[w]ith the abandonment of *National League of Cities*, all that stands between the remaining essentials of state sovereignty and Congress is the latter's underdeveloped capacity for self-restraint." Who has the better position? Why?

8. The majority acknowledged that the structural mechanisms to politically protect federalism have diminished since the Constitution was drafted and ratified. For example, senators are directly elected because of the Seventeenth Amendment. Have these changes fatally undermined the majority's conclusion?

9. The *Garcia* Court obliquely referenced a possible remaining limit on Congress' Commerce Clause power to regulate states, saying that judicial remedies must be "tailored to compensate for possible failings in the national political process." What might the Court have had in mind? Does this concession undermine the Court's claim that political safeguards are adequate to protect federalism?

10. Did the majority articulate any limits to its conclusion that the Tenth Amendment is not judicially enforceable? What are some possible limits?

11. Why did the majority not rely on the political question doctrine to bolster its conclusion?

12. Did the Supreme Court conclude that states do not retain independent sovereignty?

13. The *Garcia* Court relied on a thesis articulated by legal academics Herbert Wechsler and Jessie Choper. JESSIE CHOPER, JUDICIAL REVIEW AND THE NATIONAL POLITICAL PROCESS (1980); Herbert Wechsler, *The Political Safeguards of Federalism: The Role of the States in the Composition and Selection of the National Government*, 54 COLUM. L. REV. 543 (1954). Was it appropriate for the Court to do so? What role should legal scholarship play in Supreme Court cases?

14. Is *Garcia* faithful to the Tenth Amendment's original meaning?

15. Is it a normatively attractive interpretation of the Tenth Amendment?

16. The majority stated that "the text of the Constitution provides the beginning rather than the final answer to every inquiry into questions of federalism, for '[b]ehind the words of the constitutional provisions are postulates which limit and control.'" Is that an originalist claim? Is it an accurate claim?

17. Justice Blackmun argued that "[r]eliance on history as an organizing principle results in line-drawing of the most arbitrary sort." The question of whether history can constrain occurs in many doctrinal areas. In *Michael H. v. Gerald D.*, 491 U.S. 110 (1989), for instance, Justices Scalia and Brennan sparred over a similar question. Justice Scalia argued that using tradition would restrain the Court's substantive due process jurisprudence. *Id.* at 127 n.6. "We refer to the most specific level at which a relevant tradition protecting, or denying protection to, the asserted right can be identified." *Id.* Justice Brennan responded that, "[e]ven if we could agree . . . on the content and significance of particular traditions, we still would be forced to identify the point at which a tradition becomes firm enough to be relevant to our definition of liberty and the moment at which it becomes too obsolete to be relevant any longer." *Id.* at 138 (Brennan, J., dissenting). Which side had the better of the argument?

F. MODERN DOCTRINE

Following *Garcia*, the conventional wisdom was that few if any judicially enforceable limits on Congress' Commerce Clause power remained. *See* Richard H. Fallon, Jr., *The "Conservative" Paths of the Rehnquist Court's Federalism Decisions*, 69 U. CHI. L. REV. 429, 452 (2002) ("As recently as a few years ago, Congress's powers under Article I appeared virtually unlimited."). This applied both to the scope of Congress' power itself and to whether Congress had transgressed federalism limits. This state of affairs fit the roadmap set out in *Carolene Products* Footnote 4, covered in Volume 5. *United States v. Carolene Prods. Co.*, 304 U.S. 144, 152 n.4 (1938). There, the New Deal Supreme Court provided the jurisprudential outline that would govern American constitutional law for the next sixty years. II BRUCE ACKERMAN, WE THE PEOPLE: TRANSFORMATIONS 368–69 (1998). In *Carolene Products*, the Court stated that congressional regulation of economic activity would receive what today is labeled rational basis review. *Carolene Prods.*, 304 U.S. at 152. The Court contrasted this very deferential form of judicial review with "more exacting judicial scrutiny" of legislation that is the result of a flawed political process or infringes on a fundamental right.

Id. at 152 n.4. Commerce Clause and federalism issues fell under the sway of the deferential form of judicial review.

A mere six years after *Garcia*, however, the Court decided *Gregory v. Ashcroft*, 501 U.S. 452 (1991). Gregory involved a challenge by Missouri state court judges to a state mandatory retirement provision. The judges argued that the mandatory retirement provision violated the federal Age Discrimination in Employment Act of 1967, which prohibited employers from discharging employees "because of such individual's age." 29 U.S.C. § 623(a) (2011). Congress extended the Act to states in 1974.

In an opinion written by Justice O'Connor, the Supreme Court created a rule of construction that required Congress to "plain[ly]" state when it sought to alter the traditional federal-state balance. *Gregory*, 501 U.S. at 464. Although the Court acknowledged that the best interpretation of the Act would have subjected Missouri to the Act's requirements, *id.* at 467, the Court used its newly-crafted federalism-protective rule of construction to construe the Act so that it did not apply to Missouri state court judges. *Id.* at 470. Justice O'Connor intimated that, though the Court was not overruling *Garcia*, *Garcia* may cause "constitutional problem[s]." *Id.* at 464.

The ruling in *Gregory* set the stage for *New York v. United States*, 505 U.S. 144 (1992), and *Printz v. United States*, 521 U.S. 898 (1997), below, which articulated and applied the modern "anti-commandeering" rule.

NEW YORK v. UNITED STATES
505 U.S. 144 (1992)

JUSTICE O'CONNOR delivered the opinion of the Court.

These cases implicate one of our Nation's newest problems of public policy and perhaps our oldest question of constitutional law. The public policy issue involves the disposal of radioactive waste. The constitutional question is as old as the Constitution: It consists of discerning the proper division of authority between the Federal Government and the States. We conclude that while Congress has substantial power under the Constitution to encourage the States to provide for the disposal of the radioactive waste generated within their borders, the Constitution does not confer upon Congress the ability simply to compel the States to do so.

I

The Act [which ratified an interstate compact] provides three types of incentives to encourage the States to comply with their statutory obligation to provide for the disposal of waste generated within their borders[: (1) "monetary incentives," which permit sited States to impose a surcharge on waste accepted from unsited States, (2) "access incentives," which allow sited States to increase the surcharge and then ultimately deny access to waste generated by States that did not comply with the federal guidelines, and (3) "the take title provision," which requires States that could not dispose of low-level radioactive waste generated within its borders to take title to the waste and be liable for all damages that the generator or owner of the waste incurred.]

II

A

[The task of ascertaining the constitutional line between federal and state author-ity] can be viewed in either of two ways. In some cases the Court has inquired whether an Act of Congress is authorized by one of the powers delegated to Con-gress in Article I of the Constitution. *See, e.g., McCulloch v. Maryland*, 17 U.S. (4 Wheat.) 316 (1819). In other cases the Court has sought to determine whether an Act of Congress invades the province of state sovereignty reserved by the Tenth Amendment. *See, e.g., Garcia v. San Antonio Metropolitan Transit Authority*, 469 U.S. 528 (1985). In a case like these, the two inquiries are mirror images of each other. If a power is delegated to Congress in the Constitution, the Tenth Amendment expressly disclaims any reservation of that power to the States; if a power is an attri-bute of state sovereignty reserved by the Tenth Amendment, it is necessarily a power the Constitution has not conferred on Congress. The Tenth Amendment [therefore] restrains the power of Congress, but this limit is not derived from the text of the Tenth Amendment itself, which, as we have discussed, is essentially a tautology. Instead, the Tenth Amendment confirms that the power of the Federal Government is subject to limits that may, in a given instance, reserve power to the States.

In the end, it makes no difference whether one views the question at issue in these cases as one of ascertaining the limits of the power delegated to the Federal Govern-ment under the affirmative provisions of the Constitution or one of discerning the core of sovereignty retained by the States under the Tenth Amendment. Either way, we must determine whether any of the three challenged provisions of the Low-Level Radioactive Waste Policy Amendments Act of 1985 oversteps the boundary between federal and state authority.

B

Petitioners do not contend that Congress lacks the power to regulate the disposal of low level radioactive waste. Space in radioactive waste disposal sites is frequently sold by residents of one State to residents of another. Regulation of the resulting inter-state market in waste disposal is therefore well within Congress' authority under the Commerce Clause. Petitioners likewise do not dispute that under the Supremacy Clause Congress could, if it wished, pre-empt state radioactive waste regulation. Peti-tioners contend only that the Tenth Amendment limits the power of Congress to regulate in the way it has chosen. Rather than addressing the problem of waste dis-posal by directly regulating the generators and disposers of waste, petitioners argue, Congress has impermissibly directed the States to regulate in this field.

Most of our recent cases interpreting the Tenth Amendment have concerned the authority of Congress to subject state governments to generally applicable laws. The Court's jurisprudence in this area has traveled an unsteady path. See *Maryland v. Wirtz*, 392 U.S. 183 (1968) (state schools and hospitals are subject to Fair Labor Stan-dards Act); *National League of Cities v. Usery*, 426 U.S. 833 (1976) (overruling *Wirtz*) (state employers are *not* subject to Fair Labor Standards Act); *Garcia v. San Antonio*

Metropolitan Transit Authority, 469 U.S. 528 (1985) (overruling *National League of Cities*) (state employers are once again subject to Fair Labor Standards Act). This litigation presents no occasion to apply or revisit the holdings of any of these cases, as this is not a case in which Congress has subjected a State to the same legislation applicable to private parties.

This litigation instead concerns the circumstances under which Congress may use the States as implements of regulation; that is, whether Congress may direct or otherwise motivate the States to regulate in a particular field or a particular way.

1

As an initial matter, Congress may not simply "commandee[r] the legislative processes of the States by directly compelling them to enact and enforce a federal regulatory program." *Hodel v. Virginia Surface Mining & Reclamation Assn., Inc.,* 452 U.S. 264, 288 (1981). These statements in *Hodel* [and other cases] were not innovations. While Congress has substantial powers to govern the Nation directly, including in areas of intimate concern to the States, the Constitution has never been understood to confer upon Congress the ability to require the States to govern according to Congress' instructions.

Indeed, the question whether the Constitution should permit Congress to employ state governments as regulatory agencies was a topic of lively debate among the Framers. Under the Articles of Confederation, Congress lacked the authority in most respects to govern the people directly.

The inadequacy of this governmental structure was responsible in part for the Constitutional Convention. As Hamilton saw it, "we must resolve to incorporate into our plan those ingredients which may be considered as forming the characteristic difference between a league and a government; we must extend the authority of the Union to the persons of the citizens — the only proper objects of government." The new National Government "must carry its agency to the persons of the citizens. It must stand in need of no intermediate legislations . . . . The government of the Union, like that of each State, must be able to address itself immediately to the hopes and fears of individuals." The Federalist No. 16.

The Convention generated a great number of proposals for the structure of the new Government, but two quickly took center stage. Under the Virginia Plan, as first introduced by Edmund Randolph, Congress would exercise legislative authority directly upon individuals, without employing the States as intermediaries. 1 Records of the Federal Convention of 1787, p. 21 (M[ax] Farrand ed. 1911). Under the New Jersey Plan, as first introduced by William Paterson, Congress would continue to require the approval of the States before legislating, as it had under the Articles of Confederation.

In providing for a stronger central government the Framers explicitly chose a Constitution that confers upon Congress the power to regulate individuals, not States. We have always understood that even where Congress has the authority under the

Constitution to pass laws requiring or prohibiting certain acts, it lacks the power directly to compel the States to require or prohibit those acts. The allocation of power contained in the Commerce Clause, for example, authorizes Congress to regulate interstate commerce directly; it does not authorize Congress to regulate state governments' regulation of interstate commerce.

2

This is not to say that Congress lacks the ability to encourage a State to regulate in a particular way, or that Congress may not hold out incentives to the States as a method of influencing a State's policy choices. Our cases have identified a variety of methods, short of outright coercion, by which Congress may urge a State to adopt a legislative program consistent with federal interests.

First, under Congress' spending power, "Congress may attach conditions on the receipt of federal funds." *South Dakota v. Dole*, 483 U.S. 203 (1987). Second, where Congress has the authority to regulate private activity under the Commerce Clause, we have recognized Congress' power to offer States the choice of regulating that activity according to federal standards or having state law pre-empted by federal regulation.

By either of these methods, as by any other permissible method of encouraging a State to conform to federal policy choices, the residents of the State retain the ultimate decision as to whether or not the State will comply. Where Congress encourages state regulation rather than compelling it, state governments remain responsive to the local electorate's preferences; state officials remain accountable to the people.

By contrast, where the Federal Government compels States to regulate, the accountability of both state and federal officials is diminished. If the citizens of New York, for example, do not consider that making provision for the disposal of radioactive waste is in their best interest, they may elect state officials who share their view. That view can always be pre-empted under the Supremacy Clause if it is contrary to the national view, but in such a case it is the Federal Government that makes the decision in full view of the public, and it will be federal officials that suffer the consequences if the decision turns out to be detrimental or unpopular. But where the Federal Government directs the States to regulate, it may be state officials who will bear the brunt of public disapproval, while the federal officials who devised the regulatory program may remain insulated from the electoral ramifications of their decision. Accountability is thus diminished when, due to federal coercion, elected state officials cannot regulate in accordance with the views of the local electorate in matters not pre-empted by federal regulation.

III

C

[The Court concluded that the monetary incentives and the access incentives are constitutional but that t]he take title provision is of a different character. This third so-called "incentive" offers States, as an alternative to regulating pursuant to Congress' direction, the option of taking title to and possession of the low level radioactive waste generated within their borders and becoming liable for all damages waste generators suffer as a result of the States' failure to do so promptly. In this provision, Congress has crossed the line distinguishing encouragement from coercion.

The take title provision offers state governments a "choice" of either accepting ownership of waste or regulating according to the instructions of Congress. On one hand, the Constitution would not permit Congress simply to transfer radioactive waste from generators to state governments. Such a forced transfer, standing alone, would in principle be no different than a congressionally compelled subsidy from state governments to radioactive waste producers. The same is true of the provision requiring the States to become liable for the generators' damages. Standing alone, this provision would be indistinguishable from an Act of Congress directing the States to assume the liabilities of certain state residents. Either type of federal action would "commandeer" state governments into the service of federal regulatory purposes, and would for this reason be inconsistent with the Constitution's division of authority between federal and state governments. On the other hand, the second alternative held out to state governments—regulating pursuant to Congress' direction—would, standing alone, present a simple command to state governments to implement legislation enacted by Congress. As we have seen, the Constitution does not empower Congress to subject state governments to this type of instruction.

Because an instruction to state governments to take title to waste, standing alone, would be beyond the authority of Congress, and because a direct order to regulate, standing alone, would also be beyond the authority of Congress, it follows that Congress lacks the power to offer the States a choice between the two. Unlike the first two sets of incentives, the take title incentive does not represent the conditional exercise of any congressional power enumerated in the Constitution. In this provision, Congress has held out the threat, should the States not regulate according to one federal instruction, of simply forcing the States to submit to another federal instruction. A choice between two unconstitutionally coercive regulatory techniques is no choice at all. Either way, "the Act commandeers the legislative processes of the States by directly compelling them to enact and enforce a federal regulatory program."

Whether one views the take title provision as lying outside Congress' enumerated powers, or as infringing upon the core of state sovereignty reserved by the Tenth Amendment, the provision is inconsistent with the federal structure of our Government established by the Constitution.

IV

B

The sited state respondents note that the Act embodies a bargain among the sited and unsited States, a compromise to which New York was a willing participant and from which New York has reaped much benefit. Respondents then pose what appears at first to be a troubling question: How can a federal statute be found an unconstitutional infringement of state sovereignty when state officials consented to the statute's enactment?

The answer follows from an understanding of the fundamental purpose served by our Government's federal structure. The Constitution does not protect the sovereignty of States for the benefit of the States or state governments as abstract political entities, or even for the benefit of the public officials governing the States. To the contrary, the Constitution divides authority between federal and state governments for the protection of individuals. State sovereignty is not just an end in itself. "Just as the separation and independence of the coordinate branches of the Federal Government serves to prevent the accumulation of excessive power in any one branch, a healthy balance of power between the States and the Federal Government will reduce the risk of tyranny and abuse from either front." *Gregory v. Ashcroft. See* The Federalist No. 51.

Where Congress exceeds its authority relative to the States, therefore, the departure from the constitutional plan cannot be ratified by the "consent" of state officials. An analogy to the separation of powers among the branches of the Federal Government clarifies this point. The Constitution's division of power among the three branches is violated where one branch invades the territory of another, whether or not the encroached-upon branch approves the encroachment.

VII

[T]he Constitution protects us from our own best intentions: It divides power among sovereigns and among branches of government precisely so that we may resist the temptation to concentrate power in one location as an expedient solution to the crisis of the day. The shortage of disposal sites for radioactive waste is a pressing national problem, but a judiciary that licensed extraconstitutional government with each issue of comparable gravity would, in the long run, be far worse.

States are not mere political subdivisions of the United States. State governments are neither regional offices nor administrative agencies of the Federal Government. The positions occupied by state officials appear nowhere on the Federal Government's most detailed organizational chart. The Constitution instead "leaves to the several States a residuary and inviolable sovereignty," The Federalist No. 39, reserved explicitly to the States by the Tenth Amendment.

The judgment of the Court of Appeals is accordingly

Affirmed in part and reversed in part.

JUSTICE WHITE, with whom JUSTICE BLACKMUN and JUSTICE STEVENS join, concurring in part and dissenting in part.

I join Parts III-A and III-B, and I respectfully dissent from the rest of its opinion and the judgment reversing in part the judgment of the Court of Appeals.

I

My disagreement with the Court's analysis begins at the basic descriptive level of how the legislation at issue in these cases came to be enacted. To read the Court's version of events, one would think that Congress was the sole proponent of a solution to the Nation's low-level radioactive waste problem. Not so. The 1985 Act resulted from the efforts of state leaders to achieve a state-based set of remedies to the waste problem. They sought not federal pre-emption or intervention, but rather congressional sanction of interstate compromises they had reached.

The bill that in large measure became the 1985 Act "represent[ed] the diligent negotiating undertaken by" the National Governors' Association and "embodied" the "fundamentals of their settlement." In sum, the 1985 Act was very much the product of cooperative federalism, in which the States bargained among themselves to achieve compromises for Congress to sanction.

II

Curiously absent from the Court's analysis is any effort to place the take title provision within the overall context of the legislation. [T]he 1985 statute w[as] enacted against a backdrop of national concern over the availability of additional low-level radioactive waste disposal facilities. Congress could have pre-empted the field by directly regulating the disposal of this waste pursuant to its powers under the Commerce and Spending Clauses, but instead it *unanimously* assented to the States' request for congressional ratification of agreements to which they had acceded. The chief executives of the States proposed this approach, and I am unmoved by the Court's vehemence in taking away Congress' authority to sanction a recalcitrant unsited State now that New York has reaped the benefits of the sited States' concessions.

III

The Court announces that it has no occasion to revisit [recent] decisions, because "this is not a case in which Congress has subjected a State to the same legislation applicable to private parties." Although this statement sends the welcome signal that the Court does not intend to cut a wide swath through our recent Tenth Amendment precedents, it nevertheless is unpersuasive.

The Court's distinction between a federal statute's regulation of States and private parties for general purposes, as opposed to a regulation solely on the activities of States, is unsupported by our recent Tenth Amendment cases. An incursion on state sovereignty hardly seems more constitutionally acceptable if the federal statute that "commands" specific action also applies to private parties. The alleged diminution in state authority over its own affairs is not any less because the federal mandate restricts the activities of private parties.

[T]he more appropriate analysis should flow from *Garcia*. In *Garcia*, we stated the proper inquiry: "[W]e are convinced that the fundamental limitation that the constitutional scheme imposes on the Commerce Clause to protect the 'States as States' is one of process rather than one of result. Any substantive restraint on the exercise of Commerce Clause powers must find its justification in the procedural nature of this basic limitation, and it must be tailored to compensate for possible failings in the national political process rather than to dictate a 'sacred province of state autonomy.'" Where it addresses this aspect of respondents' argument, the Court tacitly concedes that a failing of the political process cannot be shown in these cases because it refuses to rebut the unassailable arguments that the States were well able to look after themselves in the legislative process that culminated in the 1985 Act's passage.

V

The ultimate irony of the decision today is that in its formalistically rigid obeisance to "federalism," the Court gives Congress fewer incentives to defer to the wishes of state officials in achieving local solutions to local problems. This legislation was a classic example of Congress acting as arbiter among the States in their attempts to accept responsibility for managing a problem of grave import. [T]hey sought a reasonable level of local and regional autonomy consistent with Art. I, § 10, cl. 3, of the Constitution. By invalidating the measure designed to ensure compliance for recalcitrant States, such as New York, the Court upsets the delicate compromise achieved among the States and forces Congress to erect several additional formalistic hurdles to clear before achieving exactly the same objective. Because the Court's justifications for undertaking this step are unpersuasive to me, I respectfully dissent.

JUSTICE STEVENS, concurring in part and dissenting in part.

Under the Articles of Confederation, the Federal Government had the power to issue commands to the States. *See* Arts. VIII, IX. Because that indirect exercise of federal power proved ineffective, the Framers of the Constitution empowered the Federal Government to exercise legislative authority directly over individuals within the States, even though that direct authority constituted a greater intrusion on state sovereignty. Nothing in that history suggests that the Federal Government may not also impose its will upon the several States as it did under the Articles. The Constitution enhanced, rather than diminished, the power of the Federal Government.

For these reasons, as well as those set forth by JUSTICE WHITE, I respectfully dissent.

EXERCISE 5:

1. The *New York* Court argued that the Constitution protected states via the anti-commandeering rule. What arguments did the Court use to support this conclusion?

2. The majority distinguished *Garcia*. How did it do so? Did it do so fairly?

3. Why did the Supreme Court not overrule *Garcia* (assuming you think the two cases are inconsistent)?

4. What was the take-title provision's constitutional infirmity that the other two challenged provisions lacked?

5. What is the scope of the anti-commandeering rule? Does it apply to all state actors including executive and judicial officials? If not, why not?

6. How did the Supreme Court address the operative principle from *Garcia*: that federalism limits on Congress' power are not judicially enforceable and instead are only enforceable via the federal political process?

7. A common approach in the individual rights context is to permit the federal or state government to infringe a right if it has a sufficiently powerful justification. For example, in the First Amendment context, a state government can limit free speech based on its content if it does so pursuant to a compelling state interest. The *New York* Court, however, concluded that the constitutional protection given to states against federal commandeering is not subject to federal overriding in the name of a powerful governmental interest. What arguments did the Court use to reach that result? Are they persuasive?

8. One of the frequent distinctions made in constitutional law is between formalism and functionalism. Formalism is an approach to law which holds that the law's formal legal materials—e.g., a statute's text and history—are the sole or major basis for legal decisions. Functionalism, by contrast, asks which particular legal result would work best. Which opinions fall into which categories? Which is the best approach?

––––––––––

Critics of *New York v. United States* argued that the Supreme Court had failed to justify its anti-commandeering rule. In particular, critics argued that, on the Court's own terms, it failed to show that the anti-commandeering rule is required by the Constitution's original meaning. In *Printz v. United States*, the Supreme Court took the opportunity to provide another defense of the anti-commandeering rule. As you read *Printz*, see whether the Court carried the burden of persuasion.

PRINTZ v. UNITED STATES
521 U.S. 898 (1997)

JUSTICE SCALIA delivered the opinion of the Court.

The question presented in these cases is whether provisions of the Brady Handgun Violence Prevention Act, commanding state and local law enforcement officers to conduct background checks on prospective handgun purchasers and to perform certain related tasks, violate the Constitution.

I

In 1993, Congress enacted the Brady Act. The Act requires the Attorney General to establish a national instant background-check system by November 30, 1998, and immediately puts in place certain interim provisions until that system becomes operative. Under the interim provisions, a firearms dealer who proposes to transfer a handgun must first provide the "chief law enforcement officer" (CLEO) of the transferee's residence with notice of the contents (and a copy) of the Brady Form.

When a CLEO receives the required notice of a proposed transfer from the firearms dealer, the CLEO must "make a reasonable effort to ascertain within 5 business days whether receipt or possession would be in violation of the law, including research in whatever State and local recordkeeping systems are available and in a national system designated by the Attorney General." The Act does not require the CLEO to take any particular action if he determines that a pending transaction would be unlawful; he may notify the firearms dealer to that effect, but is not required to do so. If, however, the CLEO notifies a gun dealer that a prospective purchaser is ineligible to receive a handgun, he must, upon request, provide the would-be purchaser with a written statement of the reasons for that determination. Moreover, if the CLEO does not discover any basis for objecting to the sale, he must destroy any records in his possession relating to the transfer, including his copy of the Brady Form.

Petitioners Jay Printz and Richard Mack, the CLEOs for Ravalli County, Montana, and Graham County, Arizona, respectively, filed separate actions challenging the constitutionality of the Brady Act's interim provisions.

II

Petitioners here object to being pressed into federal service, and contend that congressional action compelling state officers to execute federal laws is unconstitutional. Because there is no constitutional text speaking to this precise question, the answer to the CLEOs' challenge must be sought in historical understanding and practice, in the structure of the Constitution, and in the jurisprudence of this Court. We treat those three sources, in that order, in this and the next two sections of this opinion.

The Government contends that "the earliest Congresses enacted statutes that required the participation of state officials in the implementation of federal laws." The Government's contention demands our careful consideration, since early congressional enactments "provid[e] 'contemporaneous and weighty evidence' of the Constitution's meaning." *Bowshar v. Synar*, 478 U.S. 714, 723–724 (1986). Conversely if, as petitioners contend, earlier Congresses avoided use of this highly attractive power, we would have reason to believe that the power was thought not to exist.

The Government observes that statutes enacted by the first Congresses required state courts to record applications for citizenship, to transmit abstracts of citizenship applications and other naturalization records to the Secretary of State, and to register aliens seeking naturalization and issue certificates of registry. It may well be, however, that these requirements applied only in States that authorized their courts to conduct naturalization proceedings.

Other statutes of that era apparently or at least arguably required state courts to perform functions unrelated to naturalization, such as resolving controversies between a captain and the crew of his ship concerning the seaworthiness of the vessel, hearing the claims of slave owners who had apprehended fugitive slaves and issuing certificates authorizing the slave's forced removal to the State from which he had fled, taking proof of the claims of Canadian refugees who had assisted the United States during the Revolutionary War, and ordering the deportation of alien enemies in times of war.

These early laws establish, at most, that the Constitution was originally understood to permit imposition of an obligation on state *judges* to enforce federal prescriptions, insofar as those prescriptions related to matters appropriate for the judicial power. That assumption was perhaps implicit in one of the provisions of the Constitution, and was explicit in another. In accord with the so-called Madisonian Compromise, Article III, § 1, established only a Supreme Court, and made the creation of lower federal courts optional with the Congress — even though it was obvious that the Supreme Court alone could not hear all federal cases throughout the United States. And the Supremacy Clause, Art. VI, cl. 2, announced that "the Laws of the United States . . . shall be the supreme Law of the Land; and the Judges in every State shall be bound thereby." It is understandable why courts should have been viewed distinctively in this regard; unlike legislatures and executives, they applied the law of other sovereigns all the time.

For these reasons, we do not think the early statutes imposing obligations on state courts imply a power of Congress to impress the state executive into its service. Indeed, it can be argued that the numerousness of these statutes, contrasted with the utter lack of statutes imposing obligations on the States' executive (notwithstanding the attractiveness of that course to Congress), suggests an assumed *absence* of such power.[2] The only early federal law the Government has brought to our attention that imposed duties on state executive officers is the Extradition Act of 1793, which required the "executive authority" of a State to cause the arrest and delivery of a fugitive from justice upon the request of the executive authority of the State from which the fugitive had fled. That was in direct implementation, however, of the Extradition Clause of the Constitution itself, *see* Art. IV, § 2.

Not only do the enactments of the early Congresses, as far as we are aware, contain no evidence of an assumption that the Federal Government may command the States' executive power in the absence of a particularized constitutional authorization, they contain some indication of precisely the opposite assumption. On September 23,

---

2. Bereft of even a single early, or indeed even pre-20th-century, statute compelling state executive officers to administer federal laws, the dissent is driven to claim that early federal statutes compelled state judges to perform executive functions, which implies a power to compel state executive officers to do so as well. Assuming that this implication would follow (which is doubtful), the premise of the argument is in any case wrong. None of the early statutes directed to state judges or court clerks required the performance of functions more appropriately characterized as executive than judicial (bearing in mind that the line between the two for present purposes is not necessarily identical with the line established by the Constitution for federal separation-of-powers purposes). Given that state courts were entrusted with the quintessentially adjudicative task of determining whether applicants for citizenship met the requisite qualifications, it is unreasonable to maintain that the ancillary functions of recording, registering, and certifying the citizenship applications were unalterably executive rather than judicial in nature.

The dissent's assertion that the Act of July 20, 1790, which required state courts to resolve controversies between captain and crew regarding seaworthiness of a vessel, caused state courts to act "like contemporary regulatory agencies," is cleverly true — because contemporary regulatory agencies have been allowed to perform adjudicative ("quasi-judicial") functions. It is foolish, however, to mistake the copy for the original and to believe that 18th-century courts were imitating agencies, rather than 20th-century agencies imitating courts. The ultimate function of the judge under the Act was purely adjudicative; he was, after receiving the report, to "adjudge and determine . . . whether the said ship or vessel is fit to proceed on the intended voyage."

1789—the day before its proposal of the Bill of Rights—the First Congress enacted a law aimed at obtaining state assistance of the most rudimentary and necessary sort for the enforcement of the new Government's laws: the holding of federal prisoners in state jails at federal expense. Significantly, the law issued not a command to the States' executive, but a recommendation to their legislatures. Congress "recommended to the legislatures of the several States to pass laws, making it expressly the duty of the keepers of their gaols, to receive and safe keep therein all prisoners committed under the authority of the United States," and offered to pay 50 cents per month for each prisoner. Moreover, when Georgia refused to comply with the request, Congress's only reaction was a law authorizing the marshal in any State that failed to comply with the Recommendation of September 23, 1789, to rent a temporary jail until provision for a permanent one could be made.

In addition to early legislation, the Government also appeals to other sources we have usually regarded as indicative of the original understanding of the Constitution. It points to portions of The Federalist which reply to criticisms that Congress's power to tax will produce two sets of revenue officers. "Publius" responded that Congress will probably "make use of the State officers and State regulations, for collecting" federal taxes, The Federalist No. 36 (A. Hamilton), and predicted that "the eventual collection [of internal revenue] under the immediate authority of the Union, will generally be made by the officers, and according to the rules, appointed by the several States," id., No. 45 (J. Madison). The Government also invokes The Federalist's more general observations that the Constitution would "enable the [national] government to employ the ordinary magistracy of each [State] in the execution of its laws," id., No. 27 (A. Hamilton), and that it was "extremely probable that in other instances, particularly in the organization of the judicial power, the officers of the States will be clothed with the correspondent authority of the Union," id., No. 45 (J. Madison). But none of these statements necessarily implies—what is the critical point here—that Congress could impose these responsibilities *without the consent of the States.* They appear to rest on the natural assumption that the States would consent to allowing their officials to assist the Federal Government, an assumption proved correct by the extensive mutual assistance the States and Federal Government voluntarily provided one another in the early days of the Republic, including voluntary *federal implementation of state law, see, e.g.,* Act of Apr. 2, 1790 (directing federal tax collectors and customs officers to assist in enforcing state inspection laws).

Another passage of The Federalist reads as follows:

> "It merits particular attention . . . that the laws of the Confederacy as to the *enumerated* and *legitimate* objects of its jurisdiction will become the SUPREME LAW of the land; to the observance of which all officers, legislative, executive, and judicial in each State will be bound by the sanctity of an oath. Thus, the legislatures, courts, and magistrates, of the respective members will be incorporated into the operations of the national government *as far as its just and constitutional authority extends;* and will be rendered

auxiliary to the enforcement of its laws." The Federalist No. 27 (A. Hamilton) (emphasis in original).

The Government does not rely upon this passage, but JUSTICE SOUTER makes it the very foundation of his position; so we pause to examine it in some detail. JUSTICE SOUTER finds "[t]he natural reading" of the phrases " 'will be incorporated into the operations of the national government' " and " 'will be rendered auxiliary to the enforcement of its laws' " to be that the National Government will have "authority, when exercising an otherwise legitimate power (the commerce power, say), to require state 'auxiliaries' to take appropriate action." There are several obstacles to such an interpretation. First, the consequences in question ("incorporated into the operations of the national government" and "rendered auxiliary to the enforcement of its laws") are said in the quoted passage to flow *automatically* from the officers' oath to observe "the laws of the Confederacy as to the *enumerated* and *legitimate* objects of its jurisdiction."[4] Thus, if the passage means that state officers must take an active role in the implementation of federal law, it means that they must do so without the necessity for a congressional directive that they implement it. But no one has ever thought, and no one asserts in the present litigation, that that is the law. The second problem with JUSTICE SOUTER's reading is that it makes state *legislatures* subject to federal direction. (The passage in question, after all, does not include legislatures merely incidentally, as by referring to "all state officers"; it refers to legislatures *specifically* and *first of all*.) We have held, however, that state legislatures are *not* subject to federal direction. *New York v. United States*, 505 U.S. 144 (1992).[5]

These problems are avoided, of course, if the calculatedly vague consequences the passage recites — "incorporated into the operations of the national government" and "rendered auxiliary to the enforcement of its laws" — are taken to refer to nothing more (or less) than the duty owed to the National Government, on the part of *all* state officials, to enact, enforce, and interpret state law in such fashion as not to obstruct the operation of federal law, and the attendant reality that all state actions constituting such obstruction, even legislative Acts, are *ipso facto* invalid. This meaning accords well with the context of the passage, which seeks to explain why the new system of federal law directed to individual citizens, unlike the old one of federal law

---

4. Both the dissent and JUSTICE SOUTER dispute that the consequences are said to flow automatically. They are wrong. The passage says that (1) federal laws will be supreme, and (2) all state officers will be oath-bound to observe those laws, and *thus* (3) state officers will be "incorporated" and "rendered auxiliary." The reason the progression is automatic is that there is *not* included between (2) and (3): "(2a) those laws will include laws compelling action by state officers." It is the mere existence of *all* federal laws that is said to make state officers "incorporated" and "auxiliary."

5. JUSTICE SOUTER seeks to avoid incompatibility with *New York* (a decision which he joined and purports to adhere to), by saying that the passage does not mean "any conceivable requirement may be imposed on any state official," and that "the essence of legislative power ... is a discretion not subject to command," so that legislatures, at least, cannot be commanded. But then why were legislatures mentioned in the passage? It seems to us assuredly *not* a "natural reading" that being "rendered auxiliary to the enforcement of [the National Government's] laws" means impressibility into federal service for "courts and magistrates" but something quite different for "legislatures."

directed to the States, will "bid much fairer to avoid the necessity of using force" against the States, The Federalist No. 27. It also reconciles the passage with Hamilton's statement in The Federalist No. 36, that the Federal Government would in some circumstances do well "to employ the State officers as much as possible, and to attach them to the Union by an accumulation of their emoluments"—which surely suggests inducing state officers to come aboard by paying them, rather than merely commandeering their official services.

JUSTICE SOUTER contends that his interpretation of The Federalist No. 27 is "supported by No. 44," written by Madison, wherefore he claims that "Madison and Hamilton" together stand opposed to our view. In fact, The Federalist No. 44 quite clearly contradicts JUSTICE SOUTER's reading. In that Number, Madison justifies the requirement that state officials take an oath to support the Federal Constitution on the ground that they "will have an essential agency in giving effect to the federal Constitution." If the dissent's reading of The Federalist No. 27 were correct (and if Madison agreed with it), one would surely have expected that "essential agency" of state executive officers (if described further) to be described as their responsibility to execute the laws enacted under the Constitution. Instead, however, The Federalist No. 44 continues with the following description:

> "The election of the President and Senate will depend, in all cases, on the legislatures of the several States. And the election of the House of Representatives will equally depend on the same authority in the first instance; and will, probably, forever *be conducted by the officers* and according to the laws *of the States.*" *Id.* (emphasis added).

It is most implausible that the person who labored for that example of state executive officers' assisting the Federal Government believed, but neglected to mention, that they had a responsibility to execute federal laws. If it was indeed Hamilton's view that the Federal Government could direct the officers of the States, that view has no clear support in Madison's writings, or as far as we are aware, in text, history, or early commentary elsewhere.[9]

To complete the historical record, we must note that there is not only an absence of executive-commandeering statutes in the early Congresses, but there is an absence of them in our later history as well, at least until very recent years. The Government points to the Act of August 3, 1882, which enlisted state officials "to take charge of the local affairs of immigration in the ports within such State. The statute did not, however, *mandate* those duties, but merely empowered the Secretary of the Treasury

---

9. Even if we agreed with JUSTICE SOUTER's reading of The Federalist No. 27, it would still seem to us most peculiar to give the view expressed in that one piece, not clearly confirmed by any other writer, the determinative weight he does. That would be crediting the most expansive view of federal authority ever expressed, and from the pen of the most expansive expositor of federal power. Hamilton was "from first to last the most nationalistic of all nationalists in his interpretation of the clauses of our federal Constitution." C. Rossiter, Alexander Hamilton and the Constitution 199 (1964).

"to *enter into contracts* with such State . . . officers as *may be designated* for that purpose *by the governor* of any State." (Emphasis added.)

The Government points to a number of federal statutes enacted within the past few decades that require the participation of state or local officials in implementing federal regulatory schemes. Even assuming they represent assertion of the very same congressional power challenged here, they are of such recent vintage that they are no more probative than the statute before us of a constitutional tradition that lends meaning to the text. Their persuasive force is far outweighed by almost two centuries of apparent congressional avoidance of the practice.

III

The constitutional practice we have examined above tends to negate the existence of the congressional power asserted here, but is not conclusive. We turn next to consideration of the structure of the Constitution, to see if we can discern a principle that controls the present cases.

A

It is incontestible that the Constitution established a system of "dual sovereignty." *Gregory v. Ashcroft*, 501 U.S. 452 (1991). Although the States surrendered many of their powers to the new Federal Government, they retained "a residuary and inviolable sovereignty," The Federalist No. 39 (J. Madison). This is reflected throughout the Constitution's text. Residual state sovereignty was also implicit, of course, in the Constitution's conferral upon Congress of not all governmental powers, but only discrete, enumerated ones, Art. I, §8, which implication was rendered express by the Tenth Amendment's assertion that "[t]he powers not delegated to the United States by the Constitution, nor prohibited by it to the States, are reserved to the States respectively, or to the people."

The Framers' experience under the Articles of Confederation had persuaded them that using the States as the instruments of federal governance was both ineffectual and provocative of federal-state conflict. *See* The Federalist No. 15. Preservation of the States as independent political entities being the price of union, and "[t]he practicality of making laws, with coercive sanctions, for the States as political bodies" having been, in Madison's words, "exploded on all hands," 2 Records of the Federal Convention of 1787 (M. Farrand ed.1911), the Framers rejected the concept of a central government that would act upon and through the States, and instead designed a system in which the State and Federal Governments would exercise concurrent authority over the people—who were, in Hamilton's words, "the only proper objects of government," The Federalist No. 15. We have set forth the historical record in more detail elsewhere, *see New York v. United States*, and need not repeat it here. It suffices to repeat the conclusion: "the Framers explicitly chose a Constitution that confers upon Congress the power to regulate individuals, not States." The great innovation of this design was that "our citizens would have two political capacities, one state and one federal, each protected from incursion by the other." The Constitution thus contemplates that a State's government will represent and remain accountable to its own citizens. *See New York*, 505 U.S. at 168–69; *United States v. Lopez*, 514 U.S. 549, 576–77 (1995) (Kennedy, J., concurring).[11]

This separation of the two spheres is one of the Constitution's structural protections of liberty. "Just as the separation and independence of the coordinate branches of the Federal Government serve to prevent the accumulation of excessive power in any one branch, a healthy balance of power between the States and the Federal Government will reduce the risk of tyranny and abuse from either front." *Gregory v. Ashcroft*, 501 U.S. 452, 458 (1991).

The power of the Federal Government would be augmented immeasurably if it were able to impress into its service — and at no cost to itself — the police officers of the 50 States.

B

We have thus far discussed the effect that federal control of state officers would have upon the first element of the "double security" alluded to by Madison: the division of power between State and Federal Governments. It would also have an effect upon the second element: the separation and equilibration of powers between the three branches of the Federal Government itself. The Constitution does not leave to speculation who is to administer the laws enacted by Congress; the President, it says, "shall take Care that the Laws be faithfully executed," Art. II, §3, personally and through officers whom he appoints, Art. II, §2. The Brady Act effectively transfers this responsibility to thousands of CLEOs in the 50 States, who are left to implement the program without meaningful Presidential control (if indeed meaningful Presidential control is possible without the power to appoint and remove). The insistence of the Framers upon unity in the Federal Executive — to ensure both vigor and accountability — is well known. *See* The Federalist No. 70 (A. Hamilton). That unity would be shattered, and the power of the President would be subject to reduction, if Congress could act as effectively without the President as with him, by simply requiring state officers to execute its laws.

The dissent of course resorts to the last, best hope of those who defend ultra vires congressional action, the Necessary and Proper Clause. It reasons that the power to regulate the sale of handguns under the Commerce Clause, coupled with the power to "make all Laws which shall be necessary and proper for carrying into Execution the foregoing Powers," Art. I, §8, conclusively establishes the Brady Act's constitutional

---

11. JUSTICE BREYER's dissent would have us consider the benefits that other countries, and the European Union, believe they have derived from federal systems that are different from ours. We think such comparative analysis inappropriate to the task of interpreting a constitution, though it was of course quite relevant to the task of writing one. The Framers were familiar with many federal systems, from classical antiquity down to their own time; they are discussed in Nos. 18–20 of The Federalist. Some were (for the purpose here under discussion) quite similar to the modern "federal" systems that JUSTICE BREYER favors . . . . The fact is that our federalism is not Europe's. It is "the unique contribution of the Framers to political science and political theory." *United States v. Lopez* (Kennedy, J., concurring).

validity, because the Tenth Amendment imposes no limitations on the exercise of *delegated* powers but merely prohibits the exercise of powers "*not* delegated to the United States." What destroys the dissent's Necessary and Proper Clause argument, however, is not the Tenth Amendment but the Necessary and Proper Clause itself. When a "La[w] . . . for carrying into Execution" the Commerce Clause violates the principle of state sovereignty reflected in the various constitutional provisions we mentioned earlier, it is not a "La[w] . . . *proper* for carrying into Execution the Commerce Clause," and is thus, in the words of The Federalist, "merely [an] ac[t] of usurpation" which "deserve[s] to be treated as such." The Federalist No. 33 (A. Hamilton).

IV

Finally, and most conclusively in the present litigation, we turn to the prior juris-prudence of this Court. Federal commandeering of state governments is such a novel phenomenon that this Court's first experience with it did not occur until the 1970's, when the Environmental Protection Agency promulgated regulations requiring States to prescribe auto emissions testing, monitoring and retrofit programs, and to desig-nate preferential bus and carpool lanes. The Courts of Appeals for the Fourth and Ninth Circuits invalidated the regulations on statutory grounds in order to avoid what they perceived to be grave constitutional issues; and the District of Columbia Circuit invalidated the regulations on both constitutional and statutory grounds. After we granted certiorari to review the statutory and constitutional validity of the regulations, the Government declined even to defend them, and instead rescinded some and conceded the invalidity of those that remained, leading us to vacate the opinions below and remand for consideration of mootness.

Later opinions of ours have made clear that the Federal Government may not com-pel the States to implement, by legislation or executive action, federal regulatory programs. In *Hodel v. Virginia Surface Mining & Reclamation Assn., Inc.*, 452 U.S. 264 (1981), we sustained [a] statute[] against constitutional challenge only after assuring ourselves that [it] did not require the States to enforce federal law.

When we were at last confronted squarely with a federal statute that unambigu-ously required the States to enact or administer a federal regulatory program, our decision should have come as no surprise. At issue in *New York v. United States*, were the so-called "take title" provisions of the Low-Level Radioactive Waste Policy Amendments Act of 1985. We concluded that Congress could constitutionally require the States to do neither. "The Federal Government," we held, "may not compel the States to enact or administer a federal regulatory program."

The Government maintains that requiring state officers to perform discrete, min-isterial tasks specified by Congress does not violate the principle of *New York* because it does not diminish the accountability of state or federal officials. This argument fails even on its own terms. By forcing state governments to absorb the financial bur-den of implementing a federal regulatory program, Members of Congress can take credit for "solving" problems without having to ask their constituents to pay for the solutions with higher federal taxes. And even when the States are not forced to absorb the costs of implementing a federal program, they are still put in the position of taking the blame for its burdensomeness and for its defects. Under the present law, for example, it will be the CLEO and not some federal official who stands between the gun purchaser and immediate possession of his gun. And it will likely be the CLEO, not some federal official, who will be blamed for any error (even one in the designated federal database) that causes a purchaser to be mistakenly rejected.

Finally, the Government puts forward a cluster of arguments that can be grouped under the heading: "The Brady Act serves very important purposes, is most efficiently administered by CLEOs during the interim period, and places a minimal and only temporary burden upon state officers." [W]here, as here, it is the whole *object* of the law to direct the functioning of the state executive, and hence to compromise the structural framework of dual sovereignty, such a "balancing" analysis is inappropriate. It is the very *principle* of separate state sovereignty that such a law offends, and no comparative assessment of the various interests can overcome that fundamental defect. We expressly rejected such an approach in *New York*.

We adhere to that principle today, and conclude categorically, as we concluded categorically in *New York*: "The Federal Government may not compel the States to enact or administer a federal regulatory program." The mandatory obligation imposed on CLEOs to perform background checks on prospective handgun purchasers plainly runs afoul of that rule.

V

What we have said makes it clear enough that the central obligation imposed upon CLEOs by the interim provisions of the Brady Act is unconstitutional.

We held in *New York* that Congress cannot compel the States to enact or enforce a federal regulatory program. Today we hold that Congress cannot circumvent that prohibition by conscripting the State's officers directly. The Federal Government may neither issue directives requiring the States to address particular problems, nor command the States' officers, or those of their political subdivisions, to administer or enforce a federal regulatory program. [S]uch commands are fundamentally incompatible with our constitutional system of dual sovereignty. Accordingly, the judgment of the Court of Appeals for the Ninth Circuit is reversed.

It is so ordered.

JUSTICE O'CONNOR, concurring.

Our precedent and our Nation's historical practices support the Court's holding today. The Brady Act violates the Tenth Amendment.

JUSTICE THOMAS, concurring.

The Court today properly holds that the Brady Act violates the Tenth Amendment in that it compels state law enforcement officers to "administer or enforce a federal regulatory program." Although I join the Court's opinion in full, I write separately to emphasize that the Tenth Amendment affirms the undeniable notion that under our Constitution, the Federal Government is one of enumerated, hence limited, powers. Accordingly, the Federal Government may act only where the Constitution authorizes it to do so.

Even if we construe Congress' authority to regulate interstate commerce to encompass those intrastate transactions that "substantially affect" interstate commerce, I question whether Congress can regulate the particular transactions at issue here. The Constitution, in addition to delegating certain enumerated powers to Congress, places whole areas outside the reach of Congress' regulatory authority. I join the Court's opinion striking down the challenged provisions of the Brady Act as inconsistent with the Tenth Amendment.

JUSTICE STEVENS, with whom JUSTICE SOUTER, JUSTICE GINSBURG, and JUSTICE BREYER join, dissenting.

When Congress exercises the powers delegated to it by the Constitution, it may impose affirmative obligations on executive and judicial officers of state and local governments as well as ordinary citizens. This conclusion is firmly supported by the text of the Constitution, the early history of the Nation, decisions of this Court, and a correct understanding of the basic structure of the Federal Government.

These cases do not implicate the more difficult questions associated with congressional coercion of state legislatures addressed in *New York v. United States*, 505 U.S. 144 (1992).

I

The text of the Constitution provides a sufficient basis for a correct disposition of these cases.

Article I, § 8, grants Congress the power to regulate commerce among the States. [T]here can be no question that that provision adequately supports the regulation of commerce in handguns effected by the Brady Act. Moreover, the additional grant of authority in that section of the Constitution "[t]o make all Laws which shall be necessary and proper for carrying into Execution the foregoing Powers" is surely adequate to support the temporary enlistment of local police officers in the process of identifying persons who should not be entrusted with the possession of handguns. In short, the affirmative delegation of power in Article I provides ample authority for the congressional enactment.

Unlike the First Amendment, which prohibits the enactment of a category of laws that would otherwise be authorized by Article I, the Tenth Amendment imposes no restriction on the exercise of delegated powers. Using language that plainly refers only to powers that are "*not*" delegated to Congress, it provides:

> "The powers not delegated to the United States by the Constitution, nor prohibited by it to the States, are reserved to the States respectively, or to the people." U.S. Const., Amdt. 10.

The Amendment confirms the principle that the powers of the Federal Government are limited to those affirmatively granted by the Constitution, but it does not purport to limit the scope or the effectiveness of the exercise of powers that are delegated to Congress.[1] See *New York v. United States* ("In a case . . . involving the division of authority between federal and state governments, the two inquiries are mirror images of each other"). Thus, the Amendment provides no support for a rule that immunizes local officials from obligations that might be imposed on ordinary citizens.[2] Indeed, it would be more reasonable to infer that federal law may impose greater duties on state officials than on private citizens because another provision of the Constitution requires that "all executive and judicial Officers, both of the United States and of the several States, shall be bound by Oath or Affirmation, to support this Constitution." Art. VI, cl. 3.

It is appropriate for state officials to make an oath or affirmation to support the Federal Constitution because, as explained in The Federalist, they "have an essential agency in giving effect to the federal Constitution." The Federalist No. 44 (J. Madison). There can be no conflict between their duties to the State and those owed to the Federal Government because Article VI unambiguously provides that federal law "shall be the supreme Law of the Land," binding in every State. U.S. Const., Art. VI, cl. 2. Thus, not only the Constitution, but every law enacted by Congress as well, establishes policy for the States just as firmly as do laws enacted by state legislatures.

There is not a clause, sentence, or paragraph in the entire text of the Constitution of the United States that supports the proposition that a local police officer can ignore a command contained in a statute enacted by Congress pursuant to an express delegation of power enumerated in Article I.

---

1. Indeed, the Framers repeatedly rejected proposed changes to the Tenth Amendment that would have altered the text to refer to "powers not *expressly* delegated to the United States." This was done, as Madison explained, because "it was impossible to confine a Government to the exercise of express powers; there must necessarily be admitted powers by implication, unless the constitution descended to recount every minutia." 1 Annals of Cong. 790 (Aug. 18, 1789).

2. Recognizing the force of the argument, the Court suggests that this reasoning is in error because—even if it is responsive to the submission that the Tenth Amendment roots the principle set forth by the majority today—it does not answer the possibility that the Court's holding can be rooted in a "principle of state sovereignty" mentioned nowhere in the constitutional text. As a ground for invalidating important federal legislation, this argument is remarkably weak. The majority's further claim that, while the Brady Act may be legislation "necessary" to Congress' execution of its undisputed Commerce Clause authority to regulate firearms sales, it is nevertheless not "proper" because it violates state sovereignty, is wholly circular, and provides no traction for its argument. Moreover, this reading of the term "proper" gives it a meaning directly contradicted by Chief Justice Marshall in *McCulloch v. Maryland*, [17 U.S. (4 Wheat.) 316 (1819)]. As the Chief Justice explained, the Necessary and Proper Clause by "[i]ts terms purport[s] to enlarge, not to diminish the powers vested in the government. It purports to be an additional power, not a restriction on those already granted."

II

Under the Articles of Confederation the National Government had the power to issue commands to the several sovereign States, but it had no authority to govern individuals directly.

That method of governing proved to be unacceptable, not because it demeaned the sovereign character of the several States, but rather because it was cumbersome and inefficient. Indeed, a confederation that allows each of its members to determine the ways and means of complying with an overriding requisition is obviously more deferential to state sovereignty concerns than a National Government that uses its own agents to impose its will directly on the citizenry. The basic change in the character of the government that the Framers conceived was designed to enhance the power of the national government, not to provide some new, unmentioned immunity for state officers. Because indirect control over individual citizens was ineffective under the Articles of Confederation, Alexander Hamilton explained that "we must *extend* the authority of the Union to the persons of the citizens." The Federalist No. 15 (emphasis added).

Indeed, the historical materials strongly suggest that the founders intended to enhance the capacity of the Federal Government by empowering it — as a part of the new authority to make demands directly on individual citizens — to act through local officials. Hamilton made clear that the new Constitution, "by extending the authority of the federal head to the individual citizens of the several States, will enable the government to employ the ordinary magistracy of each in the execution of its laws." The Federalist No. 27. Hamilton's meaning was unambiguous; the Federal Government was to have the power to demand that local officials implement national policy programs.

More specifically, during the debates concerning the ratification of the Constitution, it was assumed that state agents would act as tax collectors for the Federal Government. Opponents of the Constitution had repeatedly expressed fears that the new Federal Government's ability to impose taxes directly on the citizenry would result in an overbearing presence of federal tax collectors in the States. Federalists rejoined that this problem would not arise because, as Hamilton explained, "the United States . . . will make use of the State officers and State regulations for collecting" certain taxes. *Id.*, No. 36. Similarly, Madison made clear that the new central Government's power to raise taxes directly from the citizenry would "not be resorted to, except for supplemental purposes of revenue . . . and that the eventual collection, under the immediate authority of the Union, will generally be made by the officers . . . appointed by the several States." *Id.*, No. 45.

The Court's response to this powerful historical evidence is weak. The majority suggests that "none of these statements necessarily implies . . . Congress could impose these responsibilities without the consent of the States." (emphasis deleted). No fair reading of these materials can justify such an interpretation. As Hamilton explained, the power of the Government to act on "individual citizens" — including "employ[ing] the ordinary magistracy" of the States—was an answer to the problems faced by a central Government that could act only directly "upon the States in their political or collective capacities." The Federalist No. 27. The new Constitution would avoid this problem, resulting in "a regular and peaceable execution of the laws of the Union."

This point is made especially clear in Hamilton's statement that "the legislatures, courts, and magistrates, of the respective members, will be incorporated into the operations of the national government *as far as its just and constitutional authority extends; and will be rendered auxiliary to the enforcement of its laws.*" *Ibid.* (second emphasis added). It is hard to imagine a more unequivocal statement that state judicial and executive branch officials may be required to implement federal law where the National Government acts within the scope of its affirmative powers.

The Court makes two unpersuasive attempts to discount the force of this statement. First, according to the majority, because Hamilton mentioned the Supremacy Clause without specifically referring to any "congressional directive," the statement does not mean what it plainly says. But the mere fact that the Supremacy Clause is the source of the obligation of state officials to implement congressional directives does not remotely suggest that they might be "'incorporat[ed] into the operations of the national government,'" The Federalist No. 27 (A. Hamilton), before their obligations have been defined by Congress. Federal law establishes policy for the States just as firmly as laws enacted by state legislatures but that does not mean that state or federal officials must implement directives that have not been specified in any law. Second, the majority suggests that interpreting this passage to mean what it says would conflict with our decision in *New York v. United States.* But since the *New York* opinion did not mention The Federalist No. 27, it does not affect either the relevance or the weight of the historical evidence provided by No. 27 insofar as it relates to state courts and magistrates.

Bereft of support in the history of the founding, the Court rests its conclusion on the claim that there is little evidence the National Government actually exercised such a power in the early years of the Republic. This reasoning is misguided in principle and in fact. While we have indicated that the express consideration and resolution of difficult constitutional issues by the First Congress in particular "provides 'contemporaneous and weighty evidence' of the Constitution's meaning since many of [its] Members . . . 'had taken part in framing that instrument,'" we have never suggested that the failure of the early Congresses to address the scope of federal power in a particular area or to exercise a particular authority was an argument against its existence. That position, if correct, would undermine most of our post-New Deal Commerce Clause jurisprudence.

More importantly, the fact that Congress did elect to rely on state judges and the clerks of state courts to perform a variety of executive functions is surely evidence of a contemporary understanding that their status as state officials did not immunize them from federal service. The majority's description of these early statutes is both incomplete and at times misleading. For example, statutes of the early Congresses required in mandatory terms that state judges and their clerks perform various executive duties with respect to applications for citizenship. Similarly, the First Congress enacted legislation requiring state courts to serve, functionally, like contemporary regulatory agencies in certifying the seaworthiness of vessels.

The Court assumes that the imposition of such essentially executive duties on state judges and their clerks sheds no light on the question whether executive officials might have an immunity from federal obligations. Even assuming that the enlistment of state judges in their judicial role for federal purposes is irrelevant to the question whether executive officials may be asked to perform the same function—a claim disputed below—the majority's analysis is badly mistaken.

We are far truer to the historical record by applying a functional approach in assessing the role played by these early state officials. The use of state judges and their clerks to perform executive functions was, in historical context, hardly unusual. And, of course, judges today continue to perform a variety of functions that may more properly be described as executive. The majority's insistence that this evidence of federal enlistment of state officials to serve executive functions is irrelevant simply because the assistance of "judges" was at issue rests on empty formalistic reasoning of the highest order.[11]

The Court's evaluation of the historical evidence, furthermore, fails to acknowledge the important difference between policy decisions that may have been influenced by respect for state sovereignty concerns, and decisions that are compelled by the Constitution.[12] Thus, for example, the decision by Congress to give President Wilson the authority to utilize the services of state officers in implementing the World War I draft, surely indicates that the National Legislature saw no constitutional impediment to the enlistment of state assistance during a federal emergency. The fact that the President was able to implement the program by respectfully "request[ing]" state action, rather than bluntly commanding it, is evidence that he was an effective

---

11. Able to muster little response other than the bald claim that this argument strikes the majority as "doubtful," the Court proceeds to attack the basic point that the statutes discussed above called state judges to serve what were substantially executive functions. The argument has little force. The majority's view that none of the statutes referred to in the text required judges to perform anything other than "quintessentially adjudicative tasks[s]," is quite wrong. The evaluation of applications for citizenship and the acceptance of Revolutionary War claims, for example, both discussed above, are hard to characterize as the sort of adversarial proceedings to which common-law courts are accustomed. As for the majority's suggestion that the substantial administrative requirements imposed on state-court clerks under the naturalization statutes are merely "ancillary" and therefore irrelevant, this conclusion is in considerable tension with the Court's holding that the minor burden imposed by the Brady Act violates the Constitution.

12. Indeed, an entirely appropriate concern for the prerogatives of state government readily explains Congress' sparing use of this otherwise "highly attractive," power. Congress' discretion, contrary to the majority's suggestion, indicates not that the power does not exist, but rather that the interests of the States are more than sufficiently protected by their participation in the National Government.

statesman, but surely does not indicate that he doubted either his or Congress' power to use mandatory language if necessary.[14]

Indeed, the majority's opinion consists almost entirely of arguments *against* the substantial evidence weighing in opposition to its view; the Court's ruling is strikingly lacking in affirmative support. Absent even a modicum of textual foundation for its judicially crafted constitutional rule, there should be a presumption that if the Framers had actually intended such a rule, at least one of them would have mentioned it.

III

The Court's "structural" arguments are not sufficient to rebut that presumption. The fact that the Framers intended to preserve the sovereignty of the several States simply does not speak to the question whether individual state employees may be required to perform federal obligations.

As we explained in *Garcia v. San Antonio Metropolitan Transit Authority*, 469 U.S. 528 (1985): "[T]he principal means chosen by the Framers to ensure the role of the States in the federal system lies in the structure of the Federal Government itself. It is no novelty to observe that the composition of the Federal Government was designed in large part to protect the States from overreaching by Congress."

Perversely, the majority's rule seems more likely to damage than to preserve the safeguards against tyranny provided by the existence of vital state governments. By limiting the ability of the Federal Government to enlist state officials in the implementation of its programs, the Court creates incentives for the National Government to aggrandize itself. In the name of State's rights, the majority would have the Federal Government create vast national bureaucracies to implement its policies. This is exactly the sort of thing that the early Federalists promised would not occur, in part as a result of the National Government's ability to rely on the magistracy of the States. *See, e.g.,* The Federalist No. 36 (A. Hamilton); *id.*, No. 45 (J. Madison).

With colorful hyperbole, the Court suggests that the unity in the Executive Branch of the Federal Government "would be shattered, and the power of the President would be subject to reduction, if Congress could . . . requir[e] state officers to execute its laws." Putting to one side the obvious tension between the majority's claim that impressing state police officers will unduly tip the balance of power in favor of the federal sovereign and this suggestion that it will emasculate the Presidency, the Court's reasoning contradicts *New York v. United States*.

---

14. Even less probative is the Court's reliance on the decision by Congress to authorize federal marshals to rent temporary jail facilities instead of insisting that state jailkeepers house federal prisoners at federal expense. The majority finds constitutional significance in the fact that the First Congress (apparently following practice appropriate under the Articles of Confederation) had issued a request to state legislatures rather than a command to state jailkeepers, and the further fact that it chose not to change that request to a command 18 months later. The Court does not point us to a single comment by any Member of Congress suggesting that either decision was motivated in the slightest by constitutional doubts.

That decision squarely approved of cooperative federalism programs, designed at the national level but implemented principally by state governments. *New York* disapproved of a particular *method* of putting such programs into place, not the *existence* of federal programs implemented locally.

Nor is there force to the assumption undergirding the Court's entire opinion that if this trivial burden on state sovereignty is permissible, the entire structure of federalism will soon collapse. These cases do not involve any mandate to state legislatures to enact new rules. When legislative action, or even administrative rulemaking, is at issue, it may be appropriate for Congress either to pre-empt the State's lawmaking power and fashion the federal rule itself, or to respect the State's power to fashion its own rules. But these cases, unlike any precedent in which the Court has held that Congress exceeded its powers, merely involve the imposition of modest duties on individual officers. The Court seems to accept the fact that Congress could require private persons, such as hospital executives or school administrators, to provide arms merchants with relevant information about a prospective purchaser's fitness to own a weapon; indeed, the Court does not disturb the conclusion that flows directly from our prior holdings that the burden on police officers would be permissible if a similar burden were also imposed on private parties with access to relevant data. A structural problem that vanishes when the statute affects private individuals as well as public officials is not much of a structural problem.

IV

Finally, the Court advises us that the "prior jurisprudence of this Court" is the most conclusive support for its position. That "prior jurisprudence" is *New York v. United States*.

Our statements, taken in context, clearly did not decide the question presented here, whether state executive officials—as opposed to state legislators—may in appropriate circumstances be enlisted to implement federal policy. The "take title" provision at issue in *New York* was beyond Congress' authority to enact because it was "in principle . . . no different than a congressionally compelled subsidy from state governments to radioactive waste producers," almost certainly a legislative Act.

Accordingly, I respectfully dissent.

JUSTICE SOUTER, dissenting.

I join JUSTICE STEVENS's dissenting opinion, but subject to the following qualifications. While I do not find anything dispositive in the paucity of early examples of federal employment of state officers for executive purposes, neither would I find myself in dissent with no more to go on than those few early instances in the administration of naturalization laws, for example. These illustrations of state action implementing congressional statutes are consistent with the Government's positions, but they do not speak to me with much force.

In deciding these cases, which I have found closer than I had anticipated, it is The Federalist that finally determines my position. I believe that the most straightforward reading of No. 27 is authority for the Government's position here, and that this reading is both supported by No. 44 and consistent with Nos. 36 and 45.

Hamilton in No. 27 first notes that because the new Constitution would authorize the National Government to bind individuals directly through national law, it could "employ the ordinary magistracy of each [State] in the execution of its laws." The Federalist No. 27 (A. Hamilton). Were he to stop here, he would not necessarily be speaking of anything beyond the possibility of cooperative arrangements by agreement. But he then addresses the combined effect of the proposed Supremacy Clause, and state officers' oath requirement, and he states that "the Legislatures, Courts and Magistrates of the respective members will be incorporated into the operations of the national government, *as far as its just and constitutional authority extends;* and will be rendered auxiliary to the enforcement of its laws." The Federalist No. 27 (emphasis in original). The natural reading of this language is not merely that the officers of the various branches of state governments may be employed in the performance of national functions; Hamilton says that the state governmental machinery "will be incorporated" into the Nation's operation, and because the "auxiliary" status of the state officials will occur because they are "bound by the sanctity of an oath," I take him to mean that their auxiliary functions will be the products of their obligations thus undertaken to support federal law, not of their own, or the States', unfettered choices.[1]

Madison in No. 44 supports this reading in his commentary on the oath requirement. He asks why state magistrates should have to swear to support the National Constitution, when national officials will not be required to oblige themselves to

---

1. [T]he Court reads The Federalist No. 27 as incompatible with our decision in *New York v. United States,* and credits me with the imagination to devise a "novel principle of political science," "in order to bring forth disparity of outcome from parity of language"; in order, that is, to salvage *New York,* by concluding that Congress can tell state executive officers what to execute without at the same time having the power to tell state legislators what to legislate. But the Court is too generous. I simply realize that "parity of language" (*i.e.,* all state officials who take the oath are "incorporated" or are "auxiliar[ies]") operates on officers of the three branches in accordance with the quite different powers of their respective branches. The core power of an executive officer is to enforce a law in accordance with its terms; that is why a state executive "auxiliary" may be told what result to bring about. The core power of a legislator acting within the legislature's subject-matter jurisdiction is to make a discretionary decision on what the law should be; that is why a legislator may not be legally ordered to exercise discretion a particular way without damaging the legislative power as such. The discretionary nature of the authorized legislative Act is probably why Madison's two examples of legislative "auxiliary" obligation address the elections of the President and Senators (discussing The Federalist No. 44 (J. Madison)), not the passage of legislation to please Congress.

The Court reads Hamilton's description of state officers' role in carrying out federal law as nothing more than a way of describing the duty of state officials "not to obstruct the operation of federal law," with the consequence that any obstruction is invalid. But I doubt that Hamilton's English was quite as bad as all that. Someone whose virtue consists of not obstructing administration of the law is not described as "incorporated into the operations" of a government or as an "auxiliary" to its law enforcement. One simply cannot escape from Hamilton by reducing his prose to inapposite figures of speech.

support the state counterparts. His answer is that national officials "will have no agency in carrying the State Constitutions into effect. The members and officers of the State Governments, on the contrary, will have an essential agency in giving effect to the Federal Constitution." *Id.*, No. 44 (J. Madison). He then describes the state legislative "agency" as action necessary for selecting the President, *see* U.S. Const., Art. II, § 1, and the choice of Senators, *see* U.S. Const., Art. I, § 3 (repealed by Amdt. 17). The Federalist No. 44. The Supremacy Clause itself, of course, expressly refers to the state judges' obligations under federal law, and other numbers of The Federalist give examples of state executive "agency" in the enforcement of national revenue laws.

Two such examples of anticipated state collection of federal revenue are instructive, each of which is put forward to counter fears of a proliferation of tax collectors. In No. 45, Hamilton says that if a State is not given (or declines to exercise) an option to supply its citizens' share of a federal tax, the "eventual collection [of the federal tax] under the immediate authority of the Union, will generally be made by the officers, and according to the rules, appointed by the several States." *Id.*, No. 45. And in No. 36, he explains that the National Government would more readily "employ the State officers as much as possible, and to attach them to the Union by an accumulation of their emoluments," *id.*, No. 36, than by appointing separate federal revenue collectors.

In the light of all these passages, I cannot persuade myself that the statements from No. 27 speak of anything less than the authority of the National Government, when exercising an otherwise legitimate power (the commerce power, say), to require state "auxiliaries" to take appropriate action. To be sure, it does not follow that any conceivable requirement may be imposed on any state official. I continue to agree, for example, that Congress may not require a state legislature to enact a regulatory scheme and that *New York v. United States* was rightly decided; after all, the essence of legislative power, within the limits of legislative jurisdiction, is a discretion not subject to command. But insofar as national law would require nothing from a state officer inconsistent with the power proper to his branch of tripartite state government, I suppose that the reach of federal law as Hamilton described it would not be exceeded.

Justice Breyer, with whom Justice Stevens joins, dissenting.

I would add to the reasons Justice Stevens sets forth the fact that the United States is not the only nation that seeks to reconcile the practical need for a central authority with the democratic virtues of more local control. At least some other countries, facing the same basic problem, have found that local control is better maintained through application of a principle that is the direct opposite of the principle the majority derives from the silence of our Constitution. The federal systems of Switzerland, Germany, and the European Union, for example, all provide that constituent states, not federal bureaucracies, will themselves implement many of the laws, rules, regulations, or decrees enacted by the central "federal" body. They do so in part because they believe that such a system interferes less, not more, with the independent authority of the "state," member nation, or other subsidiary government, and helps to safeguard individual liberty as well.

Of course, we are interpreting our own Constitution, not those of other nations, and there may be relevant political and structural differences between their systems and our own. But their experience may nonetheless cast an empirical light on the consequences of different solutions to a common legal problem—in this case the problem of reconciling central authority with the need to preserve the liberty-enhancing autonomy of a smaller constituent governmental entity. *Cf. id.*, The Federalist No. 42 (J. Madison) (looking to experiences of European countries); *id.*, No. 43 (J. Madison) (same).

As comparative experience suggests, there is no need to interpret the Constitution as containing an absolute principle—forbidding the assignment of virtually any federal duty to any state official.

For these reasons and those set forth in JUSTICE STEVENS' opinion, I join his dissent.

EXERCISE 6:

1. The *Printz* Court provided the most robust defense for its anti-commandeering rule. Was it persuasive? As an originalist matter? On nonoriginalist grounds?

2. On each of the three main "data" points—historical practice, constitutional structure, and Court precedent—who had the better of the argument?

3. The majority stated "[f]inally, and most conclusively in the present litigation, we turn to the prior jurisprudence of this Court." Why did the majority believe that was "most conclusive[]"?

4. After reading *Printz* and *New York*, do you think *Garcia* remains good law? If *Garcia* is no longer good law, then does that mean that *National League of Cities* is?

5. Are *New York* and *Printz* faithful to *Darby*?

6. Why did the majority cite to Justice Kennedy's concurrence in *United States v. Lopez*, 514 U.S. 549, 568 (1995) (Kennedy, J., concurring)?

7. The contending historical claims in the majority and dissenting opinions is one of the consequences of the return to originalism over the past thirty years. Does *Printz* show that the Supreme Court's use of originalist arguments is a positive or negative development? For example, regarding the contending interpretations of FEDERALIST No. 27 (Alexander Hamilton), is there a—clear?—winner?

8. Justice Scalia was a well-known proponent of originalism. *See, e.g.,* ANTONIN SCALIA, A MATTER OF INTERPRETATION: FEDERAL COURTS AND THE LAW (1997). Yet, in his majority opinion, Justice Scalia acknowledged that "there is no constitutional text speaking to this precise question." Should that be the end of his inquiry? How can an originalist determine that Congress' power is restricted by an *un*written limit? Also, is it legitimate for an originalist to divine constitutional principles as Justice

Scalia purports to do: "We turn next to consideration of the structure of the Constitution, to see if we can discern a principle that controls the present cases"?

9. Justice Scalia chided the dissent for relying on the Necessary and Proper Clause to uphold the Brady Act, and described the Clause as the "last, best hope of those who defend ultra vires congressional action." He then concluded that the Clause did not authorize the Act's conscription of state executive officers because it would not be "proper," as the Clause requires. Is Justice Scalia's approach here consistent with his approach in *Gonzales v. Raich*, 545 U.S. 1, 34–39 (2005) (Scalia, J. concurring)?

10. Justice Breyer in dissent argued that the experiences of other countries with federal governmental systems provide important information that the Court should use when interpreting the United States Constitution. To what extent, if any, is Justice Breyer right? Or does the majority have the better of the argument?

11. Did the dissents' positions permit them to retain *New York*? How? Was the majority's reply persuasive?

Keep in mind that, during this period, the Rehnquist Court handed down decisions, across a number of doctrinal categories, that indicated that the Court was, once again, serious about *judicially* enforcing federalism norms. *New York* and *Printz* dealt with the Tenth Amendment; *United States v. Lopez*, 514 U.S. 549 (1995), and *United States v. Morrison*, 529 U.S. 598 (2000), concerned Congress' Commerce Clause authority; *Boerne v. Flores*, 521 U.S. 507 (1997), governed Congress' Section 5 powers; and a series of cases, beginning with *Seminole Tribe v. Florida*, 517 U.S. 44 (1996), covered state sovereign immunity from suit. *See* John C. Yoo, *The Judicial Safeguards of Federalism*, 70 S. Cal. L. Rev. 1311, 1312 (1997) (arguing that these lines of cases "have reasserted the applicability of judicial review to questions concerning state sovereignty and the proper balance between the national and state governments").

Each of these lines of cases indicated *some* movement away from the post-New Deal consensus articulated by *Carolene Products* Footnote 4. Instead of nearly-absolute deference to congressional judgments in the context of federalism, the Supreme Court in the 1990s staked out a role for itself in adjudicating the boundaries between federal and state power. This was—and remains—a controversial move, and the four Tenth Amendment cases, beginning with *National League of Cities*, prominently display the arguments for and against this move.

G. FEDERALISM AS A RULE OF STATUTORY CONSTRUCTION

In recent years, the Court has invoked federalism in other contexts as well, such as in the interpretation of treaties and statutes. This also has occurred in the treaty power context. By way of background, Article II states: "[The President] shall have Power, by and with the Advice and Consent of the Senate to make Treaties, provided two thirds of the Senators present concur . . . ." U.S. Const., art. II, § 2, cl. 2. The most important case interpreting the scope of the treaty power was *Missouri v. Holland*, 252 U.S. 416 (1920), where the Court considered whether a non-self-executing treaty[25] between the United States and Great Britain, which regulated the capture and killing of certain birds that migrated between the United States and Canada, violated the Tenth Amendment. Congress' original attempt to regulate the killing of such migratory birds through its commerce power was struck down as a violation of the Tenth Amendment, *id.* at 432, so the government then relied on the treaty power. If the Tenth Amendment limited Congress' ability to regulate migratory birds, Missouri argued that the Tenth Amendment also precluded the government from doing the same thing pursuant to its treaty power. The Court rejected this argument, stating that "[i]f the treaty is valid there can be no dispute about the validity of the statute" that implements it "as a necessary and proper means to execute the powers of the Government." *Id.*

In the case that follows, the Court was again asked to determine whether the treaty power provides a source of authority that is not subject to Tenth Amendment limitations. The majority, however, never reached the underlying constitutional question, invoking federalism as a robust rule of statutory construction. As you read *Bond v. United States*, consider whether "principles of federalism inherent in our constitutional structure" are sufficient to avoid the underlying constitutional question regarding the proper scope of the treaty power and the Tenth Amendment. As *Bond* demonstrates, the majority and dissenting justices have very different views on this important question.

BOND v. UNITED STATES

134 S. Ct. 2077 (2014)

Chief Justice Roberts delivered the opinion of the Court.

The horrors of chemical warfare were vividly captured by John Singer Sargent in his 1919 painting Gassed. The nearly life-sized work depicts two lines of soldiers, blinded by mustard gas, clinging single file to orderlies guiding them to an improvised aid station. There they would receive little treatment and no relief; many suffered for weeks only to have the gas claim their lives. The soldiers were shown staggering through piles of comrades too seriously burned to even join the procession.

The painting reflects the devastation that Sargent witnessed in the aftermath of the Second Battle of Arras during World War I. That battle and others like it led to an overwhelming consensus in the international community that toxic chemicals should never again be used as weapons against human beings. Today that objective

---

25. A non-self-executing treaty is a treaty that is judicially enforceable only if implemented through legislation. A self-executing treaty, on the other hand, is judicially enforceable once ratified.

is reflected in the international Convention on Chemical Weapons, which has been ratified or acceded to by 190 countries. The United States, pursuant to the Federal Government's constitutionally enumerated power to make treaties, ratified the treaty in 1997. To fulfill the United States' obligations under the Convention, Congress enacted the Chemical Weapons Convention Implementation Act of 1998. The Act makes it a federal crime for a person to use or possess any chemical weapon, and it punishes violators with severe penalties. It is a statute that, like the Convention it implements, deals with crimes of deadly seriousness.

The question presented by this case is whether the Implementation Act also reaches a purely local crime: an amateur attempt by a jilted wife to injure her husband's lover, which ended up causing only a minor thumb burn readily treated by rinsing with water. Because our constitutional structure leaves local criminal activity primarily to the States, we have generally declined to read federal law as intruding on that responsibility, unless Congress has clearly indicated that the law should have such reach. The Chemical Weapons Convention Implementation Act contains no such clear indication, and we accordingly conclude that it does not cover the unremarkable local offense at issue here.

I

A

In 1997, the President of the United States, upon the advice and consent of the Senate, ratified the Convention on the Prohibition of the Development, Production, Stockpiling, and Use of Chemical Weapons and on Their Destruction. S. Treaty Doc. No. 103–21, 1974 U.N.T.S. 317. The nations that ratified the Convention (State Parties) had bold aspirations for it: "general and complete disarmament under strict and effective international control, including the prohibition and elimination of all types of weapons of mass destruction." Convention Preamble, *ibid*.

The Convention aimed to achieve that objective by prohibiting the development, stockpiling, or use of chemical weapons by any State Party or person within a State Party's jurisdiction. It also established an elaborate reporting process requiring State Parties to destroy chemical weapons under their control and submit to inspection and monitoring by an international organization based in The Hague, Netherlands.

Although the Convention is a binding international agreement, it is "not self-executing." That is, the Convention creates obligations only for State Parties and "does not by itself give rise to domestically enforceable federal law" absent "implementing legislation passed by Congress." *Medellín v. Texas*, 552 U.S. 491, 505, n. 2 (2008). It instead provides that "[e]ach State Party shall, in accordance with its constitutional processes, adopt the necessary measures to implement its obligations under this Convention." Art. VII(1), 1974 U.N.T.S. 331.

Congress gave the Convention domestic effect in 1998 when it passed the Chemical Weapons Convention Implementation Act. See 112 Stat. 2681–856. The Act closely tracks the text of the treaty: It forbids any person knowingly "to develop, produce, otherwise acquire, transfer directly or indirectly, receive, stockpile, retain, own, possess, or use, or threaten to use, any chemical weapon." 18 U.S.C. § 229(a)(1). It defines "chemical weapon" in relevant part as "[a] toxic chemical and its precursors, except where intended for a purpose not prohibited under this chapter as long as the type and quantity is consistent with such a purpose." § 229F(1)(A). "Toxic chemical," in turn, is defined in general as "any chemical which through its chemical action on life processes can cause death, temporary incapacitation or permanent harm to humans or animals. The term includes all such chemicals, regardless of their origin or of their method of production, and regardless of whether they are produced in facilities, in munitions or elsewhere." § 229F(8)(A). Finally, "purposes not prohibited by this chapter" is defined as "[a]ny peaceful purpose related to an industrial, agricultural, research, medical, or pharmaceutical activity or other activity," and other specific purposes. § 229F(7). A person who violates section 229 may be subject to severe punishment: imprisonment "for any term of years," or if a victim's death results, the death penalty or imprisonment "for life." § 229A(a).

B

Petitioner Carol Anne Bond is a microbiologist from Lansdale, Pennsylvania. In 2006, Bond's closest friend, Myrlinda Haynes, announced that she was pregnant. When Bond discovered that her husband was the child's father, she sought revenge against Haynes. Bond stole a quantity of 10-chloro-10H-phenoxarsine (an arsenic-based compound) from her employer, a chemical manufacturer. She also ordered a vial of potassium dichromate (a chemical commonly used in printing photographs or cleaning laboratory equipment) on Amazon.com. Both chemicals are toxic to humans and, in high enough doses, potentially lethal. It is undisputed, however, that Bond did not intend to kill Haynes. She instead hoped that Haynes would touch the chemicals and develop an uncomfortable rash.

Between November 2006 and June 2007, Bond went to Haynes's home on at least 24 occasions and spread the chemicals on her car door, mailbox, and door knob. These attempted assaults were almost entirely unsuccessful. The chemicals that Bond used are easy to see, and Haynes was able to avoid them all but once. On that occasion, Haynes suffered a minor chemical burn on her thumb, which she treated by rinsing with water. Haynes repeatedly called the local police to report the suspicious substances, but they took no action. When Haynes found powder on her mailbox, she called the police again, who told her to call the post office. Haynes did so, and postal inspectors placed surveillance cameras around her home. The cameras caught Bond opening Haynes's mailbox, stealing an envelope, and stuffing potassium dichromate inside the muffler of Haynes's car.

Federal prosecutors naturally charged Bond with two counts of mail theft, in violation of 18 U.S.C. § 1708. More surprising, they also charged her with two counts of possessing and using a chemical weapon, in violation of section 229(a). Bond moved to dismiss the chemical weapon counts on the ground that section 229 exceeded

Congress's enumerated powers and invaded powers reserved to the States by the Tenth Amendment. The District Court denied Bond's motion. She then entered a conditional guilty plea that reserved her right to appeal. The District Court sentenced Bond to six years in federal prison plus five years of supervised release, and ordered her to pay a $2,000 fine and $9,902.79 in restitution.

[On appeal, the Third Circuit ruled that Bond lacked standing. The Supreme Court granted certiorari and reversed, concluding that] "in a proper case, an individual may 'assert injury from governmental action taken in excess of the authority that federalism defines.'" *Bond v. United States*, 131 S.Ct. 2355, 2363–64 (2011) (*Bond I*).

On remand, Bond argued that section 229 does not reach her conduct because the statute's exception for the use of chemicals for "peaceful purposes" should be understood in contradistinction to the "warlike" activities that the Convention was primarily designed to prohibit. The Court of Appeals rejected this argument. The court acknowledged that the Government's reading of section 229 would render the statute "striking" in its "breadth" and turn every "kitchen cupboard and cleaning cabinet in America into a potential chemical weapons cache." But the court nevertheless held that Bond's use of "'highly toxic chemicals with the intent of harming Haynes' can hardly be characterized as 'peaceful' under that word's commonly understood meaning."

The Third Circuit also rejected Bond's constitutional challenge to her conviction, holding that section 229 was "necessary and proper to carry the Convention into effect." The Court of Appeals relied on this Court's opinion in *Missouri v. Holland*, 252 U.S. 416 (1920), which stated that "[i]f the treaty is valid there can be no dispute about the validity of the statute" that implements it "as a necessary and proper means to execute the powers of the Government," *id.*, at 432.

We again granted certiorari.

II

In our federal system, the National Government possesses only limited powers; the States and the people retain the remainder. The States have broad authority to enact legislation for the public good — what we have often called a "police power." *United States v. Lopez*, 514 U.S. 549, 567 (1995). The Federal Government, by contrast, has no such authority and "can exercise only the powers granted to it," *McCulloch v. Maryland*, [17 U.S.] 4 Wheat. 316, 405 (1819), including the power to make "all Laws which shall be necessary and proper for carrying into Execution" the enumerated powers, U.S. Const., Art. I, §8, cl. 18. For nearly two centuries it has been "clear" that, lacking a police power, "Congress cannot punish felonies generally." *Cohens v. Virginia*, [19 U.S.] 6 Wheat. 264, 428 (1821). A criminal act committed wholly within a State "cannot be made an offence against the United States, unless it have some relation to the execution of a power of Congress, or to some matter within the jurisdiction of the United States."

The Government frequently defends federal criminal legislation on the ground that the legislation is authorized pursuant to Congress's power to regulate interstate commerce. In this case, however, the Court of Appeals held that the Government had explicitly disavowed that argument before the District Court. As a result, in this Court the parties have devoted significant effort to arguing whether section 229, as applied to Bond's offense, is a necessary and proper means of executing the National Government's power to make treaties. U.S. Const., Art. II, § 2, cl. 2. Bond argues that the lower court's reading of *Missouri v. Holland* would remove all limits on federal authority, so long as the Federal Government ratifies a treaty first. She insists that to effectively afford the Government a police power whenever it implements a treaty would be contrary to the Framers' careful decision to divide power between the States and the National Government as a means of preserving liberty. To the extent that *Holland* authorizes such usurpation of traditional state authority, Bond says, it must be either limited or overruled.

The Government replies that this Court has never held that a statute implementing a valid treaty exceeds Congress's enumerated powers. To do so here, the Government says, would contravene another deliberate choice of the Framers: to avoid placing subject matter limitations on the National Government's power to make treaties. And it might also undermine confidence in the United States as an international treaty partner.

Notwithstanding this debate, it is "a well-established principle governing the prudent exercise of this Court's jurisdiction that normally the Court will not decide a constitutional question if there is some other ground upon which to dispose of the case." *Escambia County v. McMillan*, 466 U.S. 48, 51 (1984) (*per curiam*). Bond argues that section 229 does not cover her conduct. So we consider that argument first.

III

Section 229 exists to implement the Convention, so we begin with that international agreement. As explained, the Convention's drafters intended for it to be a comprehensive ban on chemical weapons. But even with its broadly worded definitions, we have doubts that a treaty about *chemical weapons* has anything to do with Bond's conduct. The Convention, a product of years of worldwide study, analysis, and multinational negotiation, arose in response to war crimes and acts of terrorism. There is no reason to think the sovereign nations that ratified the Convention were interested in anything like Bond's common law assault.

Even if the treaty does reach that far, nothing prevents Congress from implementing the Convention in the same manner it legislates with respect to innumerable other matters — observing the Constitution's division of responsibility between sovereigns and leaving the prosecution of purely local crimes to the States. The Convention, after all, is agnostic between enforcement at the state versus federal level: It provides that "[e]ach State Party shall, *in accordance with its constitutional processes*, adopt the necessary measures to implement its obligations under this Convention." Art. VII(1), 1974 U.N.T.S. 331 (emphasis added).

Fortunately, we have no need to interpret the scope of the Convention in this case. Bond was prosecuted under section 229, and the statute — unlike the

Convention—must be read consistent with principles of federalism inherent in our constitutional structure.

A

In the Government's view, the conclusion that Bond "knowingly" "use[d]" a "chemical weapon" in violation of section 229(a) is simple: The chemicals that Bond placed on Haynes's home and car are "toxic chemical[s]" as defined by the statute, and Bond's attempt to assault Haynes was not a "peaceful purpose." §§ 229F(1), (8), (7). The problem with this interpretation is that it would "dramatically intrude[ ] upon traditional state criminal jurisdiction," and we avoid reading statutes to have such reach in the absence of a clear indication that they do.

Part of a fair reading of statutory text is recognizing that "Congress legislates against the backdrop" of certain unexpressed presumptions. As Justice Frankfurter put it in his famous essay on statutory interpretation, correctly reading a statute "demands awareness of certain presuppositions." Some Reflections on the Reading of Statutes, 47 Colum. L. Rev. 527, 537 (1947). For example, we presume, absent a clear statement from Congress, that federal statutes do not apply outside the United States. So even though section 229, read on its face, would cover a chemical weapons crime if committed by a U.S. citizen in Australia, we would not apply the statute to such conduct absent a plain statement from Congress. The notion that some things "go without saying" applies to legislation just as it does to everyday life.

Among the background principles of construction that our cases have recognized are those grounded in the relationship between the Federal Government and the States under our Constitution. It has long been settled, for example, that we presume federal statutes do not abrogate state sovereign immunity, impose obligations on the States pursuant to section 5 of the Fourteenth Amendment, or preempt state law, *Rice v. Santa Fe Elevator Corp.*, 331 U.S. 218, 230 (1947).

Closely related to these is the well-established principle that "'it is incumbent upon the federal courts to be certain of Congress' intent before finding that federal law overrides'" the "usual constitutional balance of federal and state powers." *Gregory v. Ashcroft*, 501 U.S. 452, 460 (1991). To quote Frankfurter again, if the Federal Government would "'radically readjust[ ] the balance of state and national authority, those charged with the duty of legislating [must be] reasonably explicit'" about it. We have applied this background principle when construing federal statutes that touched on several areas of traditional state responsibility [such as qualifications for state officers, titles to real estate, and land and water use].

[I]t is appropriate to refer to basic principles of federalism embodied in the Constitution to resolve ambiguity in a federal statute. In this case, the ambiguity derives from the improbably broad reach of the key statutory definition given the term— "chemical weapon"—being defined; the deeply serious consequences of adopting such a boundless reading; and the lack of any apparent need to do so in light of the context from which the statute arose—a treaty about chemical warfare and terrorism. We conclude that, in this curious case, we can insist on a clear indication that

Congress meant to reach purely local crimes, before interpreting the statute's expansive language in a way that intrudes on the police power of the States.

B

We do not find any such clear indication in section 229. "Chemical weapon" is the key term that defines the statute's reach, and it is defined extremely broadly. But that general definition does not constitute a clear statement that Congress meant the statute to reach local criminal conduct.

In fact, a fair reading of section 229 suggests that it does not have as expansive a scope as might at first appear. To begin, as a matter of natural meaning, an educated user of English would not describe Bond's crime as involving a "chemical weapon." Saying that a person "used a chemical weapon" conveys a very different idea than saying the person "used a chemical in a way that caused some harm." The natural meaning of "chemical weapon" takes account of both the particular chemicals that the defendant used and the circumstances in which she used them.

When used in the manner here, the chemicals in this case are not of the sort that an ordinary person would associate with instruments of chemical warfare. The substances that Bond used bear little resemblance to the deadly toxins that are "of particular danger to the objectives of the Convention." The Government would have us brush aside the ordinary meaning and adopt a reading of section 229 that would sweep in everything from the detergent under the kitchen sink to the stain remover in the laundry room. Yet no one would ordinarily describe those substances as "chemical weapons."

The Government's reading of section 229 would " 'alter sensitive federal-state relationships,' " convert an astonishing amount of "traditionally local criminal conduct" into "a matter for federal enforcement," and "involve a substantial extension of federal police resources." It would transform the statute from one whose core concerns are acts of war, assassination, and terrorism into a massive federal anti-poisoning regime that reaches the simplest of assaults. As the Government reads section 229, "hardly" a poisoning "in the land would fall outside the federal statute's domain." Of course Bond's conduct is serious and unacceptable—and against the laws of Pennsylvania. But the background principle that Congress does not normally intrude upon the police power of the States is critically important. In light of that principle, we are reluctant to conclude that Congress meant to punish Bond's crime with a federal prosecution for a chemical weapons attack.

The Federal Government undoubtedly has a substantial interest in enforcing criminal laws against assassination, terrorism, and acts with the potential to cause mass suffering. Those crimes have not traditionally been left predominantly to the States, and nothing we have said here will disrupt the Government's authority to prosecute such offenses.

It is also clear that the laws of the Commonwealth of Pennsylvania (and every other State) are sufficient to prosecute Bond. Pennsylvania has several statutes that would likely cover her assault. See 18 Pa. Cons.Stat. §§ 2701 (2012) (simple assault), 2705 (reckless endangerment), 2709 (harassment). And state authorities regularly enforce these laws in poisoning cases.

In sum, the global need to prevent chemical warfare does not require the Federal Government to reach into the kitchen cupboard, or to treat a local assault with a chemical irritant as the deployment of a chemical weapon. There is no reason to suppose that Congress—in implementing the Convention on Chemical Weapons—thought otherwise.

*   *   *

The Convention provides for implementation by each ratifying nation "in accordance with its constitutional processes." Art. VII(1), 1974 U.N.T.S. 331. As James Madison explained, the constitutional process in our "compound republic" keeps power "divided between two distinct governments." The Federalist No. 51, p. 323 (C. Rossiter ed. 1961). If section 229 reached Bond's conduct, it would mark a dramatic departure from that constitutional structure and a serious reallocation of criminal law enforcement authority between the Federal Government and the States. Absent a clear statement of that purpose, we will not presume Congress to have authorized such a stark intrusion into traditional state authority.

The judgment of the Court of Appeals is reversed, and the case is remanded for further proceedings consistent with this opinion.

It is so ordered.

JUSTICE SCALIA, with whom JUSTICE THOMAS joins, and with whom JUSTICE ALLITO joins as to Part I, concurring in the judgment.

It is the responsibility of "the legislature, not the Court, . . . to define a crime, and ordain its punishment." *United States v. Wiltberger,* [18 U.S.] 5 Wheat. 76, 95 (1820) (Marshall, C.J., for the Court). And it is "emphatically the province and duty of the judicial department to say what the law [including the Constitution] is." *Marbury v. Madison,* [5 U.S.] 1 Cranch 137, 177 (1803) (same). Today, the Court shirks its job and performs Congress's. As sweeping and unsettling as the Chemical Weapons Convention Implementation Act of 1998 may be, it is clear beyond doubt that it covers what Bond did; and we have no authority to amend it. So we are forced to decide—there is no way around it—whether the Act's application to what Bond did was constitutional.

I would hold that it was not, and for that reason would reverse the judgment of the Court of Appeals for the Third Circuit.

I. The Statutory Question

A. Unavoidable Meaning of the Text

The meaning of the Act is plain. Applying those provisions to this case is hardly complicated. Bond possessed and used "chemical[s] which through [their] chemical action on life processes can cause death, temporary incapacitation or permanent harm." Thus, she possessed "toxic chemicals." And, because they were not possessed or used only for a "purpose not prohibited," §229F(1)(A), they were "chemical weapons." Ergo, Bond violated the Act. End of statutory analysis, I would have thought.

* * *

II. The Constitutional Question

Since the Act is clear, the *real* question this case presents is whether the Act is constitutional as applied to petitioner. An unreasoned and citation-less sentence from our opinion in *Missouri v. Holland*, 252 U.S. 416 (1920), purported to furnish the answer: "If the treaty is valid"—and no one argues that the Convention is not—"there can be no dispute about the validity of the statute under Article I, §8, as a necessary and proper means to execute the powers of the Government." *Id.* at 432. Petitioner and her *amici* press us to consider whether there is anything to this *ipse dixit*. The Constitution's text and structure show that there is not.

A. Text

Under Article I, §8, cl. 18, Congress has the power "[t]o make all Laws which shall be necessary and proper for carrying into Execution the foregoing Powers and all other Powers vested by this Constitution in the Government of the United States, or in any Department or Officer thereof." One such "other Powe[r]" appears in Article II, §2, cl. 2: "[The President] shall have Power, by and with the Advice and Consent of the Senate, to make Treaties, provided two thirds of the Senators present concur." Read together, the two Clauses empower Congress to pass laws "necessary and proper for carrying into Execution . . . [the] Power . . . to make Treaties."

It is obvious what the Clauses, read together, do *not* say. They do not authorize Congress to enact laws for carrying into execution "Treaties," even treaties that do not execute themselves, such as the Chemical Weapons Convention. Surely it makes sense, the Government contends, that Congress would have the power to carry out the obligations to which the President and the Senate have committed the Nation. The power to "carry into Execution" the "Power . . . to make Treaties," it insists, *has to* mean the power to execute the treaties themselves.

That argument, which makes no pretense of resting on text, unsurprisingly misconstrues it. Start with the phrase "to make Treaties." A treaty is a contract with a foreign nation *made*, the Constitution states, by the President with the concurrence of "two thirds of the Senators present." That is true of self-executing and non-self-executing treaties alike; the Constitution does not distinguish between the two. So, because the President and the Senate can enter into a non-self-executing compact with a foreign nation but can never by themselves (without the House) give that compact domestic effect through legislation, the power of the President and the Senate "to make" a Treaty cannot possibly mean to "enter into a compact with a foreign nation and then give that compact domestic legal effect." We have said in another context that a right "to make contracts" (a treaty, of course, is a contract) does not "extend . . . to conduct . . . *after* the contract relation has been established. . . .

Such *postformation* conduct does not involve the right to make a contract, but rather implicates the *performance* of established contract obligations." *Patterson v. McLean Credit Union*, 491 U.S. 164, 177 (1989) (emphasis added). Upon the President's agreement and the Senate's ratification, a treaty—no matter what kind—has been *made* and is not susceptible of any more making.

How might Congress have helped "carr[y]" the power to make the treaty—here, the Chemical Weapons Convention—"into Execution"? In any number of ways. It could have appropriated money for hiring treaty negotiators, empowered the Department of State to appoint those negotiators, formed a commission to study the benefits and risks of entering into the agreement, or paid for a bevy of spies to monitor the treaty-related deliberations of other potential signatories.

But a power to help the President *make* treaties is not a power to *implement* treaties already made. Once a treaty has been made, Congress's power to do what is "necessary and proper" to assist the making of treaties drops out of the picture. To legislate compliance with the United States' treaty obligations, Congress must rely upon its independent (though quite robust) Article I, § 8, powers.

B. Structure

"[T]he Constitutio[n] confer[s] upon Congress . . . not all governmental powers, but only discrete, enumerated ones." *Printz v. United States*, 521 U.S. 898, 919 (1997). And, of course, "enumeration presupposes something not enumerated." *Gibbons v. Ogden*, 22 U.S. (9 Wheat.) 1, 195 (1824).

But in *Holland*, the proponents of unlimited congressional power found a loophole: "By negotiating a treaty and obtaining the requisite consent of the Senate, the President . . . may endow Congress with a source of legislative authority independent of the powers enumerated in Article I." L. Tribe, American Constitutional Law § 4-4, pp. 645–646 (3d ed. 2000). Though *Holland* 's change to the Constitution's text appears minor (the power to carry into execution the *power to make treaties* becomes the power to carry into execution *treaties*), the change to its structure is seismic.

To see why vast expansion of congressional power is not just a remote possibility, consider two features of the modern practice of treaty making. [B]eginning in the last half of the last century, many treaties were "detailed multilateral instruments negotiated and drafted at international conferences," and they sought to regulate states' treatment of their own citizens, or even "the activities of individuals and private entities."

Consider also that, at least according to some scholars, the Treaty Clause comes with no implied subject-matter limitations. See, *e.g.*, L. Henkin, Foreign Affairs and the United States Constitution 191, 197 (2d ed. 1996). On this view, the treaty power can be used to regulate matters of strictly domestic concern, see Restatement (Third) of Foreign Relations Law of the United States § 302, Comment *c,* p. 153 (1986).

If that is true, then the possibilities of what the Federal Government may accomplish, with the right treaty in hand, are endless and hardly farfetched. It could begin, as some scholars have suggested, with abrogation of this Court's constitutional rulings. For example, the holding that a statute prohibiting the carrying of firearms near schools went beyond Congress's enumerated powers, *United States v. Lopez,* 514 U.S. 549, 551 (1995), could be reversed by negotiating a treaty with Latvia providing that neither sovereign would permit the carrying of guns near schools.

The Necessary and Proper Clause cannot bear such weight. As Chief Justice Marshall said regarding it, no "great substantive and independent power" can be "implied as incidental to other powers, or used as a means of executing them." *McCulloch v. Maryland,* 17 U.S. (4 Wheat.) 316, 411 (1819). No law that flattens the principle of state sovereignty, whether or not "necessary," can be said to be "proper." As an old, well-known treatise put it, "it would not be a proper or constitutional exercise of the treaty-making power to provide that Congress should have a general legislative authority over a subject which has not been given it by the Constitution." 1 W. Willoughby, The Constitutional Law of the United States § 216, p. 504 (1910).

We would not give the Government's support of the *Holland* principle the time of day were we confronted with "treaty-implementing" legislation that abrogated the freedom of speech or some other constitutionally protected individual right. We proved just that in *Reid v. Covert,* 354 U.S. 1 (1957), which held that commitments made in treaties with Great Britain and Japan would not permit civilian wives of American servicemen stationed in those countries to be tried for murder by court-martial. The plurality opinion said that "no agreement with a foreign nation can confer power on the Congress, or on any other branch of Government, which is free from the restraints of the Constitution." *Id.,* at 16.

To be sure, the *Reid* plurality purported to distinguish the *ipse dixit* of *Holland* with its own unsupported *ipse dixit.* "[T]he people and the States," it said, "have delegated [the treaty] power to the National Government [so] the Tenth Amendment is no barrier." 354 U.S., at 18. The opinion does not say why (and there is no reason why) only the Tenth Amendment, and not the other nine, has been "delegated" away by the treaty power. The distinction between provisions protecting individual liberty, on the one hand, and "structural" provisions, on the other, cannot be the explanation, since structure in general—and especially the structure of limited federal powers—is *designed* to protect individual liberty. "The federal structure . . . secures the freedom of the individual. . . . By denying any one government complete jurisdiction over all the concerns of public life, federalism protects the liberty of the individual from arbitrary power." *Bond v. United States,* 131 S.Ct. 2355, 2364 (2011).

* * *

We have here a supposedly "narrow" opinion which, in order to be "narrow," sets forth interpretive principles never before imagined that will bedevil our jurisprudence (and proliferate litigation) for years to come. The immediate product of these interpretive novelties is a statute that should be the envy of every lawmaker bent on trapping the unwary with vague and uncertain criminal prohibitions. All this to leave in place [*Holland*'s] ill-considered *ipse dixit* that enables the fundamental constitutional principle of limited federal powers to be set aside by the President and Senate's exercise of the treaty power. We should not have shirked our duty and distorted the law to preserve that assertion; we should have welcomed and eagerly grasped the opportunity—nay, the obligation—to consider and repudiate it.

Justice Thomas, with whom Justice Scalia joins, and with whom Justice Alito joins as to Parts I, II, and III, concurring in the judgment.

I write separately to suggest that the Treaty Power is itself a limited federal power. [Justice Thomas discussed "the historical evidence suggesting that the Treaty Power can be used to arrange intercourse with other nations, but not to regulate purely domestic affairs."]

* * *

In an appropriate case, I would draw a line that respects the original understanding of the Treaty Power. The parties in this case have not addressed the proper scope of the Treaty Power or the validity of the treaty here. The preservation of limits on the Treaty Power is nevertheless a matter of fundamental constitutional importance, and the Court ought to address the scope of the Treaty Power when that issue is presented. Given the increasing frequency with which treaties have begun to test the limits of the Treaty Power, that chance will come soon enough.

Justice Alito, concurring in the judgment. [Opinion omitted.]

EXERCISE 7

1. According to the majority, why is the treaty at issue in *Bond* ambiguous? Is the majority correct?

2. Did Bond violate the express terms of the legislation implementing the treaty? If so, should the majority have reached the underlying constitutional question regarding the scope of the treaty power? In *Reid v. Covert*, 354 U.S. 1 (1957), a plurality of the Court held that "no agreement with a foreign nation can confer power on the Congress, or on any other branch of Government, which is free from the restraints of the Constitution." *Id.* at 16. If that is a correct statement of the treaty power, then how could the majority avoid addressing the Tenth Amendment issue? Is it incumbent on the Court to determine whether the implementing legislation violates the Tenth Amendment? Why or why not?

3. Under the majority's analysis, if Congress had explicitly stated that it intended to infringe on the police powers of the states, would the enabling legislation have been constitutional? Would the majority have had to address the Tenth Amendment argument at that point?

4. Does it matter to the majority's analysis that the treaty was non-self-executing? To Justice Scalia in his dissent? If the treaty was self-executing, what result under the majority and dissenting opinions?

5. Articulate the rule of construction that the majority adopts in *Bond*. Should this federalism-based rule of construction affect the Court's analysis of the Tenth Amendment question if or when the Court ultimately considers that question? If so, how? If not, why not?

6. What arguments does Justice Scalia make to show that the implementing legislation is unconstitutional? Are those arguments convincing?

———————

Just one year earlier, the Supreme Court had similarly invoked federalism principles when determining the constitutionality of federal legislation. In *Shelby County v. Holder*, 133 S. Ct. 2612 (2013), the Court considered two provisions of the Voting Rights Act of 1965, 79 Stat. 437 (1965), which Congress had passed and reauthorized pursuant to its power under § 2 of the Fifteenth Amendment. The Fifteenth Amendment states: "The right of citizens of the United States to vote shall not be denied or abridged by the United States or by any State on account of race, color, or previous condition of servitude." U.S. Const. amend. XV. sec. 2 gives Congress the "power to enforce this article by appropriate legislation." *Id*. To determine whether legislation, such as the Voting Rights Act, is "appropriate," the Court typically looked to see if the legislation was "congruent and proportional" to the problem Congress sought to remedy. *See Bd. of Trustees of Univ. of Alabama v. Garrett*, 531 U.S. 356, 365 (2001) (interpreting the similar enforcement language in § 5 of the Fourteenth Amendment and holding that "legislation reaching beyond the scope of § 1's actual guarantees must exhibit 'congruence and proportionality between the injury to be prevented or remedied and the means adopted to that end.'" (quoting *City of Boerne v. Flores* 521 U.S. 507, 520 (1997)).

Under § 5 of the Voting Rights Act, certain states and local governments must obtain federal preclearance before making any changes to their voting laws or procedures. Section 4(b) specifies the coverage formula when determining whether a particular jurisdiction is subject to the preclearance requirement based on the history of discrimination in that jurisdiction. In *Shelby County*, the Court did not mention the congruent and proportional standard and, instead, struck down the formula in § 4(b) as violative of basic principles of federalism as well as the equal sovereignty of states. As you read *Shelby County*, consider: (1) how these principles shape the majority's conclusion that § 4(b) is unconstitutional and (2) whether that analysis also calls into question the constitutionality of § 5.

SHELBY COUNTY, ALABAMA v. HOLDER

133 S. Ct. 2612 (2013)

Chief Justice Roberts delivered the opinion of the Court.

The Voting Rights Act of 1965 employed extraordinary measures to address an extraordinary problem. Section 5 of the Act required States to obtain federal permission before enacting any law related to voting — a drastic departure from basic principles of federalism. And § 4 of the Act applied that requirement only to some

States—an equally dramatic departure from the principle that all States enjoy equal sovereignty. This was strong medicine, but Congress determined it was needed to address entrenched racial discrimination in voting, "an insidious and pervasive evil which had been perpetuated in certain parts of our country through unremitting and ingenious defiance of the Constitution." *South Carolina v. Katzenbach,* 383 U.S. 301, 309 (1966). As we explained in upholding the law, "exceptional conditions can justify legislative measures not otherwise appropriate." Reflecting the unprecedented nature of these measures, they were scheduled to expire after five years.

Nearly 50 years later, they are still in effect; indeed, they have been made more stringent, and are now scheduled to last until 2031. There is no denying, however, that the conditions that originally justified these measures no longer characterize voting in the covered jurisdictions. By 2009, "the racial gap in voter registration and turnout [was] lower in the States originally covered by § 5 than it [was] nationwide." *Northwest Austin Municipal Util. Dist. No. One v. Holder,* 557 U.S. 193, 203–04 (2009). Since that time, Census Bureau data indicate that African-American voter turnout has come to exceed white voter turnout in five of the six States originally covered by § 5, with a gap in the sixth State of less than one half of one percent. At the same time, voting discrimination still exists; no one doubts that. The question is whether the Act's extraordinary measures, including its disparate treatment of the States, continue to satisfy constitutional requirements.

I

A

The Fifteenth Amendment was ratified in 1870, in the wake of the Civil War. It provides that "[t]he right of citizens of the United States to vote shall not be denied or abridged by the United States or by any State on account of race, color, or previous condition of servitude," and it gives Congress the "power to enforce this article by appropriate legislation."

"The first century of congressional enforcement of the Amendment, however, can only be regarded as a failure." In the 1890s, Alabama, Georgia, Louisiana, Mississippi, North Carolina, South Carolina, and Virginia began to enact literacy tests for voter registration and to employ other methods designed to prevent African-Americans from voting. Congress passed statutes outlawing some of these practices and facilitating litigation against them, but litigation remained slow and expensive, and the States came up with new ways to discriminate as soon as existing ones were struck down. Voter registration of African-Americans barely improved.

Inspired to action by the civil rights movement, Congress responded in 1965 with the Voting Rights Act. Section 2 was enacted to forbid, in all 50 States, any "standard, practice, or procedure . . . imposed or applied . . . to deny or abridge the right of any citizen of the United States to vote on account of race or color." Both the Federal Government and individuals have sued to enforce § 2, and injunctive relief is available in appropriate cases to block voting laws from going into effect. Section 2 is permanent, applies nationwide, and is not at issue in this case.

Other sections targeted only some parts of the country. At the time of the Act's passage, these "covered" jurisdictions were those States or political subdivisions that had maintained a test or device as a prerequisite to voting as of November 1, 1964, and had less than 50 percent voter registration or turnout in the 1964 Presidential election. Such tests or devices included literacy and knowledge tests, good moral character requirements, the need for vouchers from registered voters, and the like. A covered jurisdiction could "bail out" of coverage if it had not used a test or device in the preceding five years "for the purpose or with the effect of denying or abridging the right to vote on account of race or color." In 1965, the covered States included Alabama, Georgia, Louisiana, Mississippi, South Carolina, and Virginia. The additional covered subdivisions included 39 counties in North Carolina and one in Arizona.

In those jurisdictions, §4 of the Act banned all such tests or devices. Section 5 provided that no change in voting procedures could take effect until it was approved by federal authorities in Washington, D.C.—either the Attorney General or a court of three judges. A jurisdiction could obtain such "preclearance" only by proving that the change had neither "the purpose [nor] the effect of denying or abridging the right to vote on account of race or color."

Sections 4 and 5 were intended to be temporary; they were set to expire after five years. In *South Carolina v. Katzenbach*, we upheld the 1965 Act against constitutional challenge, explaining that it was justified to address "voting discrimination where it persists on a pervasive scale."

In 1970, Congress reauthorized the Act for another five years, and extended the coverage formula in §4(b) to jurisdictions that had a voting test and less than 50 percent voter registration or turnout as of 1968.

In 1975, Congress reauthorized the Act for seven more years, and extended its coverage to jurisdictions that had a voting test and less than 50 percent voter registration or turnout as of 1972. Congress also amended the definition of "test or device" to include the practice of providing English-only voting materials in places where over five percent of voting-age citizens spoke a single language other than English. Congress correspondingly amended sections 2 and 5 to forbid voting discrimination on the basis of membership in a language minority group, in addition to discrimination on the basis of race or color. Finally, Congress made the nationwide ban on tests and devices permanent.

In 1982, Congress reauthorized the Act for 25 years, but did not alter its coverage formula. Congress did, however, amend the bailout provisions, allowing political subdivisions of covered jurisdictions to bail out. Among other prerequisites for bailout, jurisdictions and their subdivisions must not have used a forbidden test or device, failed to receive preclearance, or lost a §2 suit, in the ten years prior to seeking bailout.

We upheld each of these reauthorizations against constitutional challenge. See *Georgia v. United States*, 411 U.S. 526 (1973).

In 2006, Congress again reauthorized the Voting Rights Act for 25 years, again without change to its coverage formula. Congress also amended § 5 to prohibit more conduct than before. Section 5 now forbids voting changes with "any discriminatory purpose" as well as voting changes that diminish the ability of citizens, on account of race, color, or language minority status, "to elect their preferred candidates of choice."

Shortly after this reauthorization, a Texas utility district brought suit, seeking to bail out from the Act's coverage and, in the alternative, challenging the Act's constitutionality. See *Northwest Austin,* 557 U.S. at 200–01.

[The Supreme Court "construed the statue to allow the utility to seek bailout" and] explained that § 5 "imposes substantial federalism costs" and "differentiates between the States, despite our historic tradition that all the States enjoy equal sovereignty." We also noted that "[t]hings have changed in the South. Voter turnout and registration rates now approach parity. Blatantly discriminatory evasions of federal decrees are rare. And minority candidates hold office at unprecedented levels." Finally, we questioned whether the problems that § 5 meant to address were still "concentrated in the jurisdictions singled out for preclearance."

B

Shelby County is located in Alabama, a covered jurisdiction. It has not sought bailout, as the Attorney General has recently objected to voting changes proposed from within the county. Instead, in 2010, the county sued the Attorney General in Federal District Court in Washington, D.C., seeking a declaratory judgment that sections 4(b) and 5 of the Voting Rights Act are facially unconstitutional, as well as a permanent injunction against their enforcement. The District Court ruled against the county and upheld the Act. The court found that the evidence before Congress in 2006 was sufficient to justify reauthorizing § 5 and continuing the § 4(b) coverage formula.

The Court of Appeals for the D.C. Circuit affirmed. After extensive analysis of the record, the court accepted Congress's conclusion that § 2 litigation remained inadequate in the covered jurisdictions to protect the rights of minority voters, and that § 5 was therefore still necessary.

We granted certiorari.

II

In *Northwest Austin,* we stated that "the Act imposes current burdens and must be justified by current needs." And we concluded that "a departure from the fundamental principle of equal sovereignty requires a showing that a statute's disparate geographic coverage is sufficiently related to the problem that it targets." These basic principles guide our review of the question before us.

A

The Constitution and laws of the United States are "the supreme Law of the Land." U.S. Const., Art. VI, cl. 2. State legislation may not contravene federal law. The Federal Government does not, however, have a general right to review and veto state enactments before they go into effect. A proposal to grant such authority to "negative" state laws was considered at the Constitutional Convention, but rejected in favor of allowing state laws to take effect, subject to later challenge under the Supremacy Clause. Outside the strictures of the Supremacy Clause, States retain broad autonomy in structuring their governments and pursuing legislative objectives. Indeed, the Constitution provides that all powers not specifically granted to the Federal Government are reserved to the States or citizens. Amdt. 10. This "allocation of powers in our federal system preserves the integrity, dignity, and residual sovereignty of the States." *Bond v. United States,* 131 S.Ct. 2355, 2364 (2011). But the federal balance "is not just an end in itself: Rather, federalism secures to citizens the liberties that derive from the diffusion of sovereign power." *Ibid.*

More specifically, "'the Framers of the Constitution intended the States to keep for themselves, as provided in the Tenth Amendment, the power to regulate elections.'" *Gregory v. Ashcroft,* 501 U.S. 452, 461–62 (1991). Of course, the Federal Government retains significant control over federal elections. For instance, the Constitution authorizes Congress to establish the time and manner for electing Senators and Representatives. Art. I, §4, cl. 1. But States have "broad powers to determine the conditions under which the right of suffrage may be exercised." And "[e]ach State has the power to prescribe the qualifications of its officers and the manner in which they shall be chosen." Drawing lines for congressional districts is likewise "primarily the duty and responsibility of the State."

Not only do States retain sovereignty under the Constitution, there is also a "fundamental principle of *equal* sovereignty" among the States. Over a hundred years ago, this Court explained that our Nation "was and is a union of States, equal in power, dignity and authority." *Coyle v. Smith,* 221 U.S. 559, 567 (1911). Indeed, "the constitutional equality of the States is essential to the harmonious operation of the scheme upon which the Republic was organized." *Coyle* concerned the admission of new States, and *Katzenbach* rejected the notion that the principle operated as a *bar* on differential treatment outside that context. At the same time, as we made clear in *Northwest Austin,* the fundamental principle of equal sovereignty remains highly pertinent in assessing subsequent disparate treatment of States.

The Voting Rights Act sharply departs from these basic principles. It suspends "*all* changes to state election law—however innocuous—until they have been precleared by federal authorities in Washington, D.C." States must beseech the Federal Government for permission to implement laws that they would otherwise have the right to enact and execute on their own, subject of course to any injunction in a §2 action.

And despite the tradition of equal sovereignty, the Act applies to only nine States (and several additional counties). While one State waits months or years and expends funds to implement a validly enacted law, its neighbor can typically put the same law into effect immediately, through the normal legislative process. Even if a non-covered jurisdiction is sued, there are important differences between those proceedings and preclearance proceedings; the preclearance proceeding "not only switches the burden of proof to the supplicant jurisdiction, but also applies substantive standards quite different from those governing the rest of the nation."

B

In 1966, we found these departures from the basic features of our system of government justified. The "blight of racial discrimination in voting" had "infected the electoral process in parts of our country for nearly a century." Several States had enacted a variety of requirements and tests "specifically designed to prevent" African-Americans from voting. Case-by-case litigation had proved inadequate to prevent such racial discrimination in voting, in part because States "merely switched to discriminatory devices not covered by the federal decrees," "enacted difficult new tests," or simply "defied and evaded court orders." Shortly before enactment of the Voting Rights Act, only 19.4 percent of African-Americans of voting age were registered to vote in Alabama, only 31.8 percent in Louisiana, and only 6.4 percent in Mississippi. Those figures were roughly 50 percentage points or more below the figures for whites.

At the time, the coverage formula—the means of linking the exercise of the unprecedented authority with the problem that warranted it—made sense. We found that "Congress chose to limit its attention to the geographic areas where immediate action seemed necessary." The areas where Congress found "evidence of actual voting discrimination" shared two characteristics: "the use of tests and devices for voter registration, and a voting rate in the 1964 presidential election at least 12 points below the national average." We explained that "[t]ests and devices are relevant to voting discrimination because of their long history as a tool for perpetrating the evil; a low voting rate is pertinent for the obvious reason that widespread disenfranchisement must inevitably affect the number of actual voters." We therefore concluded that "the coverage formula [was] rational in both practice and theory." It accurately reflected those jurisdictions uniquely characterized by voting discrimination "on a pervasive scale," linking coverage to the devices used to effectuate discrimination and to the resulting disenfranchisement. The formula ensured that the "stringent remedies [were] aimed at areas where voting discrimination ha[d] been most flagrant."

C

Nearly 50 years later, things have changed dramatically. Shelby County contends that the preclearance requirement, even without regard to its disparate coverage, is now unconstitutional. Its arguments have a good deal of force. In the covered jurisdictions, "[v]oter turnout and registration rates now approach parity. Blatantly discriminatory evasions of federal decrees are rare. And minority candidates hold office at unprecedented levels." The tests and devices that blocked access to the ballot have been forbidden nationwide for over 40 years.

Those conclusions are not ours alone. Congress said the same when it reauthorized the Act in 2006, writing that "[s]ignificant progress has been made in eliminating first generation barriers experienced by minority voters, including increased numbers of registered minority voters, minority voter turnout, and minority representation in Congress, State legislatures, and local elected offices." The House Report elaborated that "the number of African-Americans who are registered and who turn out to cast ballots has increased significantly over the last 40 years, particularly since 1982," and noted that "[i]n some circumstances, minorities register to vote and cast ballots at levels that surpass those of white voters." There is no doubt that these improvements are in large part *because of* the Voting Rights Act. The Act has proved immensely successful at redressing racial discrimination and integrating the voting process.

Yet the Act has not eased the restrictions in § 5 or narrowed the scope of the coverage formula in § 4(b) along the way. Those extraordinary and unprecedented features were reauthorized — as if nothing had changed. In fact, the Act's unusual remedies have grown even stronger. When Congress reauthorized the Act in 2006, it did so for another 25 years on top of the previous 40 — a far cry from the initial five-year period. Congress also expanded the prohibitions in § 5.

Respondents do not deny that there have been improvements on the ground, but argue that much of this can be attributed to the deterrent effect of § 5, which dissuades covered jurisdictions from engaging in discrimination that they would resume should § 5 be struck down. Under this theory, however, § 5 would be effectively immune from scrutiny; no matter how "clean" the record of covered jurisdictions, the argument could always be made that it was deterrence that accounted for the good behavior.

The provisions of § 5 apply only to those jurisdictions singled out by § 4. We now consider whether that coverage formula is constitutional in light of current conditions.

III

A

When upholding the constitutionality of the coverage formula in 1966, we concluded that it was "rational in both practice and theory." The formula looked to cause (discriminatory tests) and effect (low voter registration and turnout), and tailored the remedy (preclearance) to those jurisdictions exhibiting both.

The coverage formula met that test in 1965, but no longer does so. Coverage today is based on decades-old data and eradicated practices. The formula captures States by reference to literacy tests and low voter registration and turnout in the 1960s and early 1970s. But such tests have been banned nationwide for over 40 years. In 1965, the States could be divided into two groups: those with a recent history of voting tests and low voter registration and turnout, and those without those characteristics. Congress based its coverage formula on that distinction. Today the Nation is no longer divided along those lines, yet the Voting Rights Act continues to treat it as if it were.

B

[T]he Government[] does not even attempt to demonstrate the continued relevance of the formula to the problem it targets. And in the context of a decision as significant as this one—subjecting a disfavored subset of States to "extraordinary legislation otherwise unfamiliar to our federal system"—that failure to establish even relevance is fatal.

The Government falls back to the argument that because the formula was relevant in 1965, its continued use is permissible so long as any discrimination remains in the States Congress identified back then—regardless of how that discrimination compares to discrimination in States unburdened by coverage. This argument does not look to "current political conditions" but instead relies on a comparison between the States in 1965. That comparison reflected the different histories of the North and South. It was in the South that slavery was upheld by law until uprooted by the Civil War, that the reign of Jim Crow denied African-Americans the most basic freedoms, and that state and local governments worked tirelessly to disenfranchise citizens on the basis of race. The Court invoked that history—rightly so—in sustaining the disparate coverage of the Voting Rights Act in 1966.

But history did not end in 1965. By the time the Act was reauthorized in 2006, there had been 40 more years of it. In assessing the "current need [ ]" for a preclearance system that treats States differently from one another today, that history cannot be ignored. During that time, largely because of the Voting Rights Act, voting tests were abolished, disparities in voter registration and turnout due to race were erased, and African-Americans attained political office in record numbers. And yet the coverage formula that Congress reauthorized in 2006 ignores these developments, keeping the focus on decades-old data relevant to decades-old problems, rather than current data reflecting current needs.

The Fifteenth Amendment commands that the right to vote shall not be denied or abridged on account of race or color, and it gives Congress the power to enforce that command. The Amendment is not designed to punish for the past; its purpose is to ensure a better future. To serve that purpose, Congress—if it is to divide the States—must identify those jurisdictions to be singled out on a basis that makes sense in light of current conditions. It cannot rely simply on the past.

C

In defending the coverage formula, the Government, the intervenors, and the dissent also rely heavily on data from the record that they claim justify disparate coverage. Congress compiled thousands of pages of evidence before reauthorizing the Voting Rights Act. Regardless of how to look at the record, however, no one can fairly say that it shows anything approaching the "pervasive," "flagrant," "widespread," and "rampant" discrimination that faced Congress in 1965, and that clearly distinguished the covered jurisdictions from the rest of the Nation at that time.

But a more fundamental problem remains: Congress did not use the record it compiled to shape a coverage formula grounded in current conditions. It instead reenacted a formula based on 40-year-old facts having no logical relation to the present day. The dissent relies on "second-generation barriers," which are not impediments to the casting of ballots, but rather electoral arrangements that affect the weight of minority votes. That does not cure the problem. Viewing the preclearance requirements as targeting such efforts simply highlights the irrationality of continued reliance on the § 4 coverage formula, which is based on voting tests and access to the ballot, not vote dilution. We cannot pretend that we are reviewing an updated statute, or try our hand at updating the statute ourselves, based on the new record compiled by Congress. Contrary to the dissent's contention, we are not ignoring the record; we are simply recognizing that it played no role in shaping the statutory formula before us today.

The dissent also turns to the record to argue that, in light of voting discrimination in Shelby County, the county cannot complain about the provisions that subject it to preclearance. But that is like saying that a driver pulled over pursuant to a policy of stopping all redheads cannot complain about that policy, if it turns out his license has expired. Shelby County's claim is that the coverage formula here is unconstitutional in all its applications, because of how it selects the jurisdictions subjected to preclearance. The county was selected based on that formula, and may challenge it in court.

D

[T]he dissent argues that the coverage formula can be justified by history, and that the required showing can be weaker on reenactment than when the law was first passed. There is no valid reason to insulate the coverage formula from review merely because it was previously enacted 40 years ago. If Congress had started from scratch in 2006, it plainly could not have enacted the present coverage formula. It would have been irrational for Congress to distinguish between States in such a fundamental way based on 40-year-old data, when today's statistics tell an entirely different story. And it would have been irrational to base coverage on the use of voting tests 40 years ago, when such tests have been illegal since that time. But that is exactly what Congress has done.

* * *

Striking down an Act of Congress "is the gravest and most delicate duty that this Court is called on to perform." We do not do so lightly. Congress could have updated the coverage formula [in 2009], but did not do so. Its failure to act leaves us today with no choice but to declare § 4(b) unconstitutional. The formula in that section can no longer be used as a basis for subjecting jurisdictions to preclearance.

Our decision in no way affects the permanent, nationwide ban on racial discrimination in voting found in § 2. We issue no holding on § 5 itself, only on the coverage formula. Congress may draft another formula based on current conditions. Such a formula is an initial prerequisite to a determination that exceptional conditions still exist justifying such an "extraordinary departure from the traditional course of relations between the States and the Federal Government." Our country has changed, and while any racial discrimination in voting is too much, Congress must ensure that the legislation it passes to remedy that problem speaks to current conditions.

The judgment of the Court of Appeals is reversed.

It is so ordered.

JUSTICE THOMAS, concurring.

I join the Court's opinion in full but write separately to explain that I would find § 5 of the Voting Rights Act unconstitutional as well. In spite of improvements, Congress *increased* the already significant burdens of § 5. "Section 5 now forbids voting changes with 'any discriminatory purpose' as well as voting changes that diminish the ability of citizens, on account of race, color, or language minority status, 'to elect their preferred candidates of choice.'" While the pre-2006 version of the Act went well beyond protection guaranteed under the Constitution, it now goes even further.

However one aggregates the data compiled by Congress, it cannot justify the considerable burdens created by § 5. Indeed, circumstances in the covered jurisdictions can no longer be characterized as "exceptional" or "unique." "The extensive pattern of discrimination that led the Court to previously uphold § 5 as enforcing the Fifteenth Amendment no longer exists."

While the Court claims to "issue no holding on § 5 itself," its own opinion compellingly demonstrates that Congress has failed to justify "'current burdens'" with a record demonstrating "'current needs.'" By leaving the inevitable conclusion unstated, the Court needlessly prolongs the demise of that provision. For the reasons stated in the Court's opinion, I would find § 5 unconstitutional.

JUSTICE GINSBURG, with whom JUSTICE BREYER, JUSTICE SOTOMAYOR, and JUSTICE KAGAN join, dissenting.

In the Court's view, the very success of § 5 of the Voting Rights Act demands its dormancy. Congress was of another mind. Recognizing that large progress has been made, Congress determined, based on a voluminous record, that the scourge of discrimination was not yet extirpated. The question this case presents is who decides whether, as currently operative, § 5 remains justifiable, this Court, or a Congress charged with the obligation to enforce the post-Civil War Amendments "by appropriate legislation." With overwhelming support in both Houses, Congress concluded that, for two prime reasons, § 5 should continue in force, unabated. First, continuance would facilitate completion of the impressive gains thus far made; and second, continuance would guard against backsliding. Those assessments were well within Congress' province to make and should elicit this Court's unstinting approbation.

I

"[V]oting discrimination still exists; no one doubts that." But the Court today terminates the remedy that proved to be best suited to block that discrimination. The Voting Rights Act of 1965 (VRA) has worked to combat voting discrimination where other remedies had been tried and failed. Particularly effective is the VRA's requirement of federal preclearance for all changes to voting laws in the regions of the country with the most aggravated records of rank discrimination against minority voting rights.

In the long course of the legislative process [leading up to the 2006 reauthorization], Congress "amassed a sizable record." The compilation presents countless "examples of flagrant racial discrimination" since the last reauthorization; Congress also brought to light systematic evidence that "intentional racial discrimination in voting remains so serious and widespread in covered jurisdictions that section 5 preclearance is still needed."

Based on these findings, Congress reauthorized preclearance for another 25 years, while also undertaking to reconsider the extension after 15 years to ensure that the provision was still necessary and effective. The question before the Court is whether Congress had the authority under the Constitution to act as it did.

II

In answering this question, the Court does not write on a clean slate. It is well established that Congress' judgment regarding exercise of its power to enforce the Fourteenth and Fifteenth Amendments warrants substantial deference. The VRA addresses the combination of race discrimination and the right to vote, which is "preservative of all rights." When confronting the most constitutionally invidious form of discrimination, and the most fundamental right in our democratic system, Congress' power to act is at its height.

The basis for this deference is firmly rooted in both constitutional text and precedent. The Fifteenth Amendment, which targets precisely and only racial discrimination in voting rights, states that, in this domain, "Congress shall have power to enforce this article by appropriate legislation." In choosing this language, the Amendment's framers invoked Chief Justice Marshall's formulation of the scope of Congress' powers under the Necessary and Proper Clause:

> "Let the end be legitimate, let it be within the scope of the constitution, and *all means which are appropriate, which are plainly adapted to that end,* which are not prohibited, but consist with the letter and spirit of the constitution, are constitutional." *McCulloch v. Maryland,* 17 U.S. (4 Wheat.) 316 (1819) (emphasis added).

It cannot tenably be maintained that the VRA, an Act of Congress adopted to shield the right to vote from racial discrimination, is inconsistent with the letter or spirit of the Fifteenth Amendment, or any provision of the Constitution read in light of the Civil War Amendments. Nowhere in today's opinion is there clear recognition of the transformative effect the Fifteenth Amendment aimed to achieve. Notably, the Civil War Amendments used "language [that] authorized transformative new federal statutes to uproot all vestiges of unfreedom and inequality" and provided "sweeping enforcement powers . . . to enact 'appropriate' legislation targeting state abuses."

The stated purpose of the Civil War Amendments was to arm Congress with the power and authority to protect all persons within the Nation from violations of their rights by the States. So when Congress acts to enforce the right to vote free from racial discrimination, we ask not whether Congress has chosen the means most wise, but whether Congress has rationally selected means appropriate to a legitimate end.

South Carolina v. Katzenbach supplies the standard of review: "As against the reserved powers of the States, Congress may use any rational means to effectuate the constitutional prohibition of racial discrimination in voting." Faced with subsequent reauthorizations of the VRA, the Court has reaffirmed this standard. Today's Court does not purport to alter settled precedent establishing that the dispositive question is whether Congress has employed "rational means."

III

The 2006 reauthorization of the Voting Rights Act fully satisfies the standard stated in *McCulloch*: Congress may choose any means "appropriate" and "plainly adapted to" a legitimate constitutional end. As we shall see, it is implausible to suggest otherwise.

A

I begin with the evidence on which Congress based its decision to continue the preclearance remedy. The surest way to evaluate whether that remedy remains in order is to see if preclearance is still effectively preventing discriminatory changes to voting laws.

[C]onditions in the South have impressively improved since passage of the Voting Rights Act. Congress noted this improvement and found that the VRA was the driving force behind it. But Congress also found that voting discrimination had evolved into subtler second-generation barriers, and that eliminating preclearance would risk loss of the gains that had been made. Concerns of this order, the Court previously found, gave Congress adequate cause to reauthorize the VRA. Facing such evidence then, the Court expressly rejected the argument that disparities in voter turnout and number of elected officials were the only metrics capable of justifying reauthorization of the VRA.

B

I turn next to the evidence on which Congress based its decision to reauthorize the coverage formula in § 4(b). Because Congress did not alter the coverage formula, the same jurisdictions previously subject to preclearance continue to be covered by this remedy. The evidence just described, of preclearance's continuing efficacy in blocking constitutional violations in the covered jurisdictions, itself grounded Congress' conclusion that the remedy should be retained for those jurisdictions.

There is no question, moreover, that the covered jurisdictions have a unique history of problems with racial discrimination in voting. Consideration of this long history, still in living memory, was altogether appropriate. The Court criticizes

Congress for failing to recognize that "history did not end in 1965." But the Court ignores that "what's past is prologue." Congress was especially mindful of the need to reinforce the gains already made and to prevent backsliding.

Of particular importance, even after 40 years and thousands of discriminatory changes blocked by preclearance, conditions in the covered jurisdictions demonstrated that the formula was still justified by "current needs."

[Justice Ginsburg then discussesthe ongoing differences between and among covered and noncovered jurisdictions as well as the bail-out procedure that permits a jurisdiction to "bail out by showing that it has complied with the Act for ten years, and has engaged in efforts to eliminate intimidation and harassment of voters" before concluding that] [t]his experience exposes the inaccuracy of the Court's portrayal of the Act as static, unchanged since 1965. Congress designed the VRA to be a dynamic statute, capable of adjusting to changing conditions. True, many covered jurisdictions have not been able to bail out due to recent acts of noncompliance with the VRA, but that truth reinforces the congressional judgment that these jurisdictions were rightfully subject to preclearance, and ought to remain under that regime.

IV

Congress approached the 2006 reauthorization of the VRA with great care and seriousness. The same cannot be said of the Court's opinion today. The Court makes no genuine attempt to engage with the massive legislative record that Congress assembled. Instead, it relies on increases in voter registration and turnout as if that were the whole story. Without even identifying a standard of review, the Court dismissively brushes off arguments based on "data from the record," and declines to enter the "debat[e about] what [the] record shows." One would expect more from an opinion striking at the heart of the Nation's signal piece of civil-rights legislation.

B

The Court stops any application of §5 by holding that §4(b)'s coverage formula is unconstitutional. It pins this result, in large measure, to "the fundamental principle of equal sovereignty." In *Katzenbach,* however, the Court held, in no uncertain terms, that the principle *"applies only to the terms upon which States are admitted to the Union,* and not to the remedies for local evils which have subsequently appeared."

Katzenbach, the Court acknowledges, "rejected the notion that the [equal sovereignty] principle operate[s] as a bar on differential treatment outside [the] context [of the admission of new States]." But the Court clouds that once clear understanding by citing dictum from *Northwest Austin* to convey that the principle of equal sovereignty "remains highly pertinent in assessing subsequent disparate treatment of States." If the Court is suggesting that dictum in *Northwest Austin* silently overruled *Katzenbach's* limitation of the equal sovereignty doctrine to "the admission of new States," the suggestion is untenable.

Today's unprecedented extension of the equal sovereignty principle outside its proper domain—the admission of new States—is capable of much mischief.

Federal statutes that treat States disparately are hardly novelties. Of gravest concern, Congress relied on our pathmarking *Katzenbach* decision in each reauthorization of the VRA. It had every reason to believe that the Act's limited geographical scope would weigh in favor of, not against, the Act's constitutionality. Congress could hardly have foreseen that the VRA's limited geographic reach would render the Act constitutionally suspect.

In the Court's conception, it appears, defenders of the VRA could not prevail upon showing what the record overwhelmingly bears out, *i.e.,* that there is a need for continuing the preclearance regime in covered States. In addition, the defenders would have to disprove the existence of a comparable need elsewhere. I am aware of no precedent for imposing such a double burden on defenders of legislation.

C

[T]he Court strikes § 4(b)'s coverage provision because, in its view, the provision is not based on "current conditions." It discounts, however, that one such condition was the preclearance remedy in place in the covered jurisdictions, a remedy Congress designed both to catch discrimination before it causes harm, and to guard against return to old ways. Volumes of evidence supported Congress' determination that the prospect of retrogression was real. Throwing out preclearance when it has worked and is continuing to work to stop discriminatory changes is like throwing away your umbrella in a rainstorm because you are not getting wet.

The situation Congress faced in 2006, when it took up *re* authorization of the coverage formula, was not the same [as in 1965]. By then, the formula had been in effect for many years, and *all* of the jurisdictions covered by it were "familiar to Congress by name." The question before Congress: Was there still a sufficient basis to support continued application of the preclearance remedy in each of those already-identified places? There was at that point no chance that the formula might inadvertently sweep in new areas that were not the subject of congressional findings. And Congress could determine from the record whether the jurisdictions captured by the coverage formula still belonged under the preclearance regime. If they did, there was no need to alter the formula. That is why the Court, in addressing prior reauthorizations of the VRA, did not question the continuing "relevance" of the formula.

The Court holds § 4(b) invalid on the ground that it is "irrational to base coverage on the use of voting tests 40 years ago, when such tests have been illegal since that time." But the Court disregards what Congress set about to do in enacting the VRA. That extraordinary legislation scarcely stopped at the particular tests and devices that happened to exist in 1965. The grand aim of the Act is to secure to all in our polity equal citizenship stature, a voice in our democracy undiluted by race. As the record for the 2006 reauthorization makes abundantly clear, second-generation barriers to minority voting rights have emerged in the covered jurisdictions as attempted *substitutes* for the first-generation barriers that originally triggered preclearance in those jurisdictions.

The sad irony of today's decision lies in its utter failure to grasp why the VRA has proven effective. The Court appears to believe that the VRA's success in eliminating the specific devices extant in 1965 means that preclearance is no longer needed. With that belief, and the argument derived from it, history repeats itself. The same assumption — that the problem could be solved when particular methods of voting discrimination are identified and eliminated — was indulged and proved wrong repeatedly prior to the VRA's enactment. In truth, the evolution of voting discrimination into more subtle second-generation barriers is powerful evidence that a remedy as effective as preclearance remains vital to protect minority voting rights and prevent backsliding.

After exhaustive evidence-gathering and deliberative process, Congress reauthorized the VRA, including the coverage provision, with overwhelming bipartisan support. It was the judgment of Congress that "40 years has not been a sufficient amount of time to eliminate the vestiges of discrimination following nearly 100 years of disregard for the dictates of the 15th amendment and to ensure that the right of all citizens to vote is protected as guaranteed by the Constitution." That determination of the body empowered to enforce the Civil War Amendments "by appropriate legislation" merits this Court's utmost respect. In my judgment, the Court errs egregiously by overriding Congress' decision.

* * *

For the reasons stated, I would affirm the judgment of the Court of Appeals.

EXERCISE 8:

1. Why does the majority hold that the "40 year-old facts" upon which Congress originally relied when passing the Voting Rights Act have "no logical relationship to the present day"? Because the majority struck down § 4(b) of the Voting Rights Act, no jurisdiction will be subject to § 5 preclearance unless and until Congress adopts a new coverage formula. Thus, *Shelby County* has the effect of staying § 5 even though the majority did not address the constitutionality of that provision. In light of the majority's analysis, what types of evidence must Congress rely on if it decides to create a new coverage formula?

2. Is the majority's concern with the evidentiary record on which Congress relied when passing the Voting Rights Act just another way of deciding whether the legislation is congruent and proportional (following the *Boerne* case)? Or is the majority fashioning a new standard?

3. Did the Civil War Amendments alter the relationship between the federal and state governments such that federalism principles pre-dating those Amendments do not apply (or do not apply in the same way)? What are the basic federalism principles upon which the majority relies?

4. What standard does the majority employ to evaluate § 4(b)? Is it a "congruent and proportional" standard? Rational basis? Or something else?

5. What is the principle of "equal sovereignty of the states"? Were does it come from?

6. How does the formula in §4(b) violate the "equal sovereignty of the states"?

7. Is Justice Thomas correct about that the majority's reasoning applies with equal force to §5 of the Voting Right Act such that both §4(b) and §5 are unconstitutional? Should the Court have decided the §5 question or was it proper to hold off on resolving that issue?

8. In her dissent, Justice Ginsburg contends that the Court should defer to Congress' assessment that §5 should continue in force if there is a "rational basis" for its conclusion and that Congress' concern with continuing the impressive gains under the Voting Rights Act and avoiding backsliding meets that standard. The majority counters that the dissent's position would make Congress "effectively immune from scrutiny" and permit §5 to continue indefinitely. Does the majority or the dissent have the better argument?

TABLE OF CASES

INDEX